SHARI'A IN THE WEST

Shari'a in the West

Edited by
REX AHDAR AND NICHOLAS ARONEY

OXFORD
UNIVERSITY PRESS

OXFORD
UNIVERSITY PRESS

Great Clarendon Street, Oxford OX2 6DP

Oxford University Press is a department of the University of Oxford.
It furthers the University's objective of excellence in research, scholarship,
and education by publishing worldwide in

Oxford New York

Auckland Cape Town Dar es Salaam Hong Kong Karachi
Kuala Lumpur Madrid Melbourne Mexico City Nairobi
New Delhi Shanghai Taipei Toronto

With offices in

Argentina Austria Brazil Chile Czech Republic France Greece
Guatemala Hungary Italy Japan Poland Portugal Singapore
South Korea Switzerland Thailand Turkey Ukraine Vietnam

Oxford is a registered trade mark of Oxford University Press
in the UK and in certain other countries

Published in the United States
by Oxford University Press Inc., New York

© The several contributors, 2010

The moral rights of the author have been asserted

Crown copyright material is reproduced with the permission
of the Controller, HMSO (under the
terms of the Click Use licence)

Database right Oxford University Press (maker)

First published 2010

All rights reserved. No part of this publication may be reproduced,
stored in a retrieval system, or transmitted, in any form or by any means,
without the prior permission in writing of Oxford University Press,
or as expressly permitted by law, or under terms agreed with the appropriate
reprographics rights organization. Enquiries concerning reproduction
outside the scope of the above should be sent to the Rights Department,
Oxford University Press, at the address above

You must not circulate this book in any other binding or cover
and you must impose the same condition on any acquirer

British Library Cataloguing in Publication Data

Data available

Library of Congress Cataloging-in-Publication Data
Typeset by Newgen Imaging Systems (P) Ltd., Chennai, India
Printed in Great Britain
on acid-free paper by
CPI Antony Rowe

ISBN 978–0–19–958291–4

Contents

III

Acknowledgements

The idea for this book was prompted by a now famous Foundation Lecture delivered by the Archbishop of Canterbury, Dr Rowan Williams, at the Royal Courts of Justice on 7 February 2008. Dr William's lecture was followed by an equally important address given by Lord Phillips of Worth Matravers, Lord Chief Justice of England and Wales, at the East London Muslim Centre on 3 July 2008. We thank Dr Williams and his Lordship for kind permission to reproduce their lectures as appendices to this book.

We also wish to thank Alex Flach at Oxford University Press for so enthusiastically embracing our proposal for a book that would discuss and scrutinize the suggestion that Shari'a be accommodated within Western legal systems. We owe thanks also to Natasha Knight, Glynis Dyson, and Benjamin Roberts at Oxford University Press for their tireless work in preparing the typescript for publication.

The birth of this book has had a long and, at times, difficult gestation. Our sincere thanks to our most patient contributors and to the expert navigation of Oxford University Press.

Our sincere thanks to Jude Murdoch, Simon Currie, and Emily Mayberry for their research assistance.

Rex is delighted to publicly acknowledge Nick's unstinting faith, encouragement, and perseverance in this venture (recalling the truth that, indeed, 'two are better than one': Ecclesiastes 4:9–10) and Nick, in turn, does the same.

The final touches were made to the manuscript in the days leading up to the time when Christmas is celebrated in the West. A very busy time for families, and we are therefore most grateful to our respective wives, Lidwina and Lisa, for their patience, love, and understanding. Without their support, this book would not exist.

Advent, 2009

Notes on Contributors

Rex Ahdar Professor of Law, Faculty of Law, University of Otago.

Professor Ahdar has published extensively on church-state relations and religious freedom. He is author and editor of *God and Government: The New Zealand Experience* (Otago University Press, 2000) (with John Stenhouse); *Law and Religion* (Ashgate, 2000); *Worlds Colliding: Conservative Christians and the Law* (Ashgate, 2001); and *Religious Freedom in the Liberal State* (Oxford University Press, 2005) (with Ian Leigh). His articles have appeared in journals such as *Oxford Journal of Legal Studies*, *McGill Law Journal*, *Emory International Law Review*, *The Journal of Law and Religion*, *Brigham Young University Law Review* and *The Journal of Church and State*.

Nicholas Aroney Professor of Constitutional Law, T C Beirne School of Law, University of Queensland. Fellow, Centre for Public, International and Comparative Law, University of Queensland.

Professor Aroney has published widely on constitutional interpretation, comparative constitutional law, and constitutional legal theory. He is author of *Freedom of Speech in the Constitution* (CIS, 1998) and *The Constitution of a Federal Commonwealth: The Making and Meaning of the Australian Constitution* (Cambridge University Press, 2009), and co-editor of *Restraining Elective Dictatorship: The Upper House Solution?* (University of Western Australia Press, 2008). His articles have appeared in journals such as *The American Journal of Comparative Law*, *International and Comparative Law Quarterly*, *The Journal of Legal History*, *Law and Philosophy*, *University of Toronto Law Journal*, *Archiv für Rechts- und Sozialphilosophie*, *Federal Law Review*, *Sydney Law Review*, and *Melbourne University Law Review*.

Ann Black Senior Lecturer, T C Beirne School of Law, University of Queensland. Fellow, Centre for Public, International and Comparative Law, University of Queensland.

Dr Black holds a doctorate on dispute-resolution from Brunei Darussalam and has taught and written extensively on Islamic law. Her articles have appeared in journals such as *Asian Journal of Comparative Law*, *International Trade and Business Law Annual*, *Griffith Law Review*, *Alternative Law Journal*, and *Flinders Journal of Law Reform*. She is also a past editor of the *LAWASIA Journal*.

J Budziszewski Professor, Departments of Government and Philosophy, University of Texas at Austin.

Professor Budziszewski specializes in political philosophy, ethical philosophy, and the interaction of religion with philosophy. He has written extensively on classical natural law, virtue ethics, moral self-deception and the problem of toleration. He is author of *The Resurrection of Nature: Political Theory and the Human Character* (Cornell, 1986); *The Nearest Coast of Darkness: A Vindication of the Politics of Virtue* (Cornell, 1988); *True Tolerance: Liberalism and the Necessity of Judgment* (Transaction, 1992); *Written on the Heart: The Case for Natural Law* (InterVarsity, 1997); *The Revenge of Conscience: Politics and the Fall of Man* (Spence, 1999); *What We Can't Not Know: A Guide* (Spence, 2003); *Evangelicals in the Public Square: Four Formative Voices* (Baker Academic, 2006); *Natural Law for Lawyers* (Blackstone

Fellowship, 2006); and *The Line Through the Heart: Natural Law as Fact, Theory, and Sign of Contradiction* (Intercollegiate Studies Institute Press, 2009).

Jean-François Gaudreault-DesBiens   Associate Dean, Research, and Canada Research Chair in North American and Comparative Juridical and Cultural Identities, Faculty of Law, Université de Montréal.

Professor Gaudreault-DesBiens has published widely in domestic and comparative constitutional law, legal theory and epistemology, and the sociology of legal cultures. His most recent work focuses on the legal theory of federalism, on the legal treatment of religious claims, and on the relations between the civil law and common law traditions in a globalized economy. He is author and editor of *The Response of State Law to the Expression of Cultural Diversity* (De Boeck, 2009) (with Marie-Claire Foblets and Alison Dundes Renteln); *Dilemmas of Solidarity: Rethinking Distribution in the Canadian Federation* (University of Toronto Press, 2006) (with Sujit Choudhry and Lorne Sossin); *Le sexe et le droit: Sur le féminisme juridique de Catharine MacKinnon* (Liber, 2001); and *La liberté d'expression entre l'art et le droit* (Presses de l'Universite Laval, 1996).

Erich Kolig   Honorary Fellow in Religion, University of Otago. Former Senior Lecturer in Social Anthropology, University of Otago. Former Visiting Professor of Cultural Anthropology, Vienna University.

Dr Kolig, a retired New Zealand social anthropologist, has authored and edited several books and volumes and many articles on indigenous politics, New Zealand Muslims, radical Islam in Indonesia, and Australian Aboriginal culture. He has conducted field research in Afghanistan, Australia, Austria, Indonesia, New Zealand, and Vanuatu. He is editor of *Identity in Crossroad Civilisations: Ethnicity, Nationalism and Globalism in Asia* (University of Amsterdam Press, 2009) (with Vivienne Angeles and Sam Wong) and the author of *New Zealand's Muslims and Multiculturalism* (Brill, 2010). He has written extensively on Islam and multiculturalism in journals such as *Paideuma, European Journal of East Asian Studies, Immigrants & Minorities, New Zealand Journal of Asian Studies*, and *New Zealand Journal of Sociology*.

John Milbank   Professor in Religion, Politics, and Ethics and Director of the Centre of Theology and Philosophy, the University of Nottingham.

Professor Milbank has written and co-edited several highly influential books on Christian theology, social theory, and ethics. These works include *Theology and Social Theory: Beyond Secular Reason* (Blackwell, 1990); *Radical Orthodoxy: A New Theology* (Routledge, 1999) (with Catherine Pickstock and Graham Ward); *Truth in Aquinas* (Routledge, 2001) (with Catherine Pickstock); *Theology and the Political: The New Debate* (Duke University Press, 2005) (with Slavoj Zizek and Creston Davis); and *Being Reconciled: Ontology and Pardon* (Taylor and Francis, 2007).

Tariq Modood   Professor, Department of Sociology, University of Bristol. Founding Director, Centre for the Study of Ethnicity and Citizenship, Bristol Institute for Public Affairs. Bristol Director of the Leverhulme Programme on Migration and Citizenship, University College, London.

Professor Modood has written extensively on racial equality, multiculturalism, secularism, ethnic identities, ethnic disadvantage, and the politics of being Muslim in the West. Among his many works, he is author and editor of *Secularism, Religion and Multicultural*

Citizenship (Cambridge University Press, 2009) (with G B Levey); *Multiculturalism: A Civic Idea* (Polity, 2007); *Multicultural Politics: Racism, Ethnicity and Muslims in Britain* (University of Minnesota Press, 2005); *Multiculturalism, Muslims and Citizenship: A European Approach* (Routledge, 2006) (with A Triandafyllidou and R Zapata-Barrero); *Ethnicity, Nationalism and Minority Rights* (Cambridge University Press, 2004) (with S May and J Squires); and *Ethnicity, Social Mobility and Public Policy in the US and UK* (Cambridge University Press, 2005) (with G Loury and S Teles).

Michael Nazir-Ali Former Bishop of Rochester (1994–2009) (the first non-white diocesan bishop in the Church of England). First Bishop of Raiwind in West Punjab (1984–1986).

Author of *Islam: A Christian Perspective* (Westminster John Knox Press, 1984); *Frontiers in Muslim-Christian Encounter* (Wipf & Stock, 2007); *Conviction And Conflict: Islam, Christianity And World Order* (Continuum, 2006); and *From Everywhere To Everywhere: A World View of Christian Mission* (Wipf & Stock Publishers, 2009). In September 2009 he resigned from his Bishopric to devote himself full time to defending beleaguered Christian minorities.

Abdullah Saeed Sultan of Oman Professor of Arab and Islamic Studies, University of Melbourne. Director, Asia Institute, University of Melbourne.

Professor Saeed has written widely on Qur'anic hermeneutics and Islamic jurisprudence. His publications cover Islamic finance, Muslim communities in Australia, Islamic law and freedom of religion, Christian–Muslim relations, Islamic thought in Indonesia, Islam and human rights, and Islamic law reform. His books include *Freedom of Religion, Apostasy and Islam* (Ashgate, 2004) (with H Saeed); *The Qur'an: An Introduction* (Routledge, 2008), *Islamic Thought: An Introduction* (Routledge, 2006); *Contemporary Approaches to Qur'an in Indonesia* (Oxford University Press, 2005); *Islam and Political Legitimacy* (Curzon, 2003) (with S Akbarzadeh); and *Islam in Australia* (Allen & Unwin, 2002). He is frequently engaged in interfaith dialogue between Christians, Jews, and Muslims.

Ayelet Shachar Canada Research Chair in Citizenship and Multiculturalism, Faculty of Law, University of Toronto. Previously Leah Kaplan Visiting Professor in Human Rights, Stanford Law School and Jeremiah Smith Jr Visiting Professor of Law, Harvard Law School.

Professor Shachar has written widely and influentially on legal theory, citizenship and immigration law, cultural accommodation and family law, multiculturalism and women's rights, law and religion in comparative perspective, and transnational legal process and ethics. She is author of *Multicultural Jurisdictions* (Cambridge University Press, 2001), winner of the American Political Science Association's 2002 Best First Book Award. Her most recent book is *The Birthright Lottery: Citizenship and Global Inequality* (Harvard University Press, 2008).

James W Skillen Senior Fellow and former President of the Center for Public Justice, Annapolis, Maryland.

Dr Skillen has written extensively on political thought, statecraft, and public policy. His books include *The Prospects and Ambiguities of Globalisation: Critical Assessment at a Time of Growing Turmoil* (Lexington, 2009); *With or Against the World? America's Role Among the Nations* (Rowman & Littlefield and Center for Public Justice, 2005); *In Pursuit of Justice:*

Christian-Democratic Explorations (Rowman & Littlefield and Center for Public Justice, 2004); *A Covenant to Keep: Meditations on the Biblical Theme of Justice* (CRC Publications and Center for Public Justice, 2000); *The Scattered Voice: Christians at Odds in the Public Square* (Zondervan, 1990); and *Recharging the American Experiment: Principled Pluralism for Genuine Civic Community* (Baker Books, 1994).

Sophie van Bijsterveld
Senator (Christian Democratic Party), First Chamber, Parliament of the Netherlands. Member of the ODIHR/OSCE Advisory Council on Freedom of Religion or Belief. Professor of Religion, State, and Society, School of Humanities, Tilburg University. Professor Van Bijsterveld has written widely on law and religion, human rights, and constitutional law. Her books include *The Empty Throne: Democracy and the Rule of Law in Transition* (Utrecht: Lemma, 2002); *Godsdienstvrijheid in Europees Perspectief [Religious Liberty in European Perspective]* (Deventer: WEJ Tjeenk Willink, 1998); and *Overheid en Godsdienst: Herijking van een Onderlinge Relatie [Government and Religion: Regauging a Mutual Relationship]* (Nijmegen: Wolf Legal Publishers, 2nd edn, 2009).

Jeremy Waldron   University Professor, School of Law, New York University.
Professor Waldron has written extensively and highly influentially in the fields of constitutional theory, legal philosophy, and political theory. Among his numerous works, he is author of *The Right to Private Property* (Oxford University Press, 1988); *The Law* (Routledge, 1990); *Liberal Rights* (Cambridge University Press, 1993); *Law and Disagreement* (Oxford University Press, 1999); *The Dignity of Legislation* (Cambridge University Press, 1999); *God, Locke and Equality* (Cambridge University Press, 2002); and, most recently, *Toleration and its Limits: Nomos XLVIII* (New York University Press, 2008) (edited with Melissa Williams). His numerous and widely read articles have appeared in journals such as *Harvard Law Review, Yale Law Journal, Columbia Law Review*, and *Oxford Journal of Legal Studies*.

John Witte Jr   Jonas Robitscher Professor of Law, Alonzo L McDonald Distinguished Professor and Director of the Center for the Study of Law and Religion, Emory University School of Law.
Professor Witte is a leading specialist in legal history, marriage law, and religious liberty. He is author of numerous books, including *From Sacrament to Contract: Marriage, Religion, and Law in the Western Tradition* (2nd edn, 2011); *The Sins of the Fathers: The Law and Theology of Illegitimacy Reconsidered* (Cambridge University Press, 2009); *The Reformation of Rights: Law, Religion, and Human Rights in Early Modern Calvinism* (Cambridge University Press, 2008); *Christianity and Law: An Introduction* (Cambridge University Press, 2008) (with F S Alexander); *Religion and the American Constitutional Experiment* (Westview Press, 2nd edn, 2005); *Sex, Marriage and Family Life in John Calvin's Geneva* (Eerdmans, 2005) (with R M Kingdon); *The Teachings of Modern Christianity on Law, Politics and Human Nature* (2 vols) (Columbia University Press, 2006) (with F S Alexander); *Law and Protestantism: The Legal Teachings of the Lutheran Reformation* (Cambridge University Press, 2002).

1

The Topography of Shari'a in the Western Political Landscape

Rex Ahdar and Nicholas Aroney

A. Introduction

The question whether Shari'a should be recognized and incorporated into the legal systems of the liberal democracies of the West is an imposing one. The topic is fascinating, multifaceted, and inherently complex—straddling law, politics, state-craft, history, culture, and religion. The issue has become a proverbial 'hot potato' in the corridors of power, as well as the more commonplace cafés, cyberspace chat rooms, bars, and living rooms of society. Hardly a week goes by in the West without a controversy erupting over some aspect of Muslim ritual, symbolism, belief, or practice.

Take this whirlwind global sampling of examples from 2009. In Britain, the Home Office issued a warning to civil servants not to eat lunch in front of their Muslim colleagues during the month of Ramadan.[1] A Christian couple running a guest house in Liverpool appeared in court on charges of violating a religious aggravated public order offence after offending a Muslim woman guest with their comments that Islamic dress was oppressive to women and put them into 'bondage'.[2] In Canada, Windsor police issued a public apology to the local Muslim community for the 'embarrassment' caused by its tactical officers when they conducted an arrest operation in connection with the activities of a radical Islamic group.[3] In Melbourne, Australia, Samir Abu Hamza, a Muslim cleric who instructed his male married followers to hit, and force sex upon their disobedient wives, drew

---

[1] D Gardham, 'Home Office told: "Don't eat in front of Muslims during Ramadan"', *Daily Telegraph*, 20 September 2009.

[2] J Bingham, 'Christian couple face losing hotel after criminal charges for offending Muslim woman', *Daily Telegraph*, 20 September 2009. The couple were later acquitted in the Liverpool Magistrates' Court: N Britten, 'Hoteliers cleared of abusing Muslim guest', *Daily Telegraph*, 9 December 2009.

[3] 'Windsor police apologize to Islamic community for FBI arrests', *National Post*, 12 November 2009.

a harsh rebuke from the Prime Minister, Kevin Rudd.[4] In New Zealand, the Department of Corrections revealed that all meat served to prisoners had undergone *halal* slaughter,[5] and a Muslim woman laid a complaint to the Human Rights Commission over her removal from the public gallery of a courtroom for refusing to take off her headscarf.[6] In the United States, the mass slaughter by Major Nidal Malik Hasan of 12 of his Army colleagues at Fort Hood, Texas—and who, according to witnesses, shouted 'Allahu Akbar' ('God is great') before he opened fire— sparked renewed debate on the loyalty of Muslims in the US military to American values.[7] In France, President Nicolas Sarkozy called for a ban on the *burqa* on the basis that it perpetuated the subservience of women.[8] And, as we write, there is a stormy response to the verdict of the majority of the Swiss public, by way of legally binding referendum, to ban the erection of minarets on mosques.[9]

Regrettably, calm and dispassionate reflection has not been a feature of most discussions to date. There has, as the saying goes, been 'more heat than light'. The experience in the two main Western countries to have grappled with recognition of Shari'a—Canada and the United Kingdom—bears this out. The Ontario provincial government in 2005 firmly rejected the notion of Shari'a tribunals adjudicating family and civil disputes, but only after an acrimonious debate that began immediately after a Muslim civil justice organization floated the idea in late 2003.[10] And, of course, the Archbishop of Canterbury's lecture in February 2008 elicited the fierce volley of criticism that inspired us to create this book.

As one informed commentator has pointed out, '[i]ntelligent discussion of Islamism, democracy, and Islam requires clear and accurate definitions. Without them, analysis will collapse into confusion and policymaking will suffer'.[11] The key concepts in any area require clarification, and this is especially true in this case. Accordingly, we will commence this chapter with brief definitions of the principal matters under consideration before setting out what we take to be the key issues in the debate.

However, one final opening remark. The question of the role for Shari'a is not one for specialists alone. If we operate from the premise that Shari'a makes claims

---

[4] 'It's OK to hit your wife, says Melbourne Islamic cleric Samir Abu Hamza', *The Australian*, 22 January 2009.

[5] 'Only halal-certified meat served to prisoners', *Otago Daily Times*, 9 October 2009.

[6] 'Muslim woman furious at courtroom ban', *New Zealand Herald*, 2 September 2009.

[7] 'Muslim group condemns Hood shootings', *Associated Press*, 5 November 2009. 'Fort Hood shootings: the meaning of "Allahu Akbar"', *Daily Telegraph*, 6 November 2009; J Berger, 'Army Chief Concerned for Muslim Troops', *New York Times*, 8 November 2009; J Young, 'General Casey: diversity shouldn't be casualty of Fort Hood, *Reuters: US Edition*, 8 November 2009.

[8] 'Nicolas Sarkozy pushes for burqa ban in France', *Daily Telegraph*, 12 November 2009.

[9] A Williams, 'Switzerland risks Muslim backlash after minarets vote', *Daily Telegraph*, 29 November 2009.

[10] See Gaudreault-DesBiens, Ch 4 and Shachar, Ch 8 in this collection.

[11] B Tibi, 'Islamist Parties: Why They Can't be Democratic' (2008) 19 *Journal of Democracy* 43, 43.

to function in the public square then everyone, Muslim *and* non-Muslim, has a stake in the task of what Abdullahi Ahmed An-Na'im calls 'negotiating the future of Shari'a'.[12]

B. Shari'a

References to Shari'a[13] in Western circles have, as Tariq Ramadan puts it, become something of a 'bugbear',[14] evoking dark images of floggings, stonings, amputations, women peering meekly out of eye-slits in sombre full-length garments, wide-eyed bearded imams issuing death decrees against blasphemers, and so on. What is the Shari'a? Ramadan explains there is 'not a single definition' of the term and instead provides a bifurcated definition:

1. *Ash-shari'a*, on the basis of the root of the word, means 'the way' ('the path leading to the source') and outlines a global conception of creation, existence, death, and the way of life it entails, stemming from a normative reading and an understanding of scriptural sources. It determines 'how to be a Muslim.'
2. *Ash-shari'a*, for...jurists, is the corpus of general principles of Islamic law extracted from its two fundamental sources (the Qur'an and the Sunnah) ... .[15]

The term 'Shari'a' occurs just once in the Qur'an.[16] The phrase 'Islamic law' is often used interchangeably with the Shari'a, and while this usage has its critics, others defend the equation.[17] An important related concept is *fiqh*, which literally means comprehension or understanding.[18] *Fiqh* is the body of reasoned reflection and opinion of Islamic scholars and jurists—as well as the science or method of deducing such opinions—concerning what they consider the Shari'a to require of

[12] A A An-Na'im, *Islam and the Secular State: Negotiating the Future of Shari'a* (Cambridge, MA: Harvard University Press, 2008) viii.

[13] We shall use the simplified form 'Shari'a' in this work. We recognize that many scholars insist that this term is to be more accurately rendered as 'Sharīʿa'. Other Arabic words and phrases throughout this work are also given a simplified spelling rather than the precise transcription. The editors and contributors intend no offence whatsoever. We shall alternate between the form 'the Shari'a' and 'Shari'a' as the context and discussion dictates. Again, arguably a more accurate rending would include the definite article.

[14] T Ramadan, *Islam, the West and the Challenges of Modernity* (Leicester: Islamic Foundation, 2001) 47.

[15] T Ramadan, *Radical Reform: Islamic Ethics and Liberation* (Oxford: Oxford University Press, 2009) 359–360.

[16] Qur'an 45: 18 ('We have put you on the (true) Path [Shari'a] of religion; so follow that ...'): see F Griffel, 'Introduction' in A Amanat and F Griffel (eds), *Shari'a: Islamic Law in the Contemporary Context* (Stanford: Stanford University Press, 2007) 1, 2; Tibi (n 11 above) 44.

[17] Islamic law is a shorthand expression for what scholars, when referring to the Shari'a, call 'the religious law of Islam': W Hallaq, *The Origins and Evolution of Islamic Law* (Cambridge: Cambridge University Press, 2005) 1. An-Na'im (n 12 above) 3 states: 'As a concept, [Shari'a] refers to the religious law of Islam in general, which is derived from human interpretation of the Qur'an and Sunna of the Prophet'.

[18] Ramadan (n 14 above) 72, fn 19.

Muslims in the particular time and locality they find themselves.[19] *Fiqh*, in other words, is the developing jurisprudence of the Shari'a.[20]

Some modern scholars have been at pains to distinguish between the Shari'a and *fiqh*. The latter, says Ramadan, 'respectable as they are, remain however only human attempts which cannot be convenient for all stages in history'.[21] An-Na'im similarly observes:

It is clear that there is no uniform and settled understanding of Shari'a among Muslims that can be enforced by the state. This is true even within the same school of Sunni or Shi'a jurisprudence, let alone across different schools and sects. It should be emphasized at this level that since every understanding of Shari'a, even if universal among Muslims, is a human interpretation, none should be enforced as state law in the name of Shari'a or Islam as such. At another level, because Shari'a is always the product of human interpretation of divine sources, any interpretation of it will reflect the human limitations of those who are interpreting it, despite the divinity of the sources they are working with. From this perspective Shari'a will always remain open to reinterpretation and evolution, in response to the constantly changing needs of Islamic societies and communities in different times and places.[22]

Between Ramadan and An-Na'im there is a subtle but important difference, however. Ramadan characterizes Shari'a as *derived* from the Qur'an and the *Sunna*.[23] An-Na'im characterizes it as 'a historically-conditioned *human* interpretation' of divine sources.[24] This apparently marginal difference in phraseology reflects a wider and more sharply defined disagreement between those who might be characterized as 'orthodox' or even 'fundamentalist', who would endorse certain historical understandings of Shari'a as divinely authoritative, and so-called 'reformers', 'secularists', or 'liberals', who would seek to modernize Islamic societies by reference to human rights and other standards ostensibly external to Islamic faith and tradition.[25] Plainly, views about the nature of Shari'a are shaped by both religious and scholarly considerations. Religious commitment to the revealed standards of Islam calls for an affirmation of the divine and authoritative status of the Qur'an and *Sunna*, including the Shari'a at least in its core, revealed content. However, juristic scholarship draws

---

[19] J Hussain, *Islam: Its Law and Society* (Sydney: Federation Press, 2nd edn, 2004) 28.

[20] There is the classical *fiqh*, formulated in the formative era of Islamic history (632–892) as well as *fiqh* that has developed subsequently: L A Khan, 'Jurodynamics of Islamic Law' (2009) 61 *Rutgers Law Review* 231, 232–233, fn 4.

[21] Ramadan (n 14 above) 48.

[22] An-Na'im (n 12 above) 282–283.

[23] See, further, Ramadan, *Western Muslims and the Future of Islam* (Oxford: Oxford University Press, 2004), 32–33, describing Shari'a as 'the corpus of reference in which Islamic universality is written down'. However, note also his recognition of the unavoidable human element, characterizing Shari'a as an 'expression' of the 'way to faithfulness': Ramadan (n 14 above) 34.

[24] A A An-Na'im, 'Islamic Foundations of Religious Human Rights' in J Witte, Jr and J van der Vyver (eds), *Religious Human Rights in Global Perspective: Religious Perspectives* (The Hague: Kluwer, 1996) 337, 353 (emphasis in original). See also M Fadel, 'Review Essay: Islamic Politics and Secular Politics: Can They Co-Exist?' (2009) 25 *Journal of Law and Religion* 101, 111–114.

[25] These views are canvassed in N Hosen, *Shari'a & Constitutional Reform in Indonesia* (Singapore: Institute of Southeast Asian Studies, 2007) Ch 2.

attention to differences in interpretation of Shari'a, and Islamic scholars debate the many questions of interpretation and application that inevitably arise.[26]

In this context, talk of *the* Shari'a is misleading to the extent it suggests a monolithic, fixed, and uniform body of positive norms and rules. This is to take an 'essentialist' perspective.[27] The better view is to acknowledge that there are different concepts of Shari'a in different contexts; that is, to adopt instead a 'multiplist' perspective.[28] As An-Na'im has pointed out, there are as many interpretations of Shari'a as there are schools—at least five[29] —and as many variations in its practical implementation as there are regional and cultural differences.[30] An attempt to distil the Shari'a to its core features or basic objects may simply produce a sort of lowest common denominator version that is as artificial as it is general. An-Na'im observes that one may assert:

> that all that is required is to observe the basic objectives or purposes of Shari'a (*Maqasid al-Shari'a*), while *fiqh* principles are subject to change from one time or place to another. But the problem with this view is that the so-called basic objectives of Shari'a are expressed at such a high level of abstraction that they are neither distinctly Islamic nor sufficiently specific for the purposes of public policy and legislation. As soon as these principles are presented in more specific and concrete terms, they will immediately be implicated in the familiar controversies and limitations of *fiqh*.[31]

Controversies such as these are, of course, the bread and butter of jurisprudence within any legal system, whether religious or philosophical. Modern liberalism seeks to resolve such disputes by 'bracketing' the most intractable of them out of consideration—namely, the religio-philosophical, which John Rawls called 'comprehensive doctrines'. But, while Islamic scholars continue to engage in the familiar controversies to which An-Na'im refers, it is clear that Shari'a is nothing if it is not a comprehensive doctrine in Rawls' lexicon. As An-Na'im himself puts it:

> To Muslims, Shari'a is the 'Whole Duty of Mankind,' moral and pastoral theology and ethics, high spiritual aspiration, and detailed ritualistic and formal observance; it encompasses all aspects of public and private law, hygiene, and even courtesy and good manners.[32]

---

[26] See Hallaq (n 17 above).

[27] J M Otto, 'The compatibility of *Shari'a* with the rule of law. Fundamentalist conflict: between civilisations? Within civilisations? Or between scholars?' in A Groen et al. (eds), *Knowledge in Ferment: Dilemmas in Science, Scholarship and Society* (Leiden: Leiden University Press, 2007) Ch 9, 141.

[28] Ibid.

[29] See An-Na'im (n 12 above) 14–15 and Nazir-Ali, Ch 5 in this collection. One scholar puts the total at seven (four Sunni and three Shi'a schools): A Emon, 'Conceiving Islamic Law in a Pluralist Society: History, Politics and Multicultural Jurisprudence' [2006] *Singapore Journal of Legal Studies* 331, 335.

[30] See Kolig, Ch 15 in this collection.

[31] An-Na'im (n 12 above) 35. An-Na'im goes so far as to assert that certain historical expressions of Shari'a have in particular respects been productive of serious injustice and are inadequate to 'modern' conditions. These alleged injustices are candidly addressed in his earlier work, *Toward an Islamic Reformation: Civil Liberties, Human Rights, and International Law* (Syracuse, NY: Syracuse University Press, 1990).

[32] Ibid 11.

Ramadan similarly points out that Shari'a 'touches all the aspects of existence', from the intimately personal, spiritual, and familial, through to the management of interpersonal relations at a communal level.[33] Less 'reformist' Islamic scholars would put this point even more forcefully.[34] As Joseph Schacht pointed out several decades ago:

Islamic law is the epitome of Islamic thought, the most typical manifestation of the Islamic way of life, the core and kernel of Islam itself. ... [T]he whole life of the Muslims, Arabic literature, and the Arabic and Islamic disciplines of learning are deeply imbued with the ideas of Islamic law; it is impossible to understand Islam without understanding Islamic law.[35]

Whether the 'comprehensive character' of Islamic doctrine implies that there can be no distinction between religious law and secular law, or between the private and the public, remains therefore an open question. But it is on the possibility of such distinctions that the argument over the accommodation of Shari'a in Western democracies may very largely turn.[36]

C. The West

To identify 'the West' is not a matter of reaching for an atlas.[37] There is, admittedly, an incontrovertible geographical dimension to the term, and, as an initial approximation, one could posit the West as comprising Western Europe and its colonial offspring in Canada, the United States, Australia, and New Zealand. The way one characterizes a thing depends, however, on the nature of the object of the characterization as well as the purpose for which it is being characterized. In this book we are concerned with the structure and regulation of human societies, not trade patterns or military alliances. It is befitting in a book of this nature, therefore, to quote the words of the doyen of law and religion scholarship, Harold Berman, on this point:

What is called 'the West' is a particular historical culture, or civilization.... The West is a cultural term. It is not, however, simply an idea; it is a community. It implies both a

---

[33] Ramadan (n 14 above) 33–34.

[34] Fadel (n 24 above) 115 observes: 'One can imagine, for example, a Sunni Islamist follower of Sayyid Qutb or Abu al-A'la al-Mawdudi who rejects the separation of religion and state advocated by Na'im as dismissing the historical practice of pre-modern Muslim polities as mere evidence of a failure resulting from insufficient commitment to Islamic teachings rather than as evidence of an Islamic normative ideal'.

[35] J Schacht, *An Introduction to Islamic Law* (Oxford: Oxford University Press, 1964) 1.

[36] See Milbank, Ch 9 in this collection; Gaudreault-Desbiens, Ch 10 in this collection; Fadel (n 24 above); L Abu-Odeh, 'The Politics of (Mis)Recognition: Islamic Law Pedagogy in American Academia' (2004) 52 *American Journal of Comparative Law* 789.

[37] H Berman, *Law and Revolution: The Formation of the Western Legal Tradition* (Cambridge MA: Harvard University Press, 1983) 2.

historical structure and a structured history. For many centuries it could be identified very simply as the people of Western Christendom.[38]

The people of Western Christendom adopted and over time transformed Germanic customs, Greek philosophy, Roman law, and Hebrew religion into a unique synthesis.[39] Cardinal George Pell puts it this way:

The West is the product of a dialogue between what [Pierre] Manet calls 'the party of nature'—that is, the classical inheritance of the Greco-Roman world—and the party of grace—by which he means the revelation of the Christian religion. The party of nature emphasizes pride, magnanimity and the cultivation of the virtues that are natural to man. The party of grace emphasizes humility, renunciation, and the cultivation of the soul.[40]

As Berman points out, the original idea of 'the West' lies in the distinction between the Western and Eastern divisions of the Roman Empire and of the Christian Church, a division that became especially sharp following the separation of the Roman and Orthodox communions in 1054. This separation coincided with a movement within Western Christianity 'to make the Bishop of Rome the sole head of the church, to emancipate the clergy from the control of emperor, kings, and feudal lords and sharply to differentiate the church as a political and legal entity from secular polities'.[41] Following his mentor, Eugen Rosenstock-Huessy,[42] Berman argued that the West has ever since been characterized by a commitment to ongoing 'reform', expressed by a succession of 'revolutions' that have both reshaped and revitalized its governing institutions. Each such revolution—the Papal Revolution of the eleventh century, the Reformation of the sixteenth century, the American and French Revolutions of the eighteenth century, and the Russian Revolution of the twentieth century—contributed, directly or indirectly, to the Western legal tradition as we know it today. Despite these revolutions, however, Berman thought that the tradition retained certain fundamental characteristics, the principal ones being:

(1)   a relatively sharp distinction between legal institutions and other types of institutions (religious, moral, political);

(2)   a set of legal institutions administered by a special class of legal professionals (lawyers), themselves trained in a body of legal doctrine which had been systematized into a particular legal science or jurisprudence;

(3)   a conception of the law as a body of doctrine that develops and evolves over the course of centuries, according to an inbuilt capacity for organic change

---

[38]   Ibid 2–3.   [39]   Ibid 3.

[40]   G Pell, *God and Caesar: Selected Essays on Religion, Politics & Society* (M A Casey (ed)) (Washington DC: Catholic University of America Press, 2007) 43. See also P Manet, *The City of Man* (trans M A LePain) (Princeton: Princeton University Press, 1998) 24–25.

[41]   Berman (n 37 above) 2.

[42]   E Rosenstock-Huessy, *Out of Revolution: Autobiography of Western Man* [1938] (Providence and Oxford: Berg Publishers, 1993).

shaped both by an inner logic and a felt need to adapt to new circumstances and expectations;

(4) a conception of the law as both 'constitutional' and 'constitutive' in nature, supreme over the various governing authorities (church, state, and civil society), making both necessary and possible the existence of a plurality of coexisting jurisdictions (initially of an ecclesiastical, royal, feudal, manorial, urban, and mercantile kind) which both compete and cooperate with each other within the context of an overarching legal order.[43]

As a consequence, the 'separation of church and state' has long been fundamental to the constitutional structure of the West.[44] Jesus Christ taught his disciples to render unto Caesar the things that are Caesar's and to God the things that are God's.[45] Augustine drew his famous distinction between the heavenly and earthly cities.[46] Pope Gelasius I likewise distinguished between priestly authority and the royal power.[47] Martin Luther wrote of two kingdoms, temporal and spiritual.[48] Roger Williams referred to a 'hedge or wall of Separation between the Garden of the Church and the Wilderness of the world',[49] and Thomas Jefferson wrote similarly of a 'wall of separation between church and state',[50] a formula taken up by the United States Supreme Court.[51] While each of these authors, separated by time and context, meant something specifically different, the idea of two distinct powers remained fundamental and has continued to shape Western conceptions of the relationship between church and state.[52] What has changed, rather, is the prevailing relationship between *religion* and the state.

Most pre-Christian societies drew no sharp distinction between religious authority and the governing powers.[53] Sacrificing to the genius of the Roman Emperor was enforced as a civic duty, and the early Christians were persecuted

---

[43] Berman (n 37 above) 7–10. Shari'a cannot, for this reason, be compared to the canon law of the Roman Catholic and Anglican Churches. See L C Brown, *Religion and State: The Muslim Approach to Politics* (New York: Columbia University Press, 2000) Ch 3.

[44] On this dualism of authority, see R Ahdar and I Leigh, *Religious Freedom in the Liberal State* (Oxford; Oxford University Press, 2005) 13–15, 34–36.

[45] Matthew 22:21; Mark 12:17. Likewise, John 18:36: 'My kingdom is not of this world'.

[46] Augustine, *The City of God* (413–426).

[47] Gelasius I, *Letter to Emperor Anastasius* (494).

[48] M Luther, *Temporal Authority: To What Extent It Should Be Obeyed* (1523).

[49] R Williams, *Mr Cotton's Letter Lately Printed, Examined and Answered* (1644).

[50] T Jefferson, *Letter to the Danbury Baptist Association* (1802).

[51] *Everson v Board of Education*, 330 US 1, 15-16 (1947).

[52] See B Tierney, 'Religious Rights: An Historical Perspective' in Witte and van der Vyver (n 24 above) 17. For the texts, see the collection and commentary in O O'Donovan and J Lockwood O'Donovan (eds), *From Irenaeus to Grotius: A Sourcebook in Christian Political Thought, 100–1625* (Grand Rapids MI: Eerdmans, 1999).

[53] Tierney (n 52 above) 22.

due to their refusal to participate in the imperial cult.[54] In this context, numerous appeals for religious toleration were made by both biblical[55] and patristic[56] writers. However, following the adoption of Christianity as the official religion of the Empire under Theodosius in 380, attempts were made to use Christianity as an instrument of imperial statecraft,[57] and the Church came to approve the use of secular power to exterminate heresy.[58] Persecution and suppression of religious dissent were thereafter frequently justified as 'necessary' to preserve the integrity of medieval Christendom,[59] but such voices were not the only ones to be heard. In particular, philosophical nominalists such as William of Ockham and Jean Gerson developed theories of natural rights and religious freedom founded on the idea of 'evangelical liberty',[60] and the Reformation idea of the 'priesthood of all believers' led to a moderate and incomplete form of religious toleration in some Protestant lands.[61] These ideas in turn laid the foundations for a more wide-reaching principle of tolerance, in which 'freedom of conscience' was the fundamental value.[62] Indeed, it was largely those who were descended from, or sympathetic to, the radical wing of the Reformation who first pursued and implemented policies of disestablishment and toleration.[63] Toleration was also later urged by important figures of the Enlightenment, such as Voltaire and Lessing,[64] and under that influence the disestablishment of religion and an increasing secularization has become a feature of most contemporary Western states.

As Charles Taylor has recently put it, one account of this secularization consists in the notion that:

whereas the political organization of all pre-modern societies was in some way connected to ... some faith in, or adherence to God, or some notion of ultimate reality, ... the modern Western state is free from this connection. Churches are now separate from political structures ... Religion or its absence is largely a private matter. The political society is seen as that of believers (of all stripes) and non-believers alike.[65]

---

[54] G E M de Ste. Croix, 'Why were the Early Christians Persecuted?' (1963) 26 *Past and Present* 6.

[55] Eg I Timothy 2:2.

[56] Eg Tertullian, *Apology* and *Ad Scapulam* (c 212) 2.2.

[57] C N Cochrane, *Christianity and Classical Culture* (Oxford: Oxford University Press, 1940) esp Ch 9.

[58] See, eg *Fourth Lateran Council* (1215) Canon 3; Ahdar and Leigh (n 44 above) 15–22.

[59] Eg T Aquinas, *Summa Theologica*, II:II, Q10, art 8.

[60] Tierney (n 52 above) 28–29.

[61] See J Witte Jr, *The Reformation of Rights: Law, Religion, and Human Rights in the Calvinist Tradition* (Cambridge: Cambridge University Press, 2005) Ch 1.

[62] S Smith, 'Discourse in the Dusk: The Twilight of Religious Freedom?' (2008–2009) 122 *Harvard Law Review* 1869, 1876–1869.

[63] Eg R Williams, *The Bloudy Tenent, of Persecution, for Cause of Conscience* (1644); John Milton, *Of True Religion* (1672). See Ahdar and Leigh (n 44 above) 23–25; Tierney (n 52 above) 34–43.

[64] F-M Arouet [Voltaire], *A Treatise on Toleration* (1763); G E Lessing, *The Education of Humankind* (1780).

[65] C Taylor, *A Secular Age* (Cambridge MA: Belknap Press of Harvard University Press, 2007) 1.

On this account, the public spaces of the West are now empty of religion: 'the norms and principles we follow, the deliberations we engage in, generally don't refer us to God or to any religious beliefs; the considerations we act on are internal to the "rationality" of each sphere'.[66] Secularization in this 'macro' or institutional sense[67] is compatible, as Taylor points out, with large numbers of people in a society continuing to hold religious beliefs, and indeed practising their religion vigorously—albeit in private. Institutional and structural secularization is different, however, from a second, 'micro' or individual manifestation of secularization, in which the vast preponderance of the country's citizens is no longer *personally* religious. Thus, as many have observed,[68] the United States is a country where religion is constitutionally disestablished, yet religious belief and practice appears to be thriving; whereas in the countries of Western Europe (many of which retain established churches or provide direct state funding for the incumbent traditional religious bodies), religious practice has declined to near terminal levels—except of course in the case of migrant groups, and especially among the Islamic communities of Europe.

Pace the received wisdom on secularization that dominates in the West, however, Islamic scholars such as Talal Asad caution that:

'the secular' should not be thought of as the space in which real human life gradually emancipates itself from the controlling power of 'religion' and thus achieves the latter's relocation. It is this assumption that allows us to think of religion as 'infecting' the secular domain or as replicating within it the structure of theological concepts. . . . Secularism doesn't simply insist that religious practice and belief be confined to a space where they cannot threaten political stability or the liberties of 'free-thinking' citizens. Secularism builds on a particular conception of the world.[69]

The prevailing secularization discourse thus makes the issue of the accommodation of Shari'a in Western democracies especially controversial and problematic, and not only from an Islamic point of view. As Harold Berman argued, the progressive secularization of the West has precipitated a far-reaching sense of crisis—encompassing its legal institutions, procedures, values, concepts, rules, and ways of legal thought—in which the idea of the Western legal tradition, and the very structure of Western legality, is itself under challenge. In part, this is due to forces within the West itself—its ascendant political motifs of secularism, liberalism, and individualism—but it is also in part a consequence of the West's confrontation with non-Western civilizations, theologies, and philosophies.[70] According to Berman,

---

[66] Ibid 2.
[67] R Ahdar, 'The idea of "religious markets"' (2006) 2 *International Journal of Law in Context* 49, 55–57.
[68] Ibid 57ff.
[69] T Asad, *Formations of the Secular: Christianity, Islam, Modernity* (Stanford: Stanford University Press, 2003) 191.
[70] As Asad has observed (ibid 161), '[t]he discourse of European identity is a symptom of anxieties about non-Europeans'.

virtually all of the key characteristics of the Western legal tradition are being challenged in our time, including the belief that the law transcends politics and the hope that the law retains a genuine capacity for reform. Western law—by which he meant the law of the democratic nation-states of the modern West—is thus routinely criticized from various quarters as fragmentary, as irredeemably ideological and stratified, as an instrument of raw power, and as inherently monopolistic.[71]

When considered in this context, the controversy over the Archbishop's proposal that Shari'a be accommodated in Britain was due not only to disparate views about the nature and attractiveness of Shari'a, but also exposed simmering subterranean unease about the identity of the West itself, especially given its mixed inheritance of humanistic, religious, and post-modern elements.[72] This crisis of identity takes different forms within each Western nation, of course. In France, for example, it manifests itself in the Gallic doctrine of *laïcité*,[73] whereas in Canada, on one account at least, the debate over Shari'a pivots on the Canadian polity's commitment to the principles of non-discrimination and gender equality.[74] But in both countries, as in other Western democracies, there is a felt tension, not clearly resolved, between various 'secular' principles (non-establishment of religion, governmental neutrality, equality standards, and human rights) and the problem of accommodating the diverse religious beliefs and practices of the resident population, both established and newly arrived. Further, the accommodation exercise is rendered that much more fraught when those who seek to be acknowledged are immigrants of a different race from the domestic citizenry, for then policy-makers have to contend with certain persistent xenophobic voices that seize their opportunity to be heard.

Western liberalism is supposed to offer a way in which peoples of different religious commitments and worldviews are able to live together, at least through some pragmatic *modus vivendi*—if not, as Rawls hoped for, on the basis of some more principled and enduring 'overlapping consensus'.[75] But, as the mixed and ambiguous responses to Shari'a that have emerged so far suggest, there is reason to ponder whether Western secularist statecraft has the resources to accommodate Islam without assimilating it into irreducibly Western and derivatively Christian thought-forms,[76] just as there is reason to wonder whether Muslims can find within their religious tradition the resources to accommodate themselves to Western

---

[71] Berman (n 37 above) 33–41.

[72] Archbishop Rowan Williams, 'Civil and Religious Law in England: a Religious Perspective' (see Appendix I).

[73] See O Roy, *Secularism Confronts Islam* (trans G Holoch) (New York: Columbia University Press, 2007) Ch 1.

[74] A C Korteweg, 'The Sharia Debate in Ontario' (2006) 18 *ISIM Review* 50. See also Gaudreault-DesBiens, Ch 4 and Shachar, Ch 8 in this collection.

[75] See J Rawls, *Political Liberalism* (New York: Columbia University Press, 1993); M Fadel, 'The True, the Good and the Reasonable: The Theological and Ethical Roots of Public Reason in Islamic Law' (2008) 21 *Canadian Journal of Law and Jurisprudence* 5.

[76] Cf Asad (n 69 above).

traditions and forms of life without continuing to interpret 'the West' in a confined binary fashion, as ultimately either the *dār ul-harb* (the house of war), or the *dār ul-Islām* (the house of Islam).[77] The accommodation of Shari'a in the West would seem to be a litmus test—possibly *the* litmus test—of whether anything more than a *modus vivendi* between these two forms of life is going to be possible.

D. A Slice of Demography

Islam's global adherents number some 1.2 billion and can be found on every continent. Figure 1 illustrates the territorial spread. Within the West, Islam is growing. Figures 2, 3, and 4 depict the numbers of Muslims in Western nations and the present proportions of the total population they represent.[78] This expansion, while boosted initially by immigration, is likely to be significantly enhanced in the twenty-first century by the higher birth rate of Muslims compared to the non-Muslim Caucasian majority.[79]

E. Islam, Islamism, and Reform Islam

Islam and *Islamism* are not to be confused. It would, admits Roger Scruton, 'be the greatest injustice to confuse' the two.[80] Islam, as a religion, is distinct from Islamism and the various near-synonymous expressions, such as 'radical Islam',[81] 'political Islam',[82] 'puritanical Islam',[83] and 'Islamo-fascism'.[84] Islamism is a *political* philosophy and programme—'a belligerent ideology bent on eradicating all opposition to its claims'[85] and '[a] puritanical ideology... [that] is a newly constructed version of Islam that does not necessarily have much to do with what the faith, at least from a scholarly perspective, was really all about'.[86] Further, Islamism

---

[77] Fadel (n 24 above) 115–116; and Milbank, Ch 9 in this collection. For some Muslim scholars this question is located within and secondary to a broader project aimed at revitalizing Islamic civilization: see, eg A A Allawi, *The Crisis of Islamic Civilization* (New Haven: Yale University Press, 2009).

[78] The figures are taken from the CIA World Factbook, *An Analysis of the World Muslim Population by Country/Region* (2009), available at <http://www.factbook.net/muslim_pop.php>.

[79] See C Caldwell, *Reflections on the Revolution in Europe: Immigration, Islam and the West* (New York: Doubleday, 2009) 116–119.

[80] R Scruton, *The West and the Rest* (London: Continuum, 2002) 109.

[81] Eg M Phillips, *Londonistan* (New York: Encounter Books, 2006) xxiii.

[82] Eg M S Muthuswamy, *Defeating Political Islam: The New Cold War* (Amherst, NY: Prometheus Books, 2009); the Third Section of the Chamber of the European Court of Human Rights in *Refah Partisi (No 1) v Turkey* (2002) 35 EHRR 3 at [59].

[83] Eg K A El Fadl, *The Great Theft: Wrestling Islam from the Extremists* (New York: Harper Collins, 2005) 16 ff.

[84] Eg C Hitchens, 'Defending *Islamofascism*', *Slate*, 22 October 2007.

[85] Scruton (n 80 above) 109.

[86] W Hallaq, ' "Muslim Rage" and Islamic Law' (2003) 54 *Hastings Law Journal* 1705, 1716.

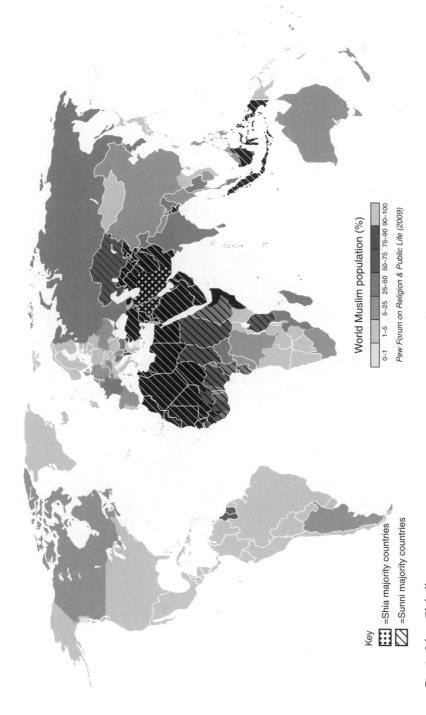

Fig. 1: Islam Globally

Rex Ahdar and Nicholas Aroney

Fig. 2: Europe

Fig. 3: North America

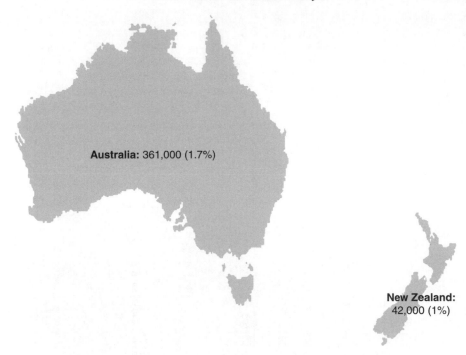

Australia: 361,000 (1.7%)

New Zealand:
42,000 (1%)

Fig. 4: Oceania

can be divided into two additional branches, according to the means used to the
same desired ends. There are, Tibi explains, the peaceful, institutional Islamists
who seek to establish *nizam Islami* (the Islamic order) based on Shari'a through
democratic and electoral means.[87] Then there are the violent Islamists who wage
jihād, in the sense of *qital* or 'violence', in order to bring about the same grand
end.[88] One of the more visible faces of Islam in Britain is 'Islam for the UK', a
group that organized a march in London in October 2009 (later cancelled in the
wake of strident counter-protests) calling for the full implementation of Shari'a.[89]
The object of the organization is 'to propagate the supreme Islamic ideology within
the United Kingdom as a divine alternative to man-made law', ie *'Izhaar ud Deen*
(Domination of Al-Islam worldwide)'.[90] However, the organization expressly disa-
vows the violation of the life or property of UK residents[91] and thus would appear
to be located within the peaceful Islamist camp.

---

[87] Tibi (n 11 above) 44.   [88] Ibid.
[89] A Jamieson, ' "Muslims want *Shari'a* law in Britain" claim', *Daily Telegraph*, 15 October 2009.
Groups opposing Islam for UK, such as the Islamic Society of Britain, welcomed the cancellation:
'Democratic Muslims pleased as *Shari'a* demo is called off', *Daily Religious.com*, available at <http://
www.dailyreligious.com/?p=23798>.
[90] See *Islam for the UK* website, at < http://www.islam4uk.com/about-us>.
[91] Ibid.

While these distinctions can be made, however, there can be no denying that Islamism is based upon Islam. It is 'a religionized ideology'.[92] Islamism may or may not be 'authentic' (in the sense of being a wholly sincere, coherent, and accurate interpretation of Islam), but it is at least a 'particular interpretation' of the faith and its roots are in Islam.[93] To what extent the core tenets and doctrines of Islam are aggressive, expansionist, and violent is thus a complex and controversial question. Islam is a 'religion of peace' cry some, while others are equally vociferous in asserting the opposite. Some say that it may be unnecessary to seek a definitive answer to this formidable question: the task can be left to historians, theologians, and others to pursue. Christopher Caldwell suggests:

How Islamism is related to Islam is beside the point. We can know that Islamism is a serious enemy of the modern liberal state before we have a clear sense of its religious logic and before we know what, if anything, it has to do with 'real' Islam. Proving that Islamism is not the same thing as Islam will not make it less dangerous.[94]

A related theme concerns the so-called 'clash of civilizations' thesis. The phrase is so firmly embedded that we forget its very recent coinage and heuristic character. Samuel Huntington's original 1993 article bore a question mark[95] and in our view that marker remains apt. To recap, Huntington's thesis posited the emergent global 'fault lines' as conflicts between civilizations instead of the political and ideological boundaries and flashpoints of the Cold War. He saw the principal clash as that between the West and a grand alliance of Islamic and Confucian civilizations. Events after 11 September 2001 have subsequently focused more on the Islamic half of the Harvard professor's putative Western nemesis. Criticism can of course be made that the real clash was something entirely different.[96] For our purposes, the main attack has been that Huntington, Bernard-Henri Lévy,[97] George Weigel[98] and others succumbed to a fallacious 'essentialist' understanding of Islam.[99] For broad-brush predictions of civilizational conflict to be postulated, 'Islam' and 'the Muslims' must first be seen as having a unity of mind and purpose and a relatively cohesive shared core. But for the critics, this sort of reductionism

---

[92] Ibid.   [93] Phillips (n 81 above) 168.   [94] Caldwell (n 79 above) 282–283.

[95] S Huntington, 'The Clash of Civilizations?', *Foreign Affairs*, Summer 1993, 22. Interestingly, his book version, *The Clash of Civilizations and the Remaking of the World Order* (New York: Simon & Schuster, 1996), omits the question mark.

[96] See, eg J Kurth, 'The *Real* Clash', *National Interest*, Fall 1994, 3. Kurth argues that the real conflict will take place within the West itself in the form of a clash between Western civilization and a different grand alliance of multiculturalists and feminists. Others maintain that it is more a 'clash of perceptions', and that 'little about our cultures, religions or ways of life…suggest coexistence to be impossible; rather, it is our perception of this impossibility that drives discord': F Rusuf, 'A Clash of Perception, not Civilisations', *Daily Telegraph*, 9 June 2008.

[97] B-H Lévy, *La Pureté Dangereuse* (Paris: Grasset, 1994).

[98] G Wiegel, *Faith, Reason and the War Against Jihādism* (New York: Doubleday, 2007).

[99] Otto (n 27 above) 141–142.

is not just inaccurate,[100] it unwittingly fuels the very conflict it seeks to avert. As Ramadan observes, 'The theses of Huntington and Lévy have, moreover, their parallels in the Muslim world. Incidentally, these feed into one another and each reinforces itself with its alter ego'.[101]

Discussion of Islamism, 'clash of civilizations', and so forth brings into focus the role of the ordinary, 'moderate' Muslim.[102] Like the vast majority of people of whatever faith, the predominant focus of the typical Muslim is not political. Rather, theirs is the perennial mundane task of earning a livelihood, paying bills, providing for the needs of their family, and, quite simply, minding their own business.[103] Moderate Muslims, by definition, do not subscribe to Islamism. Indeed, some even suggest that they are the most frequent and numerous victims of this 'clerical fascism'.[104] If that is so, however, others wryly note that they are a rather silent majority.[105] Liberal governments eagerly awaiting firm denunciations by Muslim community spokesmen of *Al-Qaeda* terrorist attacks have been consistently disappointed: 'condemnation of terrorism has never been frequent or full-throated enough to assure their fellow citizens. There was a collective test of loyalty. Muslims for the most part failed it'.[106] The extent to which this silence represents tacit acquiescence and support for the radicals remains a moot point.[107]

On both sides, if 'sides' there must be, mutual understanding is required. Gross injustices have been perpetrated by (and against) Muslims, Christians, and secularists alike, and those who have suffered most find it difficult to forget. But beyond the injustices and underlying the mutual suspicions are theological and philosophical differences that need to be understood, especially when we consider issues such as the possible accommodation of Shari'a within Western legal systems.

---

[100] Huntington's *Clash of Civilizations* '[f]rom an academic standpoint is a shoddy performance' castigates one critic: A Ahmad, 'Islam, Islamisms and the West' (2008) 44 *Socialist Register* 1, 20. His 1993 'clash' thesis (n 95 above) is found wanting both empirically and theoretically according to another: R P Mottahedeh, 'The Clash of Civilizations: An Islamicist's Critique' (1995) 2 *Harvard Middle Eastern and Islamic Review* 1.

[101] Ramadan (n 14 above) 266–267. See also W T Cavanaugh, 'Clash Course', *Commonweal*, 15 January 2008, 21, 23.

[102] Khaled Abou El Fadl (n 83 above), as part of his mission to 'wrest Islam from the extremists', draws a clear distinction between Muslim 'moderates' and Muslim 'puritans'. In his view (ibid 18), 'the majority of Muslims are moderates'. Those 'described by various writers as fundamentalists, militants, extremists, radicals, fanatics, jihadists, and even simply Islamists' he prefers to call 'puritans, because the distinguishing characteristic of this group is the absolutist and uncompromising nature of its beliefs' (ibid).

[103] Otto (n 27 above) 150.   [104] Phillips (n 81 above) xviii.

[105] El Fadl (n 83 above) 6 comments: 'Moderates constitute the silent majority of Muslims in the world, but puritans have an impact upon the religion that is wildly disproportionate to their numbers'.

[106] Caldwell (n 79 above) 287.

[107] Muthuswamy (n 82 above) opines: 'even though many ordinary Muslims are busy eking out a living, without their support political Islam's vision of Islamic conquest would be a nonstarter'.

To begin with, it is important for liberal secularists in the West to appreciate the 'indelible connection that Muslims feel with their God, a tie that the Christian West for the most part severed long ago'. Wael Hallaq points out:

The idea of giving to Caesar what is Caesar's and to God what is God's does not wash in the Muslim world-view, for Caesar is only a man, and men, being equal, cannot command obedience to each other. Obedience therefore must be to a supreme entity, one that is eternal, omnipotent, and omniscient.[108]

Because committed Muslims think in theological terms, the nature and character of God and His revealed instructions for humankind fundamentally shape Islamic attitudes to all issues of life, including those of law and politics. As Wael Hallaq has pointed out, mainstream Sunni jurisprudence, influenced by the theology of Abu al-Hasan al-Ash'ari (d 324 AH/936 AD) and working from the premise that the nature of God is radically inscrutable, has traditionally considered the rationale behind God's revealed laws to be beyond human comprehension. Accordingly, the rationales for the rules in the revealed texts could be discovered only to the extent that God chose explicitly to declare the *ratio legis* of each case; without divine revelation, the human mind is utterly incompetent to judge whether an act is good or bad. As a consequence, traditional Islamic jurisprudence has tended to be literalistic in its interpretation of the Qur'an and *Sunna*.[109]

A second important characteristic of Islamic and especially Sunni jurisprudence is that it has historically been administered by a body of jurists that is generally independent of state regulation.[110] There is no jurisdictional hierarchy within Islam, unlike the canon law systems of the Roman Catholic *curia* and other Christian churches.[111] In contrast to Roman and European civil law, which is primarily legislative in character, and unlike English common law, which is essentially judicial in origin, Islamic law is a law of jurists and legal scholars.[112] In this connection, Hallaq argues that the characteristic response of Sunni jurisprudence to the problem of regulating the opinions issued by Islamic jurists was to fix upon certain canonical works, with each school favouring its particular authoritative authors, thus contributing to the highly conservative character of traditional Islamic jurisprudence.[113]

---

[108] Hallaq (n 86 above) 1706.
[109] W Hallaq, *A History of Islamic Legal Theories: An Introduction to Sunni Usul Al-Fiqh* (Cambridge: Cambridge University Press, 1997) 135-136, 207.
[110] Ibid 208.
[111] See J A Brundage, *The Medieval Origins of the Legal Profession: Canonists, Civilians, and Courts* (Chicago : University of Chicago Press, 2008).
[112] M C Bassiouni and G M Badr, 'The *Shari'ah*: Sources, Interpretation, and Rule-Making' (2002) 1 *UCLA Journal of Islamic and Near Eastern Law* 135, 136–137.
[113] Hallaq (n 17 above) 208.

Thirdly, Islamic jurisprudence offers a comprehensive framework for the whole of life: no area of human endeavour is untouched by the Shari'a.[114] As Hallaq observes:

[Islamic] law defined not only the Muslim way of life, but also the entire culture and psyche of Muslims throughout fourteen centuries. Islamic law governed the Muslim's way of life in literally every detail, from political government to the sale of real property, from hunting to the etiquette of dining, from sexual relations to worship and prayer. It determined how Muslims conducted themselves in society and in their families; how they designed and ordered their cities and towns; and, in short, how they viewed themselves and the world around them.[115]

As in the medieval and modern West, there is, fourthly, a strong insistence within traditional Islam on the rule of law: according to classical and medieval Islamic thought, all political authorities are bound by the law and responsible to administer it. Thus, although many Muslim jurists were customarily appointed to administrative and judicial positions, the body of law that they studied and expounded operated very largely outside of state influence and provided a kind of counter-balance to it.[116] And yet, there was not the same separation of life into different spheres governed by distinct jurisdictions that emerged in medieval Christendom; the pluralism in the Islamic tradition lay in the variety of schools of interpretation and the multiplicity of states in which Shari'a was applied.

As Hallaq also points out, however, Western colonization of the Islamic world during the nineteenth and early twentieth centuries led to the creation of 'sovereign' nation-states and the enactment of 'positive' legal codes embodying 'secular' legal values. These codes, on the model of nineteenth-century legal positivism, displaced the Islamic jurists and their Shari'a. Hallaq argues that this does much to explain not just the fundamentalist resurgence with its emphasis on the reinstitution of Islamic law, but also why so many contemporary Islamic states are oppressive regimes: the institutional and social roots of the old Shari'a-based rule of law have been severed and not yet restored.[117]

Into this context, 'Reformist' scholars within the Islamic tradition have, in the last century or so, sought, through various techniques of Qur'anic interpretation and jurisprudential logic, to carve out a middle way between Islamist literalism and secularist modernism. Without attempting to pronounce upon the cogency of these techniques or to predict how successful they are likely to be in the long term,

---

[114] Christianity struggles to recapture this insight—that all of life in all its dimensions is lived by faith and invested with religious significance—and to overcome well-entrenched dualistic tendencies to compartmentalize life into neat boxes marked 'the sacred' and 'the secular/profane'. See A Wolters, *Creation Regained: Biblical Basics for a Reformational Worldview* (Grand Rapids MI: Eerdmans, 1985) 49–54.
[115] Hallaq (n 86 above) 1707.
[116] Ibid 1708–1710. See, further, Hallaq (n 17 above) Ch 8.
[117] Hallaq (n 86 above) 1711–1715. Cf N Feldman, *The Fall and Rise of the Islamic State* (Princeton: Princeton University Press, 2008).

it seems to us to be of great significance that these projects are not simply juristic or philosophical, but are fundamentally theological in character. Reformists characteristically seek to identify the 'spirit', as distinct from the 'letter', of the law, thus avoiding the literalism of the traditional schools. But such reformism, as Hallaq points out, is premised upon a rejection of the fundamental principle of Ash'arite theology, in which it is asserted that human reason is independently incapable of distinguishing between right and wrong and of discerning the *ratio legis* of the Shari'a. On the contrary, the reformists follow the lead of path-breakers such as Muhammad 'Abduh (d 1905), who maintained that there is an inherent harmony between the deliverances of sound reason and the dictates of divine revelation: if there appears to be a contradiction it is because one or the other has been misunderstood.[118] We note, here, that such a move is remarkably reminiscent of the synthesis of reason and revelation inaugurated in profoundly influential terms by St Thomas Aquinas in thirteenth-century Europe.[119]

F. Liberal Democracies and Shari'a: The Broad Policy Options

Any comprehensive philosophy or ideology must deal with those who oppose its basic tenets—what Larry Alexander calls the 'foreign policy problem'.[120] Liberalism is no exception. Like medieval Christianity or traditional Islam, contemporary liberal democracy will defend itself when its fundamental premises or major institutions are directly challenged. As US political theorist, William Galston, observes: 'A liberal democracy must have the capacity to articulate and defend its core principles, with coercive force if needed'.[121] Liberalism has, necessarily, an in-built antipathy to religions that oppose its teachings about truth, goodness, and meaning.[122]

A landmark case of direct relevance to this point is the unanimous 2003 decision of 17 judges of the European Court of Human Rights in *Refah Partisi (No 2) v Turkey*.[123] Refah Partisi (the Welfare Party) was the largest political party in Turkey's Parliament, and in a coalition Government, when in January 1998 it was dissolved and its assets confiscated. The Constitutional Court of Turkey at first instance

[118] Hallaq (n 109 above) 212.
[119] Aquinas, *Summa contra Gentiles* (1259–1265), Bk I, esp chs 3, 7, and 8. See, further, Budziszewski, Ch 11 in this collection.
[120] L Alexander, 'Liberalism, Religion and the Unity of Epistemology' (1993) 30 *San Diego Law Review* 763, 763–764.
[121] W Galston, 'Expressive Liberty, Moral Pluralism, Political Pluralism: Three Sources of Liberal Theory' (1999) 40 *William & Mary Law Review* 869, 904.
[122] 'A liberal society must be intolerant and nonneutral towards the forms of life that are inconsistent with or threatening to its liberal values of human society and the values necessary for its preservation': P Ikuenobe, 'Diverse Religious Practices and the Limits of Liberal Tolerance' in D Odell-Scott (ed), *Democracy and Religion: Free Exercise and Diverse Visions* (Kent OH: Kent State University Press, 2004) 309, 316 (original emphasis omitted).
[123] (2003) 37 EHRR 1.

justified this action on the ground that the Party was a 'centre of activities contrary to the principle of secularism'. This decision was in turn upheld by four votes to three in the Third Section of the Chamber of the European Court of Human Rights at Strasbourg on 31 July 2001, and reaffirmed unanimously by the Grand Chamber of that Court on 13 February 2003. The Strasbourg Courts' grounds for upholding such drastic action were that the Refah Party had been shown to advocate and intend the introduction of Shari'a, either for everyone or as part of a plural system of laws for citizens of different faiths, *and* that its leaders' statements about *jihād* did not clearly rule out resort to force to achieve its aims. Significantly, the Court observed that even in the absence of threats of force, both Shari'a and plural religiously based legal systems were in themselves inherently incompatible with the European Convention on Human Rights and the conceptions of democracy and the rule of law that it enshrines. The following key passage of the lower court was adopted by the Grand Chamber:

Like the Constitutional Court, the [Third Section of the Chamber of the European] Court considers that Shari'a, which faithfully reflects the dogmas and divine rules laid down by religion, is stable and invariable. Principles such as pluralism in the political sphere or the constant evolution of public freedoms have no place in it. . . . It is difficult to declare one's respect for democracy and human rights while at the same time supporting a regime based on Shari'a, *which clearly diverges from Convention values*, particularly with regard to its criminal law and criminal procedure, its rules on the legal status of women and the way it intervenes in all spheres of private and public life in accordance with religious precepts. . . . In the Court's view, a political party whose actions seem to be aimed at introducing Shari'a in a State . . . *can hardly be regarded as* an association *complying with the democratic ideal that underlies the whole of the Convention.*[124]

The Court here invoked what has been described as the principle of 'militant democracy'.[125] This was explained in the Third Section's summary of the Turkish Government's case against Refah Partisi:

The Government asserted that, when confronted with the risk which political Islam represented for a democratic regime based on human rights, that regime was entitled to take measures to protect itself from the danger. 'Militant democracy', in other words *a democratic system which defended itself against all political movements which sought to destroy it*, had been born as a result of the experience of Germany and Italy between the wars with fascism and national-socialism, two movements which had come to power after more or less free elections. In the Government's submission, militant democracy required political parties, its indispensable protagonists, to show loyalty to democratic principles, and accordingly to the principle of secularism.[126]

---

[124] Ibid at [123] (emphasis added).
[125] For an illuminating critique of the concept, see P Macklem, 'Militant Democracy, Legal Pluralism, and the Paradox of Self-Determination' (2006) 4 *International Journal of Constitutional Law* 488.
[126] *Refah Partisi (No 1) v Turkey* (2002) 35 EHRR 3 at [62] (emphasis added).

A more forceful response by the European Court of Human Rights to the advocacy of Shari'a by a European political party can hardly be imagined. The Court's response is comparable to those who are sceptical, if not openly antagonistic, to the recognition of Shari'a in any form. For them, state acknowledgment and adoption of Shari'a is a dangerous folly, even if allowed only in limited form and even if democratically adopted. Over time, they contend, the familiar slippery slope will operate: the ambit of Shari'a law will incrementally expand, an inexorable outworking of its comprehensive scope and the theonomic logic on which it is based. The altered demographics, and consequent greater political clout of the swelling Muslim communities, convince these commentators that this is one slippery slope that will actually materialize.[127]

There are others, however, working also within the framework of liberal democratic politics, who support the recognition of Shari'a, at least to some extent. In its strongest variant, this accommodation takes the form of a fully fledged parallel system of justice operating alongside existing state law. More qualified accommodations (such as that advocated by Archbishop Rowan Williams) involve certain 'safeguards' to the admission and enforcement of Shari'a, including restrictions on its jurisdiction, maintenance of its entirely voluntary nature, and subordination of religious rules and judgments to human rights norms. Thus, for example, some suggest that Shari'a should govern certain areas of law only—most commonly only civil law, family and financial affairs—and not criminal law. In addition, some insist that Shari'a must not be *imposed* upon persons, especially upon the vulnerable or oppressed: hence the rights of Islamic women to opt out of Islamic adjudication and appeal to the secular courts must be maintained. Relatedly, there are those who argue that the operation of Shari'a must be subject to anti-discrimination principles. On this view, historically hard-won protections of women's rights—to equal treatment, for instance—cannot be jettisoned simply because we want to accord religious law limited autonomy.

Lying behind these specific policy responses to Shari'a are different attitudes to the state's treatment of minorities and their religious and cultural needs. Within the framework of liberal-democratic political thought, the various views can be spread along a continuum.[128]

At one end is assimilation. In its pure form, assimilation allows no exceptions at all for minorities. The law is the law and 'when in Rome, one must do as the Romans do'. Migrants and their offspring, as well as indigenous peoples, are to blend into the dominant culture. When believers of a particular religion find themselves in conflict with the general law, then it is *them,* and not the state, which

---

[127] Eg Muthuswamy (n 82 above).
[128] We draw here from Ahdar and Leigh (n 44 above) Ch 3 and W Cole Durham Jr, 'Perspectives on Religious Liberty: A Comparative Framework' in J Witte, Jr and J van der Vyver (eds), *Religious Human Rights in Global Perspective: Legal Perspectives* (The Hague: Kluwer, 1996) 1.

must yield. And if they will not, or cannot,[129] the believers will have to face the consequences—fines, arrest, imprisonment, de-registration, and so on. Now it is true that assimilation in its strict and undiluted form has probably never been practised. States have invariably been prepared to grant the occasional ad hoc exception where these sorts of concessions do not cost the state too much—in terms of both loss of face and derogation from significant societal objects that would otherwise be met by the law.

This leads us to the accommodation model. In the West, the long-standing policy of assimilation has been replaced by multiculturalism as the preferred governmental stance toward minorities and migrants. Multiculturalism has come under a sustained critique of late, but this debate cannot be pursued in depth here.[130] The point of present concern is that self-consciously multicultural societies seek to make *due* allowance for difference. A liberal and tolerant state on this view recognizes religious pluralism and the genuine call of conscience by making *reasonable* accommodation of cultural and religious minorities, *within* the framework of a comprehensive system of law. But note the italicized words. It is not accommodation at all costs, but only an allowance that is 'due' and 'reasonable'. And in the modern West, what is reasonable is for the powers-that-be to determine—given all the usual exigencies and countervailing concerns such as public health, safety, order, and the rights of others. Further, accommodation is located firmly within the existing legal framework of constitutional norms. Accommodation is seen as a gracious *concession* conferred by the framers of the single overarching law for all citizens and decidedly not the acknowledgment of a rival legal order that some citizens, by virtue of their faith, can avail themselves of.

Any yet, accommodation is 'an elastic term'.[131] As Jeremy Waldron has expertly clarified,[132] it may take two broad forms: (a) exemptions from the general law; and (b) enforcement of transactions governed by religious norms. Exemptions from the law of the land are familiar and usually uncontroversial—Sikh motorcycle riders are permitted not to wear crash helmets and devout doctors may be excused from having to perform or counsel abortions.[133] Sometimes the exemptions are more

---

[129] For example, Muslims in Britain have a strong preference for marrying spouses from abroad, leading Caldwell (n 79 above) 225 to warn that large numbers of marriage migrants is 'evidence of a collective choice *against* assimilation [and] indicates that an "ethnic minority" is waiting patiently not until it is welcome enough to assimilate, but until it is strong enough to separate' (emphasis in original).

[130] For a valuable discussion, see A Rubenstein, 'The Decline, but not Demise of Multiculturalism' (2007) 40 *Israeli Law Review* 763. Stanley Fish provides a characteristically provocative and searching analysis in his 'Boutique Multiculturalism, or Why Liberals Are Incapable of Thinking about Hate Speech' (1997) 23 *Critical Inquiry* 378.

[131] See Budziszewski, Ch 11 in this collection.

[132] See Ch 7 in this collection.

[133] See Ahdar and Leigh (n 44 above) Ch 6.

contentious, however—one thinks here of the sacramental use of narcotics such as marijuana for Rastafarians or peyote for native American Indian tribes.[134]

What the Archbishop of Canterbury meant in his lecture when he referred to 'supplementary jurisdictions'[135] was the recognition and enforcement of trans-actions by religious tribunals according to religious norms, the second form of accommodation identified by Professor Waldron. In simple terms, he envisioned tribunals with limited powers being able to resolve certain kinds of disputes accord-ing to their own religious law, and the state cooperating by enforcing those judg-ments. However, the existing UK arbitration law, the Arbitration Act 1996, already embraces religious tribunals within its framework—a context which implies that the Archbishop's proposal was either positively 'otiose'[136] or directed to something significantly more than merely affirming the rights of individual believers to agree to submit their disputes to the arbitration of religious courts. Indeed, Dr Williams referred explicitly to 'something like a delegation of certain legal functions to the religious courts of a community',[137] suggesting a kind of *permanent* recognition of a *standing system* of religious courts having a form of *presumptive jurisdiction* over all persons identified with that religion. However, at the same time he proposed this subject to the bedrock condition that any religious court process must have in-built safeguards, such as the right of appeal to the regular civil courts, and be subject to continual 'monitoring' by the state in order to ensure that the 'rights' and 'liberties' of vulnerable individuals are protected.[138]

Such an arrangement, if secured on these grounds, does not *quite* amount to a comprehensive regime of devolution and autonomy, or what the Archbishop referred to (and expressly refused to support) as 'parallel' jurisdictions,[139] but it may, over time, come close. Notably, Dr Williams considered the recognition of religious tribunals to be properly understood as a matter of 'communal rights' and 'public' legitimacy, and he rejected the idea that the state be conceived as a 'sovereign order' which confers upon other, subordinate orders the merely positive right to exist.[140] Rather, he suggested that the ultimate ground of such accom-modation ought to be a commitment to 'human dignity as such'—no matter how any particular community might understand itself and its rights.[141] However, as Jean-François Gaudreault-DesBiens points out,[142] conceiving the question of the accommodation of Shari'a courts in this way runs the serious risk of over-simplification and a failure to grapple with the much stronger claims that may be made, involving a kind of autonomous self-government, or what Gaudreault-Desbiens characterizes as a form of personal federalism.[143] Autonomy of this

---

[134] See K Greenawalt, *Religion and the Constitution, Vol 1: Free Exercise and Fairness* (Princeton NJ: Princeton University Press, 2006) Ch 5.
[135] See Appendix 1 at [10], [11], [13], [14], and [20].
[136] A Tucker, 'The Archbishop's unsatisfactory legal pluralism' [2008] *Public Law* 463, 466.
[137] Appendix 1 at [8].
[138] Ibid at [10], [11], [14], [16], [19], and [29].   [139] See ibid at [30].
[140] Ibid at [8], [12], and [15].   [141] Ibid at [17].   [142] See Ch 4 in this collection.
[143] See Ch 10 in this collection.

kind is what Professor Budziszewski in this volume distinguishes as a third level of accommodation.[144] Under this stronger model, religious courts are in no sense subordinate or subject to review by the ordinary civil courts.[145] Under such a regime, a wider range of possibilities emerges, which could include the imposition of punishments for violations of distinctly religious norms and rules (fines, corporal and even capital punishment for blasphemy, apostasy and adultery, for example), or punishments that are even more severe than those issued by the general law as a response to the perpetration of certain crimes (amputation for theft, for instance).

G. The Essays

As we have sought to show, the issues raised by the accommodation of Shari'a within Western countries are simultaneously legal, political, sociological, religious, and philosophical. For this reason, the essays collected in this volume are a deliberately eclectic mix, representing diverse perspectives on the topic. There are contributions from a range of disciplines (political philosophy, law, theology, sociology), written from the perspective of several religions and worldviews (Christian, Muslim, Jewish, agnostic), various political persuasions ('liberal', 'conservative', 'communitarian'), and diverse geographical locations (Europe, North America, and Australasia). We have endeavoured to secure as wide a range of views as possible. As is often the case, however, supply did not quite meet demand and the reader will have to judge where the gaps in coverage and analysis lie.

By way of a very brief overview of the essays we start with Tariq Modood. Professor Modood is at the forefront of British discussions of multiculturalism. With the benefit of the effluxion of a year or so, he reflects upon his initial defence of Archbishop Williams' lecture and his condemnation of the vitriolic Islamophobic outcry that followed. He finds that his initial assessment was sound and builds his case for a British instantiation of what he terms, 'multicultural citizenship', based on a 'multilogical' dialogue among equal citizens of all faiths, operating within the context of a 'moderate secularism' which accommodates religion in many and varied ways.

Professor Modood's essay is the first of several in this collection that discuss the arguments in Archbishop Williams' lecture directly and seek to place it in its context. In a most penetrating and original analysis, leading Christian theologian John Milbank dissects the Archbishop's lecture further, going well beneath the surface cut-and-thrust of the all-too ephemeral, if not intestinal, commentary of

---

[144] See Ch 11 in this collection.
[145] One version of parallel jurisdictions is the Malaysian model. For trenchant criticism, see J Neoh, 'Islamic State and the Common Law in Malaysia: A Case Study of *Lina Joy*' (2008) 8 *Global Jurist* (Article 4), available at <http://works.bepress.com/joshua_neoh/1/>.

the day, to the man himself and his theology. Professor Milbank notes that Dr Rowan Williams' erudition and ability to see all sides of an argument, as well as the many subtle nuances of the issues at stake, has paradoxically been his Achilles heel. While perfect for the Oxford don (which Williams once was) this same fair-mindedness and courage can land Williams the Primate (and leader of the Anglican communion) in hot water. Williams, in Milbank's opinion, deserves better.

Professor Jean-François Gaudreault-DesBiens, in turn, analyses the Archbishop's lecture in largely jurisprudential terms. He identifies and clarifies the main thrust of the Archbishop's lecture in its recommendation of an accommodation of Shari'a courts in the form of a kind of 'delegation' of state authority subject to 'conditions' and 'monitoring'. Then, as a prelude to a more substantive analysis and critique (published as a second chapter in this volume), Gaudreault-DesBiens draws attention to certain undeveloped themes and resulting problems in Williams' argument. Williams adopts a primarily individualist and private law-centered framework, he says, which tends to conceal the potential public law implications of the accommodation of Shari'a. There is a significant difference, he explains, between 'opting out of state institutions on religious grounds and asking the state to institutionalize, through positive law, faith-based jurisdictional authorities'. The Archbishop, he suggests, does not fully grapple with the implications of his call for the recognition of a positive and collective, and not merely negative and individual, conception of religious freedom and identity. To illustrate this, Gaudreault-DesBiens recounts in some detail the way in which calls for the accommodation of Shari'a in Ontario, especially given the 'prescriptive and hegemonic tone' of the language in which these calls were made, were very difficult to distinguish from demands for a kind of 'quasi sovereignty'.

Dr Michael Nazir-Ali is perhaps better known as the Bishop of Rochester, a post he held with great distinction until he resigned in 2009. His public persona is also linked to brave media utterances stating what many already knew, but were afraid to declare—that certain suburban enclaves of Britain were now 'no go' areas for non-Muslims. In his lucid essay, Dr Nazir-Ali clarifies the meaning, sources, and interpretive principles governing Shari'a. Several important concrete topics—the role of women, blasphemy, apostasy, *jihād*, Islamic banking and finance, and so on—are also explored. Nazir-Ali does not rule out Shari'a 'councils' or tribunals of limited jurisdiction provided the rights of the vulnerable are protected, but he cautions that if admitted their operation would need to be carefully monitored.

In the last of the essays in this collection which focus particularly on the Archbishop's lecture, James Skillen artfully identifies and interrogates the possible meanings that Dr Williams might have intended in his lecture as a way of opening several crucial questions about the nature of religious communities and other non-governmental institutions, their relation to systems of public law and governance, and the meaning of legal and governmental universality. It is important for Dr Skillen that, although traditional Shari'a offers a kind of rule of law and balance of powers between the authority of the jurist-scholars and the political and judicial authority of the state, it is also true that Shari'a's reach is 'as wide and deep as the whole community' and that it is not evident in any of the schools what the limits of a government's authority ought to be. The key question for Skillen is whether Islam has the resources within its own theology to provide a justification for and a defence of a differentiated society and a pluralized authority structure.

Skillen's essay forms a kind of bridge between essays focussed on Dr Williams' lecture and its context and those which undertake broader theoretical and policy analyses of the 'Shari'a in the West' issue. The second part of the collection contains a series of essays which lay out broad theoretical frameworks for the assessment of what it would mean for the West to 'accommodate' Shari'a.

Professor Jeremy Waldron draws upon his formidable command of liberal political theory to burrow down to the animating principles and models of accommodation of religious minorities that policy-makers ought to be pondering. Difficult but unavoidable questions recur: Is there room for an accommodation at all? If so, how ought this concession to be distributed among the citizenry? And are those exempted from the general law (and governed instead by religiously based norms) adequately protected from exploitation? The answers to these are hardly self-evident or straightforward but, as Waldron says, 'No one ever said that thinking about accommodations would be easy'.

Professor Ayelet Shachar's book, *Multicultural Jurisdictions*, is a seminal work in the field. Her notion of 'transformative accommodation' (reform within the religious tradition in response to inescapable cultural forces) featured prominently in the Archbishop's lecture. In what will be another keenly read piece, Dr Shachar revisits the pitfalls of 'privatized diversity' in the form of state-approved, faith-based arbitration tribunals. She calls for a greater measure of 'regulated interaction' between the state and the religious community to ensure that a baseline of citizen-guaranteed rights is preserved. This safeguarding of hard-won rights is especially crucial, she says, for devout female members of the religion concerned.

Professor Milbank picks up from his earlier essay in this volume by traversing some very deep and difficult intellectual terrain. Readers will need to strap themselves in for an exhilarating ride. His thesis is that the entire idea of group rights is rooted in a medieval 'corporatist' and nineteenth-century 'organicist, pluralist' tradition that is indubitably Christian. In this context he presents the striking argument that only a distinctly Christian polity—not a secular postmodern one—can actually accord Islam the respect it seeks *as a religion*. For Milbank, the answer to many of the apparently intractable questions bedevilling liberal polities in the face of insistent claims by religious communities to public recognition may be found in something that resembles a Christendom *redux*.

Gaudreault-DesBiens, in his second essay in this collection, asks whether it is possible to accommodate Shari'a courts without engaging in a reconfiguration of the political structure of the state as a whole, particularly in the form of a kind of 'personal federalism'. After reciting several common criticisms of personal federalism arrangements, Gaudreault-DesBiens draws attention to the fact that such arrangements have, to date, been implemented almost exclusively within Middle Eastern or Asian societies. While such schemes may in practice have worked tolerably well in the circumstances of those societies, Gaudreault-DesBiens points out that the adoption of similar systems within Western countries may possibly present the kinds of 'unintended consequences' typical of 'legal transplants' generally. This kind of 'reverse Orientalism' needs to be assessed carefully for its likely consequences, not just in 'the West', but in the particular circumstances of each country. Something that *might* work in the United Kingdom may not work so well in Canada, or in France, for example.

Professor Budziszewski subjects the idea of separate jurisdictions to yet another penetrating analysis and critique. Although delivered in an at times ironic style, his intent is very serious. Premised upon a most helpful explication of the three levels of civil accommodation, he shows that the argument that separate jurisdictions might provide a kind of *modus vivendi* is not only unprincipled, but potentially chaotic, if not also quixotic and dangerous. It provides no ground upon which to determine which religious and other groups should be entitled to their separate courts, and it is naive about the potential that separate jurisdictions of this kind might have for gaming and manipulation by those who have ulterior motives. For different reasons, Budziszewski also shows that 'principled' defences of jurisdictional plurality are internally self-contradictory: grounding the argument on the 'equal treatment' of all religions is problematic for there is no 'universal' concept of equal treatment, only 'partial' ones, so to implement equal treatment is to impose a particular conception of equality about which religions disagree. Budziszewski proposes, on the contrary, that the natural law tradition can, in principle, make possible an authentic dialogue about the rule of law between Christians, Jews, and Muslims in a manner consistent with their respective theologies. However, he is also aware of potential problems with this proposal in practice—including questions whether the Islamic religion, properly understood, recognizes some acts as intrinsically evil, whether it authorizes holy war, and whether it justifies religious coercion and the death penalty for conversion from Islam.

The collection next turns to a series of essays that are primarily focussed on the question of the accommodation of Shari'a within particular jurisdictions.

Senator Sophie van Bijsterveld brings a unique perspective to this volume as a current member of a European legislature. As a law professor at Tilburg University and leading academic on Dutch church-state relations, she explains how the Netherlands has responded to the growth of its Muslim community. The key theme, as the old song went, is one of 'getting to know you'. As the Dutch authorities become more familiar with the Muslim culture and worldview, she argues, the ongoing process of contestation and accommodation—that marked the hard-won settlements between the state and the Christian and Jewish communities—is being repeated. This is an unglamorous but necessarily incremental, case-by-case, concrete exercise, she says, one that is best seen through the sociological microscope rather than through a wide-angled lens of abstract policy.

Professor Abdullah Saeed in turn considers whether there is room for Shari'a courts or tribunals in Australia. The issue has hardly been free from acrimonious debate in the Great Southern Land, some seeing it as a complete non-starter and antithetical to the somewhat nebulous concept called 'Australian values'. Saeed believes that most Australian Muslims are 'participants' (a term from his own cultural taxonomy) who can contextualize the requirements of their faith to fit into a liberal democracy guided by human rights norms. In this context he carefully unpacks the practicalities and logistics of Shari'a courts, and the law administered therein.

In her essay, Ann Black, another long-time student of Islamic law, shows that in relation to the possible transplantation of Shari'a law into a Western country such as Australia it is relevant not only to consider social, political, and legal conditions within the 'receiving' country generally, but also the situation of Islamic peoples within that country. Dr Black points out that Shari'a is already practised within Australia 'in the shadow', as it were, of the legal system, and that although further accommodation might be both 'empowering' and 'educative', it remains important to recognize the diverse and indeed factionalized nature of the Islamic 'community' within the country. Black therefore cautions against any premature state recognition of Shari'a courts, given especially that there are serious questions at the threshold about the representative character of any such system of courts. *Whose* Shari'a should be implemented, she in effect asks, and *who* will do the implementing? Until the Islamic community itself resolves these questions, she concludes, it is best for Shari'a to continue to operate within the lives of those for whom it is personally obligatory, without engaging the power of the state to enforce its dictates.

The two last essays provide a kind of conclusion to the collection.

Dr Erich Kolig is a cutting-edge social anthropologist specializing in matters multicultural and Islamic. His comprehensive essay captures the issues central to the entire topic and also addresses a large and thorny question with much vigour and no small panache. Leave aside questions of accommodation and compromise by the dominant secular liberal legal order of the Muslim 'other'. These are but 'small beer'. Instead ask yourself, what if the law of the land were to be 'Shari'aticized'? Professor Kolig makes a cogent case why this would not be a good idea. He concludes with a tantalizing glimpse of a future that navigates past the Scylla of 'liberal sycophantism' and the Charybdis of rampant Islamophobia.

Professor John Witte Jr draws the book to a close. The tireless Director of Emory University's outstanding Centre for the Study of Law and Religion distils the major themes in the book and adds a penetrating discussion of the fate of a central construct in any human society: marriage. 'Marriage is a contract; living together is an arrangement; seeing each other from time to time is simply an understanding.' So goes the immortal quip from that prodigious author, Anonymous. Marriage as a legal construct bears little resemblance to its predecessors from a century, if not a generation, ago. Muslim diaspora communities in the West, Witte argues, quite reasonably seek firmer constitutional ground for the regulation of their own marital and familial relationships and the Archbishop was quite right to say that these are 'unavoidable' questions. Witte elucidates the key lessons that both Western states and minority religious communities will need to learn if they are to craft workable and just public policies for the recognition and regulation of marriage in a multicultural context.

2

Multicultural Citizenship and the Shari'a Controversy in Britain

Tariq Modood

An intense public debate and media controversy was triggered in Britain after a lecture delivered by the Archbishop of Canterbury on 7 February 2008.[1] The lecture raised important questions of law, state, faith, and citizenship in a modern, plural society; and its bitter, polarizing aftermath equally highlights the issue of what kind of civic discourse about these questions is necessary if they are to be properly addressed. This essay responds to the debate and controversy by viewing them in the perspective of 'multicultural citizenship', a concept which allows for nuanced understanding of the inter-relationship of 'secular' and 'religious' notions in civic life.

Dr Rowan Williams' careful address explored the 'growing challenge' presented by 'the presence of communities which, while no less "law-abiding" than the rest of the population, relate to something other than the British legal system alone';[2] raised the question of 'what degree of accommodation the law of the land can and should give to minority communities with their own strongly entrenched legal and moral codes';[3] and included a developed and highly sensitive reflection on the reality and potential of 'plural jurisdiction',[4] particularly in relation to the experience of and discussions about 'Shari'a courts', their capacity to rule on such matters as family disputes and claims, and their relationship to the 'statutory law of the United Kingdom'.[5]

It may seem astonishing that a lecture at the Royal Courts of Justice in London, academic both in atmospherics and language, should generate such passionate denunciation. It is less so if seen in a context where the 'legal recognition of communal religious identities'[6] conjures the worst suspicions and prejudices of those already attuned by a hostile public discourse to regard Islam-based practices, codes, or ideas as by definition extreme or dangerous. Such sentiments are reinforced by a situation where criticism of multiculturalism—often focusing on its

---

[1] See Appendix 1.   [2] Ibid at [1].   [3] Ibid at [2].
[4] Ibid at [11].   [5] Ibid at [3].   [6] Ibid at [14].

alleged socially divisive tendencies and supposed empowerment of reactionary religious forces—has become both routine and (often) ill-informed. In turn, they fuel the argument that a turn towards a more or less rigorous secularism that would exclude recognition of religion in the public sphere is desirable. This line of argument, however, offers a false diagnosis and therefore a flawed prescription.

A particularly stark vision of these alternative social models was presented by David Hayes in the weeks after the terrorist attacks in London on 7 July 2005: the attacks, he argued, opened a new period in Britain's development where the choice was between 'radical multiculturalism' and 'radical secularism'.[7] But these are not the only choices; indeed, they are not realistic choices at all, because they deny the complex but definite reality of a deep resonance between citizenship and multicultural recognition. Together, these elements presuppose complementary notions of unity and plurality, and of equality and difference; and they are further linked by the fact that central to citizenship is respect for the group self-identities that citizens value. This is the context, I suggest, within which this latest 'multiculturalism' versus 'secularism' storm can best be understood.

A. Citizenship and Multicultural Citizenship

Multicultural citizenship is based on the idea that citizens have individual rights, but as individuals are not uniform, their citizenship contours itself around the specific individuals that make up a citizenry of a particular time and place. Citizenship is not a monistic identity that is completely apart from or transcends other identities important to citizens. Their group identities are ever-present, and each group has a right to be a part of the civic whole and to speak up for itself and for its vision of the whole.[8]

Hence citizenship is a continuous dialogue. As the parties to these dialogues are many, not just two, the process may be described as 'multilogical'. The 'multilogues' allow for views to qualify each other, overlap, synthesize, modify one's own view in the light of having to coexist with others, hybridize, allow new adjustments to be made, new conversations to take place. Such modulations and contestations are part of the internal, evolutionary, work-in-progress dynamic of citizenship. Thus, civic inclusion does not consist of an uncritical acceptance of an existing conception of citizenship, of 'the rules of the game' and a one-sided 'fitting-in' of new entrants (or 'new equals'—mostly ex-subordinates of the colonial experience). To

[7] 'What kind of country?', *Open Democracy*, 28 July 2005, available at <http://www.opendemocracy.net/conflict-terrorism/britain_2713.jsp>.
[8] For a fuller statement of this understanding of citizenship, see T Modood, *Multiculturalism: A Civic Idea* (Cambridge: Policy Press, 2007).

be a citizen, no less than to have just become a citizen, is to have a double right: to be recognized, and to debate the terms of recognition.

Citizenship consists of a number of coterminous processes: a framework of rights and practices of participation; discourses and symbols of belonging; ways of imagining and remaking ourselves as a country and expressing our sense of commonalities; and differences in the ways in which these identities qualify each other and create inclusive public spaces. Change and reform do not all have to be brought about by state action, laws, regulation, or prohibitions; they are also the result of public debate, discursive contestations, pressure-group mobilizations, and the varied and (semi-) autonomous institutions of civil society.

Citizenship, then, is not confined to the state but dispersed across society, compatible with the multiple forms of contemporary group identity. It is sustained through dialogue, new and reformed national identities, and plural forms of representation that do not privilege one group as the model to which all others have to conform.

The ideal of multicultural citizenship is a critique of the cultural assimilation traditionally demanded by nation-states of migrants and minorities, as well as of that liberal individualism that has no space for groups. Nevertheless, it is clearly grounded in, and is a development out of, the ideas of individual equality and democratic citizenship. It is not about pre-democratic arrangements such as the Ottoman accommodation of minorities through the *millet* system. It seeks to pluralize, and hence adapt, not undermine, the unity and equality of citizenship and national identity.

B. Multicultural Citizenship and Religion

What implications does this have for religious groups? It means that secularism pure and simple—the absolute and dogmatic separation of citizenship and religion—appears to be an obstacle to pluralistic integration and equality. This is a big implication but not as radical as it sounds. For secularism *simpliciter* is not what exists in Britain, nor indeed in any democratic country. Britain is a secular country and a version of secularism is indeed hegemonic; but it is of a moderate kind that accommodates organized religion, religious identities, and conscience.

This is evident in many areas: constitutional arrangements, schools, government support for welfare by religious agencies, and ministerial consultations with religious groups, etc. These arrangements reflect a particular history to the point of idiosyncrasy, but moderate secularism is the secularism of all democracies (as opposed to, say, the Soviet Union or communist China)—even though each draws the religion-politics linkages and separations in its own way.

Multicultural citizenship's relation to the state, and to the varied areas of civil society and local government that shape and make meaningful our civic identities, is broad rather than narrowly defined. This means that a focus on legal provisions is not the beginning or end of multicultural citizenship. But it is an important area, and so everything the Archbishop said about the need to explore accommodating aspects of Muslim principles and laws (the heterogeneous collection of texts and forms of reasoning summed up as Shari'a) within UK law is relevant to the task of multiculturalizing citizenship. The Archbishop was thinking about how the work of the existing Shari'a councils (which adjudicate on personal and civil matters such as divorce) could be extended and given legal recognition in the way that their Jewish equivalents have enjoyed for decades or longer.

He was quite clear that this was not a matter of separate or parallel legal systems, for the Shari'a tribunals would not be able to go against UK laws, both on specific areas or cases and on individual and human rights in general. The decision to go to such Muslim adjudication services has, of course, to be voluntary by both parties, and above all the Archbishop rightly emphasized the importance of gender equality in these contexts. These courts would not have the power to punish or fine individuals and so would concern only civil matters, and have nothing to do with criminal justice. Many people, willfully or otherwise, misunderstood Dr Williams' position and thought (sincerely or otherwise) that he was sanctioning the stoning of adulterers, hands-chopping for theft, and beheadings for apostasy. Even some of those who recognize that he was not doing so still argue that his intentions here are not relevant, for granting anything to Muslims in this area would encourage extremists and unreasonable demands and propel the entire society down a slippery slope to the 'Talibanization' of British law.

This is not an argument, but scaremongering on a large scale. To avoid discussing and conceding what is reasonable because someone else might later demand something unreasonable is irrational. And to associate a whole group, in this case Muslims, with their extremist elements is a kind of political demonization that may appropriately be called anti-Muslim racism.[9] Of course, some Muslims may, just as anybody may, make unreasonable demands; but to therefore dismiss all Muslim demands is surely to draw the line between what is acceptable and unacceptable in the wrong place. As a matter of principle, each proposal should be considered on its own merits; and there is wisdom in discussing and implementing proposals on a gradual basis so that their practical effects can be seen and lessons can be learned.

---

[9] It is not unusual for communities defined by religious traditions and families to be 'racialized'. It is the historic experience of the Jews, and can be seen in the Catholic-Protestant non-doctrinal communalism in Northern Ireland, as well as in the 'ethnic cleansing' of Muslims by Serbs in Bosnia. For a discussion of ways in which Muslims in Britain are being racialized, see T Modood, *Multicultural Politics: Racism, Ethnicity and Muslims in Britain* (Minneapolis, MN: University of Minnesota Press, 2005).

C. Legal Positivism and Critical Interpretivism

This is not just a matter of pragmatism and practical wisdom. It flows out of the ethics of multicultural citizenship: the imperative to seek the inclusion of marginal groups through dialogue, a commitment to seek mutual under-standing and find accommodation. There is a yet deeper philosophical basis for what I am advocating. We should not ideologize Shari'a and secular law into rival, exclusive, and inflexible systems. They have much in common both at the level of principles as well as the capacity to live together. Those who think the opposite are likely to be influenced by a form of reasoning I will call legal positivism.

Positivists understand principles, bodies of thought and practice, and tra-ditions as if they were self-evident, and that once learned all that is needed is to apply them in a legalistic way to a specific situation. Legal reasoning itself highlights the distortion of reasoning that this view embodies. For laws are not self-evident; otherwise why are there enormous legal libraries that contain volu-minous commentaries, analyses, and interpretations, as well as stacks of case law and precedent?

Interpretation and sensitivity to context are always essential to the application of a rule or law to a specific case. Understanding the rule depends upon reading it with other rules and principles that illuminate and qualify it. These rules and principles are not self-evident but rationally provoke questions which have to be critically engaged with. If the situation to which the rule has to be applied is to be understood, a capacity must exist both to identify what is similar in that situation to all the other cases to which the rule applies and what is distinctive or new about the context, and which may require a questioning or refinement of the relevant body of principles and rules. In short, it requires the critical reason-ing that Muslim jurists call *ijtihād*. A simple illustration lies in the fact that at the time of the founding texts of Islam, there was no tobacco in Muslim socie-ties. Hence the question of what attitude a believer should have to tobacco—its cultivation, trade, and consumption—is a matter of identifying the relevant rules and principles and showing in what ways and to what extent and under what conditions they apply to tobacco. To do that is to critically interrogate the texts and to extend the structure of thought and practice built upon them. The conclusion of the process may entail more than simply reflecting on a new case: it may open the way to a new understanding of the principles involved, their interrelationships, ambivalences, and contradictions—perhaps even to a reinterpretation of what had been considered settled. Some principles may thus be tightened and given greater definition, others loosened to widen their range of applicability; and there can thus be implications for other cases and questions of behaviour.

D. Practical Multiculturalism

There are significant practical difficulties in giving public recognition and legal incorporation of Shari'a councils. They must of course work within UK law, only delivering judgments that are consistent with it, including human rights, gender equality, and child protection legislation. There must be no compulsion or social pressure to go to them in preference to civil courts or other lawful remedies. The adjudicators need to be properly trained and qualified, both in terms of Islamic knowledge and authority but also in terms of their understanding of UK law and society, and the complex context in which the cases arise and within which they must be understood and resolved.

As there is no single ecclesiastical authority in Islam, certainly not in Sunni Islam, these problems cannot be addressed simply at the top and filtered down through a hierarchy. Yet it is a fact that Shari'a adjudication councils do exist and operate in Britain and so it is very likely that some of the problems just mentioned are problems that already exist. These must be addressed, but in sensitive and feasible ways; that is, not by picking a fight with Muslims but by bringing them deeper into British institutions and practice, and by equitable treatment that extends to Muslims the opportunities and resources that other groups enjoy.

This issue has some parallel with that of faith schools. In England there are thousands of Christian and Jewish schools largely funded by the public purse and which teach about one-quarter of all pupils. So, when some private Muslim schools sought to enter this voluntary-aided sector their inclusion was reasonable and just and an appropriate elaboration of multicultural citizenship. But the process has been neither simple nor automatic. The schools had to teach within a national curriculum, have competent teachers, appropriate facilities and governance, meet a local need, and be open to professional inspection. Some private Muslim schools have been able to meet these criteria—indeed, they meet them better than many comprehensives; others are working to reach these standards and most are outside the system.

This is a good model for finding ways to respond to the existence of Shari'a adjudication panels. The principle of their incorporation as a feature of the developing multicultural citizenship should be accepted. The existence of comparable Christian and Jewish institutions (such as the *Beth Din*) should be used as a benchmark—though not inflexibly nor as a perfect model; then the practical issues can be considered, including the safeguarding of individual rights, especially those of women and children, with each application being examined on its own merits. Some applications may not be able to meet the requisite standards, others may not seek this formalization (though that is not to say that they should be beyond all regulation and support if there is a cause for concern). A trial-and-error basis should operate with existing arrangements as a guide; yet out of this the emergence of some institutional innovation is likely, so, as always, caution is needed. This would be both a pragmatic way to proceed and an appropriately British form of multicultural integration, something that works with the grain of what already exists (just as other countries may want to do it their own way).

The storm that the Archbishop's views provoked is in many ways more instructive than what he himself said. The reaction was immediate and was wholly disproportionate. Part of the problem is language. The mere fact of saying something positive about Shari'a leads to knee-jerk hostility among many people. Regrettably, and in a similar fashion, the term 'secularism' is understood by some Muslims as a policy of atheism, colonialism, or post-colonial despotism. The use of either of these terms can lead to the closing of minds, however reasonable and qualified what is being said.

Beyond this, it is clearly indicative of deep insecurities and fears about Islam among many non-Muslim British citizens. The resulting tendency to demonize and victimize Muslims is deeply regrettable; yet the ethic of dialogical citizenship offers Muslims a basis both to stand up for equal status in a dignified way and to seek to address these fears sensitively and in the spirit of mutual concern and solidarity. It is not easy to be sympathetic and considerate when under attack, but a shared future depends upon handling even Islamophobic hysteria in the spirit of common citizenship. For Britain belongs equally to all its citizens, its problems no less than its gifts. In mutual recognition of this shared ownership lies the hope of a secure and inclusive future.

E. Retrospection

The foregoing was written (taking a couple of days out of a busy academic schedule) in the heat of the moment, when the furore over Archbishop Williams' lecture was still in the airwaves.[10] Yet there is nothing in it that with hindsight—enriched by further reading and reflection, as well as the knowledge of subsequent developments—that I would wish to change. I continue to think that much of the 'debate' was driven by stereotypes and fear of Muslims, and some of it by wilful scaremongering. I maintain that what the Archbishop argued was sensible as well as learned and not anything as radical as his critics thought. The latter is vindicated by the fact that journalists have now discovered that Shari'a councils already operate in England. These usually comprise informal bodies of local *imams* providing a mediation and arbitration service covering mainly marriage and divorce matters—though in the case of the most organized body, the Muslim Arbitration Tribunal (MAT), it also resolves disputes between business partners or mosques. The MAT currently only operates in five cities but it intends to expand to other cities and also

---

[10] T Modood, 'Multicultural Citizenship and the Anti-Sharia Storm, *openDemocracy*, 14 February 2008, available at <http://www.opendemocracy.net/article/faith_ideas/europe_islam/anti_sharia_storm>.

to train *imams* from other bodies. Shari'a councils are completely voluntary and operate within the law of England and Wales as an arbitration service under the Arbitration Act 1996 and their judgments are not legally binding without the support of a county court. That they are not a challenge to English law was made clear by the Chief Justice, Lord Phillips' endorsement of them as vehicles for alternative dispute-resolution, the Chief Justice noting that 'our system already goes a long way towards accommodating the Archbishop's suggestion'.[11]

I would, however, point to a fact that was quite visible at the time and yet which some, including myself, failed to highlight. This is that the controversy was not started by Muslims. They, together with the Archbishop, faced a barrage of criticism, for which they were completely unprepared as the controversy was sprung upon them out of the blue. Indeed, it was unclear to what extent the call for the legal incorporation of Shari'a councils was of importance to most Muslims. For British Muslims the issue aroused nothing like the passion that some controversies had. Think of *The Satanic Verses* uproar, the Danish cartoon affair, the international and domestic 'War on Terror', the Israeli attacks on Lebanon and Gaza, and ongoing debates about female dress. The passion unleashed by the Archbishop's Lecture was very largely one-way: it consisted of mainly non-Muslims expressing outrage at Rowan Williams and at things Islamic. In this context, while there seems to be a growing demand by some Muslims, not least women in relation to issues surrounding divorce, for *halal* conflict-resolution and that this demand is being met by an expansion in the number of Shari'a councils in Britain, I would like to acknowledge that not all Muslims fully agree with the kind of support I have given above to this development. At one level it is obvious that not all Muslims agree on this (or indeed any other) matter. But I am thinking of people with whom I normally have wide areas of agreement and so would have expected to have agreement on this issue.

For example, Samia Bano has probably done the most systematic research on the use of Shari'a councils in Britain by women. In a thoughtful article she makes a number of cautionary points. Her research suggests that while some women want the provision of Shari'a arbitration, in many cases the actual practice of the arbitration services reflects patriarchal assumptions and power relations. She believes that the institutionalization of Shari'a bodies should not proceed without a proper examination of the position of women and without the involvement of women.[12] I think the difference between us is not very great. As I originally argued, the vulnerability of women (and children) in the process must be highlighted and their rights safeguarded. So I would fully support the involvement of women at every level of consultation and institutional design. I would perhaps hesitate to make that a necessary condition of approval of a Shari'a body. Requiring such bodies to

[11] See Appendix II and 'Sharia law "could have UK role"', *BBC News*, 4 July 2008, available at <http://news.bbc.co.uk/2/hi/uk_news/7488790.stm>.
[12] S Bano, 'In Pursuit of Religious and Legal Diversity: A Response to the Archbishop of Canterbury and the "Sharia Debate" in Britain' (2008) 10 *Ecclesiastical Law Journal* 283.

publish their *fatawa* would go some way to alerting women's organizations, professional advisers, and individual supplicants about the track record of a council and so enable women-friendly bodies to be selected and hopefully to proliferate over time. For me, the bottom line is that if such bodies already exist and are growing in number and scale then it is better to bring them into the system and regulate them. Creating barriers to that by instituting a regulatory regime that deters bodies from making themselves fully public and legal, especially if it is perceived that greater demands are being made on Muslims than on others, will not protect the interests of Muslim women (nor would it be consistent with equity and multicultural citizenship). It will only lead to 'back-street Shari'a councils' that may do more harm than recognized bodies whose processes can be publicized and monitored.

Perhaps a more fundamental disagreement is with Tariq Ramadan. Even though he was quoted at length by Dr Williams, Ramadan did not appreciate the Archbishop's intervention on this issue. This was partly because he saw how the lecture—however far this was from Dr Williams' intentions—whipped up fears among non-Muslims. But more fundamentally, Ramadan baulked because he believed that talk of Shari'a in Britain was steering Muslims away from the importance of abiding by a singular law of the land.[13] This is wholly consistent with his French republicanism, which has always made him warn against minority rights and 'victim mentality', be lukewarm about multiculturalism, and consistently stress the importance of the shared rights and duties of common citizenship.[14] I believe, as argued above, that this is too simplistic a view of citizenship, especially in a context of ethno-religious diversity. Our common citizenship should not swamp our other identities (that is usually a recipe for cultural majoritarianism) but should allow difference to coexist, and interact, with commonalities.[15] I suspect that Ramadan also feels that Shari'a is currently interpreted in too many different ways and is often applied in ways described above as legal positivist and inconsistent with its core principles. For Ramadan, Shari'a needs serious scholarly reform and consensual modernization and without this it is in no fit state to be brought into contact with English law.

[13] W Woodward and R Butt, 'Williams Defiant over Islamic Law Speech', *Guardian*, 9 February 2008, available at <http://www.guardian.co.uk/politics/2008/feb/09/uk.religion>.
[14] T Ramadan, *Western Muslims and the Future of Islam* (Oxford: Oxford University Press, 2004). Unfortunately, some French intellectuals completely fail to see this. In a translation of a co-authored article of mine for publication in a book by Presses de Sciences Po, the publisher (despite the efforts of the French editors) refused to publish the original footnote. This read: 'It is sadly ironic that such an integrationist is reviled by many French intellectuals and has been denied entry into the US, and was the target of a boycott attempt by the National Union of Students, who tried to exclude him from the 2004 European Social Forum (www2.mpacuk.org)'. Instead, the publisher suggested: 'It ought to be remembered that Tariq Ramadan is a controversial scholar, that he has been under a lot of criticism from French intellectuals, and that his participation in the European Social Forum (2004) generated a great deal of controversy too'. Such academic censorship is a reflection of the demonization of one of the leading European Muslim intellectuals. I did not accept their footnote though offered to withdraw it but Sciences Po refused to accept the inclusion of my article in the book and it was ejected.
[15] For an elaboration of this view, see Modood (n 8 above).

If so, I do not disagree with that description, but I do not draw the same conclusion. One of the ways forward can be through piecemeal application (say, in relation to marriage and divorce) and through engagement with the principles and practice of contemporary English law. I differ from Ramadan here. Such interaction—which can be influential in both directions—is part of my understanding of citizenship in a multicultural society.

3

The Archbishop of Canterbury: The Man and the Theology Behind the Shari'a Lecture

John Milbank

A. The Lecture and the Aftermath

Over the first two weeks of February 2008 in the United Kingdom, a sizable controversy was stirred up by a lecture given to the Royal Courts of Justice by the Anglican Archbishop of Canterbury, the Rt Rev Rowan Williams, entitled 'Civil and Religious Law in England: A Religious Perspective',[1] and a prior interview which he gave to the BBC Radio 4 news programme, 'The World at One'.[2] In the course of both the talk and the interview, the Archbishop suggested that certain extensions of Shari'a law in Britain were both 'unavoidable' and also desirable from the double point of view of civil cohesion and the defence of the 'group rights' of religious bodies.

Public reactions to this pronouncement were both swift and overwhelmingly negative. The Prime Minister distanced himself from the remarks, declaring that there could be but one common law for all in Britain, which must be based upon 'British values'.[3] Most political leaders from all the main British political parties more or less followed suit. The popular press suggested that the Archbishop was clearly as mad as his hirsute appearance had always led them to suppose,[4] while the quality press by and large accused him of extreme political naivety, obscurity, and misplaced academicism.[5] Certain commentators at the higher end of the

---

[1] See Appendix 1.
[2] The transcript of the BBC interview with Christopher Landau on 7 February 2008 is available on the Archbishop's official website at <http://www.archbishopofcanterbury.org/1573>.
[3] R Butt, 'Gordon Brown backs archbishop in sharia law row', *Guardian*, 11 February 2008, available at <http://www.guardian.co.uk/world/2008/feb/11/religion.islam>.
[4] Eg Jeremy Clarkson railed at the Archbishop's 'idiocy' and his behaving 'like some deranged Duracell rabbit': 'I'll follow laws of MY religion', *Sun*, 9 February 2008, available at <http://www.thesun.co.uk/sol/homepage/news/columnists/clarkson/836484/Jeremy-Clarkson-JEREMY-Clarkson-says-ignore-the-idiocy-of-the-Archbishop-of-Canterbury.html>.
[5] Eg N Johnson, 'A threat to cohesion', *Guardian*, 9 February 2008, available at <http://www.guardian.co.uk/commentisfree/2008/feb/09/athreattocohesion/print>.

media spectrum dissented from the latter verdict, and allowed that Dr Williams had bravely raised issues of great future importance.[6] They also conceded to him that some supplementary elements of the religious law of all three monotheistic traditions were already incorporated by British justice and that further extensions of this accommodation should not be ruled out.

Yet, with near unanimity they declared that he had gone too far in apparently condoning parallel legal systems with an option for people to have certain cases considered either by a civil or religious tribunal. Any such possibility was also condemned by the Catholic Cardinal Archbishop of Westminster, the Rt Rev Cormac Murphy-O'Connor,[7] and this was discretely echoed by the majority of even the Anglican bench of bishops. It was reported that only three per cent of the members of the Synod which helps to govern the Anglican Church in England favoured the Archbishop's opinion, while up and down the country, on the Sunday following the initial furore, priests found themselves forced in their sermons to make some sort of allusion to it, and were only received well by their congregations if they wholeheartedly confirmed their support for one common law for all people resident in England.[8] The population at large, encouraged by some sections of the media, predictably associated the word 'Shari'a' with the chopping-off of hands and the punishment of raped women as fornicators—a reaction which, it seems, the Archbishop's advisors had predicted and warned him against.

Why he went ahead with his remarks in unmodified form in the face of this advice remains something of a mystery.[9] For, unquestionably, it weakened, if only for the short-term future, his standing in the church and in the nation. In addition, the very same African Anglicans threatening (in the summer of 2008 at the Lambeth Conference) to split the Anglican communion over the homosexual issue were further alienated from Williams: several of them operate in countries where Shari'a law is not only applied in a draconian fashion, but is also used as a weapon against the freedoms and customs of Christians. Not surprisingly, in the face of such implications, the Queen herself—who is the ultimate head of the Church of England (though not of the Anglican communion, which nonetheless informally acknowledges the primacy of the See of Canterbury)—was reported in *The Times* to have expressed grave concern over the impact of the row upon the standing of her Archbishop.[10]

---

[6] Eg B Cathcart, 'Omigod! They'll come and chop our heads off!', *New Statesman*, 18 February 2008, 24.

[7] See J Wynne-Jones, 'Sharia law may result in "legal apartheid"', *Daily Telegraph*, 10 February 2008, available at < http://www.telegraph.co.uk/news/uknews/1578211/Sharia-law-may-result-in-legal-apartheid.html>.

[8] Scotland is governed by a different, Roman law-based, civil code and the Anglican Church is not established in either Scotland or Wales.

[9] One commentator speculates that it was not naivety but 'stubbornness': M Bunting, 'A noble, reckless rebellion', *Guardian*, 9 February 2008, available at <http://www.guardian.co.uk/commentisfree/2008/feb/09/religion.politics>.

[10] D Brown and R Gledhill, 'Archbishop faces fresh pressure over Queen's "worry" at Sharia speech', *The Times*, 13 February 2008, available at <http://www.timesonline.co.uk/tol/comment/faith/article3360742.ece.>.

B. Muslims' Reaction

Meanwhile, the reactions of Muslims themselves were such as must surely have left Williams feeling somewhat dismayed. Publicly articulate Muslim women were overwhelmingly hostile. Most moderate Muslims, from spokespersons to those in humble walks of life, said that the issue of Shari'a was of little relevance to them, while one or two heads of mosques—Mohammed Chisti, the Central Oxford *imam*, for example—declared that the Archbishop had endangered the lives of Muslims by stirring up Islamophobia.[11] Even Tariq Ramadan, the well-known Muslim academic (whom Williams had cited in his speech), while welcoming much of it, appeared to distance himself from any endorsement of parallel jurisdictions. The Muslim Council of Great Britain did, however, offer approval while, significantly, expressing concern for Williams' qualified support for Dr Michael Nazir-Ali, the Bishop of Rochester's (truthful, if rhetorically overheated) declaration that certain Muslim-dominated areas of British cities were in effect 'no-go areas' for those of other cultures.[12]

Here, on the side of both the Archbishop and the Council, one detected apparent inconsistencies which may be of some significance. On the one hand, Williams' apparent sympathy for Islamic aspirations was conjoined to a certain fear of multicultural ghettoization of Muslims in particular. On the other hand, the Council's attitude suggested a covert welcome for such segregation, which may call into question its 'moderate' standing. This standing has, in any case, been questioned before by commentators, who point out the degree to which the qualified, 'do-not-use-violence' support for the position of Sayeed Qutb (a crucial Egyptian theorist of modern Islamism)[13] affects the Council's policies and strategies.

As to the 'moderate' character of other Muslims who welcomed Williams' comments, this is more than debatable. At least one cleric insisted, on television, that a Shari'a-regulated marriage law would have to accept polygamy—on the grounds that otherwise an excess of Islamic women left many of them with only the option of becoming either prostitutes or nuns (with the latter being scarcely an Islamic option). All this left Williams wide open to the charge that he had in fact encouraged Muslim extremism and only made the position of the majority of moderate Muslims in Britain more uncomfortable. Most opinion was divided only as to whether he was simply foolish or dangerously adrift from sanity in his

[11] See D Harrison, 'Sharia in Britain: Unease in Oxford', *Daily Telegraph,* 10 February 2008, available at <http://www.telegraph.co.uk/news/uknews/1578215/Sharia-in-Britain-Unease-in-Oxford.html>.
[12] J Wynne-Jones, 'Bishop warns of no-go zones for non-Muslims', *Daily Telegraph,* 6 January 2008, available at <http://www.telegraph.co.uk/news/uknews/1574694/Bishop-warns-of-no-go-zones-for-non-Muslims.html>.
[13] S Qutb, *Milestones* (originally published 1964; later edition: Birmingham, UK: Maktabah Publishers, 2007).

substantive opinions. There were several calls for his resignation[14]—a more or less unprecedented circumstance for an Archbishop of Canterbury.

C. After the Initial Furore

A week or so after the Shari'a lecture, the heat started somewhat to evaporate, and some commentators who took the trouble to read the original speech, wrote that they were surprised by both its subtle seriousness and relevance—even if aspects of it still seemed very ill-judged.

The latter verdict was finally endorsed by Williams himself before a session of the Synod at York—at least to the degree that he was able to do so without seriously losing face (which, most conceded, was fair enough). He confessed to 'clumsiness' and 'unclarity', and crucially denied that he had ever intended to endorse 'parallel' jurisdictions.[15] Yet he proceeded to repeat positions that, in the opinion of many, remained open to such an interpretation. The concession seemed, however, to be enough to ensure a rallying-round by the British establishment in the interests of not allowing any besmirching of the dignity of Williams' office. The Prime Minister endorsed his worth as a person and a leader, while the Synod itself offered surprisingly unqualified support—for reasons both pragmatic and sentimental.

The long-term impact of this public argument remains to be seen—it may well be very short term and limited. However, the broader concerns that Williams rightly and courageously sought to address will not go away and the various reactions to his talk themselves cast an interesting light upon those issues. Just what was Williams trying to say, and why was it received with such incredulity and hostility? What does all this tell us about the situation of cultural and religious diversity in the United Kingdom today?

D. Rowan Williams

It must first be acknowledged that, for some reason or other, the personality of Rowan Williams is itself an issue for the British media. This largely unprecedented fact may itself reveal certain dominant trends within contemporary British culture. His very appearance is an issue, even in the 'quality' press. Alone among prominent public figures, it would seem, the Archbishop is indifferent to personal grooming—despite the best efforts of his aides. His hair, beard, and eyebrows have

---

[14] R Gledhill and J Sugden, 'Archbishop of Canterbury "should resign" over Sharia row', *The Times*, 8 February 2008, available at <http://www.timesonline.co.uk/tol/news/uk/article3335026. ece>.

[15] 'Presidential Address to the opening of General Synod', 11 February 2008, available at <http://www.archbishopofcanterbury.org/1583>.

the unkempt length of an ascetic, not a public executive. In robes he looks naturally magisterial, like a Roman in a toga, but always oddly uncomfortable in trousers. This blatant refusal of any concern whatsoever with image and fashion clearly riles some among the metropolitan *cognoscenti*. His style also appears to hark back to an era of political critique and questioning in the early 1960s, which most of them now assume to be over forever. Perhaps Williams galls them with the emblems of a lost youth, supposedly outgrown yet secretly regretted. But still more fundamentally, the long shaggy beard looks *foreign,* more like the appendage of an Orthodox patriarch than an Anglican cleric.

Here we are never far away from the thought that after all he *is* 'foreign'—a member of the Celtic tribe perhaps least respected by the English, the Welsh, whose nationhood the English vanquished and yet who retain against England the weapon of an esoteric language and impenetrable (in fact, extremely sophisticated) literary culture. Like many Celts, Williams is far more European in his range of reference than the English, and far more overtly intellectual. When he publicly concludes to complexity, hesitation, or even *aporia*,[16] the less educated commentators of the English 'quality' press tend to take this for mental confusion, lack of civil polish, or refusal of evident common sense. English metropolitan culture[17] tends to think that there should be simple, bold answers, elegantly expressed with a few witticisms, like the ideal Oxford undergraduate essay. Williams, who cannot be placed in any convenient box ('liberal' or 'conservative' etc) is an affront to all that, just as he fails to conform to the usual image of the bumbling, non-intellectual Anglican clergyman unable to talk about much except rugby, gardening, detective fiction, and a little light party politics.

In many ways, responses to Williams echo those to the leaders of the Oxford Movement in the nineteenth century and their successors, among whom he was certainly in his youth to be numbered. As a young man he nearly became a Catholic monk and much of his thinking remains basically Catholic or Eastern Orthodox in character—something which people dimly sense as a further 'foreign' element in his make-up. Indeed, his Royal Courts of Justice lecture reveals clearly, to those in the know, a fundamentally Catholic approach to social and political affairs—even if this approach also has a long tradition in Anglo-Catholic, besides Roman Catholic, reflection.

---

[16] *Aporia* is an ancient Greek term meaning hesitating doubt between two opposite opinions, where each opinion appears to be equally problematic. For a good consideration of characteristics of Williams' thought and personality, see Rupert Shortt, *Rowan's Rule: the Biography of the Archbishop* (London: Hodder & Stoughton, 2008).

[17] It is arguable that outside the South-East, most of England itself—especially 'upland England' north of Trent and west of Bristol—is much nearer to 'Celtic' characteristics of delight in rowdiness, dreaming, and debate than inhabitants of the 'Home Counties' surrounding London usually imagine.

E. Wellsprings of the Archbishop's Theology and Ecclesiology

Dr Williams has gradually ceased (though to what precise extent remains unclear) to be an entirely emphatic Anglo-Catholic. One senses, and this is something which commands respect (if not assent), that he feels he can only be head of the Church of England with integrity if he does justice to all the wings of Anglican theological tradition and attempts a certain synthesis. Such unifying attempts tend to show the incoherence of Anglicanism (if we conceive it in this manner, and not in the revisionary Anglo-Catholic sense of regarding it as fully within the same tradition as the Catholic and Orthodox churches). I find that Williams sounds convincing and heartfelt when talking about Maritain, Augustine, Aquinas, David Jones, Dostoyevsky, and Bulgakov, but somewhat more strained when praising the insights of William Tyndale. Attempts to arrive at an Anglican synthesis seem most like muddle when he addresses certain neuralgic issues of the nature of fallenness, grace, sacraments, ecclesiology, and miracles, even though he remains a superb and truly great theologian when he speaks about the Trinity, Creation, Christology, and spirituality. Most crucially, from the point of view of the present set of issues, Williams sometimes curiously shies away from Pauline notions of the Church as an organism ('the body of Christ') and from the orthodox Catholic view that Christ is only mediated to the individual via participation in this corporate body (however generously understood its bounds may be).[18]

But despite Williams' generally stern resistance to qualifications of the divine *apatheia* (impassibility),[19] he echoes in his own way the over-anguished fallacies of earlier Anglican kenoticists[20] when he appears to speak as if the good can *only*

---

[18] See R Williams, 'Foreword' to the (seriously dreadful) report of a 'working group' of the Church of England, *Mission-Shaped Church* (2004), which reflects neither real work nor serious reflection, since it proposes a supposedly 'evangelical' surrender to secularity by abandoning the integral scope of parish mission and liturgical worship in favour of 'niche marketing' and pious gossip. Here, Williams (p vii) suggests that something called 'church' (lower-case) may possibly be (though he has apparently hedged his bets with a preceding 'if') 'what happens when people encounter the Risen Jesus [upper-case and not "Christ"—which panders to evangelical Nestorianism] and commit themselves to sustaining and deepening that encounter in their encounter with each other'. To which one must reply that 'the Church' (Paul's *ecclesia,* which means 'the presiding assembly of the cosmopolis') is rather *already* the collective and interrelational event of the sacramental (non-identical) repetition of the resurrection of the God-Man. By entering within the portals of its microcosm—in whatever manner—the individual begins to share in this event. For the Church, as the Kingdom in embryo, *is* the reality of salvation, not just its medium. This is classic nineteenth-to-twentieth-century High Church Anglican theology (and there is in truth no *other* Anglican theology) later echoed by crucially influential Roman Catholics like Henri de Lubac and Romano Guardini. Why Williams at times compromises this theology is something of a mystery.

[19] This is the orthodox Christian doctrine that God cannot and does not suffer, since, as infinitely 'active', he cannot be said to passively receive anything either from outside or within himself.

[20] Adherents of a 'kenotic' Christology, which derives from Martin Luther and Lutheran tradition stress, follow St Paul, the divine 'self-emptying' in the Incarnation and Passion. Sometimes, in nineteenth-century Lutheran and then late nineteenth-century to early twentieth-century Anglican theology, this involved a heterodox suggestion that God temporarily 'put off' his omnipotence

be fully manifest when it is exhibited in a tragic and ambivalent world where it is bound to fail. For all his formal acknowledgement of resurrection, there is always a sense that he is more at ease with a doomed ethical constancy and that for him (following Hegel, whose orthodoxy he has dubiously defended) finitude as such is fated to engender ambivalence and irresolvable perplexity.[21] The problem with this is that while, indeed, for St Paul, there may be something of our original created flesh that cannot be saved (for we are raised in a new 'spiritual body', implying that the spoiled physical body inherited from Adam is never fully repaired), this is seen as a contingently engendered situation lightened by the fact that the resurrected life will salvage all that really matters. Nor can we ever set *a priori* bounds to the way in which the resurrected life, already begun now, will renew and transform even the damaged earthly paradise. Hence, while Williams is profoundly and uniquely insightful in seeing that there is *some* generally unacknowledged tragic dimension to the Pauline outlook, this should not be taken so far that (a kind of Stoic) resignation in the face of difficulty becomes the last word. For if one so consecrates mere constancy, then one must *also* consecrate difficulty. The ever-present danger in Williams' theology is that he regards conscientious hesitation as the most righteous and holy thing imaginable. The problem then, of course, is that the merely ethical stance of the atheist appears more 'religious' (since it is without false consolation) than the stance of the religious themselves.

Significantly, Williams at times appears to allow that the idea of a non-religious ethic is coherent. But this is to miss the validity of a Nietzschean critique of either a Kantian or a Levinasian stance in their secularized guises: why should the other be seen as sacred in a meaningless universe? What 'good' am I willing for the other besides the amoral goods of self-determination and contentment? It is also to miss the importance of Kierkegaard's 'religious beyond the ethical' as that which paradoxically marks the specificity of the Christian ethical. The 'untested' good that we ascribe to the infinite God is an unimaginable good whose innocence we must take as apophatically[22] exceeding in goodness any 'tested' good which we may

---

through total enclosure within finitude (this having been already somewhat dubiously suggested by Luther, though in terms of paradoxical—and more or less 'monophysite'—identity between human and divine natures which did not affirm any suspension of eternal attributes). In more orthodox versions, as favoured by recent Roman Catholic theology (Hans urs von Balthasar) and High Anglican theology (Donald Mackinnon), it means that divine omnipotence is itself paradoxically kenotic in terms of the 'active reception' that occurs within God between the persons of the Trinity who are fully constituted by their mutually relational giving and receiving. Formally, Williams adheres to the latter position; substantively, he at times still echoes the former.

[21] See R Williams, 'Between Politics and Metaphysics: Reflections in the Wake of Gillian Rose' (1995) 11 *Modern Theology* 3.

[22] 'Apophatically' means 'negatively' in the sense of 'negative' or 'apophatic' theology. According to this essential moment within orthodox theology (for it is not, as sometimes thought, some sort of 'alternative tradition') God is said to be 'good' (and true, one, wise, beautiful, etc) in a manner infinitely exceeding what we are able to think about goodness. In this way the divine 'goodness' etc is denied as well as affirmed.

experience. But it is a trusting confidence in this good that allows us to see the image of this God in the other, and to go on hoping that the real good can be *actualized*: that good and being can once more coincide in human history as they really do, ontologically. For this reason the Christian good is always new, always fresh, always exceptional, even though exemplary. It is a good *beyond the law*, and *only* good because beyond the law in any usual sense.

F. The 'Tragic' Dimension

The broader significance of the 'tragic' bias of Rowan Williams' theology is that it can encourage a sacralization of hesitation and even vacillation. This is only compounded by the mode of very negative Hegelianism which he has imbibed from the British philosopher Gillian Rose, which tended to accord finality to a 'broken', unfinished mode of social mediation, attempting (quite rightly, beyond postmodernism) to link the universal with the particular, the general with the different. Of course, there has to be truth in this, but it is also clearly true that there can be relatively stable social and political resolutions which intimate something of perfection—and that these can sometimes arise by partially refusing or outflanking the generally inherited carapace of our society. Not to allow enough for this sort of relative completion, or to refuse all real countercultural thinking as the delusion of a 'beautiful soul', is to lapse after all into the postmodern promotion mainly of the inevitably aporetic.[23]

Such a tendency in Williams' thought combines in a somewhat fateful way with the admittedly almost irresolvable dilemmas that have confronted him over the homosexual issue. At times he can sound almost as if the complexity of these dilemmas proved the tragic worth and authentic ecclesiality of the Anglican Communion. He can come across as not surprised that the world and the Church turn out to be like this—hopelessly intractable and then doubly intractable to his own wise advice. As Andrew Brown perceptively but sympathetically remarked in the *Guardian*,[24] it sometimes seems that Williams does not grasp the contradiction in first of all recognizing the hopeless evil and ambivalent muddle of the world and then talking as if he can nonetheless appeal to people's most reasonable and subtle sensibilities. The failure consistently to think *politically* here—to be 'as wise as serpents' albeit 'as innocent as doves'[25]—is palpable. For the specifically political yet still Christian question is always: 'who can I persuade and how, if I am to make at least a small advance towards the objective good?'

---

23 For Rose and Anglicanism, see A Shanks, *Against Innocence* (London: SCM Press, 2008).
24 A Brown, 'Laws of the Land', *Guardian*, 7 February 2008.
25 Matthew 10:16.

To return to the gay controversy, it can seem that Williams has lapsed from the pragmatic need to pursue a consistent line: this is especially evidenced in the near-catastrophic about-turn, early in his primacy, over the consecration of Jeffrey John as Bishop of Reading—a decision which Williams eventually vetoed, even though John was a declared celibate homosexual (albeit in a civil partnership with another man) within the terms of the Church's standing rules. Arguably, there was the issue of John's apparent non-repentance for earlier behaviour—but if that was seen to be decisive, then his nomination should have been squashed at an earlier stage, and if this was politically impossible (because of the testing behaviour of the liberal Bishop of Oxford, Richard Harries), then the appointment had to be stuck with, as the lesser of two evils. In the event, vacillation cost Williams both the initiative over the whole issue, as well as the ability to impose a theological vision which would override the contending arguments—something he alone is manifestly capable of doing. (Indeed, it is highly likely that it was this perception which in part led to his appointment.) On the other hand it may be, as Andrew Shanks (Canon-theologian of Manchester Cathedral) and others have suggested, that Williams has not sufficiently considered the possibility of riding the issue out, minimizing international meetings of primates, and endorsing some measure of traditional Anglican local autonomy. Many believe that in this way he would have called the bluff of the African conservatives (whose 'anti-gay' stance is actually a mask for a very non-Anglican biblical fundamentalism).

This, however, is arguable. Williams may, to the contrary, be right in his implicit judgement that, in a newly globalized era, the Anglican communion has to be a more palpably organized reality. But in certain ways the very notion of an 'Anglican communion' is problematic from an Anglo-Catholic or even a 'High Church' perspective. From this point of view, the Anglican Church simply *is* the Catholic Church in England, whose relationship to the Catholic Church elsewhere (the Roman Church, the Eastern Orthodox churches, etc) has become sadly inhibited or temporarily sundered. Hence, an Anglo-Catholic response to an attempt more closely to unite the worldwide Anglican churches would be that this venture cannot stop there. If unity is paramount over any principled stance on an issue such as the homosexual one, then the Anglican Church must once more seek the reunification of all the episcopally based churches, and perhaps newly take the lead in this endeavour.

But there are some signs that this is Williams' conclusion also, and that in the face of double hostility from liberals and evangelicals, he is recalled to his Anglo-Catholic roots. For how else can he make any positive, visionary sense of the seemingly intractable pass to which events (and his response to events) has brought him? He appears to get on well with Pope Benedict XVI, with whose Augustinian and Lubacian theology he indeed shares a great deal in common. Furthermore, certain recent remarks would seem to be trying to pave the way for renewed ecumenical ventures. Thus, Williams now treats with caution the once half-officially recommended Church of England position which held that lay (not clerical) homosexuals could be in faithful same-sex relationships. And far more remarkably, he once suggested, prior to a visit to the Pope, that the Anglican ordination of women was 'only an experiment' and had not been productive of 'all that might have been hoped for'.

All in all, perhaps these particular 'about-turns' are less signs of vacillation than of a new strategic vision. That might seem well and good, yet Williams' dismissal of his earlier essays written while a professor at Oxford—views that were strongly and bravely in support of gay sexual practice (and heterosexual sex outside marriage in certain circumstances)—as merely tentative academic exercises seems at best disingenuous. Moreover, the remarks about women priests imply the possibility of a reversed decision which is beyond the pale of any practical politics. Half of Church of England clergy are female and any such reversal would entirely blow asunder the communion as we know it. Since these remarks about female ordination Williams has made others which clearly go back on them in turn.

One is left then with the perception that, for all the secular press's self-shaming refusal to take seriously a man whose intellectual level is way above their own, it nevertheless (along with many ordinary people outside the Church) picks up certain features of Williams' personality and outlook which Anglican Church-goers perhaps prefer to ignore. As is so often the case, it would seem, serious flaws are the tragic reverse-face of unusually shining virtues. Ability to see all sides of a case also verges on inconsistency. A humble preparedness to listen encourages a failure to back his own unrivalled abilities and supply a strong lead: at this point he can appear more 'arrogantly' concerned to sustain his own quietist mode of complex reflective leadership than to take the strategic and 'simplifying' risks that a leader must take and has been appointed to take. A loyalty to his vision of the good, which we all know would carry him unswervingly through martyrdom (whereas most of the rest of us must be extremely unsure of ourselves in this respect), can also teeter on the brink of unconsciously seeking out a martyrdom which would test his steadfastness. An ability to travel alone in integrity and shape a vision also translates into an occasional inability to seek out advice and engage in genuine (heated, noisy, raucous, Celtic) debate with his intellectual equals. He is, indeed, a Brithonic bard and not a Gaelic dialectician. These flaws have only appeared when a fine and able man is placed in the pole position of exercising power (and one can think here of analogies with Gordon Brown). It is a test, indeed, that almost no one survives. But feeble men fail feebly, strong men spectacularly, and they retain a unique capacity, as Williams still does, to turn failure to ultimate good account.

What I am trying to hint at is that there is a certain symbiosis between Williams' tendency to consecrate uncertainty, and the sheer impossibility of achieving any 'Anglican' synthesis between Catholicism and Protestantism, theological conservatism and theological liberalism, nationhood and ecclesial universality. If he *is* involved in any tragic drama of which he is the representative, then this is it. But most crucially, I think that the ecclesial perplexities in which he is caught up fail to temper his personal tendency towards a hesitancy punctuated by over-abrupt, isolated interventions concerning sometimes quirkily selected, albeit very important topics. And equally, his relative desertion of a consistently Anglo-Catholic position fails to temper the Anglican problematic in the radical manner which that position might allow.

Yet all of the foregoing indicates that the most crucial background to the 'Shari'a controversy' is *neither* the personality of the Archbishop *nor* the current character of the Anglican Church. Rather, it concerns the *theology* of the Archbishop and its sheer mismatch with the general thinking of the people of England (and most likely of Britain) as a whole.

Here, once more, I want to suggest a difficult double-verdict. On the one hand, it is the authentic *Catholicity* of Williams' thinking which stuns and perplexes an ancestrally Protestant and now extremely secular people. On the other hand, their sense of confusion is not altogether at fault. But it is nothing to do with Williams' prose style, which, although idiosyncratic and excessively prolix, is generally clear and sometimes highly forceful—incomprehensible only to those British journalists who left university too soon (before they had read any 'great books') or to British academics apparently lacking the metaphysical part of the human brain. It is rather somewhat to do with a tendency that is the very reverse of what the media supposes—his tendency not to push conceptual inquiry *far enough,* a kind of ultimate yielding on his part to English politeness (perhaps out of a subconscious over-awe, despite himself, for the Oxbridge ethos). It is also to do with a certain surprising lack of relish on his part (beyond a certain point) for the knockabout of argument, but, more fundamentally, with an occasional mixture of incompatible positions which prevents rigorous adherence to *one* view with all its logical consequences. This mixture seems sometimes to cause him to evade relatively obvious conceptual considerations, while elaborating subtle new ones which indeed may have a promising import.

G. The Archbishop's Broader Religio-Political Philosophy

During the same period as the 'Shari'a' speech, Williams delivered two other remarkable addresses: 'Europe, Faith and Culture' (in Liverpool)[26] and 'Religious Hatred and Religious Offence' (in London).[27] Given within a very short span of time, the three lectures can be regarded as a religio-political triptych which

[26] Delivered on 6 January 2008 at the Anglican Cathedral, Liverpool, available at <http://www.archbishopofcanterbury.org/1547>.
[27] Delivered on 29 January 2008 in London (at the James Callaghan Memorial Lecture), available at <http://www.archbishopofcanterbury.org/1561>.

share many of the same themes. They also stand within a much longer series of substantive addresses he has given on the subject of socio-political 'pluralism'.[28]

To put things in highly schematic terms, one could say that, in all three of these addresses, Williams implicitly considered three different ways of considering the place of religion in the modern state and in modern society and culture. The first way is purely secular, in terms of traditions of secular norms which either 'bracket' or deny questions of religious truth. The second is sheerly Christian, appealing to a long and largely consistent Christian tradition of thinking about the nature of the human person and the place of the legal and the political. The third, however, must be described as 'religious *in general*'—indeed he described his controversial Shari'a lecture as offering a 'religious' perspective—and not, be it noted, a theological one. The claim to do so was strongly reinforced before the York Synod, when he argued that part of the responsibility of the Archbishop of Canterbury was to speak on behalf of people of all faiths in Britain. This statement might be considered to be at variance with his strong rebuke to Prince Charles' wish to be designated on his coronation as 'defender of faith', not 'defender of *the* faith' (this faith being none other than the Catholic faith—since this was a title awarded to Henry VIII prior to his defection for a royal theological treatise attacking Martin Luther). The statement, of course, raises the question of what exactly *is* a 'religious perspective in general'?

Whatever the answer to that question, in two of the lectures—'Shari'a' and 'Religious Hatred'—it is this 'pan-religious' perspective which finally dominates (along with an important role given to the first, secular, enlightened way of thinking about the place of religion). In the Liverpool 'Europe' lecture, by contrast, it is the second, Christian perspective which dominates (along with, again, a very significant role for the secular perspective).

What is striking here is the isomorphism between this conceptual tripartition, on the one hand, and the responses of the British public to the Shari'a lecture, on the other. Overwhelmingly, the speech was rejected because the 'pan-religious' perspective was either not understood, or else actively disdained. Most of Williams' opponents defended the universal application and non-exceptionality of British law for British citizens in secular terms, appealing either to 'enlightenment' or to 'British tradition'. The government itself took the latter tack, proclaiming in loud 'bulldog' fashion its unqualified jurisprudential adherence to 'British values'— while at the same time reminding the populace that it had set up a committee in order to discover just what these might be. As Christopher Caldwell rightly notes, it is too late in the day for this sort of call to come from European secular

[28] See 'Secularism, Faith and Freedom', speech given at the Pontifical Academy of Social Sciences, Rome on 23 November 2006, available at <http://www.archbishopofcanterbury.org/654>; 'Christianity: Public Religion and the Common Good', speech given at St Andrew's Cathedral in Singapore on 12 May 2007, available at <http://www.archbishopofcanterbury.org/495>; 'Multiculturalism: Friend or Foe', speech given at Toynbee Hall on 16 May 2007, available at <http://www.archbishopofcanterbury.org/1602>.

governments. Having for the first time abandoned Christian culture at the *mass* level during the 1960s and 1970s, these governments in the 1980s and 1990s then proceeded to give a postmodern preference to the values of all and every 'other'— to the detriment of the European legacy and its fragile sophistication.[29]

However, a surprisingly large number of those who called up talk-radio or wrote to newspapers insisted (with an imperial half-measure of truth) that British law was based upon the 'Judeo-Christian' tradition and should not be 'contaminated' with alien Islamic imports. Moreover, the dominant reaction in Anglican parishes was that the Archbishop of Canterbury should be speaking up in the name of Christian values and Christian-based law—even if an often ageing, 1970s educated clergy tried to explain to them how *kenosis* (humble receptivity) towards the entirely alien 'other' (and especially other religions) was the real kernel of the gospel. Naturally, the laity did not listen to this, silently and rightly excusing their pastors on the grounds of their consistent gospel charity in practice. It would be too hasty to accuse the laity of religious atavism. I also detected a sense that it might be presumptuous for Williams to claim to speak on behalf of Muslims. And clearly a large number of Muslims thought so too.

H. The 'Pan-Religious' Stance

In practical political terms, the claim to speak in a 'generally religious' idiom proved highly problematic. Basically, the Archbishop's only significant united audience here was religious studies lecturers, plus a number of the more liberal, metropolitan laity (whose theological instincts are generally flimsier and more mired in the urban grime of false sentiment than those of 'Middle England'). Here we see yet another irony of Rowan Williams' personal predicament: he may have compromised with the very metropolitan forces that find his Celtic marginality and linked global culture hard to stomach.

This failure to find an audience that supports his positions, and so potentially encourages their implementation, clearly relates to the sporadic lack of a specifically political 'savvy' referred to earlier. Williams was apparently not thinking ahead and asking himself: 'just who is likely to support this?' If, on the other hand, he knew that very few would, was it not counter-productive, in practical terms, to say what he said and when he did? However, he seems more or less to have conceded this point.

Nevertheless, it seems that the Archbishop still thinks that it is ethically and theologically right to think in 'pan-religious' or 'generally religious' terms. He may well believe that he must persist in doing so, even though it proves unpopular. But in this case, as in many others, may it not be true that the (dual) *vox populi* intuits

[29] C Caldwell, *Reflections on the Revolution in Europe: Can Europe be the Same with Different People in it?* (New York: Doubleday, 2009) 88.

a certain intellectual incoherence which it is rightly refusing? Does it actually *out-think* the Primate, albeit in an almost instinctual manner? I think that this may well be the case.

For a start: what is this 'generally religious' position? Does it represent a pluralist theology or is it simply a twist on the secularist argument that accords more respect for 'group rights' alongside individual rights?

Under the first option Williams indicates in a general way that the faiths should respect each other. If this implies for him, as I suspect it does, that any supposition of sheer incommensurability between religions is just as silly as the opposite 'liberal' position (which imagines that religions all exemplify a religious 'essence' in different ways) then this is fair enough. It is also fair enough if it means, as he indeed indicates, that it would be *impossible* to be a good and orthodox (as opposed to fanatical) Jew, Christian, or Muslim without recognizing a great deal in the beliefs and practices of the other two faiths, which one would wholeheartedly endorse, and indeed could hope to learn from.

Nonetheless, this does *not* mean that one might not find differences (perhaps painful ones) from the other two faiths to be equally important. For example, to the frequent exasperation of Jews and Muslims, Christians think that monotheism is vastly preferable to polytheism, but they also think that a *more radical* monotheism is opened up by the doctrines of the Trinity and the Incarnation. They do not regard these doctrines as 'tacked on' to the doctrine of the One God; they think of them as redefining what 'oneness' means (oneness as love, the One God as only able to reveal himself through unity with humanity) in a way that escapes certain spiritual and political dangers of an apparently 'purer' monotheism. Jews and Muslims (especially of the more non-mystical persuasions) think just the reverse—and not without some highly plausible reasons: for them the monotheism of Christians is to be welcomed, but equally (especially according to Muslims) is to be disparaged as an idolatrous and semi-polytheistic dilution of monotheistic purity which encourages neo-pagan social tendencies.

Of course, Williams knows all this—but I am pointing it out in order to indicate the limits to a 'shared faith' perspective, one which also applies to vastly different cultural attitudes (for example towards music, female dress, and pictorial composition). Moreover, the 'resemblances' are only ever detected from a *specific* faith stance, not from a fantasized 'general' religious position. Again, I am sure that Williams would assent to this. It is nonetheless worth making this clear, because it turns out that his 'pan-religious' discourse has far more to do with a secular recognition of 'group rights', allied to a somewhat pathos-filled request that secular people try harder to 'imagine' what it is like to be religious.

It is here that I think Rowan Williams' perspective is weakest and it is here also that I think one can locate the element of incoherence in his thinking that has got him into trouble— an incoherence that is more to blame for the outcome than even his lack of political judgement or the admitted crassness of the media.

It can be argued that little can be built upon a desire for sympathetic imagination for the religious outlook, and that a demand for a *secular* recognition of group rights is like whistling in the wind on a cultural night that is far closer to the nihilistic chime of midnight than Williams perhaps imagines. This is regrettable, because I entirely endorse his crucially important defence of group rights and his critique of the assertion of absolute state sovereignty over other allegiances.

By contrast, I would insist more strongly than Williams that the entire idea of 'group rights' derives from a medieval 'corporatist' and nineteenth century 'pluralist' tradition that is essentially Christian in inspiration. But elaboration of this thesis awaits another essay.[30]

---

[30] See Ch 9 of this collection.

4

Religious Courts' Recognition Claims: Two Qualitatively Distinct Narratives

Jean-François Gaudreault-DesBiens

In 2008, Rowan Williams, Archbishop of Canterbury, shook the United Kingdom when he suggested that it was unavoidable that Shari'a be granted some form of recognition to respond to the needs and expectations of the country's growing Muslim population. Urban legends notwithstanding,[1] he was not arguing in favour of a full-fledged application of the Shari'a in the United Kingdom, but he was rather pleading in favour of a better inclusion of religious sensitivities into the British legal process characterized by a form of uneasiness about religion. In this context, Williams' lecture first and foremost consisted of a critique of legal universalism and of its exclusionary consequences, especially for religious individuals, and he used the example of English Muslims to make his point. As he observed:

If the law of the land takes no account of what might be for certain agents a proper rationale for behaviour—for protest against certain unforeseen professional requirements, for instance, which would compromise religious discipline or belief—it fails in a significant way to *communicate* with someone involved in the legal process (or indeed to receive their communication), and so, on at least one kind of legal theory ... [it] fails in one of its purposes.[2]

This is an important observation, as it points to the need for a constant, intersubjective, legitimization of legal norms in political regimes where the rule of law serves as a governing constitutional principle. Indeed, such a regime is first and foremost one where 'citizens conceive of themselves as the authors of the legislation they must obey'.[3] Therefore, the actual or perceived exclusion of a particular group, religious or otherwise, becomes an important issue from the standpoint of legitimacy and democracy. In Williams' view, this exclusion stems from a refusal

---

[1] In view of attempting to dissipate some of these legends, I deem it important to quote extensively from Williams' text.

[2] R Williams, 'Civil and Religious Law in England: a Religious Perspective' (see Appendix I in this volume).

[3] J Habermas, *Après l'État-nation: une nouvelle constellation politique* (Paris: Fayard, 2000) 108 (author translation).

in many secular states to acknowledge the multiplicity of identities, individual and collective, that all persons carry.[4] In other words, he faults Western legal systems for their monopolistic claims over socio-political identities and for the exclusionary monism that the ideology of abstract legal universalism has brought about. At the same time, he recognizes the danger of having faith-based monopolistic claims replacing secular ones. As he notes regarding the case of Muslims, 'the Muslim, even in a predominantly Muslim state, has something of a dual identity, as citizen and as believer within the community of the faithful'.[5] The logical consequence of such an intellectual stance is to question the sharp private/public dichotomy, often established in officially secular states, between religion and state, the former being relegated to the private sphere and the latter being presumed always to act in a neutral fashion.[6] The next step that Williams takes is to recommend the accommodation of those believers who wish to exercise 'the liberty of conscientious opting-out from collaboration in procedures or practices that are in tension with the demands of particular religious groups'.[7]

It is thus by taking the problems plaguing legal universalism as a starting point that Williams delves into institutional questions, including that of whether or not to recognize in religious courts some form of autonomous jurisdiction. In this context, he envisages 'something like a *delegation* of certain legal functions to the religious courts of a community; and this latter question, it should be remembered, is relevant not only to Islamic law but also to areas of Orthodox Jewish practice'.[8] The use of the word 'delegation' must be stressed here. Indeed, a delegation implies some monitoring and control on the part of the delegator, who, in any event, is always free to put an end to the delegation. Therefore, we would not be talking

---

[4] Williams states: 'There is a recognition that *our social identities are not constituted by one exclusive set of relations or mode of belonging*—even if one of those sets is regarded as relating to the most fundamental and non-negotiable level of reality, as established by a "covenant" between the divine and the human (as in Jewish and Christian thinking; once again, we are not talking about an exclusively Muslim problem)': Williams (n 2 above) at [6].

[5] Ibid at [5].

[6] Williams argues as follows: 'But the point of defining legal universalism as a negative thing is that it allows us to assume, as I think we should, that the important springs of moral vision in a society will be in those areas which a systematic abstract universalism regards as "private"—in religion above all, but also in custom and habit. The role of "secular" law is not the dissolution of these things in the name of universalism but the monitoring of such affiliations to prevent the creation of mutually isolated communities in which human liberties are seen in incompatible ways and individual persons are subjected to restraints or injustices for which there is no public redress. The rule of law is thus not the enshrining of priority for the universal/abstract dimension of social existence but the establishing of a space accessible to everyone in which it is possible to affirm and defend a commitment to human dignity *as such*, independent of membership in any specific human community or tradition, so that when specific communities or traditions are in danger of claiming finality for their own boundaries of practice and understanding, they are reminded that they have to come to terms with the actuality of human diversity—and that the only way of doing this is to acknowledge the category of "human dignity as such"—a non-negotiable assumption that each agent (with his or her historical and social affiliations) could be expected to have a voice in the shaping of some common project for the well-being and order of a human group': ibid at [16]–[17].

[7] Ibid at [19].   [8] Ibid at [8].

about an unchecked implementation of religious law. On the contrary, Williams establishes as a precondition 'for recognising and collaborating with communal religious discipline' that religious jurisdictions do not 'actively interfer[e] with liberties guaranteed by the wider society in such a way as definitively to block access to the exercise of those liberties'.[9] In this context, state courts would not be entirely displaced but somehow 'supplemented'.[10] This explains why he ends up advocating a model devised along the lines proposed by Ayelet Shachar in her seminal book *Multicultural Jurisdictions*,[11] which recognizes in individual believers the liberty to opt out of the state court system in certain 'core' legal areas, from an identity standpoint, without affecting their right to remain within that state system if they so choose. Such a regime, according to Shachar, could provoke a competition between religious and state systems that could lead to the 'transformative accommodation' of both. In sociological terms, the desired outcome of the interaction between the two systems would be mutual acculturation, one that would make each system more sensitive to the core values of the other. This obviously includes basic liberties as far as religious systems are concerned, and particularly those that are exercisable by vulnerable individuals.

Archbishop Williams' starting assumption, ie that some communities 'relate to something other than the British legal system',[12] is an interesting reminder that Western secular societies such as the United Kingdom, Canada, and others have somehow forgotten what it is to evolve in a religious environment. They may also have forgotten that they themselves used to be societies where a majority of the population related to 'something other than the domestic legal system'. In this way, Williams' lecture is not only a call for a deeper accommodation of religious minorities but also, arguably, a call to revisit Western secular societies' religious roots, as well as an appeal to take stock of the discrete persistence of these roots in a series of allegedly 'neutral' norms. Fundamentally, through his questioning of abstract legal universalism, he promotes a state-sponsored reconciliation of believers' multiple identities and loyalties. In this respect, the challenge, in my view, lies in finding a way to structure the interplay between religious and positive legal orders so as to encourage the predominance of the most liberal strands of interpretation available within all religious traditions. The further question is whether conferring upon religious courts some reserved areas of jurisdiction, subject to state monitoring, is the best way to proceed.

That being said, although he refers at times to religious legal traditions other than Islamic law, he is at pains to treat this particular body of law entirely on a par with other religious *corpi juris* that could also seek some form of institutional

---

[9] Ibid at [19].

[10] The Archbishop speaks of 'a scheme allowing for *supplementary* jurisdiction': ibid at [20] (emphasis added).

[11] A Shachar, *Multicultural Jurisdictions: Cultural Differences and Women's Rights* (Cambridge: Cambridge University Press, 2001).

[12] Williams (n 2 above) at [1].

recognition. While laudable, this discursive posture obscures the fact that the theology of a particular faith may be different from that of another and that this may end up affecting the nature, scope, and justification of what I would call 'jurisdictional recognition claims'. Shari'a may very well pose qualitatively different obstacles in that regard, in that it serves as a springboard, *at least in some interpretations*, to claims that question the political structure of secular societies. Arguably, this can be attributed to the rejection, in Islam, of the more or less sharp divide that has been established over the centuries between the secular and religious realms in liberal societies,[13] as well as by the embrace by some Muslim leaders in the West of a strong conception of the politics of recognition. As a result, their claims are often markedly different from those made by other religious groups such as Hassidic Jews or Anabaptist Christians (such as the Amish). To use Kymlicka's typology, the latter will more likely tend to claim 'polyethnic rights', which fundamentally remain anti-discrimination rights (however grounded on a substantive rather than formal conception of equality), while the former may also claim 'self-government rights', which imply some level of recognition.[14] This highlights the dual nature, religious and political, of the claims made by some Muslim leaders. Acknowledging this dual nature does not mean, however, that only Muslims can make, or have made, such 'stronger' claims. For instance, the Ultramontane stream of Roman Catholicism, which emerged in Italy[15] in the early nineteenth century and which more or less dominated until the Vatican II Council, promoted a theology that envisaged the relations between the secular and religious spheres in a manner broadly akin to the said 'strong' Muslim claims. Indeed, Ultramontanism not only rejected the separation of Church and state, but advocated the Church's normative primacy over the state on political questions carrying a moral connotation.[16] Since so many political questions overlap with moral ones, this was clearly a far-reaching claim. In practice, this vision led to numerous fights between the Catholic Church and various

---

[13] To discuss an Islamic rejection of the division between the religious and the secular may to some extent be misleading, as such an assertion relies on an ideal type that tends to reduce the much more complex reality of the law as experienced in contemporary Muslim states. Suffice it to say that at least since the colonial era, acculturation to Western legal models has created a distinction between Shari'a in its traditional sense and the various positive legal systems that have emerged as a result of this acculturation dynamic. In other words, the laws of Muslim states are often much more secular than imagined, even when they claim to be inspired by Shari'a. See E Moosa, 'Colonialism and Islamic Law' in MK Masud, A Salvatore, and M van Bruinessen (eds), *Islam and Modernity* (Edinburgh: Edinburgh University Press, 2009) 158, 173.

[14] W Kymlicka, *Multicultural Citizenship* (Oxford: Oxford University Press, 1995) 27–31.

[15] 'Ultramontane' means 'beyond the mountains', ie the Alps. The reference to the Alps comes from the opposition, in the nineteenth century, between Ultramontanism and Gallicanism, a doctrine of French origins which accepted the separation of the spiritual and temporal realms. So, while Ultramontanism affirmed the Pope's ultimate and unlimited authority in almost all matters (given, as mentioned, the number of questions with a moral connotation), Gallicanism defended the autonomy of local churches vis-à-vis Rome and sought to place limits on the Pope's authority, precisely in favour of national churches.

[16] Y Lamonde, *Histoire Sociale des Idées au Québec 1760–1896* (Montreal: Fides, 2000) 290–291.

states over whose law would, or should, prevail in cases of conflict between secular and religious rules.[17]

Archbishop Williams' lecture unfortunately downplays the potentially stronger component of Shari'a courts' recognition claims. It does so in part because it adopts an essentially individualist and private law-centered grid for analysing such claims. As I will comment in Chapter 10, this constitutes an obstacle to a genuinely complex grasp of these claims. Paradoxically, however, while adopting such an individualist framework, Williams seems to reconceptualize freedom of religion, which has traditionally been understood as a primarily negative and individual freedom, as a positive and possibly collective freedom.[18] Indeed, when he speaks of 'the liberty of conscientious opting-out from collaboration in procedures or practices that are in tension with the demands of particular religious groups',[19] an ambiguity remains. Can this liberty be exercised absent state intervention, or does it necessitate such an intervention to be fully realized? There is a significant leap between opting out of state institutions on religious grounds and asking the state to institutionalize, through positive law, faith-based jurisdictional authorities. Let us not forget that in most, if not all, liberal states, nothing precludes a believer from opting out of the state court system in view of referring a dispute, for example a matrimonial dispute, to a religious authority whose decision will not be legally binding from a positive law angle. However, when examined from the standpoint of religious law and bearing in mind the circumstances in which decisions to opt out of one's religious community are often taken, it can actually be considered binding on the believer who will have little choice but to comply if he or she is to remain within his or her faith-based community. The absence of positive law recognition may not be entirely satisfying, but, as a matter of principle, it does not infringe freedom of religion on a negative understanding of that freedom.[20] This is where the collective (yet not fully articulated) dimension of Williams' conception of that freedom reveals itself: what is in fact sought through claims for the positive law recognition of faith-based decisions in core areas such as family law is the opportunity for a community of believers to access a particular, legally binding system of justice (in the positivist sense) to which they will individually and collectively submit. Providing such an opportunity is intended to protect or promote a certain religious identity which may itself overlap with a cultural and even a

---

[17] For an account of the legal battles between Ultramontanes and secularists in the originally deeply Catholic Canadian province of Québec, see M Morin, 'De la reconnaissance officielle à la tolérance des religions: l'état civil et les empêchements de mariage de 1628 à nos jours' in J-F Gaudreault-DesBiens (ed), *Le droit, la religion et le 'raisonnable': Le fait religieux entre monisme étatique et pluralisme juridique* (Montreal: Éditions Thémis, 2009) 54, 73–84.

[18] Freedom of religion has always had a collective dimension. However, from a liberal perspective, that dimension derives from the prior recognition of that freedom in individual believers.

[19] Williams (n 2 above) at [19].

[20] For a more detailed version of this argument in the Canadian legal context, see J-F Gaudreault-DesBiens, 'Constitutional Values, Faith-Based Arbitration, and the Limits of Private Justice in a Multicultural Society' (2005) 19 *National Journal of Constitutional Law* 155.

political identity, actual or desired. Thus, presenting such claims *solely* as seeking to maximize the religious freedoms of individual believers is misleading.

The collective and political nature of religious courts' recognition claims appears in a more straightforward way in other narratives, which, when examined in context, reveal that the judicial autonomy that they superficially seek aims instead at a sharing of sovereignty within the state, thereby progressing beyond mere 'accommodation' claims. One of these narratives was voiced in the context of the now famous 'Ontario Shari'a courts debate'. By and large, the interest of the recognition claim at stake in this case lies in the intellectual presuppositions that inspired it.

The debate arose as a result of the realization that the legal framework governing contractual arbitration in the Canadian province of Ontario allowed private arbitrators to decide family-related or personal status-related disputes on the basis of religious law.[21] Although this possibility had existed since 1991, it was only much later, in 2003, that a debate ensued about the merits of legally acknowledging faith-based arbitration in family or personal status disputes. This development came about following the announcement by the Society of Canadian Muslims, a private association, of the creation of an Islamic Institute of Civil Justice,[22] under the auspices of which arbitrations based on Islamic law would be conducted and expertise in Islamic law would be pooled. Emphasizing family-related and personal status-related disputes,[23] the Institute did not advocate the systematic primacy of Islamic law over Canadian norms. For example, mandatory state norms such as the prohibition of polygamy would not have yielded to Islamic norms allowing for such a practice.[24] But the Institute's understanding of the exact interplay of Islamic norms perceived as fundamental and Canadian norms enjoying a similar status was not clear. Nor was its proponents' understanding of the interpretation to be given to Shari'a norms. They were rather conservative Muslims, and although being conservative is not per se a problem, the prescriptive and hegemonic tone of their discourse, especially about what is good for 'the' Muslim community, as well as their vision of that community's place within Canadian society, hardly heralded the application of a liberal version of Islamic law.

---

[21] At the time of the debate, the Arbitration Act 1991, SO 1991, cl 17, did not exclude family-related or personal status-related disputes from arbitration, nor did family law legislation, except in respect of certain formal conditions and substantive exceptions dealing with court powers concerning the education, moral training, custody and access to children, and the protection of the children's best interests. Further limits were introduced after the debate, the most important being the decision to restrict the recognition of family arbitrations to those conducted exclusively in accordance with the laws of Ontario or of another Canadian jurisdiction. See, eg Family Statute Law Amendment Act 2006, SO 2006, cl 1.

[22] Information on this project is available at <http://muslim-canada.org>.

[23] Generally speaking, personal laws or personal status laws refer to norms relating to marriage, divorce, separation, inheritance, alimony, custody of children, etc.

[24] In the particular juridical context of the Institute's proposal, which was that of a provincial legislation over family law and arbitration, it bears noting that any proposal for the repeal of the criminal ban on polygamy would have had to be directed to the federal Parliament, which possesses constitutional jurisdiction over criminal law. The same is true with respect to divorce.

For instance, in a position paper demanding the recognition of Islamic personal laws instead of the imposition of state norms in that field,[25] one of the promoters of the Islamic Institute, Syed Mumtaz Ali, had earlier questioned (with co-author Anab Whitehouse) the allegedly secular bias of public institutions in Canada and argued that the imposition of state personal laws constituted a secular interference in the exercise by Muslims of their freedom of religion and that the appropriate remedy was the recognition by the state of relatively autonomous religious tribunals, whose decisions would be legally binding.[26]

Their demonstration proceeds as follows. After acknowledging that some Muslims 'are enamoured with the Canadian way of dealing with and arranging issues of family/personal law', Ali and Whitehouse argue that '[t]here are many other people in the Muslim community, on the other hand, who feel that their sovereignty as human beings, in general, and as Muslims, in particular, has been intruded upon, undermined and marginalized through being prevented from following the requirements of their own religious tradition'.[27] This view is grounded on the belief that '[t]his is the obligation that we have as Muslims, both individually and collectively, to seek to establish an environment which, to the extent that it is feasible and practical in a non-Muslim country, is conducive to living in accordance with the way in which Allah would wish Muslims to live'.[28] But what can be the content of such an obligation? Having stated that 'Muslims are informed in the Qur'an that one cannot consider oneself a Muslim—one who submits to the command of God—unless one adheres to the guidelines, counsel, principles, beliefs and practices that are related to human beings through the Qur'an and the Prophet Muhammad (p.b.u.h.)', they specify that '[p]art of the guidelines, counsel and principles to which Muslims must adhere are the spectrum of constraints and degrees of freedom which give expression to Muslim personal/family law'.[29] Thus, according to that view, having free access to binding Islamic personal/family law is at the core of the freedom of religion of Muslims. They then state their understanding of that freedom:

We do not believe that freedom of religion can be restricted to meaning only that one is free to think what one wants about religious issues or that one is free to perform acts of worship in one's home or place of community worship. The very nature of religion has *everywhere and at all times* been intended to extend into realms which fall beyond the boundaries of the home or the mosque, temple or church. Religion is a way of life, a set of values, a

---

[25] S Mumtaz Ali and A Whitehouse, 'The Reconstruction of the Constitution and the Case for Muslim Personal Law in Canada', available at <http://muslim-canada.org/case.pdf>. Interestingly, the vision of Shari'a espoused in this document tends to present a kind of pure, untouched Shari'a which stands in stark contrast to the Shari'a implemented in most Muslim states, where it is mixed with many other legal influences, including secular influences.

[26] It is interesting to note that complaints about Western liberal societies' secular bias or aggressive secularism are commonly made by conservative religious communities, irrespective of their creed.

[27] Mumtaz Ali and Whitehouse (n 25 above) 8.

[28] Ibid.   [29] Ibid.

framework which is intended to penetrate into, shape, colour and orient all facets of an individual's life.[30]

This assumption brings the Shari'a courts' advocates to conclude that a particular state-sanctioned regime is necessary to ensure the spiritual, political, and cultural well-being of 'true' Muslims, who therefore need the required legal space to blossom as obedient members of a community of believers. The existence of that legal space, it is to be noted, is dependent upon the positive intervention of the state, through statutory recognition and binding legal effect being given to faith-based arbitral awards. Again, religious freedom is conceptualized differently from its classical understanding, which essentially imposes upon the state the duty not to interfere in religious affairs.

Moreover, the desired outcome—the state recognition and binding legal effect—is depicted as a necessity, as Muslims place themselves into an invidious situation should they submit to another set of rules:

If the governmental authorities and judicial system of a non-Muslim country have in place methods of conflict resolution that are rooted in principles and values that are governed by motives other than the intention to please God or which do not serve the best interests of the Muslim community or which contain less wisdom than do the guidelines which have been given by Allah and His Prophet, then Muslims place their spiritual and social lives in dire peril when they submit to that which is other than what Allah has ordained for those who wish to submit themselves to Him.[31]

From this standpoint, the imposition of certain compulsory state norms upon religious arbitration processes can only be viewed as undue intrusions from a foreign system into a system that defines itself as autonomous, if not quasi-sovereign. Religious freedom is thus taken to imply a right to the recognition of that sovereignty, understood as a God-given natural right from which the law derives.[32]

In such a discourse, autonomy does not refer so much to personal autonomy, conceptualized as guaranteeing an individual space where one's religious inclinations will be expressed without external interference, but rather to a form of functional, personality-based autonomy the scope of which can hardly be restricted to religious, family, and educational issues.[33] There is a subtle shift here from autonomy to sovereignty. Let us recall that Ali and Whitehouse contend that Muslims cannot fully live as Muslims in Canada[34] without the particular type of individual and collective self-determination regime that the state recognition of Islamic personal laws would allow, and that the failure to provide such

---

[30] Ibid 10.   [31] Ibid 9.   [32] Ibid.
[33] For a typology of levels of autonomy, see M Weller, *Towards a General Comment on Self-Determination and Autonomy* (working paper), UN Sub-Commission on the Promotion and Protection of Human Rights, Working Group on Minorities (UN Doc E/CN.4/Sub.2/AC.5/2005/WP.5) (2005) 4–6.
[34] Mumtaz Ali and Whitehouse (n 25 above) 8.

recognition, or the withholding of it, further violates their freedom of religion. Moreover, they make clear that the recognition of Islamic personal laws is a tool to protect and promote a Muslim identity in a non-Muslim world, and that since a good Muslim is one who submits to Shari'a, any real Muslim would support its application. They thus finally situate the claim for the recognition of Islamic personal laws within the broader context of a debate on the modes of exercising and sharing sovereignty in Canada. Of course, by so doing, Ali and Whitehouse are not advocating such a thing as the break-up of Canada. They simply advocate, under the guise of what looks like a much more modest jurisdictional demand, what they themselves characterize as a 'radical reconstruction of the Canadian Constitution'.[35] But in all likelihood, such a reconstruction would have to be made on the basis of a regime of *personal federalism,* organized around a set of contractualized statuses. This goes far beyond mere judicial autonomy in specific areas of life.

In a way, these views constituted the sub-text of the claim made by the Islamic Institute of Civil Justice in favour of 'Shari'a courts' in Ontario, even though the text of that claim, ie official documents formally published under the auspices of the Institute, was never as straightforward as those articulated by Ali and Whitehouse under their personal names. In any event, it is hard not to come to the conclusion that the Islamic Institute of Civil Justice's project involved more than merely taking stock of the desire of some individual Muslims to resort to a private religious adjudicator in relation to their family disputes; a collective dimension was extant in that project, which pointed to the political aspect of what superficially looked like a mere religious claim. Clearly, the type of legal pluralism underlying the Institute's project had the potential of becoming somewhat 'stronger' than the one envisaged by Rowan Williams. That being said, the nexus between the individual and the collective established through the Ontario Shari'a courts' claim was perfectly understandable. Indeed, for conservative Muslims, separating the temporal from the spiritual is unthinkable.[36] Shari'a is thus much more than a set of legal norms: it is a way of life, a form of *ethos.*[37]

The claim of the Islamic Institute of Civil Justice was ultimately rejected (in spite of a government-sponsored report that recommended maintaining faith-based arbitration in the field of family law under the condition that an increased monitoring of such arbitral processes be implemented).[38] In this process, all religious groups,

---

[35] Ibid 1.

[36] T Oubrou, 'La *chari'a* et/dans la laïcité' (2005) 48 *Archives de philosophie du droit* 156.

[37] See, generally, S A Aldeeb Abu-Salieh, *Religion et droit dans les pays arabes* (Bordeaux: Presses Universitaires de Bordeaux, 2009).

[38] M Boyd, *Dispute Resolution in Family Law: Protecting Choice, Promoting Inclusion*, December 2004, available at <http://www.attorneygeneral.jus.gov.on.ca/english/about/pubs/boyd/fullreport. pdf>. The so-called 'Boyd report' attempted to locate a middle ground between recognizing the legitimacy of individual choices to resort to religious arbitration and the incorporation of minimal safeguards designed to regulate the consequences of making such choices. For example, it suggested

and not only Muslims, were affected by the Ontario government's decision because all lost the opportunity, afforded since 1991, to have state-sanctioned binding arbitral awards in that field of law.

It is beyond the purpose of this essay to examine either the reasons for that rejection, or the particular constitutional and legal problems the Shari'a courts' recognition claim faced, or even the consequences of, and reactions to, that rejection. Suffice it to say that while some level of post-9/11 Islamophobia[39] contributed to the demise of the Islamic Institute of Civil Justice's project, it would be unduly simplistic to settle for such a monocausal explanation. I would like to use instead the opportunity offered by what I have called the 'sub-text' of that debate to draw attention to the fact that in some narratives, religious courts' recognition claims may imply much more than the mere accommodation of individual choices made by religious believers. In passing, this sheds light on the nature of a particular set of religious claims. Indeed, some of these claims are as much political as they are religious; in the name of freedom of religion (whether or not their understanding of that freedom is legally correct), they seek to establish a *rapport de forces* or to shift the balance of power between religious groups and the state.

In this sense, in spite of being an identity marker among others, religion does not exactly raise, qualitatively speaking, the same stakes as most other identity markers. Because it revolves around the acceptance of, or the submission to, a comprehensive doctrine[40]—the mission of which is to impact the lives of believers in most, if not all, their dimensions—religious identity tends to blur the border between what is political and what is not political, as well as what is 'private' and what is 'public'. It is instructive in this respect to remember that the consecration of freedom of religion in the modern history of the Western state, and the separation of the spiritual and temporal realms that it underlies, by and large resulted from attempts to *tame* religious ambitions to regulate both of these realms. In other words, what could be called religious identity's 'monopolistic temptation' is always present, even when its ambitions are limited to the particular segment of society

the creation of a special judicial review procedure in order to reduce the risk of abuse in religious arbitrations, as well as another under which the authenticity of the consent given by the parties to the arbitration would have been examined by a secular, independent third-party. The report's aim to protect the most vulnerable parties to faith-based arbitrations by linking religious norms and processes to state law—which would have allowed for a form of dialogical pluralism—was clearly commendable, although its appreciation of the concrete circumstances in which individual choices are often made was rather naive.

[39] See, eg R A Macdonald and A Popovici, 'Le catéchisme de l'Islamophobie' in M Jézéquel (ed), *La justice à l'épreuve de la diversité culturelle* (Cowansville, QC: Éditions Yvon Blais, 2007) 19; S H Razack, *Casting Out: The Eviction of Muslims from Western Law and Politics* (Toronto: University of Toronto Press, 2008) 145–172; M Williams, 'The Politics of Fear and the Decline of Multiculturalism' in J E Fossum, P Magnette, and J Poirier (eds), *Ties That Bind: Accommodating Diversity in Canada and the European Union* (Brussels: PIE Lang Publishers, 2009) 53. Although Islamophobia certainly influenced some discourses during the Ontario Shari'a debate, it bears noting that the most vocal and vehement opposition to the Islamic Institute of Civil Justice's proposal came from *within* the Muslim community.

[40] J Rawls, *Political Liberalism* (New York: Columbia University Press, 1993) 146.

formed by the adherents to the creed. Thus, the comprehensive nature of religious doctrines, which today is nowhere better exemplified than in the writings of some fundamentalist Muslims (without being restricted to fundamentalist Islam), entails consequences for one's understanding of freedom of religion and sheds light on the ideal-typical, social-constitutional organization that informs demands for the state's full recognition of religious courts' decisions in matters pertaining to family law. It would be falling upon an epistemological obstacle[41] to blind ourselves to that political dimension of religious claims, as it would also be stumbling over such an obstacle not to take stock of the potential difficulties a society might face in implementing a personality-based federalism in a context that is *a priori* not receptive to it.[42]

---

[41] On the notion of epistemological obstacle, see G Bachelard, *La formation de l'esprit scientifique: Contribution à une psychanalyse de la connaissance objective* (Paris: Vrin, 12th edn, 1983) 14.

[42] See Jean-François Gaudreault-DesBiens, Ch 10 in this collection.

5

Islamic Law, Fundamental Freedoms, and Social Cohesion: Retrospect and Prospect

Michael Nazir-Ali

The aim of the chapter is to provide a basic understanding of the sources and branches of Islamic law and to suggest how 'the principles of movement' in the various schools of law can be used to relate Shari'a to contemporary situations in the Muslim world and more widely. There is particular consideration of penal law and its applicability in present-day societies, and also of the status of women and of non-Muslims. I have given some attention to the hotly debated subject of apostasy and its punishment, as well as the notorious blasphemy law in countries like Pakistan, of which I have some personal experience. This leads to a wider consideration of the status of non-Muslims in Islamic societies. Again, much of this is based on living as a Christian in a predominantly Islamic society. The chapter goes on to consider the scope of Shari'a and the extent of its applicability in non-Muslim societies, especially the West. I suggest that Muslims should be free to order their lives according to the tenets of their faith but that there should be no recognition of Shari'a in terms of public law since the assumptions of the latter are quite different from those of the former. Like others, Muslims would be free, however, to contribute to public discussion from the point of view of their own tradition. My comments here have arisen from the debate in Britain which was initiated by leading figures in the Church and state.

A. The Origins of Shari'a

The term 'Shari'a' is rooted in the general Semitic notion of a way (*sharᶜ*) which leads to a place of safety, to a site where there is water and sustenance for the weary traveller. In modern Arabic, the word *Shāriᶜ* (meaning a thoroughfare or main road) is also derived from the basic verb. In religious terminology, it came to mean the path which believers are to follow to ensure they reach their goal of fulfilling the divine purpose marked for them. The associated term *shirᶜa* at first designated the customs of a people, but in the Qur'an it came to mean a law which had been given to each people (5:51[1]). The Qur'an explicitly says that Jewish people have their own law (*Torah*) by which to make moral and legal judgments (5:46) and, similarly, Christians are to judge by what God has revealed in the Gospel (5:50). In 42:13 it is said that The Way or religion enjoined on Muhammad is the same as the one given to Noah, Abraham, Moses, and Jesus.

In its most general sense, Shari'a is simply the Way of God, as it has been—according to the Muslim point of view—revealed to their Prophet. However, both the Qur'an and the *hadith* (reports of what the Prophet had said about various matters) contain a considerable number of injunctions not only about matters like worship and pilgrimage, but also the regulation of marriage and divorce, war and peace, diet, trade, and a host of other matters. If Muslims were to observe them, they would have to be codified so that they could be studied and made available to those in the community who had a responsibility for their implementation.

It was this that gave rise to the discipline of *fiqh*, or codified Islamic law. When people refer to the provisions of the Shari'a on family issues, penalties, religious freedom, etc, they are often referring to such a codification. The main interest was in the codification of the *ʿibādāt*, that is, matters such as worship, ritual, prayer, fasting, and pilgrimage, where Muslims have an obvious duty towards God. The other area of early interest was the *muʿāmalāt*, regulating the daily lives of Muslims, their social relations, and matters having to do with the governance of the state and relations between states. Gradually, the codifications come to include the most varied of matters—vessels for eating and drinking, the use (or not) of music, art, sport, clothing, and so on—for which provision was made in minute detail.[2]

It appears that the earliest codification was *Shīʿa*, from the *Zaidī* branch of that group. This is in spite of the fact that, in *Shīʿa* doctrine, the *imam* has a continuing prerogative to pronounce on the sources of law—and thus the content of law, of necessity, remains dynamic and fluid. It has, however, been pointed out that such a prerogative remained largely theoretical and did not affect the actual development of *fiqh*.[3]

---

[1]   All numerical references are to the Qur'an. Thus, 5.51 is shorthand for *Sura* (Chapter) 5 (the title of this *Sura* being, *Al- Ma'ida,* the Table Spread), *Ayah* (Verse) 51 of the Qur'an.

[2]   M Geijbels, *An Introduction to Islam: Muslim Beliefs and Practices* (Rawalpindi: Pakistan Committee for Theological Education, 1977) Vol I, 72ff and Vol 4, 444ff; Wael Hallaq, *Authority, Continuity and Change in Islamic Law* (Cambridge: Cambridge University Press, 2001) ixff. See also articles on *fiqh* and Shari'a in H A R Gibbs and J H Kramers (eds), *Shorter Encyclopaedia of Islam* (Leiden: Brill, 1974).

[3]   Geijbels (n 2 above) Vol 4, 357ff; *The Encyclopaedia of Islam* (n 2 above) and especially the reference to E Griffini's translation of *Majmu'a Zaid binʿAlī* (Milan 1919).

B. The Sources and Schools of Law

In about 200 years or so, most of the classical codifications of *Sunnī* law were completed. In their work, the founders of the so-called law schools (or *madhāhib*) used the four sources of law (or the *usūl Al-fiqh*). They are: (i) the Qur'an itself, (ii) the *hadith*, (iii) *Qiyas* (analogical reasoning) which allowed them to transpose judgment about one set of circumstances to another similar set, and (iv) *Ijmāʿ*, which was originally the consensus of those who had been with Muhammad, but later became the consensus of the early lawyers themselves.

In addition to those 'roots' or 'sources' of law, there were the *furūʿ Al-fiqh*, or the 'branches' of the law, that is, the systematic elaboration of how the law, derived from the sources, was to be applied. This was developed from master to pupil and handed down as the tools needed for the practice of *fiqh*. *Qiyas* is a strict method for using the sources in deciding questions which arise in new situations. In addition, there is also the use of *ra'y*. At first, this was the use of the judges' own deliberation and judgment on a particular matter where no precedent could be found.

Gradually, however, in the *Hanafiyya* (or *Hanafī*) School the application of *ra'y* was allowed—even where analogical reasoning could be used in relation to the sources—if practical considerations demanded it and if the judgment suggested by such use was 'better' for the conditions in question. Such a use of opinion by the jurist is known as *istihsān*. Among the *Mālikī* School *ra'y* could also be used and here it is known as *istislāh*. For *Mālikī* jurists, judgments suggested by a strict use of the sources of law, based on *qiyas*, can be set aside if the jurist believes that another course would benefit society more—or at least cause less harm. By contrast, the *Hanbalī* School rejected any use of private opinion by the jurists and insisted on deducing all case law from the traditional sources. A mediating position on these issues was taken by the *Shāfiʿī* School with its doctrine of *istishāb*. These jurists held that a particular application of Shari'a remains as long as it is not certain that conditions have changed. This is clearly a more conservative principle than that of *istihsān* or *istislāh* and, indeed, the founder of this school was critical of these. This tendency was further magnified in the Hanbalite *fiqh* which rejected all subjective and speculative elements and confined itself to the application of deductions based strictly on the traditional sources of law.[4] Such a strict following of the sources of law could, on the one hand, be simply a mechanical reproduction of the school's teaching (as set out by the founders and systemizers of the school) or, on the other hand, it could be a creative engagement of the authoritative texts with a particular situation. As Wael Hallaq has shown, *taqlīd* (the following of a legal precedent) need not be the blind following of a legal authority but can be, rather, the attempt to apply it to individual cases in creative ways.[5]

---

[4] See M Nazir-Ali, *Islam: A Christian's Perspective* (Philadelphia: Westminster Press, 1983) 48ff.
[5] Hallaq (n 2 above) 86ff.

C. The Interpretation and Development of Islamic Law

As discussed above, to a greater or lesser degree there are principles of 'movement' in the four *Sunnī* law schools (*Hanafī, Mālikī, Hanbalī,* and *Shāfiʿī*) as well as the *Shīʿa* School. These certainly do not amount to brand new *ijtihād,* literally self-exertion or effort, but referring here to independent legal judgments (based directly on the Qur'an and the *Sunna*). They do, however, represent flexibility in applying the rules of a particular school of law to specific situations. Faced with present realities, such flexibility may be practically very useful. Muhammad Iqbal, the great philosopher, lawyer, politician, and poet (who is regarded as the ideological founder of Pakistan) affirms the great adaptability of the *Hanafī* school. But he also bewails the imitative bent of its jurists, at least in the South Asian context, who work against the spirit of their own tradition. As might be expected, Iqbal regards this school as the most suitable for modern times and conditions.[6] On the other hand, a case has recently been made for using the *Mālikī* principle of *maslaha,* or the public good. This requires the jurist to take account of human welfare and the common good in reaching any decision. Such a principle may be more acceptable where the people and the scholars are traditional in outlook, as it works within the parameters of a particular school of law.[7] The great Egyptian activist and reformer, Muhammed Abduh, while advocating radical reform of the Shari'a, in fact used the more conservative principle of *maslaha* in the *fatwās* he had to issue as Grand *Muftī.*[8]

Both Abduh and Iqbal, however, were, in the end, ardent advocates of a new *ijtihād*—a radical remaking of Shari'a from basic principles—and of the emergence of a new *ijmāʿ* (consensus) suitable for modern times. Iqbal claims that the use of *raʾy* in relationship to *qiyas* (analogical method) is already *ijtihād.* Hallaq also has pointed out that the emergence of schools of law did not mean that 'ijtihādic' activity, as he calls it, came to an end. It continued within the framework of the law schools, and *mujtahids*—who could frame law simply by reference to its sources and without relying on legal precedent—continued to appear. Hallaq himself lists some from the tenth and eleventh centuries AD.[9] The late Fazlur Rahman has shown in some detail how the thirteenth-to-fourteenth-century reformer, Ibn Taimiyya, both regarded himself, and is widely regarded, as a *mujtahid.*[10] It is indeed remarkable that reforming movements in Islam, both liberal and fundamental, go back to him for inspiration and direction. Similarly, Iqbal mentions the work of Sheikh Ahmad Sarhandi in criticizing the prevalence

---

    [6] M Iqbal, *The Reconstruction of Religious Thought in Islam* (Lahore: Ashraf, 1971) 176ff.
    [7] See further M Baderin, *International Human Rights and Islamic Law* (Oxford: Oxford University Press, 2003); and M Nazir-Ali, *Conviction and Conflict: Islam, Christianity and World Order* (London: Continuum International, 2006) 146.
    [8] Nazir-Ali (n 4 above) 105.
    [9] Hallaq (n 2 above) 62.
    [10] F Rahman, *Revival and Reform in Islam* (E Moosa ed) (Oxford: OneWorld, 2000) 132ff.

of *Wahdat Al-Wujūd* (monistic Sūfism) in India. Sarhandi attempted to turn Sūfīs back to Islamic orthodoxy and used his Sūfī order itself as a vehicle for his ideas far beyond the sub-continent. Because he appeared at the beginning of the second Islamic millennium, he is often known as the *Mujaddiad-i-alf-i-thānī*, or the Reformer of the Second Millennium.[11] Iqbal also mentions the work of the eighteenth-century Sūfī and theologian, Shāh Walīullāh of Delhi, who distinguished between the eternal principles involved in prophetic teaching and the way in which the Prophet embodies and applies them in the life of the particular people to whom he is sent. The former, naturally, are valid for all times and all places, whereas their application can vary according to time and place. It is interesting to note that Iqbal refers specifically to the penal law of Islam. The penalties used to enforce the principles of Islam in the seventh century cannot just automatically be transferred to other places and other ages. Rather, account must be taken of the state of society, the prevalence of justice and compassion in it, the extent to which the judicial and correctional system has developed, and so on. In the light of this, it is very unlikely that Iqbal (or Shāh Walīullāh, for that matter) would have agreed with the rather crude and literalistic way in which Islamic penal law was reintroduced into Pakistan in the 1980s.[12] Having experienced this myself, and having opposed it at the time, it is indeed gratifying to note that the Council of Islamic Ideology is itself having second thoughts about such laws and proposing a revision.[13]

Drawing inspiration from modern Turkey, Iqbal began to see how *ijtihād* could be exercised not by a particular *mujtahid* (however learned), but by the representative assembly of a nation. Such an exercise of *ijtihād* would also exemplify a fresh *ijmāᶜ* (consensus of the community). There were of course problems. For example, would the 'lay' members of such an assembly be qualified to engage in *ijtihād* themselves or would they need 'guidance' by the ᶜ*Ulamā*? In this connection, Iqbal considers and rejects the *Wilāyet-i-Faqīh* solution of the *Shīᶜa* in force then—and currently the theological underpinning for post-revolutionary Iran. He cannot see how the ᶜ*Ulamā* can establish their claim to represent the absent Imam and his authority. He can, however, in a *Sunnī* or mixed context, see a temporary role for the ᶜ*Ulamā* as a source of information and of assistance for an assembly. For him, the lasting remedy lies in better education in the sources and principles of the Shari'a for the representatives themselves. He saw the difficulties that his view would pose for Parliament in undivided India, where the majority of members would not be Muslim. This may have been one of the reasons for his demand for a separate Muslim state. He does not, however, consider what role, if any, the non-Muslim members of a Muslim-majority assembly would have in such matters.[14]

---

[11] Iqbal (n 6 above) 192. See also A M Schimmel, *Gabriel's Wing: A Study into the Religious Ideas of Sir Muhammad Iqbal* (Lahore: Iqbal Academy, 1989) 7.

[12] Iqbal (n 6 above) 171.

[13] See further Nazir-Ali (n 4 above), 126ff; and the report of the Council of Islamic Ideology, Khalid Masud, *Hudood Ordinance 1979, An Interim Brief Report* (2006).

[14] Iqbal (n 6 above) 157, 173.

D. The Status of Women

According to Iqbal, the scope for the exercise of *ijtihād* is very wide and its exercise must, in the end, lead to a radical reconstruction of *fiqh* itself. In the meantime it can be exercised, for example, in relation to the status of women in society. The Turkish Revolution led to demands for female emancipation and equality. As Colin Chapman notes, there are three great inequalities in the Islamic legal tradition: disparities between men and women, between Muslims and non-Muslims, and between the free and slaves.[15] The Turkish revolutionaries were asking for equality in divorce, separation, and inheritance. Iqbal, while he has sympathy with these demands, argues that, in Islamic law, a woman can have the right of divorce delegated to her by her husband and that inequality in the law of inheritance is only apparent, as it is a husband's duty to maintain his wife. He does not comment on the situation of single women or the vexed question of how *mahr* (bridal dowry) is manipulated in such a way as to leave many women penniless after divorce, and without the pos-sibility of alimony. In addition to the *talāq-i-tafwīd*, mentioned by Iqbal, there is also the possibility of a woman obtaining *khulʿ* (a decree of divorce by the courts) with an accompanying exchange of property or other rights. In certain circum-stances, there is also the possibility of divorce by mutual agreement (*mubāraʾa*). It seems then that there may be resources in the tradition, which the exercise of *ijtihād* could use, to bring about greater fairness in the context of divorce.[16]

A review by the Council of Islamic Ideology in Pakistan has shown the vulner-ability of women under the *Hudūd* laws. A woman reporting rape, for instance, may find herself accused of adultery if she cannot fulfil the rigorous requirements for Muslim male witnesses to the rape. It is such unforeseen consequences that have led the Council to conduct a large-scale consultation on these laws and their revision or even repeal. It is interesting here to note that the scholars who were consulted recognized the need for a thorough exercise of *ijtihād* in this area.[17] As we have seen, there is already much material available from Walīullāh to Iqbal on what the fruits of such an exercise might be.

Even where a strict exercise of *ijtihād* has not taken place, there have sometimes been improvements in women's status because of a perception, for instance, that Islam encourages economically useful activity among women, that it requires their presence in representative assemblies, or that access to education should not be withheld from them. On the other hand, extremist forces, like the *Tālibān* in Pakistan and Afghanistan, have campaigned hard and brutally against any role for women outside the home.

[15] C Chapman, *Islam and the West: Conflict, Co-existence or Conversion?* (Carlisle: Paternoster, 1998) 125.

[16] Iqbal (n 6 above) 168ff; L Carroll and H Kapoor (eds), *Talāq-i-Tafwīd: The Muslim Woman's Contractual Access to Divorce: Women Living Under Muslim Law* (Lahore, 1996).

[17] Masud (n 13 above) 75.

E. Apostasy

Whilst the Qur'an condemns apostasy (*ridda*) and the apostate (*murtadd*), their 'dreadful penalty' is for the life to come (eg 16:106). There seems to be no punishment for them in this life. Against this, all the schools of *fiqh* (*Sunnī* as well as *Shīʿa*) prescribe the death penalty for apostates—with the *Hanafis* and the *Shīʿa* exempting women from the extreme penalty, and requiring instead their confinement until they have once again accepted Islam. Naturally, the disparity between the prima facie teaching of the Qur'an and that of *fiqh* has to be explained. This is done in two ways: verses such as 2:217 (which speak of the futility (*habata*) of an apostate's life and work, whether in this world or the next) are interpreted as meaning that there is punishment for apostates in both this world and the next. Other passages, like 4:88–4:89, are taken as the justification for inflicting capital punishment on apostates. There is also evidence from the *hadith* that the apostate is to be put to death. This is confirmed by the *Sunna*, or the practice of his closest companions. The only question here is the method of execution.

The *Encyclopaedia of Islam*, reporting practice in the earlier part of the twentieth century, can claim that the death penalty for apostasy had been abolished in many parts of the Muslim world because of Western influence (though imprisonment, deportation, and lynching by the mob remained possibilities).[18]

In the latter years of the twentieth century, however, there have been concerted moves to bring the punishment for apostasy back onto the statute books. Movements such as the *Jamāʿat-i-Islāmī*, have always argued for the implementation of penalties for apostasy, as it is regarded by them as undermining the *Umma* (the community of Muslims—understood as a socio-political, as well as religious, entity).[19]

There have been attempts, under extremist pressure, in Egypt and in Pakistan to reintroduce the death penalty for apostasy but in both cases the proposals have quietly been shelved because of international pressure.[20] The Iranian *Majlis* recently passed a law putting the death penalty for male apostates onto the law of the land. This would mean that judges would not have to appeal to the provisions of Shari'a to sentence an apostate but could do so directly from the public law of the country. A parliamentary review body has, however, directed that the *Majlis* should reconsider its earlier decision. The Sudan has, notoriously, executed one of its leading Islamic scholars, Mahmūd Taha, on a charge of apostasy because he was advocating a thorough reform of Islam based on what he called 'abrogation in reverse' (an approach that grants priority to the non-violent preaching of the Prophet at Mecca over the later conflict at Medina).[21] Many other examples can be given of attempts to bring back the traditional penalties for apostasy in a number of Islamic countries.

---

[18] H A R Gibbs and J H Kramers (eds), *Shorter Encyclopaedia of Islam* (Leiden: Brill, 1974) 413.
[19] A A Maudūdī, *Rights of Non-Muslims in an Islamic State* (Lahore: Islamic Publications, 1961).
[20] Nazir-Ali (n 4 above) 127.
[21] Chapman (n 15 above) 142.

At the same time, there is a growing number of scholars and activists who take, as their point of departure, their claim that the Qur'an is silent on punishment in this world for apostasy. They minimize the force of the traditions that speak of the extreme penalty for apostasy. It is said, for example, that these traditions are weakly attested as they fall under the category of *ahad gharib* (a tradition which has a single source and only one chain of narrators and is rare) or that they are from an unreliable source, or both. Similarly, it is argued that even the *Hadith* and the *Sunna* cannot trump the Qur'an, and that one *Hadith* must cohere with all the others.[22] It is also claimed that the second Caliph^c Umar disliked the death penalty for apostasy and preferred imprisonment. In this, he is said to have been followed by a number of the early *fuqahā* or canon lawyers.

The late Dr Zaki Badawi has traced the development of thought about *ridda* among the Egyptian *'Ulamā*. He shows how Muhammad ^cAbduh himself and his disciple, Rashid Ridā (the mentor, no less, of the *Ikhwān Al-Muslimīn*, the Muslim Brotherhood) argued that the Qur'an guarantees freedom of religion. Badawi shows how this idea has taken root in the thought of leading scholars at Al-Azhar, the university (and mosque) in Cairo and the premier place of *Sunnī* learning in the world. According to this kind of thinking, the apostate is to have freedom of religion and should be treated like one who has never been a Muslim.[23] In line with such a view, an important Al-Azhar committee has recommended that an apostate should be given a whole lifetime to repent instead of the three days normally allowed in *fiqh*. These are indeed encouraging developments, but at the same time, attacks on prominent personalities, such as Naguib Mahfouz, and legal action against dissidents, like Nasr Abū-Zayd and Nawwāl Al-Sa'adāwī, continue. Most recently, a young woman, Inas Rafaat As-Sa^cīd Muhammad Hassan, was arrested because she had converted to Christianity. In such situations, we have to ask exactly what is the cash value of *fatwās* from even revered institutions like Al-Azhar As-Sharīf?

My own experience is that an apostate's life remains in danger—whether from extremists, neighbours, relatives, or over-zealous members of law enforcement agencies—even if there is no formal provision for the punishment of apostasy.

F. Blasphemy

The crime of apostasy (and its penalties) clearly apply only to Muslims, whereas the offence of *Sabb* (insulting the Qur'an or the Prophet) applies also to non-Muslims.

[22] On the debate regarding the relative importance of the *ahad gharib*, see Y Al-Qaradāwī, 'Apostasy, Major and Minor' on the website, *Islam Online*, 13 April 2006; and MT Ahmad, *Murder in the Name of Allah* (1989) 74ff. See also the article on *Hadith* in the *Encyclopaedia of Islam* (n 2 above).

[23] Z Badawi, 'Freedom of Religion in Islam', an unpublished paper presented to a closed gathering of Muslim and Christian leaders in London in 2003.

Once again, there is unanimity among the lawyers that anyone who blasphemes against Muhammad is to be put to death, although *how* the execution is to be carried out varies from one person to another.

It is this unanimity on capital punishment that led the Federal *Sharīʿat* Court in Pakistan to rule that the death penalty was mandatory for blaspheming the Prophet of Islam. I can testify that the so-called Blasphemy Law has caused great suffering for Christians and other non-Muslim communities and individuals in Pakistan, as well as for some Muslims. The law has become a way of settling scores and of gaining advantage in matters like property disputes. It has also seriously affected research, teaching, and freedom of expression. There have been many convictions in the lower courts though, fortunately, the higher courts have, to date, overturned these verdicts. Nonetheless, meanwhile the accused has been held in custody (even if mainly for his or her own protection), the accused's family is left destitute, and the community from which the accused comes faces harassment and intimidation. Furthermore, even if an accused is acquitted, he or she is not safe from the mob, and judges who acquit alleged blasphemers have been attacked and even murdered.

Again, as with apostasy, there seems to be no provision in the Qur'an for such a draconian punishment. At the most, the Qur'an threatens those who insult God and the Prophet with God's curse in this life and in the next and 'a humiliating punishment' (33:57). It is claimed that the execution of poets, such as Kaʿb ibn Ashraf (who used poetry to insult the Prophet), sets a precedent for executing blasphemers. But, in reply, it is pointed out that the poets were not put to death for blasphemy, but for seditious conduct which was causing unrest in the *umma*.[24] Tradition also records that while some were punished for insulting the Prophet, others were pardoned by Muhammad himself. Which of these attitudes is to prevail in Muslim communities and nations today?

Successive governments in Pakistan, realising how the law has affected their reputation internationally, have sporadically tried to blunt the full force of the law through various administrative and judicial measures. None of these has been wholly successful and the law constantly returns to haunt the politicians and the legal community. In my view, the only real solution is to find resources in Islamic tradition itself to question the very basis of the law and thus to lead to its repeal. Pending this, it may be necessary to suspend or abolish the death penalty altogether. In the case of blasphemy, this would still leave available other penalties for insulting people's beliefs or inciting religious hatred. Such penalties existed before the current law was promulgated and there is no evidence to suggest that they were not enough. Again and again, I have urged the government, at the highest levels, to take swift action. Much has been promised but little has been delivered so far.

---

[24] Ahmad (n 22 above) 93ff.

It is claimed that some *'Ulamā* will object to the abolition or suspension of the death penalty as Islamic law prescribes the *lex talionis* (the law of retaliation) or *qisās* for murder. The relatives of the murdered person have the right to seek life for life or, alternatively, compensation (*diya*). If the death penalty is suspended or abolished for all serious crime, how will this condition be met? Currently, the state determines the nature of the crime and the punishment due for committing it. Personal vengeance by the relatives is excluded. They can, of course, accept the *diya* in place of the killer's execution. Would it not be possible for the state, representing the *Umma* as a whole, to decide—and drawing an analogy with criminal injuries compensation—the appropriate *diya* to be paid by the state itself? Would it not be preferable for the state to decide what penalty to impose on the killer? Such questions need to be explored further, but plainly, the current blasphemy law is neither just nor compassionate nor (some would say) even Islamic. It should not be allowed to continue causing incalculable suffering to mostly innocent people and also tarnishing the image of Pakistan in the international community.

G. The Plight of the *Dhimmi*

One of the leading features of Islamic policy is the *dhimma*. The word means 'protection' or 'responsibility' and, in Islamic law, applies to non-Muslims who accept the conditions for living under Muslim rule. This involves, *inter alia*, paying special taxes, being unable to enter military service or to serve in the higher echelons of the civil service, and being able to maintain their places of worship (but not to build new, or to repair existing, places of worship without permission). Occasionally it has involved instances of systemic humiliation, such as: special dress, houses that are more modest than those of Muslims, not being able to ride horses but only asses or mules, and, in some cases, paying the poll-tax (*jizya*) with some accompanying ritual humiliation (such as being struck on the neck in symbolic fulfilment of Qur'an 9:29 and 47:4)[25]

There have been strikingly different assessments of the *dhimma* situation. On the one hand, Colin Chapman sees it as an improvement in comparison with medieval Europe.[26] On the other, the sustained work of the Egyptian-Jewish scholar, Bat Ye'Or, has shown not only the discriminatory nature of the *dhimma*, but also its role in the numerical, social, and political decline of non-Muslim communities in the Muslim world. She has spoken of a *dhimmī* 'mentality'—a mindset which acknowledges, perhaps implicitly, the superiority of Muslims and seeks to accommodate and even to promote the desirability of an Islamic hegemony. More controversially,

---

[25] B Ye'or, *The Dhimmi: Jews and Christians Under Islam* (London: Associated University Presses, 1985) 201.
[26] Chapman (n 15 above) 32 and *passim*.

she detects the emergence of such a mentality even in some Western dealings with resurgent and radical Islam.[27]

Historically, the reduction of the Jewish fort of the Khaibar, during the Prophet's lifetime and after a siege of six weeks duration by the Muslim forces, and the agreement of its inhabitants to pay *kharāj* (land tax) to the early Muslim conquerors presages the rise of the *dhimma* as the Muslim armies swept across much of the ancient world. Muhammad's treaty with the Christians of Najrān, who were given immunity from attack on payment of a ransom, is another example of the way in which the *dhimma* was to develop. Both of these instances of dealing with non-Muslim populations became patterns for applying the *dhimma* in varied situations across the world. In addition to Jews and Christians, it was extended to the Zoroastrians (perhaps on the basis of 22:17) and later, as the *Chachnāmah* (the ancient chronicle of the Muslim Conquest of the Sindh) recounts, it was further extended to include Buddhists and Hindus.[28] Many of the provisions of the *dhimma*, and, indeed, the development of *fiqh* as a whole, relate to the previously existing Byzantine Codes of Theodosius and Justinian and also to the ancient Persian provision of the *millet* system. In some respects they represent an improvement on previously existing systems—for example, in the treatment of Jews. But in other respects, the *dhimma* regime introduces regrettable innovations, such as the wearing of special dress by the *dhimmis* and the ritual humiliations they had to face in their daily life.[29] Even if the *dhimma* in the early days marked an improvement on what had existed before the advent of Islam—and this cannot be said to be a foregone conclusion—there remain questions about how it developed and the kinds of mentality it produced, both among Muslims and the subjugated peoples.

Today, moreover, there are powerful voices, such as those of the followers of Maudūdī and some of the Ulamā of the Iranian Revolution, advocating a return to the *dhimma*. Some measures have already been enforced—systems of separate electorates, laws of evidence relating to non-Muslims, marriage between Muslims and non-Muslims, and so on. These developments threaten to reverse the progressive dismantling of the *dhimma* since the decrees of the Ottoman Caliph in the nineteenth century. I have seen how non-Muslim citizens have progressively been turned into subjects in a number of countries because of the application of *dhimma*-like conditions on them.

The *Khatt-i-Sharif* of Gulhane and the *Khatt* of Humāyūn set in train expectations of emancipation which, in turn, gave rise to various nationalisms, Arabic, Turkish, Indian, etc, in the Muslim world. These nationalistic visions have become the basis for the polities of many countries in the Arab world, of Turkey, Pakistan,

---

[27] See also B Ye'or, *Islam and Dhimmitude: Where Civilisations Collide* (Madison/Teaneck, NJ: Dickinson University Press, 2001); B Ye'or, *The Decline of Eastern Christianity under Islam: From Jihad to Dhimmitude* (London: Associated University Presses, 1996).
[28] Alī Kūfī, *The Chachnāmah* (trans Mirza Kalichbeg) (Karachi: Commissioner's Press, 1985) vi.
[29] Ye'or (n 25 above) 49, 65; Chapman (n 15 above) 31ff.

and elsewhere. In the Arabic world, Christian Arabs played a very significant part in the articulation of Arab consciousness which, while recognizing the due place of Islam in Arab culture, gave considerable attention to factors like language, history, custom, and so on.[30]

'Islamism', by its very nature, is a rejection of these ideologies, which it sees as Western-inspired accretions. In its various forms, Islamism seeks a return to an earlier form of Islam and Islamic polity and very often this in turn means a return to the *dhimma*. Whether this *should* be so—even on the premises consciously adopted and propagated by the Islamists—is a question that Muslims need to answer. We have seen how the *dhimma* developed out of the Prophet's own *Sunna* with respect to the Jews of the Khaibar and the Christians of Najrān. Within this same *Sunna*, however, another model is available: the *Sahīfat Al-Medīna* (the Constitution of Medina) promulgated after Muhammad had arrived in Medina. Although an exclusive reading is possible, the usual reading includes Jews, Christians, and even non-Muslim Arabs in the *umma* and guarantees their proper freedoms and rights, as well as delineating the responsibilities of each towards the others. It is true that this covenant or constitution was soon rendered obsolete by changing circumstances but might it not serve as a model for polities in Muslim countries in which non-Muslims play an equal part as citizens rather than as *dhimmīs*?[31]

H. Finance

One urgent area for '*ijtihādic*' activity is Islamic finance. The fundamental reason why this assumes the forms it does is, of course, the Qu'ranic prohibition on *riba* (2:275). *Riba* is a term which occurs in a number of Semitic languages, and generally denotes usury or interest (in the sense of making a profit by lending money or goods to someone who needs them). The prohibition has had a huge influence on *fiqh*, as well as on piety among Muslims. Various ways of avoiding the prohibition were developed by jurists, but the modern form of Islamic finance, as it is practised today, was elaborated by Maudūdī and Qutb. For them, the prohibition of *riba* meant a total ban on all interest, whether in cash or in kind.

A number of 'instruments' have been developed to assist Muslims in both observing this prohibition and actively engaging in trade.[32] It seems that the main business of Islamic banks is *murābaha*. This enables a customer to make a purchase

---

[30] M Nazir-Ali, *Conviction and Conflict: Islam, Christianity and World Order* (London: Continuum International, 2006) 87; K Cragg, *The Arab Christian: A History in the Middle East* (Louisville, KY: Westminster/John Knox Press, 1991) 145ff.

[31] The constitution is reproduced in A Guillaume's translation of Ibn Ishāq's *Sīrat Rasūl Allāh (The Life of Muhammad)* (Oxford: Oxford University Press, 1955) 231. See also Nazir-Ali (n 30 above) 61.

[32] See, eg *The Elimination of Interest from the Economy*, Report of the Council of Islamic Ideology, Islamabad, CII (1980); and P Sookhdeo, *Understanding* Shari'a *Finance* (McLean VA: Isaac Publishing, 2008).

without having to take out an interest-bearing loan. The bank purchases the goods itself and then sells them to the customer on a deferred basis, with a mark-up built in that both meets the bank's operational costs, as well as having an element of profit. The question remains: is this interest by another name? Similarly, other instruments, such as *mushāraka* and *mudāraba* are about the financing of ventures by entrepreneurs, with the banks sharing in the profits (or losses) of these ventures and, at least in theory, passing these on to their own profit-and-loss account depositors. Once again one may ask: are they so very different from venture-capital schemes where a customer borrows for a specific project and the scheme shares, in a pre-agreed way, with any profits or losses? *Ijāra* is very like lease financing and the bank's risk in owning the equipment is covered by insurance for which the client pays.[33] *Sukūk* bonds raise a different kind of problem: unlike conventional bonds they are not debt but asset based. Here the bond holder shares in the underlying assets for the acquiring or developing of which the bonds have been issued. In the case of government and other strategic organizations, the question that arises concerns the extent to which strategic assets may be exposed as a result of raising capital in this way.[34]

There is growing unease in the Islamic world about conventional insurance. It is said that the uncertainty of outcome that insurance addresses introduces an element of gambling which is forbidden by Shari'a. Further, it is claimed that because the premium received by insurance companies is usually invested in interest-bearing ventures, Muslims cannot profit from the income produced by such ventures. Some now propose an Islamic form of insurance called *takāful*, which is based on the concept of social solidarity.[35]

If all interest is regarded as *riba* and, therefore, unlawful, the question is to what extent should 'interest-free' transactions be engaged in. If, for example, banks provide Shari'a-compliant products to their Muslim customers, can these be provided from funds generated conventionally (by interest-bearing activities) or will such funds also have to be generated through 'interest-free' activity? Logically, the latter conclusion would require the establishment of free-standing institutions which engaged only in Shari'a-compliant activity. This would have the effect of isolating Muslims from the mainstream of economic life in a country, and even globally. It is, of course, possible that some of those who promote such an economic system would gladly do so as yet another identity marker to distinguish Muslims from others.

It is perhaps for these reasons that a long line of scholarly opinion in Egypt—beginning with the great reformer, Muhammad ʿAbduh, and continuing to the present luminaries such as Dr Tantāwī, the Sheikh of Al-Azhar, and Sheik ʿAlī

---

[33] See A Meleagrou-Hitchens, 'Banking on Allah', *Standpoint*, July/August 2009, 51.

[34] See further HM Treasury, *The Development of Islamic Finance in the UK: the Government's Perspective*, 10 December 2008, available at <http://www.hm-treasury.gov.uk/fin_islamic_finance.htm>.

[35] Here, a group of persons or institutions agree jointly to indemnify loss or damage inflicted upon any one of them out of a fund to which all contribute. The fund itself is invested in Shari'a-compliant ventures and any profits are distributed in accordance with pre-agreed ratios.

Gomaᶜa, the present Grand Muftī—declares that interest paid and received by banks is *not* contrary to Islam. For them it is not *riba*, which is identified by them as usury and exploitation of the poor. The Pakistan government, similarly, has petitioned the courts to reverse their earlier decisions declaring all interest to be *riba*. It argues that there is no hard-and-fast definition of *riba*, that the Qur'an seems to refer to *exploitative* usury and to *punitive* sums being added to the original loan, and, interestingly, that a completely 'interest-free' economy would isolate Pakistan from the global economy.[36]

If due weight were to be given to Qur'anic commentators such as Yusuf ᶜAlī (on the meaning of 2:275), the teaching of Al-Azhar, and the stance of the government of Pakistan, the case for a distinct Islamic financial system would be undermined. If legitimate interest is not *riba*, there would be no need for the elaborate products and accompanying super-structure to avoid interest in all forms. In the Western world and elsewhere, it may still be possible to provide Shari'a-compliant products for those with traditional scruples, but any such regime should be regulated by the law of the land—with recourse to the usual civil courts maintained. Any official recognition of Shari'a-related financial and commercial law would be fraught with difficulties, both foreseeable and unforeseeable. Muslim countries themselves have experienced serious problems in this area and we should learn from them in this regard.

I. The Ambit of Shari'a

We should not imagine that Muslim-majority polities are, or always have been, theocratic with Shari'a as the only, or even the main, body of law. While the *Qāḍīs*, or Islamic judges, have always been appointed to administer Shari'a law, rulers have sometimes limited their jurisdiction. At the same time, secular or police courts also emerged. The temporal powers often took over areas like constitutional law, international relations, and law relating to conflict between states. The *Qāḍīs* maintained their authority over religious and family law, but even under the Ottomans, large areas of law were governed by statute, or the so-called *Qānūn-Nāmas*. In addition to such restrictions of the application of Shari'a, there has also been widespread recognition of law deriving from *ᶜada* or *dustūr* (the customs of a particular people or nation). This has especially been so in South-East Asia and East Africa. In modern times, a number of states have deliberately borrowed from European codes of civil, criminal, and even family law. The *ᶜUlamā* have often resisted such borrowing as being contrary to Islam, but, at the same time, they have also been involved in the modification of Islamic law by employing the procedural device of *maslaha* (applying or withholding application of the law in terms of the public good) or by constructing laws

---

[36] For a fuller account see Sookhdeo (n 32 above) 18.

necessary for contemporary needs through, what Sir Norman Anderson used to call, *talfīq* or the creation of 'patchwork' of law by borrowing from the different law schools.

J. Muslims in Non-Muslim States

One of the key questions facing both Muslims and the rest of the world is how Muslims will adapt to living as minority communities in non-Muslim polities. This is a pressing question not only in the Western world, where Muslims numbers have swelled due to relatively recent immigration, but also in the Balkans, the Caucasus, and in countries like India, Sri Lanka, Thailand, and the Philippines, where the issue is a long-standing one. One should not forget Africa also, where there are significant indigenous Muslim minorities in many countries.

The classical division of the world into the *Dār ul-Islām* (the abode of Islam) and the *Dār ul-Harb* (the abode of conflict or war) implied that it was the obligation of Muslims to turn as much of the latter into the former. This is one of the primary reasons for *jihād*. If a Muslim finds himself or herself in the *Dār ul-Harb*, it is his or her duty to withdraw from it. Naturally, such an uncompromising position has been impossible to maintain through the course of history and various measures have been devised to assist Muslim communities in developing trading and political relations with non-Muslim neighbours as well as those further afield. These range from the *hudna* (a more or less temporary truce, for the sake of trade) to the recognition of certain territories being *Dār ul-Sulh* (the abode of peace by agreement) or *Dār ul-Ahd* (the abode of covenanted treaty). Even here, however, it is assumed that, at least in theory, these territories and peoples are in a tributary relationship to the Muslims. Gifts sent by them, for instance, to seal or renew a treaty, can be regarded as *kharāj* (tribute). This means that historically there is little by way of a truly plural doctrine of international relations, and Muslim states have had to rely on fictive measures to order their relationships with non-Muslim states. Surely, an urgent requirement of the international political order is that Muslim states be willing to give reassurance that their entry into treaties (international, regional, or bilateral) reflects a permanent commitment, not a mere transient arrangement. There is further discussion on how Muslims should conduct themselves when in a non-Muslim polity in the next section.

K. *Jihād*

If Islam is to acknowledge and respect an abiding plurality, much will turn on a reinterpretation of the notion of *jihād*. It is true that the term has come to have a number of meanings: the *Sūfīs*, for example, take the *jihād Al-Akbar* (the greater *jihād*) to be a struggle against one's meaner and weaker tendencies. Armed struggle in the cause of Islam is, for them, the lesser *jihād* (the *jihād Al-Asghar*). In the same way, Ibn Taimiyya distinguished between the *jihād Makki* and the *jihād Madanī*. The former is about persuasion through preaching, as exemplified by the Prophet at Mecca, while the latter denotes armed conflict, akin to the struggles of the Muslim community at Medina. The Prophet regarded each of them as important for Muslims.

Later reformers, such as the Islamic socialist Ubaidullāh Sindhī, claiming the authority of Shāh Walīullāh, took *jihād* to mean a social revolution which destroys the hegemony of the rich and powerful and nullifies the imperialism of one nation over another. For Sindhī, *jihād* represented the Muslim response to the call for Marxist revolution. Curiously, and while disagreeing with his fundamental outlook, many contemporary *jihādists* from Kashmir to Chechenya would agree. Certainly, in South Asian Islam, a consensus has been growing since the time of the nineteenth-century reformer, Sir Syed Ahmad Khan, that *jihād*, in the sense of armed struggle against an enemy, is justifiable only in self-defence and specifically when Islam is itself in danger. Thus, the *wahhabī*-inspired *jihād* against the British in India was unlawful because the British did not wish to destroy Islam. Quite the opposite: they were its supporters and wanted Muslims to develop politically, economically, and socially.[37] If *jihād* can be seen very much as a defensive war and as a struggle against social evils, this would, indeed, create a new context for Muslims in the modern world. For the time being, however, we must also take account of interpretations of *jihād* which remain aggressive in intent—even if there are alleged or real grievances which are cited as the *casus belli*.[38]

The theory remains that Muslims should either withdraw from the *Dār-ul-Harb* or, through *jihād* of one kind or another, seek to turn it into the *Dār-ul-Islām*. As I have pointed out, it has been claimed that historical circumstances have put pressure on the theory and ways have been devised of allowing Muslims to continue living in non-Muslim polities. The situation is highly ambiguous and the research inadequate. Most of the known cases concern Muslims falling under non-Muslim rule rather than choosing to live under it. The classical consensus seems to be that Muslims should not remain in the *Dār-ul-Harb*. Where exceptions are made, it is demanded, for example, that they should be able to live as distinct and separate communities, and that they should be able to have their own law, their own judges, and even their own governors. Further, they must not contribute to the wealth and

---

[37] See further Nazir-Ali (n 4 above) 102ff; Nazir-Ali (n 30 above) 155ff; P M Holt, A Lambton, and B Lewis (eds), *The Cambridge History of Islam* (Cambridge, Cambridge University Press, 1970) Vol 2A, 82ff.

[38] See G Kepel, *Jihad: The Trail of Political Islam* (Cambridge, MA: Harvard University Press, 2002).

strength of a non-Muslim polity and should not serve in the military, especially against Muslims.[39]

Whatever the logical position may have been, it was soon recognized that a country does not become *Dār ul-Harb* until Islamic values are completely abandoned and Muslims are no longer protected. The point about values is an important one, since integration depends not only on sharing a language, for example, but also on the sharing of at least some values and aspirations. One of Sir Syed Ahmad Khan's contemporaries, Deputy Nazīr Ahmad, urged Indian Muslims to respect the laws of British India because they promoted the underlying values of Islam.[40] Even Muhammad Iqbal, in an early article, described the British Empire as 'the greatest Muhammadan Empire in the world' because (as he saw it) it embodied within it vital Islamic principles such as freedom of expression, the rule of law, democracy, etc.[41]

In the West today, Muslims, along with other religionists, enjoy the right to practise and propagate their faith. Their religious leaders, moreover, should be free to guide them according to the tenets of the faith, and this includes the Shari'a (as codified by the various schools of law, with their differences and similarities). We must also expect that Muslims will seek to influence public policy in accordance with the teachings of Islam.

There is, however, another side to the coin. The autonomy of the public law of the land must be upheld. In most Western contexts this law is derived from the Judaeo-Christian tradition, as interpreted and clarified by aspects of the Enlightenment. The Shari'a, even if influenced by the laws of Byzantine, is actually founded on quite different assumptions. Its recognition or incorporation into public law could cause not only confusion, but an undermining of the fundamental assumptions undergirding the general law. Family law, for example, is often mooted as an area of Islamic law that might, somehow, be recognized by public law in the West. But what would be the consequences? I noted earlier the unequal position of Islamic women in the context of divorce. Similar questions would arise with respect to the custody of children, the laws of inheritance and of evidence, the legality of polygamy, and so on.

To repeat: Muslims should be free to order their lives, including their family lives, according to Islamic teachings. As with other communities, there may be arrangements for the restoration of disputes which arise within Muslim communities. They should not, however, take on a quasi-legal form, nor can their jurisdiction be acknowledged in matters that are for the courts to address. If any question arises

---

[39] See the detailed discussion in Khalid Abou el Fadl, 'Islamic Law and Muslim Minorities: The Juristic Discourse on Muslim Minorities from the Second/Eighth to the Eleventh/Seventeenth Centuries' (1994) 2 *Journal of Islamic Law and Society* 1. See also S Gertz, 'Permission to Live under Christian Rule? The Views of a Medieval Muslim Jurist', *Newsletter of the Centre for Muslim-Christian Studies*, Oxford, No 2, Summer 2010.

[40] Holt, Lambton, and Lewis (eds) (n 37 above) 87.

[41] M Iqbal, 'Islam as a Moral and Political Ideal' in S A Vahid (ed), *Thoughts and Reflections of Iqbal* (Lahore: Ashraf, 1964) 51.

about the fundamental rights and responsibilities of a citizen or resident, there must continue to be free access to the courts to enable such matters to be settled in accordance with the law of the land. The possibility of some persons, such as women or young people, being coerced into accepting the decisions of so-called Shari'a 'councils' or 'tribunals' has to be monitored carefully. Moreover, it should not be possible for the structures and institutions of any religion to deal with criminal matters—domestic violence and rape come to mind here. We have noted the difficulties surrounding the operation of Islamic finance in Muslim countries, let alone in the West. Once again, Muslims should be free to comply with Shari'a teaching on this subject and financial institutions can offer products that Muslims judge to be Shari'a-compliant. But equally again, any dispute must be settled according to the commercial law of the land.

What else can be said in this regard? While the autonomy and integrity of public law must be preserved, governments and parliaments must also recognize the importance of the rights of conscience for believers. There is, of course, a long and varied history as to the extent of the recognition of religious liberty and freedom of conscience. If the needs of the law are to be balanced by due respect for the sincere beliefs of citizens, there will have to be an increasing awareness of, and provision made for, genuine claims based on religious or other belief. Such questions will need to be addressed in matters such as participation in armed conflict, the status of the unborn foetus (at different stages of development), euthanasia and assisted suicide, the nature and structure of family life, as well as the understanding, portrayal, and regulation of human sexuality.

The incorporation of Shari'a into the public law of states, or of groups of states (such as the EU), cannot, in my view, be supported. Nonetheless, Muslims should of course be free to advance arguments and proposals in public policy debates, arguments based on the values of Shari'a (as exemplified, for instance, in the *maqāsid,* or principal objectives). Both Iqbal and Tariq Ramadan, relying on the mediaeval Spanish jurist, Imām Shātibī, list various *maqāsid* which are to be protected and implemented in any society. These policy objectives or principles concern pivotal matters such as *dīn* (belief, religion, or worldview), *nafs* (the person), *ʿaql* (the mind), *nasl* (everything connected with the propagation of humanity), and *māl* (property). Some would add *ʿizza* (dignity) to this list. This kind of contribution to public discussion, based on such principles, must be permitted. Democratic participation of this sort is to be welcomed. Importantly, however, it does *not* require, in any way, an alignment of quite different systems of law.[42] The key question is whether such an understanding of polity will be seen by Muslims as being in accordance with their own tradition. Much in international order and national cohesion depends on the answer given.

---

[42] See further Iqbal (n 6 above) 169ff; and Tariq Ramadan, 'Islamic Views of the Collective' in M Ipgrave (ed), *Building a Better Bridge: Muslims, Christians and the Common Good* (Washington DC: Georgetown University Press, 2008) 73ff.

L. Conclusion

We have briefly traced the origins of Shari'a and its development, as well as its effects on the lives of ordinary people and, in particular, on non-Muslims who came within the orbit of Islam. We have seen also how Shari'a has influenced relations between Muslim and non-Muslim states, and the implications of this for current world order. I have quickly surveyed the principles of the development of Shari'a in the various schools of law and how the techniques of interpretation and application might assist Muslims in addressing the opportunities and problems of the contemporary world. I have examined various aspects of Islamic law, for example family law, Islamic finance, the penal laws, and *jihād,* and considered how some Muslim scholars have dealt with difficulties that arise in the implementation of Islamic law in these fields. Finally, I have asked how all of this relates to Muslims living in largely non-Muslim societies, including those in the Western world.

How can the state ensure that Muslims may continue to freely practise their faith, while also preserving the integrity of public law and the maintenance of central democratic institutions? How can all this be achieved, even as Muslims (and others) seek to make a real contribution to public discussion and debate? Public contributions by Muslims advocating Shari'a principles, rules, or solutions present a particularly acute and poignant test of this commitment to participatory democracy. The debate will no doubt continue. One thing upon which there can be no debate, however, is the necessity of good scholarship, both Muslim and non-Muslim, in the areas traversed in this chapter. Let us hope it will be forthcoming.

6

Shari'a and Pluralism

James W Skillen

A. Introduction

In the lead-up to parliamentary elections in Indonesia in April 2009, a young woman and devout Muslim studying at an Islamic school told an interviewer that she would not vote for one of the Islamic political parties: 'The wisest choice is a government not dependent on Islamic law...Islam actually guides our lives, but it doesn't seem to be shown in the way we vote'.[1] Her attitude toward voting reflected that of the majority in her culturally diverse country whose population is 90 per cent Muslim. The reasons for this include the syncretistic nature of South-East Asian Islam and Indonesia's peculiar political history. With some similarities to the division between religious practice and secular politics in the West, there is a degree of separation between Muslim ritual and national politics in Indonesia. According to Amin Abdullah, head of the Muslim state university in Yogyakarta, 'Politics is not ritual, it is public service, public governance...So the [recent] rise in popularity of ritual can't be linked with parties' popularity'.[2]

Indonesia's system of government, now democratic, is somewhat like that of Turkey, which is also a Muslim-majority country. It makes room for diverse faiths (even if not with equal treatment of all) and the government at the national level does not operate with allegiance to Islamic law. Indonesia, like Turkey, gained its twentieth-century shape under authoritarian, nationalistic rule, which was often at odds with Islam.[3]

By contrast with Indonesia, also early in 2009, the Afghan Parliament passed a law that would allow the Shia minority in Afghanistan to enforce Shari'a, even making it illegal for wives to refuse to have sex with their husbands. On 13 April 2009, Pakistan's president, Asif Zardari, with bipartisan support in the National

---

[1] R Shulman, 'Indonesia Holds Fast to Secular Politics', *Washington Post*, 9 April 2009.

[2] J Aglionby, 'The Call of Islam Loses Allure for Voters in Indonesia', *Financial Times*, 7 April 2009.

[3] An authoritative assessment of Indonesia's Pancasila-based system, a form of nationalist civil religion or public religion, can be found in BF Intan, *'Public Religion' and the Pancasila-Based State of Indonesia* (New York: Peter Lang, 2006).

Assembly, gave approval to the use of Shari'a by Taliban-related commanders who have gained control in the Swat Valley of the North West Frontier Province.[4] While Afghanistan and Pakistan, which are also Muslim-majority countries, are different from one another in culture and governance, both are more influenced by radical Islamism today than are Indonesia and Turkey.

Given these very different circumstances and developments in Muslim countries, how shall we assess what is genuinely Islamic with respect to law and governance? Are the systems in Indonesia and Turkey the wave of the future, or does the degree of separation between Muslim piety and democratic governance in those countries represent a corruption of authentic Islam? If the latter is true, then are the radically reforming Islamists correct, that only a return to strict observance of Shari'a will save Islam?

And what about the compatibility of Shari'a with democratic governance in religiously diverse societies that do not have Muslim majorities and have legal systems quite different from anything ever practised in Muslim societies? What should Muslims, as minorities in those countries, be seeking? Is it conceivable that in the name of religious freedom and diversity some aspects of Muslim law could be recognized by, or incorporated into, the governance systems of a European country or of the United States? Would Muslims be happy with that, or must they forever be uncomfortable living in non-Muslim societies?

B. Anglican Archbishop Rowan Williams

As a way of joining the discussion of Islam (particularly Shari'a) and pluralism, I will begin with the comments in 2008 of Rowan Williams, the Anglican Archbishop of Canterbury, in a lecture exploring the possibility of Shari'a being accommodated within the British legal system.[5] Leaving to one side a consideration of the distinctive character of the British system of law and institutions, I will consider just two elements of his lecture: (1) its references to 'religious communities'; and (2) the argument about the relation of 'universal secular law' to 'social pluralism'.

The Archbishop's references to religious communities are equivocal. Primarily, he appears to be concerned with 'minority communities' such as Muslims and Jews, who 'relate to something other than the British legal system alone'. In other places, he has in view particular institutions that are different from the Church of England but which have a function in Muslim and Jewish communities similar to that of the Church in Britain. And at yet other points he seems to have in view

---

[4] See P Constable, 'Afghan Law Ignites Debate on Religion, Sex', *Washington Post*, 11 April 2009; J Hoagland, 'The War Within Islam', *Washington Post*, 12 April 2009; and D Gardner, 'Democracy Denied', *Financial Times*, 11/12 April 2009, 1–2.

[5] R Williams, 'Civil and Religious Law in England: a Religious Perspective' (see Appendix I).

a broad theology of law and society that is (or might be) shared by all Abrahamic faith communities.

The problem created by this equivocation shows up in the phrase—just quoted—about communities that 'relate to something other than the British legal system alone'. Part of what he is suggesting is that anyone in Britain, not just Muslims, should be free to belong to non-state organizations. He opposes a 'monopolistic' conception of 'universal secular law' that would force people to choose between 'cultural loyalty' and 'state loyalty'. Insofar as this is his point, Dr Williams apparently intends by 'something other' simply those arenas of life in which parents, educators, publishers, and church leaders bear responsibilities different from those of Parliament and the courts. In that case, everyone, and not only minority communities, have freedom to relate to something other than the British legal system alone. And pluralism of that kind is already recognized in British law, so the law may simply need to be refined or expanded slightly within the British legal system to accommodate some new types of non-government organizations such as mosques and Muslim schools.

Following a different line of argument, however, if Archbishop Williams intends by 'something other' a realm of divine law or moral constraints that transcend the entire British system of law, then, again, 'minority religious communities' in Britain are not peculiar. Christians themselves acknowledge the higher authority of God above both the Crown and the Church of England. Perhaps, therefore, the equivocation arises because the Church's law, as Williams says, is 'the law of the land' in a way that Shari'a is not. If that is what he is struggling with, then he may be looking for a way to allow Muslims to heed those precepts that they revere as divine mandates which are not currently recognized or allowed by the British legal and ecclesiastical systems. To make that possible, however, may involve more than minor legal adjustments. It could require either the disestablishment of the Church of England, so that it would become merely one among many 'religious communities' alongside Islam, or it might require the pluralization of the Church itself to the point where the Church would make room, under its authority, for Muslim practice of at least some elements of Shari'a.

Seen from a Muslim point of view, however, the religious community of Islam (the *umma*) can never be understood as a minority community *within* a modern state. The *umma* is a worldwide transnational people practicing faithful obedience to Allah. Its identity is more like the worldwide body of Christ in Christian understanding, a community that is not reducible to a subset of some other institution, community or political order. There may be local expressions of the *umma* in mosques and communities around the world, but the Muslim community, even in its local expressions, cannot be thought of as a 'minority community', or as a sub-unit within the United Kingdom, or even as the established religion of a particular state the way the Church of England is connected to Great Britain. In Muslim understanding, the whole of humanity should turn to follow the way of Islam in order to constitute the *Dār ul-Islām* (the house of faithfulness and surrender to Allah) that will triumph over the *Dār ul-Harb* (the house of conflict and disobedience). Neither of these 'houses' is understood in terms of states or ethnic nations. The *Dār ul-Islām* is a universal community. Earthly governments, to have any legitimacy, will show their submission to Allah by contributing to the advance of Islam, typically by showing respect for the higher authority of Shari'a, about which we will say more below. Thus it could be that Archbishop Williams is trying to fit a square peg in a round hole by asking how Britain might accommodate Shari'a.

This brings us to Williams' second point about universal secular law and social pluralism. His argument toward the end of the lecture suggests that he wants to reconceive the universality of public law more restrictively in a 'negative rather than a positive sense'. In other words, what should remain universal about it, in his estimation, is the protection of every person's basic human dignity, while beyond that, people should be free to pursue social and cultural pluralism in marriage, finance, and perhaps education and other spheres of life. 'The role of "secular" law', he says, 'is not the dissolution of these things [religion, custom, and habit] in the name of universalism but the monitoring of such affiliations to prevent the creation of mutually isolated communities in which human liberties are seen in incompatible ways and individual persons are subjected to restraints or injustices for which there is no public redress'.[6]

This line of argument presupposes the existence of something more than just a human-rights monitor, however; it presupposes a British *political community* in which every citizen is a member and in which the government governs for the common good of all. After all, who decides when a particular community within Britain has become too 'isolated'? Who is to judge when the 'restraints' on citizens are unjust and demand public redress? Who decides when different ways of understanding human liberties are 'incompatible' enough to require public action? The answer, of course, is that the national community's government and courts will decide. Therefore, even if the 'secular law' does not function in a totalitarian or omnicompetent way but only in a monitoring way, it must still set boundaries for the whole of society in some kind of universal fashion.

Perhaps what the Archbishop is trying to argue in his lecture is, first of all, that diverse religious communities, including Muslims, who give allegiance to Allah above and beyond allegiance to the Crown and Church, should be equally as free as British citizens to conduct certain rituals in their mosques and in the privacy of their homes. The next step, then, would be for public 'secular' law to recognize the right of British citizens, including Muslims, to engage in diverse practices in the non-governmental spheres of worship, marriage, private finance, education, and so forth, as long as those practices do not undermine the dignity of persons, or lead to a community's troubling isolation, or come into conflict with human liberties. If this is an accurate statement of what Williams wishes to suggest about the

---

[6] Ibid at [16].

place of religious communities in Britain, then it is his idea of the role of universal secular law that appears to be problematic. For the foundation on which that kind of religious freedom and institutional pluralism depends is the obligation of *all* citizens, as members of the *same* political community, to abide by the public laws of the nation that protect religious freedom (pluralistically) and uphold societal pluralism (offered equally to all). If any group of citizens wants to change the laws that stipulate these conditions and obligations of citizenship, it will have to participate in the open democratic process to try to do so. In other words, short of changing the British system of government entirely, no part of Shari'a could be admitted that aimed to displace the universal public law of Great Britain, or that curtailed or eliminated the religious freedom of British citizens, or that abridged the equal opportunity of all citizens to enjoy independent responsibility in non-governmental organizations.

This brief consideration of Williams' lecture sets up three important questions that I want to take up in the remainder of this essay. The first question concerns the nature of religious communities and their relation to systems of public law and governance. The second concerns the nature of non-governmental institutions and the way they are recognized in public law and served by government. And the third concerns the meaning of legal and governmental universality. We will take them up in that order, but only after first saying more about the nature of Shari'a.

C. Shari'a

Noah Feldman provides a helpful overview of the classical Muslim view of the 'rule of law'.[7] Shari'a is not, as some Westerners imagine, the expression of arbitrary despotism or paternalistic authoritarianism. It is a system of judging cases that developed over time, deriving from Muhammad's authority as the recipient of divine revelation. 'With Muhammad's death', Feldman explains, 'revelation to the Muslim community stopped'.[8] Authority over the community in the following decades passed on to a 'substitute or stand-in' (*khalifa*, or 'caliph') for the Prophet. Years of judging cases led to the development of a legal system that was based on (1) the revelatory text of the Qur'an; (2) oral-tradition reports (*hadith*) of Muhammad's actions and sayings (his path or *Sunna*); (3) analogical reasoning from the first two; and (4) the consensus of legal scholars about the meaning and implications of the first three. With increasing complexities of the growing Muslim empire the need arose for an 'organised legal system' as Feldman explains, and a self-appointed group of those who spent their lives studying the law 'got the caliphs

---

[7] The comments in this and subsequent paragraphs draw from N Feldman, 'Rule of Law and Balance of Power in Classical Islam' (2008) 6(4) *The Review of Faith and International Affairs* 3, which is an excerpt from his book, *The Fall and Rise of the Islamic State* (Princeton: Princeton University Press, 2008).

[8] Ibid 5.

to acknowledge them as the guardians of the law'. This group came to be called simply 'the scholars'. The process that developed, in other words, was something like the English common law tradition in the sense that ongoing rulings on cases established a body of precedents and applicable laws that served as the foundation for subsequent rulings and legal discoveries. Again, the process, like that of the common law, was more one of discovering the law than of making the law. Only God could make law.[9]

This is the juncture at which the relation of law and governance comes to the fore, as Feldman points out. Islamic law, Shari'a, was arrived at by jurist-scholars, but it had to be applied and enforced. Those who enforced the law were judges appointed by the caliph. Thus, a three-part division of labour gradually emerged: the caliph had supreme authority to 'command the right and forbid the wrong' with the help of judges who enforced judgments as interpreted by the scholars. This established a considerable source of authority on which the caliph himself was dependent. A judge had to be qualified in knowing the law, although he did not have to know everything the way the scholars did. So, it followed that 'judges should be drawn from among the scholars'. And even though as judges they were acting to fulfil the caliph's will, they were obligated to heed the law. 'Judicial authority came from the caliph, but the law to be applied came from the scholars'.[10]

This led in the early classical era to a system that Feldman describes as a balance of power between the scholars and the caliph. The scholars had a tool to keep the caliph in line—at least to some degree. Given the uncertainty of who would succeed a passing caliph, the role of the scholars grew in importance. Any new claimant to the authority of caliph needed public affirmation of his legitimacy. That affirmation could be given or withheld by the scholars who might also be called upon in other important circumstances to approve or disapprove the caliph's actions. 'Without a single soldier under their command', says Feldman, 'the scholars nonetheless represented a crucial source of power in the Islamic constitutional structure'. Their authority 'derived from their understanding of [the law] as God's law, greater certainly than the ruler, but also greater than themselves'.[11]

With this helpful overview we can see that Shari'a—the tradition of making judgments together with the body of law that emerged—has more checks and balances, more rigor and carefulness than we in the West might imagine. On the other hand, and at the same time, it is apparent from Feldman's remarks that the reach of Shari'a in its classical development is as wide and deep as the whole community. It is not surprising, then, that this body of law and those with continuing responsibility to discover and apply it bear some responsibility for anything and everything that touches the behaviour of the Muslim community, from sexual practice to finance to foreign policy. It is not evident within any of the branches of Islam what the limits of a government's authority should be in its enforcement of Shari'a. In principle a single caliphate could and should govern the whole earth in

---

[9] Ibid 5–6.   [10] Ibid 7.   [11] Ibid 11.

keeping with Shari'a. Wherever Islam spreads, Shari'a should abound. This implies undifferentiated, omnicompetent legal governance for a universal, undifferentiated *umma*.

In practice today, however, Muslims are spread throughout most of the world, with some living in states like Indonesia and Turkey, others in places like Afghanistan, Iran, and Saudi Arabia, and still others in non-Muslim states of Europe and North America. Moreover, there are diverse schools of scholars who offer diverse interpretations of Shari'a. And there are different kinds of rulers and judges who make different uses of Shari'a, if they make use of it at all. In what sense, then, can we judge what normative Islam should be today, and how much pluralism can exist among Muslim communities and within different states where Muslims live, without frustrating or even destroying the meaning of the *umma*, the Muslim community?

D. Three Questions

With that background, let us return to our three questions about the nature of religious communities, societal pluralism, and legal universality. Religious communities both today and historically have been understood by their members in many different ways. For some, religion is an all-encompassing way of life dependent on a single, highest human authority under God. For others, religion is an all-encompassing way of life but with different human authorities responsible before God in different arenas of life such as family, business, education, and government. For yet others, religion is more narrowly a mode of worship, piety, and moral guidance that may have a wide impact but is generally distinguished from so-called secular realms of life. And finally, there are those for whom religion functions only as an institutional practice of ritual and piety at certain times and places and in prescribed ways.

Islam is certainly an all-encompassing way of life in which the whole of reality falls under the sovereignty of Allah. Shari'a entails law-making and the judging of cases covering the full extent of life. As Feldman explains, 'the goal that is always placed first in the political platform of those who call for an Islamic state [is] the restoration of the Shari'a to its central role in Islamic society'.[12] In practice, however, we can see that today Muslims who want strict adherence to Shari'a throughout society are very different from those, in places like Indonesia, who want Shari'a restricted to non-governmental spheres of life, if it is used at all. Muslim practice, then, appears to be diverging, as have Christian and Jewish practices, along all four lines of religious practice just mentioned.

How essential, then, is Shari'a to Islam? It seems clear that classical Islam did not allow for the privatizing of faith and piety and leaving public governance in

12 Ibid 4.

the hands of those who practise a secular mode of decision-making. Yet that is part of what constitutes the life of some Muslim communities today. Does that mean, then, from an Islamist point of view, that Indonesia and Turkey are not really Muslim countries?

The chief question about the meaning of the Muslim *umma* today would appear to be whether it can exist apart from public governance under Shari'a. If Islam can develop in that way, then the classical meaning and enforcement of Shari'a is not essential to the Muslim *umma*'s contemporary identity, and it may well be that 'minority Muslim communities' in countries such as Great Britain can maintain strong communities of private faith. In that case, it may also be possible for the law in Britain to make room for some distinctive institutional expressions of Islam in family life, education, finance, and the media without doing injustice to either Muslims or non-Muslims.[13]

However, the question arises whether Muslims who are dissatisfied with a society not governed entirely by Shari'a will feel compelled to use force to try to achieve the kind of society they want or will be willing to work non-violently to try to achieve their goals by persuasion. For the most part, Christians have come to accept open societies and peaceful democratic processes for government, yet that was not always the case. Evidence, both historical and Qur'anic, suggests that Islam does not have a rationale of its own to justify the submission of Muslims to governments that do not recognize Allah and Shari'a. There is also some evidence to the contrary, according to recent scholarship.[14] There are those like David Gardner who argue that the 2003 petition, 'A Vision for the Present and Future of the Homeland', signed by leading liberals and Islamist reformers in Saudi Arabia, point the way to pluralism. In Gardner's view, 'the 2003 "Vision" document is as suggestive of a path forward as the 1969 Jordanian National Charter or the still unrealised Iraqi constitution of 2005. They all draw on and revisit the sources of renewal that are and will remain Islamic, and in important ways, Islamist'.[15]

---

[13] For differing views of the malleability and adaptability of Islam and Shari'a, see C Caldwell, *Reflections on the Revolution in Europe: Immigration, Islam, and the West* (New York: Doubleday, 2009); R Ramadan, *What I Believe* (New York: Oxford University Press, 2009); J Aglionby, 'Islamic Banks Urged to Show West the Sharia Way Forward', *Financial Times*, 3 March 2009; R Aslan, '"A" Source of Law?' (2008) 36(3) *Harvard Divinity Bulletin* 14; A A An-Na'im, *Islam and the Secular State: Negotiating the Future of Shari'a* (Cambridge, MA: Harvard University Press, 2008); D Gartenstein-Ross, 'The Role of Consensus in the Contemporary Struggle for Islam' (2008) 6(4) *Review of Faith and International Affairs* 13; A Afsaruddin, 'Absolutism vs. Pluralism in Islam Today' (2008) 6(4) *Review of Faith and International Affairs* 23; T F Farr, 'Islam's Way to Freedom' (2008) 187 *First Things: A Monthly Journal of Religion and Public Life* 24; and R L Wilken, 'Christianity Face to Face with Islam' (2009) 189 *First Things: A Monthly Journal of Religion and Public Life* 19.

[14] See, eg Andrew March, *Islam and Liberal Citizenship: The Search for an Overlapping Consensus* (Oxford: Oxford University Press, 2009); Mohammad Fadel, 'The True, the Good and the Reasonable: The Theological and Ethical Roots of Public Reason in Islamic Law' (2008) 21(1) *Canadian Journal of Law and Jurisprudence* 5; Khaled Abou El Fadl, 'Islamic Law and Muslim Minorities: The Juristic Discourse on Muslim Minorities from the Second/Eighth to the Eleventh/ Seventeenth Centuries' (1994) 1(2) *Islamic Law and Society* 141.

[15] Gardner (n 4 above), 2.

What the reformers in Saudi Arabia articulate, says Gardner, is the desire for 'free elections, freedom of expression and association, an independent judiciary and a fairer distribution of wealth—in short a constitutional monarchy, if not a bicycling monarchy'.[16] If these ideas gain power in Saudi Arabia, the system might indeed be opened up, but the question remains about how pluralistic a Muslim state of this kind can become.

Abdullahi Ahmed An-Na'im goes even further than Gardner, claiming 'the Qur'an never mentions the idea of a state and does not prescribe a particular form of government'.[17] 'The premise of my proposal', he says, 'is that Muslims every-where, whether minorities or majorities, are bound to observe Shari'a as a matter of religious obligation, and that this can best be achieved when the state is neutral regarding all religious doctrines and does not claim to enforce Shari'a principles as state policy or legislation.'[18] Yet if Shari'a touches every sphere of life, how are Muslims to observe it when the laws and governments of 'neutral' states inhibit or prohibit its observance?

This leads to our next big question, which relates to what I would call the pluralism of societal structures and authorities in a differentiated society. Part of what constitutes public law and governance in the United States and Great Britain, for example, is a constitutional limitation of the state that makes room for non-governmental organizations and institutions such as families, universities, businesses, and religious bodies. This does not mean that public governance has nothing to do with those organizations but rather that public law recognizes their non-governmental identity and allows for their self-governance in non-political or non-public ways. Parental authority in the home, academic authority in the university, and business authority in the corporate enterprise are limited in each case to a differentiated responsibility. This means that there is room for diverse economic philosophies to guide different enterprises, for some couples to practice Christian marriage and others to practice Jewish or Hindu marriages, and for uni-versities to shape their programs by Christian or Marxist or liberal secular philoso-phies. Public law makes room for that structural diversity even as it accepts its own lack of omnicompetence in a legal sense. A constitutionally limited government of this kind means that government lacks legal competence to act as if it were the ultimate authority *within* families, universities, business enterprises, and churches, synagogues, and mosques. This is, in essence, what characterizes a structurally pluralistic society.

Does Shari'a admit to this kind of limitation of its boundaries and authority? And on the other side, would a Western constitutional state be ready to allow Shari'a to govern Muslim marriages, financial practices, schooling, and family life? These questions reach to the heart of different views of society. From what

[16] Ibid.
[17] These are the words of Geneive Abdo in her review of An-Na'im's book, *Islam and the Secular State* (n 13 above). See G Abdo, 'Islamic Democracy', *Washington Post Book World*, 27 July 2008.
[18] Ibid.

we understand of Shari'a, it does not appear that the governance of marriage and family practices can be disengaged from public governance, although it is conceivable that some Muslims in non-Muslim countries are willing to accept a mode of public governance that does not accord with Shari'a as long as they are allowed some measure of internal freedom as Muslim families. Yet, how narrowly or broadly should public law define the responsibilities of marriages and families? And how great can be the diversity of such practices within the same society? Should the law permit polygamy, same-sex marriages, abortion, or any restrictions on the education, employment, and individual freedoms of women?

Archbishop Rowan Williams seems to suggest in this regard that there might be more room for Muslim practices in Britain than now exists. But he also wants to maintain a universal umpire role for public law and governance that would set limits of a non-Shari'a type for all marriages and families. That is precisely the rub. If Muslims can accept the contextualization of parts of Shari'a within a pluralistic society that denies Shari'a the role of highest public legal authority, then there might be room for accommodation. But if, for Islam, Shari'a must be the authority above and behind all public law, including the internal life of marriage and family, then that would eliminate the possibility of a structural differentiation of families from the state and any publicly protected pluralism for families who are committed to other faiths.

This brings us to our third and final question. What does it mean to argue, as Williams does, for diverse cultural groups to enjoy a measure of freedom within a system of universal law that functions negatively to protect citizens from threats to their dignity and the danger of isolation in a community that could deny them access to legal redress of their grievances? Williams seems clearly to have in view a Western type of differentiated society in which the very possibility of the relative independence of families, schools, businesses, and religious institutions depends on a universal public law and authority that guarantees their relative independence. Yet that system of governance must function as the highest public law-making authority. That is incompatible with classical Islam's system of Shari'a.

E. Conclusion

From what has been said above we can draw together the following threads. To the extent that religions such as Islam and Christianity are ways of life and not merely modes of worship, they will require public access and expression in many if not all areas of life. At the same time, if such religions are to be able to coexist with others in the same political communities, they need an internal rationale for public coexistence or public pluralism. In other words, they will need to have a motive of their own to support the kind of political and legal system that at least tolerates other religions and at best assures equal treatment of all faiths in diverse spheres of life. It appears that Islam does not have that kind of internal rationale or motive, though there have been periods in Muslim history when its control of people and territory included toleration of Christians and Jews. Today, in those states where Muslims are in the majority but where Shari'a is not the recognized legal system, the political systems are grounded in variations of nationalism and civil religion. In other words, Muslims living in those political communities are compelled by something other than Shari'a to accept a more limited public role for Islam. This is not unlike the way in which Christians in the West from the end of the Middle Ages through to the high point of the Enlightenment accepted a degree of private religious freedom at the expense of a desired ecclesiastical establishment. Yet, within Christianity's founding documents there is a basis for equal-treatment pluralism in public life. Jesus tells his disciples through a parable (Matthew 13:24–30, 36–43) and instruction (Matthew 5:45) that they do not bear responsibility to remove or discriminate against unbelievers in the 'field of the world' but are to recognize that God mercifully sends rain and sunshine to the just and unjust alike. And the apostles teach Christians that they should seek to live at peace with everyone, insofar as that is up to them and to leave final judgment in the hands of God (Romans 12:18). There is within Christianity a basis for accepting equal treatment of religious communities in the public life of this age while awaiting the return of Christ and God's final judgment. Can Islam find in its classical resources or generate from within itself a firm commitment to, and not merely a grudging acquiescence in, religious pluralism?

The history of Islam clearly shows that diverse organizational and institutional responsibilities emerged and were honoured within the *umma*, including family life, scholarship, inventive technologies, education, and much more. The question is whether then or now Shari'a can be conceived as a system that allows for and encourages the differentiation of those responsibilities into spheres of independence from the scholars and judges who have traditionally ruled on everything within the *umma*. If such differentiation is possible, then we can imagine not only a greater expansiveness and flourishing of Muslim societies, no longer constrained by the control of an omnicompetent human authority, but also a more expansive engagement of Muslims in societies that are not Muslim-majority societies.

Finally, it would seem that the only way a universal public legal system can function well is in connection with a differentiated society and constitutional limitation of the governing system. In other words, the universality of public law does not entail a totalitarian or omnicompetent government. Its universality goes hand in hand with distinguishing the public commons (which embraces everyone universally) from all those non-governmental or non-political organizations and institutions that are recognized as having their own freedom and authority to act. In that sense, there can be no compatibility between a British public legal system and a Shari'a system, if the latter lays claim to society-wide omnicompetence. If a Shari'a system requires omnicompetent authority for the government, judges, and scholars, then it will be incompatible with a differentiated society in which non-governmental institutions enjoy relative independence from the public authorities while the government is constitutionally limited to a particular range of public-legal adjudication. On the other hand, if elements of traditional Shari'a that have guided Muslims in worship, family life, finance, and education can be disengaged from an omnicompetent Shari'a system and fitted into a differentiated system of public governance and non-governmental societal freedoms, then a minor synthesis of systems may be possible. In fact, these are the very experiments now contending with one another in Indonesia, Turkey, Iraq, Jordan, Great Britain, France, the Netherlands, the United States, India, Pakistan, Afghanistan, and other countries. We will see what develops.

7

Questions about the Reasonable Accommodation of Minorities

Jeremy Waldron

A. Introduction

The furore following the lecture by the Archbishop of Canterbury in early 2008—where Dr Rowan Williams discussed the prospect of some limited form of Shari'a being introduced into Britain—reminds us that the accommodation of minorities is seldom an uncontroversial or straightforward subject. The UK debate quickly degenerated into a heated and polarized discussion that, with few exceptions, neglected to undertake a constructive analysis of the underlying issues and policy concerns. In this brief essay I hope at least to partly redress that shortcoming by illuminating some key questions that a modern liberal state confronts in legally accommodating the religious and cultural claims of minority groups.

The title of this essay refers to the 'reasonable accommodation of minorities'. I take this to mean accommodation within a modern legal system of the norms and requirements of their culture or religion or of the law associated with their culture or religion or associated elsewhere with a political community of which they and their ancestors were once a part. I shall assume that the accommodation occurs within the framework of a comprehensive system of law in a modern democratic state. Among other things, 'accommodation' might include (i) exemptions from generally applicable prohibitions or requirements to permit actions (or omissions) required by minority norms but presently prohibited by general law, or (ii) giving legal effect to transactions (such as certain types of marriage or property transactions) structured and controlled by norms other than those used to structure and control similar transactions in the general system of law. (An example of (ii) might be the introduction and recognition of marriage as defined by Shari'a law within the general framework of British law or Israeli law or the law of Ontario.) I assume that 'accommodation' does not include devolution of government, in a sense that would allow a minority community to determine, for example, (iii) the imposition of punishments for crimes that were more severe than, or different in character from, the punishments imposed by the general legal system (amputation for theft, for example). Possibly accommodations of type (i) might have something in common with accommodations of type (iii)—for example, allowing minority groups freedom from constraints on corporal punishment imposed generally on parents. But the idea of devolution and regional autonomy, with different legal systems (what the Archbishop of Canterbury in his Shari'a Lecture called 'parallel jurisdictions'), is in principle separable from the idea of accommodations within the framework of a *single overarching* legal system associated—importantly here— with a single state in control of the legitimate means of coercion. So I shall not discuss accommodations of type (iii).

B. When Are Accommodations 'Reasonable'?

When are accommodations of types (i) and (ii) 'reasonable'? This includes— though it is not exhausted by—the question: when are accommodations of types (i) and (ii) 'just' (in perhaps the conservative sense of 'not unjust in their effects on certain persons', as opposed to the more liberal sense of 'permitted by a compre- hensive theory of justice')?

In a 2002 essay, 'One Law for All', I argued that there is some considerable ten- sion between accommodations of types (i) and (ii), on the one hand, and the idea of the rule of law—one law for all—on the other. I said:

Our belief in the rule of law commits us to the principle that the law should be the same for everyone: one law for all and no exceptions. It would be quite repugnant if there were one law for the rich and another for the poor, one law for black Americans and another for whites. Formally at least we repudiate all such classifications, and to the extent they still exist in our law or in the way our legal system is administered, we believe they disfigure, or at least pose grave difficulties for, our commitment to the rule of law ideal.[1]

There is also tension between the idea of these accommodations and the idea of strongly deliberative democracy. Surely the thing to do in a democracy is for the members of the minority to put forward their views about the criminal law, or about marriage, to the polity at large in a debate about how the polity should shape its general laws.[2] For instance, in many countries—for example New Zealand recently—there has been a national debate about the use of corporal punishment by parents in the upbringing of children.[3] Various minority groups contributed

---

[1] J Waldron, 'One Law for All: The Logic of Cultural Accommodation' (2002) 59 *Washington and Lee Law Review* 3, 3.

[2] See J Waldron, 'Status versus Equality: The Accommodation of Difference' in Omid A Payrow Shabani (ed), *Multiculturalism and Law: A Critical Debate* (Cardiff: University of Wales Press, 2007) 129, 152–155.

[3] Some 87.4 per cent of 1.682 million voters in a 2009 national referendum responded 'no' to the question, 'Should a smack as part of good parental correction be a criminal offence in New Zealand?' See 'Final smacking results released', *New Zealand Herald*, 25 August 2009, available at <http:// www.nzherald.co.nz/the-smacking-debate/news/article.cfm?c_id=1501165&objectid=10593090>.

to this debate, some arguing that there should not be a blanket ban on 'smacking' but rather that the matter should be left to the wisdom and judgment of parents (which might include their acceptance of certain traditions of child-rearing not necessarily accepted in other segments of society). Surely this is healthier than minority members withdrawing from such a debate, but demanding an exemption from whatever laws result from the debate for their own child-rearing practices. Of course, it is likely that members of minority groups might participate in *both* ways by (a) contributing to the debate about whether to impose a blanket ban on 'smacking' children, and (b) demanding an accommodation of type (i) (above) for the minority group's own child-rearing practice in the event that a blanket ban on 'smacking' children is imposed. The combination of (a) and (b)—a sort of political 'double-play'—might seem objectionable to some democrats, for whom it reeks of the posture of a 'sore loser', an attempt to have it both ways, and participating in bad faith in the national debate.

But both points can be answered. The rule of law is not incompatible with the idea of there being complex as opposed to simple laws, nor laws riddled with exceptions of various sorts set up to accommodate purely commercial or material interests. Often these are the products of shady political deals. So long as these are allowed, it seems unfair not to countenance the prospect of 'accommodations' for the sake of a people's culture, religion, or traditions, especially if these can be presented as just and reasonable.[4] The democratic 'double-play' mentioned above is used all the time by business and commercial interests to oppose various forms of regulation and argue for favourable exceptions in the event that regulation is imposed. It seems unjust to allow it for commercial interests, but not for the cultural or religious interests of minority groups.

In the 'One Law for All' essay I tried to set out some principles to help define the reasonableness of accommodations of type (i).[5] I defined two questions to ask: (1) Is there room for an exemption? (2) Is the benefit of that exemption distributed fairly if it is assigned to members of the minority group?

C. Question 1: Is There Room for an Exemption from the General Law?

The aims and purposes of general legislation are not always all-or-nothing matters. For instance, we might want to protect the lawns around public buildings. We could do so with a blanket ban: 'No walking on the grass'. But we know that a complete ban is actually unnecessary: it will be sufficient if most people stay off the grass; it is not necessary that all do so; the grass can stand a little bit of walking. Or consider a law regulating the hunting of some species. We may want to protect

---

[4] Waldron (n 1 above) 4.   [5] Ibid 18–23 and 29–30.

some species of deer, say, in the breeding season. We could enact a general ban on hunting in that season. But maybe our aim—eg preserving sufficient number of deer for hunting in the open season—could be achieved provided *most* hunting, even if not all hunting, is prohibited in the breeding season. In these cases there is room for an exemption. So there is space in the second example that might be made available, say, to members of an indigenous group who have a cultural or religious imperative of sacrificing a deer on the Spring solstice.

But this is not always true. Compare—forgive the flippancy—the ban on hunting with the ban on homicide. The ban on hunting admits of room for exemption because the preservation of the species is a matter of degree and probably one deer more or less does not matter. With a general prohibition on murder, the case is quite different. It is true that the law's policy is to reduce the number of homicides, preferably to zero (or as close to zero as possible), and some aspects of the law's operation—such as punishment of homicide for the sake of general deterrence—are connected to this aim. But the law also has a more immediately focused relation to any *particular* homicide or potential homicide: it is a matter of the utmost urgency that *each one* be prevented. More generally, we want the law to prohibit, prevent (as far as possible), and punish each and every murder that might be committed. There is no room for any exception (though we have some conditions of justification, such as law-enforcement or self-defence).

So, for example, if I am about to kill Dr Rowan Williams (and I am certainly not, but let us hypothesize), the law's attitude toward me is much more focused than its attitude toward my hunting out of season. The ban on murder gives law enforcement officials an immediate and powerful reason to stop me from killing Dr Williams, and if need be, they will devote enormous resources to this end. As far as the specific-prevention aim of the law is concerned, there is no room for any exemption: Dr Williams is not to be killed.

Another way of putting this is to say that some of the most important aspects of the law's ban on homicide are 'right-based': they are oriented to the interests of individuals (their interest in not being killed) one-by-one, rather than *en masse* in the spirit of minimizing killing. As far as the possible killing of Rowan Williams is concerned, the duties that the law imposes exist for the sake of preventing (or, if it cannot be prevented, for the sake of punishing) *that* killing. In this regard, it is quite unlike the ban on hunting, which—to say the least—is never focused on the lives of *particular* deer in the same way.[6]

---

[6] In Waldron (n 1 above) 30–31, I also developed a more complex argument about the ban on homicide that distinguished between issues of exemption and issues of excuse, and the relevance of cultural factors to each:

'[S]uppose... the law fails and I do kill [Rowan Williams]. Then the law must punish me. Now part of the point of this punishment is general deterrence. Insofar as *that* policy is concerned, there might be room for exemption. The policy of generally deterring homicide will go forward only marginally less effectively if I am let off from punishment for killing [Rowan]. However, punishing me also would have a more focused aim—doing justice to [Rowan] posthumously, or maybe to his loved ones. There, once again, there may be much less room for compromise.... This helps us understand

So, for question 1, the first thing to figure out is whether the general law in question admits of space for exemption. Is it more like the murder example or the deer-hunting example?

D. Question 2: How Should the Benefit of the Exemption be Distributed?

Assume there is space for exemption. Question 2 invites us to consider how the benefit of that space should be *distributed*. All sorts of people would like to go hunting in the closed season: why should the benefit be given to a specific minority group?

I think this question can sometimes be answered, especially in the case of those who might otherwise have to choose between compliance to general laws and satisfaction, not just of their own preferences, but of deeply felt religious obligations.[7] The place of the norms or custom in the life of an individual or a community might be important. The question might also be answered on broader grounds of justice, like those raised by Will Kymlicka and others,[8] concerning the raw deal that minorities have received generally in the setting-up of our legal and political arrangements: this might give them an edge in the accommodation stakes over those who, for example, simply would rather like to have the benefit of an accommodation.

These questions are not always easy to answer, and the answers may be contestable. But the difficulty of answering them in the case of accommodations

---

certain things about proposals for a cultural defense. In areas like homicide, no one *ever* proposes the cultural defense as anything other than an excuse or an ingredient in an excuse. No one who believes in the cultural defense would oppose a police officer intervening to prevent Mr. Chen from killing his wife. Similarly, no one, whatever their cultural sensitivity, would suggest that our respect for diversity and individualized justice requires us to stand back and let Mrs. Kimura drown her children. There is no room for that sort of exemption. The only room for exemption ... is at the level of punishment, when combinations of plea-bargaining, excuse, and mitigation kick in. (So Mr. Chen and Mrs. Kimura both find that murder charges are reduced to charges of second degree manslaughter, and they do not face incarceration.) And even then, as feminist critics of the decision have emphasized, there is injustice to the rights of the victim; full vindication of the victims' rights would leave no room for exemption at all, not even at the level of punishment.'

The *Chen* and *Kimura* references are to *People v Dong Lu Chen*, No 87-7774 (New York Supreme Court, 2 December 1998) and *People v Kimura*, No A-091133 (Santa Monica Supreme Court, 21 November 1985). Both were cases in which it was argued that extreme reactions to a spouse's adultery (bludgeoning the spouse to death with a hammer in *Chen*, and drowning her own children in *Kimura*) should be excused on account of extraordinary cultural sensitivity to marital infidelity. See further C W Chen, 'A Critique of "Loss of Face" Arguments in Cultural Defense Cases: A Comparative Study' in M-C Foblets and A D Renteln (eds), *Multicultural Jurisprudence: Comparative Perspectives on the Cultural Defense* (Oxford: Hart Publishing, 2009) Ch 10.

[7] See Waldron (n 1 above) 22–29.

[8] See W Kymlicka, *Liberalism, Community and Culture* (Oxford: Oxford University Press, 1989).

of type (i)—exemptions from generally applicable prohibitions—pales in comparison to the difficulty of answering the same or similar questions in the case of accommodations of type (ii)—giving effect to transactions (such as certain types of marriage or property transactions) structured and controlled by norms other than those used to structure and control similar transactions in the general system of law. I did not even attempt this in my earlier work. But I want to say something about the difficulty now.

E. Accommodation of Arrangements Structured by Different (Religious) Norms

It may be considered easier to figure out when to countenance transactions and relationships of this kind because in most cases they are set up by *consent*. I will focus on the case of marriage. Marriage, we sometimes say, is a contract and surely—like any other contract—the important thing to do is to ensure that people enter into the relationship (however it is defined) willingly and with full knowledge of what it involves. So we police the issue of informed consent and we impose age-restrictions to ensure that only those people are eligible to marry who are old enough to understand what they are getting themselves into.

Someone might say: if these factors are taken care of, what does it matter whether people are entering into civil marriage or Christian marriage or marriage defined by Shari'a law? After all, many jurisdictions allow and enforce prenuptial contracts, which have the effect of varying the terms of a marriage and in particular the terms that apply in the unfortunate event that the marriage is dissolved. The state imposes certain default rules (eg for the division of property); but in many jurisdictions parties may bargain around these in their pre-nuptial agreements. What is the difference between that and an agreement to enter into marriage as understood and controlled not by norms one has made up for the purposes of a pre-nuptial agreement, but by the norms of a specific culture or religious tradition? As we asked earlier, if variations and exemptions are good enough for people seeking to promote their own *material* interests, why are they not also good enough for people seeking to promote their own cultural or *religious* views?

One possible response—if this line is taken—is that what we have established is not strictly speaking an exemption, but rather a *permission* for members of minority groups, like everyone else in society, to exercise certain rights or powers as they please, within broadly defined limits.[9] The law of (say) California gives everyone the power to enter into a marriage governed by a pre-nuptial agreement—whether

---

⁹ But the debate about same-sex marriage indicates limits on this also.

it is a materialist pre-nup, a Christian covenant[10] pre-nup, or a Shari'a pre-nup. There is no question of any special exemption here. As I have argued elsewhere, general provision for liberty is a different kind of strategy for dealing with cultural difference than accommodations and exemptions.[11]

F. Ensuring Fairness in Religiously Contoured Arrangements

A more serious response relates to the way in which the general law will want to interrogate and supervise the fairness of these arrangements. Though we talk loosely of marriage as a contract, it remains formally a matter of legal status— which means that the law retains an interest in regulating and controlling the relationship as a package and over the whole time of its formation, duration, and dissolution.[12] The reason for the law's ongoing concern can be subdivided into three distinct interests:

[A] There is a perceived societal interest in the institution itself, both as a social presence and in its public-good benefits (so far as social stability, the mental, spiritual, and material well-being of the population, the regulation of sexuality, the reproduction of the species, and the nurturing of the next generation, are concerned).

[B] There are 'externalities'. The interests of persons other than the parties entering into the relationship need to be considered: most obviously, the interests of children.

[C] Finally, there are well-founded concerns about the reality of 'consent'.

In this latter area (as in some others), the law is by no means fully and confidently committed to the principle of *ex ante* consent as sufficient for underwriting the interest of the parties. As with the employment relation and some other long-term relations with complex and multiple impacts on a party's well-being, it is the view of the law that parties may have interests—long-term future interests, interests in the interests of others (children and parents), and interests predicated on radical and perhaps unforeseeable changes in affection and attitude—that cannot properly or in all (or most) cases be taken care of by upfront bargaining, negotiation, and consent. It may even be the law's attitude in some jurisdictions that justice—eg as between parties exiting a marriage—is not determined by what

---

[10] For the idea of Christian 'covenant marriage', see J Witte and J Nichols, 'More Than a Mere Contract: Marriage as Contract and Covenant in Law and Theology' (2008) 5 *University of St Thomas Law Journal* 595.

[11] See Waldron (n 2 above) 144–147.

[12] For discussion of the idea of legal status in this connection, see J Waldron, 'Does "Equal Moral Status" Add Anything to Right Reason?', paper presented at the American Political Science Association Annual Conference, Chicago, 2 September 2004, 5–14, available at <http://tiny.cc/ WaldronStatusAPSA >.

they have bargained for, no matter how informed or far-seeing their consent was. Contractualism is an arguable, but far from a self-evident, theory of justice.

These are among the reasons why some jurisdictions will not countenance or enforce pre-nuptial agreements or will limit their ambit to certain matters and not allow them to determine others.[13] One can imagine that they would be among the reasons why the law in any jurisdiction might want to look very closely (and indeed sceptically) at any suggestion that minority communities should be permitted to follow and enforce their own customs in an area like this.[14]

Some of the considerations mentioned in [A], [B], and [C] above can perhaps be brought under the auspices of questions 1 and 2, discussed earlier. For example, the social goals mentioned in [A] might be like the goals discussed in the first part of question 2 (the room for any exemption question)—goals that can be pursued to a greater or lesser degree, leaving some room for exemption.

But considerations [B] and [C] are not like that. They raise important issues, but they are not like the very specific distributive issue covered by question 2, which requires us to consider *who* should receive the benefit of such space for exemption or variation as there is.

Considerations [B] and [C] raise broader issues of justice. They seem to suggest that we should add a further question to our list. That is, we should ask not only:

(1) Is there space for exemption or variation so far as the purpose served by the general law is concerned?
     and

(2) If there is space for exemption or variation, is it fair to give the benefit of that to the members of the minority group who are seeking the exemption or variation as opposed to other members of society?
     but also

(3) Is there no danger that the exemption or variation will harm or impose injustice upon any member of society (including, for example, young children or even including some of those are currently seeking the benefit of the exemption or variation)?

---

[13] For a helpful and provocative discussion, see C Sanger, 'A Case for Civil Marriage' (2006) 27 *Cardozo Law Review* 1311.

[14] It is interesting that we do not permit even members of mainstream religions to bind themselves legally to conceptions of marriage sponsored by their faith. Roman Catholic doctrine forbids divorce in most cases: but a respondent may not set up his or her Catholic faith or his or her partner's Catholic faith at the time of marriage to block an otherwise valid divorce petition.

G. Question 3: Averting Injustice and Safeguarding the Vulnerable

What counts as satisfying question 3 will certainly be contestable and, on any account, difficult. Apart from anything else, it seems unfair to hold the proposed accommodation to a higher level of justice than that established under the status quo. To persist with our example: existing marriage law works injustice in many cases; arguably what we should ask is whether the proposed variation would be worse. But this is a delicate and difficult matter because it may involve comparing the injustice that one arrangement might do to persons of type X against the (qualitatively different) injustice that the proposed variation might do to persons of type Y. There is no way of avoiding this difficulty. No one ever said that thinking about accommodations would be easy.

It may be said that there is a further difficulty with questions 2 and 3 in that there will be some contestation about whether to use the *broader society's* conception of justice to settle these issues or whether to qualify that with the *minority's* conception of justice. For example, from the broader perspective, it may seem oppressive to expose a woman to the will of her husband in matters like separation and the division of matrimonial property; but from a conception of justice influenced by Shari'a jurisprudence it may not seem unjust at all.[15]

There are difficulties along these lines, but they are not exactly this difficulty. The decision as to whether to accommodate some minority arrangement within the fabric of the broader legal system is a matter for the people of the broader society (citizens, legislators, judges, etc). They must make that decision the best way they can, using whatever criteria of justice seem true or right to them. To put it another way, questions 2 and 3 are *for them* to answer—for the citizens, legislators, judges of the whole society—and they must answer them directly in *their own* voice. An accommodation is not shown to be reasonable simply because the members of the minority judge it to be so.

On the other hand, we should expect there to be disagreement about justice among the citizens, legislators, judges of the wider society—especially since this category includes all the members of the minority. *Their* views about justice—as much as anyone's—will be there in the political maelstrom, and if anything is to emerge as *the* criteria of justice of the broader society, it will emerge as a resultant of the minority's views along with everyone else's.

---

[15] Bear in mind too that the members of the minority may be divided among themselves on these matters.

H. Minorities' Democratic Opportunity to
Shape the General Law

This takes us back to the point made earlier. There I raised the possibility that it is more appropriate for a religious or cultural minority to contribute its perspective and customs to a democratic debate about what the larger society's laws ought to be, than to treat the larger society's laws as alien and demand an exemption from them. I suggested that even though there was force in that point, a quest for accommodations still might not be inappropriate. But now we see a version of this point returning. In order to decide whether a demand for accommodations is appropriate, there is no choice but to introduce the minority's views about justice into the mix of general democratic debate, along with all the other views about justice in the society. As I cautioned in an earlier essay:

> If we are going to strut around…announcing, and where possible enforcing, universal human rights claims, the only thing that can possibly entitle us to do that is that we have carefully considered *everything* that might be relevant to the moral and political assessment of such claims. It is not enough that we have considered what Kant said to Fichte, or what Bruce Ackerman said to John Rawls. The price of legitimizing our universalist moral posturing is that we make a good faith attempt to address whatever reservations, doubts, and objections there are about our positions out there, in the world, *no matter what society or culture or religious tradition they come from*. Apart from that discipline and that responsibility, we have no more right to be confident in the universal validity of our intuitions than our opponents in another culture have to be confident in theirs. And that is a difficult assignment, because such doubts and reservations and objections will often challenge not just the content of our conclusions, but our whole way of thinking about the issues that we address in our human rights concerns.[16]

Eventually it is the whole society that needs to make a judgment about the fairness and reasonableness of accommodations, and the members of the minority—with their distinctive views—must play a full and complex part in that debate at least.

One final and perhaps mischievous point. In some modern democracies, debating the answers to questions 2 and 3 may amount in effect to applying—rather than qualifying—the general norms of the society.

Consider marriage again. The marriage laws of a capitalist democracy like (say) California (or a California-of-the-future) may evolve to the point where the only regulations imposed upon private arrangements *anyway* are those that are required by the consent principle— as supplemented by questions 2 and 3. I have presented these as principles for supervising the accommodation of alternative norms of marriage as exemptions or variations. But they may be *all there is* to the local marriage laws. Any marriage-like arrangement, pre-nuptial contract, religious covenant,

---

[16] J Waldron, 'How to Argue for a Universal Claim' (1999) 30 *Columbia Human Rights Law Review* 305, 313.

or minority custom may be permitted provided these concerns are addressed and satisfied. Depending on how you look at it, the meta-law for determining which laws apply becomes the law that applies, or the law that applies becomes the meta-law for determining which laws should apply.

If so, is this unfair to the minority—representing yet again the hegemony of the majority's view? No. Something like this is morally to be expected. We cannot be required, in the name of accommodating cultural and religious minorities, to abandon what we really care about, nor what matters to us in the way of justice, fairness, and rights, and concern for all of those who are vulnerable to decisions being made in this area. Those concerns ought to inform our laws anyway. And they ought equally to inform our receptiveness to other customs, particularly if those customs are going to be upheld and enforced in our name.

8

State, Religion, and the Family: The New Dilemmas of Multicultural Accommodation

Ayelet Shachar

Arguments over the public recognition of cultural differences, and especially the degree and type of accommodation that ought to be afforded to religious faiths, have risen to the forefront of public debate. This essay highlights the centrality of women, gender, and the family in the spate of state and religion contestations in Europe and North America. This is illustrated, for example, by the veiling controversies in France and elsewhere. These legal and cultural contestations partake in delineating the boundaries of accommodation (or restriction) of expression of diversity in the *public sphere*. After investigating these debates, I will turn to explore a new type of challenge on the horizon: the call for 'privatized diversity'. By this I refer to increased demands by members of religious minorities to rely on *private law* mechanisms, including alternative dispute resolution and contractual provisions, to 'import' religious norms into dispute resolution between consenting parties occurring under the jurisdiction of the secular state. By focusing on these topical issues, we are faced with a larger puzzle: what might the new engagement between state and religion in the twenty-first century look like? Would it permit a path to accommodating diversity *with* equality? These are the questions I address in the following pages.

A. Religious Dress and Citizenship

State and religion contestations are rife. In England, a scholarly lecture by none other than the Archbishop of Canterbury—where the Archbishop contemplated the option of allowing British Muslim communities the freedom to regulate certain legal functions (especially those dealing with family law)—provoked zealous criticism across the political spectrum. This response echoed a similarly acrimonious one in Canada that broke out following a community-based proposal to establish a private 'Islamic Court of Justice' (*Darul-qada*) to resolve family law disputes among consenting adults according to faith-based principles. A further vivid illustration is the ongoing debate surrounding the Islamic headscarf (*hijab*) in Europe, from Germany to Turkey and to France. These debates have engulfed schoolhouses, courts and legislatures, even reaching the European Court of Human Rights on several occasions over the last decade.[1] The House of Lords, too, was called upon in 2006 to determine whether a school board that permitted the donning of the *hijab* had the authority to ban a more conservative and extensive form of covering called the *jilbab* (a garment that usually covers the whole body except for the hands and sometimes part of the face). The House of Lords upheld the Luton school's *jilbab* ban.[2] France also returned to the headlines. After passing national legislation in 2004 that prohibited ostentatious religious symbols from public schools[3] (widely interpreted to interdict the *hijab*), the Conseil d'État upheld a decision to decline citizenship in 2008 to a Muslim woman who spoke French, was married to a citizen, and had three French children, because 'she had adopted a radical practice of her religion, incompatible with essential values of the French community, particularly the principle of equality of the sexes'. This legal ruling was based on Article 21-4 of the Civil Code as it applied in 2005, stating that '[b]y a decree in the Conseil d'État, the Government may, on grounds of indignity or lack of assimilation other than linguistic, oppose the acquisition of French nationality by the foreign spouse'.[4]

The documentation brought before the court demonstrated that Faiza Silmi (the woman at the heart of this controversy) was engaged, in Paris' outskirts, in 'a life that is almost reclusive and apart from French society'. She wore a full body cover and the *niqab* (a face veil that leaves only the area around the eyes clear), declared that she had no knowledge of France's semi-sacred principle of *laïcité* (secularism) or the right to vote. Her reclusive and domestic-centred life was seen by the Conseil d'État as a sign of submission to the male figures in her family, which rendered her 'insufficiently assimilable' into French life.

This is surely not the first time, nor the last, that administrative agencies around the world get embroiled in the muddy waters of defining what is a legitimate form

---

Author's note: An earlier version of this essay was delivered as a distinguished lecture at the University of Leipzig on the occasion of its 600th anniversary. It was also presented at Harvard Law School's Religion, Citizenship, and Multiculturalism Conference. A shorter version appeared as 'Faith in Law? Diffusing Tensions between Diversity and Equality', (2010) 36 *Philosophy & Social Criticism* 395.

[1] *Karaduman v Turkey*, Application No 1628/90 (1993) 74 DR 93; *Dahlab v Switzerland*, Application No 42393/98 (15 February 2001); *Sahin v Turkey* (2005) 41 EHRR 8.

[2] *R (Begum) v Headteacher and Governors of Denbigh High School* [2006] UKHL 15.

[3] Law No 2004-228, 15 March 2004. See M Idriss, '*Laïcité* and the banning of the "hijab" in France' (2005) 25 *Legal Studies* 260.

[4] All countries impose restrictions on naturalization. Applicants must comply with a list of predefined requirements, such as establishing permanent residence, demonstrating adequate knowledge of the country's official language(s), and, in the case of foreign spouses of citizens, establishing the validity of the marriage. As Patrick Weil reports, the vast majority of spouses of French citizens who seek naturalization obtain it. The government does, however, occasionally sign decrees of opposition due to lack of assimilation, as was the situation in this case. See P Weil, *How to be French: Nationality in the Making since 1789* (Durham: Duke University Press, 2008), 230–237.

of the 'family' for purposes of allotting immigration or social welfare benefits. However, this decision was different: it focused on the degree of commitment to gender equality (or lack thereof) within a nuclear family, a traditionally private domain, as a foundation for denying the immigrant woman—who was clearly the dependent partner in this relationship—access to the most public of state entitlements: citizenship. This raises significant questions about the limits that can, and should, be imposed upon the exercise of such regulatory authority in respect of the parties' individual autonomy and religious freedom. No less significant, it is hard to imagine that Silmi is alone in being (alarmingly) uninformed about the basic values and rights of citizenship in the adoptive country, or involved in a marriage relationship that strays from the ideal of gender equality.

Alas, if the empowerment of Silmi, an orthodox Muslim woman, was the end goal of this decision, then it is hard to square how denying her request for full inclusion and membership in the state—a status that is *independent* of her husband (once bestowed upon her)—is conducive to that goal. Instead, we can interpret this decision as a more general, socio-political statement about: (a) what behaviour is expected of 'free' (as opposed to submissive) women in France, of whatever religious background or national origin; and (b) the statist interpretation of the veil, and especially its more extensive covering variants, as a symbolic affront to European countries' self-definition as liberal and secular. No one stated this sentiment better than urban affairs minister, Fadela Amara, herself a practising Muslim, who in a press interview endorsing the Conseil d'État ruling described Silmi's religious attire as 'a prison, it's a straightjacket'. In a society formally committed, since the French Revolution, to *liberté*, *égalité*, and *fraternité*, denial of citizenship must remain a rare, last-ditch resort. Better to first invest heavily in putting women's interests and special needs at the heart of the analysis, for instance by providing them with advice about their legal rights or the cultural and social know-how to allow them the basic means to stand on their own feet in the new country of residence. This is a more promising route than turning them into pawns in renewed battles between state and (minority) religion. By denying an immigrant woman citizenship this is precisely what happened. It left her in a dependent position vis-à-vis both her partner, who already had a secure legal status, and a community that has some more radical elements that wish to politicize the debate over *laïcité* by placing much of its burden on women's (covered) heads and bodies.[5]

The same sentiments now inform calls in France to ban the wearing of the *niqab* and the *burqa*, the most restrictive of all Islamic veils, which covers the face in addition to the full body.[6] A similar anti-veiling proposal was made in the Netherlands in 2006, but never passed the initial stages of legislation. In 2010, Belgium introduced

[5] L Volpp, 'The Culture of Citizenship' (2007) 8 *Theoretical Inquiries in Law* 571, 594.
[6] Law No 2010-2050, 19 May 2010 (passed in the National Assembly on July 13, 2010; the draft bill awaits ratification by the Senate to become law).

legislation that bans partial or total covering of faces in public places. This nation-wide ban—the first in Europe—is now echoed in various other jurisdictions. What does persist in these different examples of state-religion tensions is the focus on a visual marker of identity that is ascribed to the *female body*.

This particularized gaze has ignited political activism on behalf of conservative religious leaders as well as secularist state officials. The former often seek to impose a rigid and strict reading of what is arguably a more flexible and malleable tradition, claiming their authority to define and enforce a 'pure' or 'authentic' manifestation of a distinct cultural or religious identity in the face of real or imag-ined threats. State officials, for their part, have interpreted the veil as representing a global rise of political Islam, the challenge of Muslim integration into European societies, and as yet another justification to retreat from multiculturalism. What often get lost in all this are the real pressures facing women who cover: both in negotiating their position *within* their religious minority and *across* communal boundaries in secularized societies that increasingly view them as vanguards of religious extremism.

These legal battles over the veil (in its various manifestations) are also steeped in deep anxieties about the painful renegotiation of the once-hierarchal relations between the metropolitan centre and colonized populations, some of which later became immigrants and citizens of the very countries that once oppressed them. The blurring and intermixing of 'here' and 'there'—especially in times of political upheaval or social tension and under conditions of globalization—inspire not only minority communities, but majorities as well, to make claims to *their* distinctive cultural or national values, norms, and traits. This has led many European countries to tighten their immigration policies and place heavier emphasis on civic integration tests that require newcomers to demonstrate linguistic proficiency and knowledge of the shared values of the admitting society. These mega transformations force, as one scholar put it, 'the French, the British, and the German to see who they are and to rethink the kinds of societies and public institutions they wish to have.'[7] The turn to collective identity claims by the majority has, however, a sharp edge: making it potentially harder for non-dominant members of minority religions to gain full inclusion or even mere legal admission (if they are not yet citizens).

B. Privatized Diversity

As if these charged dilemmas do not present enough of a hurdle, we are also starting to see a new type of challenge on the horizon: the request by members of religious minorities already present on the territory of a secular state to *privatize diversity*.

---

[7] C Joppke, *Veil: Mirror of Identity* (Cambridge: Polity Press, 2009), X, 115; L Orgad, 'Illiberal Liberalism: Cultural Restrictions on Migration and Access to Citizenship in Europe' (2010) 58 *American Journal of Comparative Law* 53.

By this I refer to the recent proposals raised by self-proclaimed 'guardians of the faith' to establish private arbitration tribunals in which consenting members of the group will have their legal disputes resolved in a binding fashion—according to religious principles—under the secular umbrella of alternative dispute-resolution. While formally deploying the logic of alternative dispute resolution, this new development is potentially far-reaching. The main claim raised by advocates of privatized diversity is that respect for religious freedom or cultural integrity does not require inclusion in the public sphere, but *exclusion* from it. This leads to a demand that the state adopt a hands-off, non-interventionist approach, placing civil and family disputes with a religious or cultural aspect 'outside' the official realm of equal citizenship. This potential storm must be addressed head on. This is the case because privatized diversity mixes three inflammatory components in today's political environment: religion, gender, and the rise of a neo-liberal state. The volatility of these issues is undisputed; they require a mere spark to ignite.

Privatized diversity's potentially dramatic alterations to the legal system increasingly revolve around the regulation of women and the family, placing them at the centre of larger debates about citizenship and identity. These challenges cannot be fully captured by our existing legal categories; they require a new vocabulary and a fresh approach. I begin to sketch here the contours of such an approach by asking what is owed to women whose legal dilemmas (at least in the family law arena) arise from the fact that their lives have already been affected by the interplay between overlapping systems of identification, authority, and belief: in this case, religious and secular law.[8]

The standard legal response to this challenge is to seek shelter behind a formidable 'wall of separation' between state and religion, even if this implies turning a blind eye to the concerns of religious women caught in the uncoordinated web of secular and religious marriage bonds. I advance a different approach. By placing these once-ignored agents at the centre of analysis, this essay explores the idea of permitting a degree of *regulated choice and interaction* between religious and secular sources of obligation, so long as the baseline of citizenship-guaranteed rights remains firmly in place.[9] Despite the understandable desire to disentangle law from religion by metaphorically 'caging' each in its appropriate sphere or domain, it is worth contemplating whether a carefully regulated recognition of multiple legal affiliations (and the subtle interactions among them) can allow devout women to benefit from the protections offered by the state to other citizens—yet without

---

[8] The core arguments advanced here are addressed at greater length in A Shachar, 'What We Owe Women? The View From Multicultural Feminism' in D Satz and R Reich (eds), *Toward a Humanist Justice: The Political Philosophy of Susan Moller Okin* (New York: Oxford University Press, 2009) 143–145; A Shachar, 'Privatizing Diversity: A Cautionary Tale from Religious Arbitration in Family Law' (2008) 9 *Theoretical Inquiries in Law* 573; A Shachar, 'Religion, State, and the Problem of Gender: New Modes of Citizenship and Governance in Diverse Societies' (2005) 50 *McGill Law Journal* 49.

[9] 'Citizenship rights' here apply to anyone who resides on the territory, regardless of their formal membership status.

abandoning the tenets of their faith. I demonstrate the possibility of implementing such a vision by reference to a recent decision of the Supreme Court of Canada, *Bruker v Marcovitz*, which breaks new ground.[10]

I will then reflect on the government's chosen policy to ban any type of family arbitration by such faith-based tribunals, thus reaffirming the classic secular-religious divide. While this decision is politically defensible and symbolically astute, it does not necessarily provide adequate protection for those individuals most vulnerable to their community's formal and informal pressures to push them to accept 'unofficial' dispute-resolution forums in resolving family issues. The decision may instead thrust these tribunals underground where no state regulation, coordination, or legal recourse is made available to those who may need it most.

Before we turn to alternative remedies, it is important to first articulate the privatized diversity challenge in greater detail. In discussions about citizenship, we repeatedly come across the modernist and liberal schema of separate spheres: we are expected to act as citizens in the public sphere, but remain free to express our distinct cultural or religious identities in the private domain of family and communal life. Yet multiple tensions have exposed cracks in this separate-spheres formula. In Faiza Silmi's case, for example, where precisely does the 'private' end and the 'public' begin? Who is to bear the burdens if the modern state's desire to keep religion out of the public sphere indirectly inspires calls to limit access to citizenship or, conversely, to create unregulated 'islands of jurisdiction' that immunize the practices of certain religious communities because they occurred under the cover of privatized diversity? In the remainder of this essay I try to provide some concrete institutional answers to these queries by reliance on recent and creative attempts by courts and legislatures to forge ahead.[11]

Family law serves as an excellent illustration to these simmering gender and religion tensions. It demonstrates that for some observant women, the claim for achieving greater gender equality and legal protection as female citizens may in part be informed by their claim for religious recognition and accommodation. Consider, for example, the situation of observant religious women who may wish (or feel bound) to follow their faith community's divorce requirements in addition to the rules of the state that remove barriers to remarriage. Without the removal of such barriers, women's ability to build new families, if not their very membership status (or that of their children), may be adversely affected. This is particularly true for observant Jewish and Muslim women living in secular societies who have entered marriage through a religious ceremony—as permitted by law in many jurisdictions. For them, a civil divorce—which is all that a secular state committed to a separation of state and church can provide—is simply part of the story; it does not, and cannot, dissolve the religious aspect of the relationship. Failure

---

[10] [2007] 3 SCR 607.
[11] For an illuminating comparative discussion of such creative responses by civil courts, see T Einhorn, 'Jewish Divorce in the International Arena', in J Basedow et al. (eds), *Private Law in the International Arena* (The Hague: T.M.C. Asser Press, 2000), 135-153.

to recognize their 'split-status' position—of being legally divorced according to state law, but still married according to their faith tradition—may leave these women prone to abuse by recalcitrant husbands. These men are often well aware of the adverse effect this split-status situation has on their wives—women who fall between the cracks of the civil and religious jurisdictions.[12]

Add to this the recognition that, for a host of complex historical, political, and institutional path-dependency reasons, family law has become crucial for minority religions in maintaining their definition of membership. Religious minorities in secularized democracies are typically non-territorial entities, unlike certain national or linguistic communities (think of the Québécois in Canada, the Catalans in Spain, and so on). They have no semi-autonomous sub-unit in which they constitute a majority, nor have they power to define the public symbols that manifest, and in turn help preserve, their distinctive national or linguistic heritage. Religious minorities, as non-territorial communities, are thus forced to find other ways to sustain their distinct traditions and ways of life. With no authority to issue formal documents of membership, regulate mobility, or hold the power to collect mandatory taxes, religious personal laws that define marriage, divorce, and lineage have come to serve an important role in regulating membership boundaries. These laws demarcate a pool of individuals endowed with the collective responsibility to maintain the group's values, practices, and distinct ways of life (if they maintain their standing as members in that community). I label this family law's *demarcating* function. For some religious minorities it comes close to serving the same core purposes as citizenship law does for the state. It delineates who is legally affiliated to the community and thus strengthens the bonds of continuity between past and future by identifying who is considered part of the tradition. This is why gaining control over the religious aspects of entry into (or exit from) marriage matters greatly to these communities; it is part of their membership demarcation and intergenerational project. At the same time, family law is also the area in which women have historically and traditionally been placed at a disadvantage by both states and religious communities, in part because the recognition of female members plays a crucial role in 'reproducing the collective'—both literally and figuratively. Although this core contribution to the collective could, in theory, have empowered them, in most places and legal traditions it led to tight control and regulation of women, treating them, by law, as less than equal.

With this background in mind, we can now see more clearly why the Archbishop of Canterbury's lecture has provoked such an unwieldy storm of response, as did the Shari'a tribunal controversy in Canada, where a bitter debate erupted after a small and relatively conservative non-governmental organization, the Canadian Society of Muslims, declared in a series of press releases its intention to establish

---

[12] Related concerns can also arise for Roman Catholic couples in the context of a civil divorce. In certain cases, the Catholic Church has nullified the religious marriage bond so as to avoid the split-status situation.

a faith-based tribunal that would operate as a forum for binding arbitration on consenting parties.[13] The envisioned tribunal (which never came into operation for reasons explained below) would have permitted consenting parties not only to enter a less-adversarial, out-of-court, dispute-resolution process, but also to use choice of law provisions to apply religious norms to resolve family disputes, according to the 'laws (*fiqh*) of any [Islamic] school, eg *Shiah* or *Sunni* (*Hanafi, Shāfiʿi, Hanbalī,* or *Mālikī*)'.[14]

The proposal to establish a tribunal of this kind was perceived as challenging the normative and juridical authority, not to mention legitimacy, of the secular state's asserted mandate to represent and regulate the interests and rights of *all* its citizens in their family matters, irrespective of communal affiliation. In this respect, it raised profound questions concerning hierarchy and lexical order in the contexts of law and citizenship: which norms should prevail, and who, or what entity, ought to have the final word in resolving any value-conflicts between equality and diversity. No less significant for our discussion is the recognition that the proposal to establish a non-state arbitration tribunal of this kind does not by itself provide a conclusive answer to determining how secular and religious norms should interact in governing the family. To the contrary, it serves to provoke just such a debate. As an analytical matter, secular and religious norms may stand in tension with one another, point in different directions, lead to broadly similar results, or directly contradict one another. It is the latter outcome that is seen to pose the greatest challenge to the superiority of secular family law by its old adversary—religion.

A rigid dichotomy between either rejecting or accepting such religious arbitration characterizes these debates. The wholesale capture of jurisdictional authority over family affairs by 'alternative' tribunals is indeed objectionable, even if we accept the force of the argument for non-intervention on the grounds of allowing communities as much associational freedom as possible to pursue their own visions of the good in a diverse society. The reason is as simple as it is powerful: hardly anyone suggests that religious liberty is absolute; it may be overridden or restricted by other liberties or compelling state interests. Without such limitations in place, the state becomes an implicit accomplice in tolerating infringements of women's basic citizenship protections that may occur in the name of respecting cultural and religious diversity. Furthermore, the privatized diversity framework relies on an artificial and over-simplified distinction between private and public, culture and citizenship, and contractual and moral obligation. This vision is not only inaccurate on a descriptive level; it is normatively unattractive as well. It is blind to the intersection of overlapping affiliations in individuals' lives. These parallel 'belongings' are often the significant source of meaning and value for religious women; at the same time, they may also make them vulnerable to a double or

---

[13]   See N Bahkt, 'Were Muslim Barbarians Really Knocking on the Gates of Ontario? The Religious Arbitration Controversy—Another Perspective' [2006] *Ottawa Law Review* 67.

[14]   S M Ali, 'Establishing an Institute for Islamic Justice (Darul Qada)', Canadian Society of Muslims News Bulletin, October 2002.

triple disadvantage, especially in a legal and governance system that permits little interaction and dialogue between their overlapping sources of obligation. Women situated in minority religious communities are often especially hard hit by the privatized diversity framework and are left to fend for themselves under structurally unfavourable conditions.

C. The Predicament Facing Vulnerable Members of Religious Communities

The established strict separation approach asks religious women to adhere to the civil rules on the dissolution of marriage and divorce, leaving it up to each individual woman to somehow negotiate a termination of the religious aspect of the relationship—a task that may prove extremely difficult if the husband is recalcitrant.[15] Another response, often presented by well-meaning philosophers and political theorists, is to recommend that these members simply 'exit' their home communities if they experience injustice within.[16] However, this recommendation provides little solace. If pious women wanted to leave their communities, the central legal dilemmas that haunt them—the challenge of adhering to both secular and non-state religious requirements of forming and dissolving marriage—would not arise in the first place. Clearly this is not the situation we are dealing with.

Into this vacuum enters the privatized diversity approach. It takes a diametrically opposed path to that of strict separation, placing the need to address the religious side of the marriage at the heart of the non-statist legal response: for instance, by recommending that parties move the 'full docket' of their disputes from public state-provided courtrooms to private faith-based tribunals that may (or may not) comply with statutory and constitutional protections of rights and obligations. Blanket acceptance of privatized diversity would thus amount to a dramatic redefinition of the relationship between state and religion under the guise of mere procedural reliance on private alternative dispute resolution mechanisms. The price to be paid for such a move might prove dangerously high—forfeiting women's hard-won protections through democratic and equity-enhancing legislation, itself achieved as a result of significant social mobilization by women's groups and other justice-seeking individuals and communities. While offering opposing solutions, the strict separation and privatized diversity approaches rely on a common matrix of denying their *shared* responsibility and obligation to assist women whose

---

[15] This position informs, for example, the minority opinion in *Marcovitz* [2007] 3 SCR 607 at [102]–[106].

[16] For a critical discussion of the exit option, see S M Okin, ' "Mistresses of Their Own Destiny": Group Rights, Gender and Realistic Rights of Exit' (2002) 112 *Ethics* 205; A Phillips, *Multiculturalism Without Culture* (Princeton: Princeton University Press, 2007) 133–157.

marriage regulation is grounded in an uneasy amalgam of secular and religious traditions. Between them, the two approaches compel devout women to make an all-or-nothing choice between these sources of law and identity.

This punishing dilemma can be avoided, or at least mitigated, if the option of regulated interaction is contemplated. The core issue for us to assess is whether, and under what conditions, women's freedom and equality can be promoted (rather than inhibited) by law's recognition of faith-based obligations that structure marriage and divorce for religious citizens. The additional challenge is to develop a legal approach that can foster viable institutional paths for cooperation that begin to match the actual complexity of women's lived experience.

The standard legal response to such dilemmas is of course different. It tends to relegate civil and family disputes with certain religious aspects beyond the reach of the secular courts—and thus outside the realm of provision of the safeguards provided by the state to other litigants or vulnerable parties. This need not, however, be the sole or even primary response to such dilemmas, especially when 'non-intervention' effectively translates into immunizing wrongful behaviour by more powerful parties. In the deeply gendered world of intersecting religious and secular norms of family law, these more powerful parties are often husbands who may refuse to remove barriers to religious remarriage (as in the Jewish *get* (bill of divorcement), elaborated later) or who may seek to retract a financial commitment undertaken as part of the religious marriage contract (as might be the case with deferred *mahr* in certain Islamic marriages). Such retaliation impairs the woman's ability to build a new family or establish financial independence after divorce. The broader concern here is that while their multiple affiliations might offer religious women a significant source of meaning and value, they may also make them vulnerable to a double or triple disadvantage, especially in a legal system that categorically denies cooperation between their overlapping sources of obligation.

Is it possible to find a more fruitful engagement that overcomes this predicament by placing the interests of these historically marginalized participants at the centre of the analysis? Arguably, the obligation to engage in just such renegotiation is pressing in light of growing global demands to re-evaluate the crucial social arena of family law. From the perspective of women caught in the web of overlapping and potentially competing systems of secular and sacred law, the almost automatic rejection of any attempt to establish a forum for resolving standing disputes that address the religious dimension of their marriage might respect the protection-of-rights dimension of their lived experience, but unfortunately does little to address the cultural or religious affiliation issue. The latter may well be better addressed by attending to the removal of religious barriers to remarriage, obstacles that do not automatically disappear following a civil divorce. This is particularly true for observant women who have solemnized marriage according to the requirements of their religious tradition, and who may now wish—or feel obliged—to receive the blessing of this tradition for the dissolution of the relationship.

In the Canadian debate, this constituency also reflected a transnational element. In families with roots in more than one country, a divorce agreement that complies with the demands of the faith (as a non-territorial identity community)—in addition to those of the state of residence—appears somehow more 'transferable' across different Muslim jurisdictions.[17] In technical terms, this need not be the case—private international law norms are based on the laws of states, *not* of religions. But what matters here is the perception that a faith-based tribunal may provide a valuable legal service to its potential clientele, a service that the secular state, by virtue of its formal divorce from religion, simply cannot provide.

I believe we also face the urgent task of investigating and highlighting the importance of state action (or *in*action) in shaping, through law and institutional design, the context in which women can pursue their claims for equity and justice. Viewed through this perspective, the rise of privatized diversity mechanisms to implement religious principles should rightly be perceived with a healthy dose of scepticism, particularly if the parties lose the background protections and bargaining chips they are otherwise entitled to under secular law. One may well wonder whether this development represents a whole new and convenient way for the neo-liberal state (and its 'rolled-back' public institutions) to avoid taking responsibility for protecting the rights of more vulnerable parties precisely in that arena of social life, the family, that is most crucial for realizing both gender equality and collective identity.

In order to militate against such a result, it is high time to search for new terms of engagement between the major players. They have a stake in finding a viable path that accommodates diversity *with* equality, a path that includes the faith community, the state, and the individual. Any tractable solution, however, must work in ways that will benefit religious women, while duly acknowledging that they are members of intersecting (and potentially conflicting) identity- and law-creating jurisdictions.

D. Forging a New Path

Any new path requires a delicate balance. On the one hand, it demands vigilance to address the serious communal pressures that make 'free consent' to alternative dispute resolution a code name for thinly veiled coercion. On the other hand, it requires avoidance of any hasty conclusion that the answer to such complex legal and identity challenges lies in turning a blind eye to the problems confronting women who wish to maintain good standing in both their religious and non-religious communities.

---

[17] Similar misconceptions are also traced in England: L Carroll, 'Muslim Women and "Islamic Divorce" in England' (1997) 17 *Journal of Muslim Minority Affairs* 97, 100–111.

A number of alternative ideal-type responses present themselves. I will discuss just two promising alternatives: (a) democratic deliberation and intercultural dialogue in civil society, and (b) changing the background conditions that shape such intra- and inter-cultural negotiations.[18]

The democratic deliberation path emphasizes the importance of dialogue in civil society and involves formal and informal intercultural exchanges. This route permits revealing the internal diversity of opinions and interpretations of the religious and secular family law traditions in question. Deliberation and contestation can also promote agency and direct empowerment through political participation.

While I fully endorse and support these civil society avenues, 'something else' might be required in terms of institutional design to address situations of negotiation breakdown, imbalance of power, and restoration or establishment of rights. That 'something else' translates into a focus on legal-institutional remedies that respond to the fact that erosion of women's freedom and autonomy is increasingly the 'collateral damage' of charged state-religious showdowns. To avert this disturbing result, I will briefly explore how, despite the fact that the strict separation approach still remains the standard or default response, courts and legislatures have recently broken new ground by adopting what we might refer to as 'intersectionist' or 'joint governance' remedies.

One example is the case mentioned earlier, *Bruker v Marcovitz*,[19] in which the Canadian Supreme Court explicitly rejected the simplistic 'your culture or your rights' formula. Instead, it ruled in favour of '[r]ecognizing the enforceability by civil courts of agreements to discourage religious barriers to remarriage, addressing the gender discrimination those barriers may represent and alleviate the effects they may have on extracting unfair concessions in a civil divorce'.[20] In that case, a Jewish husband made a promise to remove barriers to religious remarriage in a negotiated, settled agreement, which was incorporated into the final divorce decree between the parties. He said he would give his wife a *get*—a bill of divorcement. This contractual obligation thus became part of the terms that enabled the civil divorce to proceed. Once the husband had the secular divorce in hand, however, he failed to honour the signed agreement to remove the religious barriers to his wife's remarriage, claiming that he had undertaken a moral rather than legal obligation. The Supreme Court was not in a position to order specific performance (forcing the husband to grant a *get*); instead, the court ordered the husband to pay monetary damages for breach of the contractual promise, a breach that had harmed the wife personally and the public interest generally. What *Marcovitz* demonstrates is the

---

[18] This categorization fits well with Seyla Benhabib's 'dual track' approach: S Benhabib, *The Claims of Culture: Equality and Diversity in the Global Age* (Princeton: Princeton University Press, 2002) 130–132. A similar distinction between the 'legal track' and 'citizen track' is found in a major report recently published in Quebec on the boundaries of reasonable accommodation: G Bouchard and C Taylor, *Report: Building The Future—A Time for Reconciliation* (Québec City: Gouvernement du Québec, 2008).

[19] [2007] 3 SCR 607.

[20] Ibid at [3], [92].

possibility of employing a standard legal remedy (damages for breach of contract, in this example) in response to specifically gendered harms that arise out of the intersection between multiple sources of authority and identity—religious and secular—in the actual lives of women.

The significance of the *Marcovitz* decision lies in its recognition that both the secular and religious aspects of divorce matter greatly to observant women if they are to enjoy gender equality, articulate their religious identity, enter new families after divorce, or rely on contractual ordering just like any other citizen. This joint-governance framework offers us a vision in which the secular law may be invoked to provide remedies for religious women to protect them from husbands who might otherwise 'cherry-pick' their religious and secular obligations. This is a clear rejection of a punishing 'either/or' approach, and instead offers a more nuanced and context-sensitive analysis that begins from the 'ground up'. It identifies who is harmed and why, and then proceeds to find a remedy that matches, as much as possible, the need to recognize the (indirect) intersection of law and religion that contributed to the creation of the very harm for which legal recourse is sought.

E. Regulated Interaction

The last set of issues I wish to address relates to the thorny challenge of tackling the potential conflict between secular and religious norms governing family disputes. The fear of religious law as a competing normative system that resists the lexical superiority of the statist rule of law clearly played a significant part in the anxiety that surrounded the Shari'a tribunal debate. Given the deference typically afforded to out-of-court arbitration procedures, critics of the tribunal charged that nothing less than an attempt to use a technique of privatized diversity to redefine the relationship between state and religion was underway. This posed an existential threat that no secular state authority is likely to accept with indifference—not even in tolerant, multicultural Canada.[21] Therefore, after much contemplation, the chosen response to the challenge was to quash the proposed tribunal with all the legal force the authorities could muster. This took the shape of an absolutist solution: prohibiting by decree the operation of any religious arbitration process in the family law arena.[22] This universal ban effectively shuts down, rather than encourages, dialogue between civil and religious authorities. A less heavy-handed approach might have been worth exploring, especially once the idea of granting unrestricted immunity in the name of religious freedom to any kind of dispute-resolution forum is rejected.

[21] R Hirschl and A Shachar, 'The New Wall of Separation: Respecting Diversity, Prohibiting Competition' (2009) 30 *Cardozo Law Review* 2535.
[22] The government adopted this solution with the enactment of the Family Statute Law Amendment Act 2005 (amending the Arbitration Act 1991) and the subsequent regulations that followed in 2007: Family Arbitration, O Reg 134/07 (Ontario).

The alternatives include a range of options that permit a mixture of *ex ante* and *ex post* regulatory oversight in the service of human rights protections, mandatory provisions that no party is permitted to waive, and enhanced access to whatever public-sponsored resources are normally available to anyone facing a family breakdown. Regulated interaction envisions a new way of allocating and sharing jurisdiction between states and religious minorities.

The major insight here is that today's most contested social arenas—education, family law, criminal justice, and immigration, to mention but a few key examples—are internally divisible into parts or 'sub-matters'—multiple, separable yet complementary, legal components. Existing legal and normative models rarely recognize that most contested social arenas encompass multiple functions, or diverse sub-matters. Rather, they operate on the misguided assumption that each social arena is internally *indivisible* and thus should be under the full and exclusive jurisdiction of one authority—either the state or faith community. On this account, there is always a winner and loser in the jurisdictional contest between state and religion. But if power can be divided into sub-matters within a single social activity, it becomes possible to have a more creative, nuanced, and context-sensitive basis for coordination.

Take marriage. Here at least two sub-matters should be identified. There is a *demarcating* function, mentioned earlier, which regulates, among other things, the change of one's marital status or one's entitlement to membership in a given community. Then there is a *distributing* function which covers, among other things, the definition of the rights and obligations of married spouses, together with a determination, in the event of divorce or death, of the property and economic consequences of this change in marital status. These demarcation and distributive sub-matters parallel the two key legal aspects of marriage and divorce rules: status and property relations. This division permits ample room for legal creativity. Recent studies have shown, for example, that Muslim women in Britain have turned to non-state institutions in order to gain a religious-authorized release from a dead marriage—one, that in certain cases, no longer legally existed because a state divorce decree had already been granted.[23] For these women, the religious councils were performing the crucial communal demarcating function of removing religious barriers to remarriage. These 'end users' were seeking specialized religious-oriented divorce services that the secular state is, by definition, barred from supplying. At the same time, the women who turned to these religious councils expressed no interest in (and, indeed, some explicitly rejected) the idea of delegating control over the distributive components of their fractured marriage. They did not want their post-divorce property relations—controlling matters such as the rights and obligations owed by each former spouse to the other, to the children (if

---

[23] S Bano, 'In Pursuit of Religious and Legal Diversity: A Reply to the Archbishop of Canterbury and the "Sharia Debate" in Britain' (2008) 8 *Ecclesiastical Law Journal* 283, 309.

any), and to various third parties—determined by these non-state institutions.[24] Such division of responsibility fits well with the idea of sub-matter jurisdictions. It rejects transferring the 'full docket' or 'package' to privatized-diversity entities and, instead, demands that some degree of coordination occur between religious and civil institutions in the allocation of shared responsibility and its subsequent implementation.[25]

In addition to the recommended division of authority according to component functions, the literature on institutional design distinguishes between different forms or techniques of oversight. The classic approach envisages minimal oversight: the rationale here is that the consenting parties intentionally removed their dispute from the public system, preferring instead an out-of-court process. In the case of severe breaches of procedural justice, however, laws governing alternative dispute resolution routinely permit the arbitrating parties to seek judicial review.[26] This is characterized in the literature as the 'fire alarm' response (a decentralized and *ex post* review initiated by individual complainants or public interest groups) as opposed to 'police control' (a more centralized, governmental *ex ante* mode of regulation).[27] The fire-alarm technique decentralizes regulation; the burden of monitoring alleged violations in the arbitration process, for example, rests upon the parties themselves. They are the ones best informed about the process and possess the strongest interest in identifying and reporting such breaches.

While the fire-alarm model might suit commercial or civil arbitration (with its strong emphasis on party autonomy, agency and parity) it may fail miserably in the family arbitration context. Here, there is a real concern about power and representation inequalities—asymmetries that disrupt the *ex post* judicial review model's basic assumption about both parties being equally positioned to 'pull' the fire alarm and call attention to potential breaches in the arbitration process. Given the gendered concerns identified above, the idea of placing the burden of initiating the process of *ex post* review on the more vulnerable party—someone who may have been semi-coerced into consenting to a religious tribunal's authority in the first place—is implausible. If anything, it provides a (unintended) guarantee that very few, if any, of the most serious violations will ever be reported. This result stands in direct contravention of the logic of 'active agency' that lies at the basis of

---

[24] Ibid.
[25] This is not the present legal reality in England. Instead, these non-state entities operate outside the official system of law, remaining 'non-existent' from the state's perspective, notwithstanding the fact that they operate within its territory and affect its citizens. This situation spells potential trouble for women and their hard-won equality rights because there is no guarantee that the unregulated religious councils will not try to extend their reach to re-open legal matters that have already been dealt with by civil courts. This represents precisely the kind of deleterious situation that the regulated interaction approach seeks to prevent.
[26] Eg, the provisions (prior to its amendment in 2006) of the Arbitration Act, 1991 SO, ch 17, §§ 6, 19, 45-47.
[27] These two models are described in M McCubbins and T Schwartz, 'Congressional Oversight Overlooked: Police Patrols Versus Fire Alarms' (1984) 28 *American Journal of Political Science* 165.

this oversight mechanism and thus makes it a less attractive mechanism to address the complex gendered and communal pressures at issue.

Once we enter the realm of family dispute resolution, we cannot rely solely on *ex post*, 'fire alarm', judicial review; rather, the *complementary* technique of *ex ante* or 'police control' oversight is needed. This may include requirements such as subjecting arbitrators or mediators dealing with such matters to a licensed training process, demanding that they keep records containing both the evidence presented and notes taken at the hearing, ensuring that both parities receive adequate counselling by an independent legal advisor before entering the family arbitration process, and so on.[28] These protections can assist individuals by reducing information asymmetries and power imbalances; regrettably, however, just like any other legal measure that respects individual choice, they may fall short of providing a *full* guarantee that no communal (or other) pressure was imposed on those utilizing an ADR forum. To address these real concerns, any *ex ante* oversight scheme must ensure that women are not dispossessed of whatever rights and protections they have as citizens when they raise a legal claim that incorporates the religious dimension as well. That is precisely what the *Marcovitz* ruling clarifies. Notably, this shift in regulatory emphasis does not require, or entail, total abandonment of the *ex post* review model. The two models can live happily side-by-side.

With these conditions firmly in place, we can appreciate the dynamism and behaviour-alteration potential of the regulated interaction approach. For instance, communal decision-makers (ideally trained in *both* civil and religious law) have the opportunity to enjoy the benefits of state recognition of their decisions—including the coveted public enforcement of their awards—when dissolving a religious marriage in accordance with the tenets of the relevant faith. The state retains the power to issue a civil divorce and to define the thresholds or default rules in matters such as the post-divorce distribution of matrimonial and other property, matters that inevitably concern all citizens facing a marriage breakdown. These safeguards typically establish a baseline or 'floor' of protection, above which significant room for variation is permitted. These protections were designed, in the first place, to address concerns about power and gender inequities in family relations—concerns that are not absent from religious communities either. If anything, these concerns probably apply with equal force in the religious context as in the individualized, secular case.

---

[28] These *ex ante* requirements now apply in Ontario based on regulations that came into effect in 2007. These regulations recognize family arbitration agreements that are conducted in accordance with (i) the law of Ontario, and the law of Canada as it applies in Ontario, or (ii) the law of *x* (another Canadian jurisdiction), and the law of Canada as it applies in that jurisdiction. See s 4(1) of O Reg 134/07. This definition does not permit family arbitration to proceed in accordance with any law other than that of a recognized Canadian jurisdiction, thus prohibiting the application of purely faith-based principles.

This then is the basic structure of the regulated interaction model, one that offers an alternative to the 'top-down' prohibition model. Provided the resolution by a religious arbitration body falls within the reasonable margin of discretion permitted a family law judge or secular arbitrator, there is no reason to discriminate against that tribunal solely for the reason that the decision-maker used a different tradition to reach a permissible resolution. The operative assumption here is that, in a diverse society, we can safely assume that at least some individuals might wish to turn to their 'communal' institutions, knowing that their basic state-backed rights are still protected by these alternative fora. Against this backdrop, permitting community members to turn to a non-state tribunal may, perhaps paradoxically, nourish the motivating conditions for promoting a more dynamic, context-sensitive, and moderate interpretation of the tradition that is acceptable to the faithful, as endorsed by religious authorities themselves.

The prospect for such 'change from within'—or what I have elsewhere labeled *transformative accommodation*[29]—in this context does not rely merely on good will. It also incorporates a more calculated, rational act or logic to it, namely: if religious arbitrators operating within a secular constitutional state wish to issue binding and compelling decisions (which permit parties to turn to the civil system for enforcement where needed), they must recognize that they cannot breach the basic protections to which each woman is entitled by virtue of her equal citizenship status.[30] Ignoring these entitlements would lose them the ability to provide enforceable legal services to members of the community. Such a result would be unattractive for religious authorities if they strive to provide distinct legal services that no secular agency can offer. If they wish to see their faith community survive (and, indeed, flourish), and if they wish to continue to define who belongs within the faith community's membership boundaries, these basic protections cannot be spurned. Such a result would also fail to provide a remedy to the individual who turns to this specialized forum in order to bring closure to a family dispute that bears a religious aspect that categorically cannot be addressed by the secular court system.

As we saw earlier, religious marriage and divorce rules play a crucial role in fulfilling this identity-demarcating function. The obligation to comply with minimal standards defined by the larger community in governing the distributive obligations between the separated or divorced parties (and toward relevant third parties) does not have to cripple the new-found authority gained by the religious community and its tribunals. They may maintain their identity through

---

[29] A Shachar, *Multicultural Jurisdictions: Cultural Differences and Women's Rights* (Cambridge: Cambridge University Press, 2001) 117–145.

[30] This division of authority respects the vital demarcating interests of the group while upholding the commitment of the state to equally protect the distributive needs of all its citizens, irrespective of religious affiliation or national origin. Once defined, these guidelines can be implemented by a civil court, through negotiated agreement between the parties (or their legal counsels) or via an arbitrated award.

control over the demarcating aspect of marriage and divorce (for those members who desire such an affiliation). By ensuring that incidents of 'split status' are reduced within a diverse plural society, both the community at large and the specific women involved benefit by having all barriers to remarriage removed in a conclusive and non-ambivalent manner. Such processes could plant the seeds for meaningful reform that falls within the interpretative margins and methodologies for innovation permitted by the religious tradition and improves women's bargaining position and rights protection. This creates an alignment of interests between the group, the state, and the individuals at risk. In this fashion, regulated interaction can address the multiple aspects of the marriage and its breakdown. Counterintuitively, a qualified recognition of regulated interaction may generate effective, non-coercive encouragement of more egalitarian and reformist changes from within the religious tradition itself.

The state system, too, is transformed from strict separation to regulated interaction. It is no longer permitted to categorically relegate competing sources of authority to the realm of unofficial, exotic, if not outright dangerous 'non-law'. The regulated interaction approach discourages an underworld of unregulated religious tribunals. It offers a path to transcend the 'either/or' choice between culture and rights, family and state, citizenship and islands of 'privatized diversity'.

F. Conclusion

Despite persistent, and at times oppressive, attempts by the modern state to monopolize the power to regulate the family, other communities and values have retained a hefty influence in this significant realm of life. As the belligerent responses to the Archbishop of Canterbury's lecture on the relationship between civil and religious law in England, and the public outcry following the proposal to establish a faith-based tribunal in Canada dramatically revealed, these issues touch a raw nerve. Alas, the almost automatic response of insisting on the *dis*entanglement of state and church (or mosque, synagogue, and so forth) in regulating the family may not always work to the benefit of female religious citizens—persons who are deeply attached to, and influenced by, *both* systems of law and identity. Their complex claim for inclusion in both the state and their faith group as full members derives from their multilayered connections to both systems. Some insight into this complex phenomenon was evident in the *Marcovitz* case, where the Supreme Court challenged the very assumption that it is impossible to grant consideration to religious diversity and gender equality at the same time.

Existing legal strategies offer a false sense of confidence. They draw uncompromising lines that aim to compartmentalize sacred from secular, private from public—despite the fact that the social reality they regulate no longer fits this bill (if it ever did). While some, perhaps many, are accustomed to seek shelter behind a high 'wall of separation' between state and religion, a qualified yet dynamic 'entanglement' between these old rivals—under a combined *ex ante* and *ex post* regulatory framework (coupled with due recognition of interlocking and complementary sub-matters)—may present the best hope for expanding recognition to, and equal citizenship for, once-marginalized religious women who now seek recoginition as *both* culture bearers *and* rights bearers.

9

Shari'a and the True Basis of Group Rights: Islam, the West, and Liberalism

John Milbank

A. Introduction

In this essay, and in the wake of the recent Shari'a furore in Britain, I shall argue that religious group rights need to be defended from a specifically theological position. If the Archbishop of Canterbury, the Rt Rev Dr Rowan Williams, had adopted a Christian theological defence of group rights, then he could not have endorsed any notion of 'rival' or 'parallel' jurisdictions. The kind of pluralism undergirding parallel jurisdictions—secular, liberal, multiculturalist—is alien to the specifically *organic* plurality of the Christian tradition. Furthermore, justifying religious group rights from a secular perspective, especially if this requires that one perform the contortion of respectfully 'imagining' what it would be like to be religious, is doomed. I contend that the entire idea of 'group rights' derives from a medieval 'corporatist' and nineteenth-century 'pluralist' tradition that is entirely Christian (or ultimately Christian) in inspiration.

The spectre of rival jurisdictions is only raised by the 'postmodern' application of liberal secular thought to the group rather than the individual. Treating a group as a 'personality' within a liberal regime involves one in multiple and irresolvable *aporiae*[1] in the following manner.

The liberal polity—taking 'liberal' in the standard, modern sense (as opposed to an older understanding that means roughly 'constitutionalism')—is premised upon the notion of the freely choosing, and self-determining, individual. If one treats the group as such an individual, then how can the group take precedence over the members of the group who have contracted into it—and therefore must be free to break their 'original' contracts at any time in the face of new collective developments?

---

[1] *Aporia* is an ancient Greek term meaning hesitating doubt between two opposite opinions, where each opinion appears to be equally problematic.

On this view, a Catholic should have been able to sue the Pope for excommunication if he or she had objected to the new doctrine of the Assumption in the 1950s!

As to relations of the group with other groups (and the public at large), then if, as Rowan Williams says, these are 'procedurally secular', then all those outside the group can do is treat the group like a self-determining collective will. But Rowan Williams wants more than that: he wants general public respect for the 'otherness' of religion according to the latter's collective mystical character. And this must mean, in terms of such a 'Levinasian' model,[2] either as 'appearing', or as 'non-appearing'.

If as 'appearing', then those outside the religion might find it to be (in some ways) admirable. However, imagination is not here finally decisive. Let us fervently hope with Rowan Williams for a much more generous exercise of sympathetic imagination toward 'the other', and let us heartily agree with him that this might foster social peace (and ensure that Richard Dawkins sold no more books). But imagining something does not guarantee sympathizing with it. Given the increasing secular rejection of any truths outside those guaranteed by science, little admiration for any values other than those of extending freedom of choice, and 'happiness' defined as a consistent intensity of sensation (rather than 'flourishing'), it is most unlikely that this will be forthcoming. After all, religion relies on taking that which you imagine seriously; secularity can be *defined* by the view that such imagined realities are mere delusory diversions (or else 'paradigms' subject to empirical testing of one sort or another).

If, to take the other fork of the *aporia*, we take the otherness of the religious group as ineffably 'non-appearing', then further conundrums arise. One can universally respect the freedom of the other insofar as this is publicly verifiable. But respect for something that does not appear is a blank cheque: such respect might be considered admirable, or it might equally be deemed deplorable. Moreover, there can be no real parity of the group with the individual here. An individual is born, not humanly constructed, and it is possible that he or she always has potential for goodness, however defined. By contrast, the very nature and purpose of a group might be considered malign.

Hence *either,* in the latter case, one implausibly legitimates any group *qua* group (ignoring its possibly anti-civil purpose), *or,* in the former case, there is a kind of public imperative towards 'imaginative sympathy' with literally 'exotic' outlooks, especially religious ones. But as I have just pointed out, this is illogical in secular terms and cannot, within those terms, ever trump respect for individual freedom.

---

[2] Emmanuel Levinas argues that an acknowledgement of 'the other' in their non-theoretically graspable 'otherness' is the foundation not just of ethics, but of subjectivity as such. See especially E Levinas, *Totality and Infinity: an Essay on Exteriority* (Pittsburgh: Duquesne University Press, 1969).

B. Liberalism's Atomistic Character

Rowan Williams appears not to grasp this point—that liberalism is *incorrigibly* atomistic. Liberal recognition of group identity must always logically give way before the recognition of individual rights. Those nineteenth-century liberals in France (Constant, Tocqueville, Guizot) and in Britain (W H Gladstone, T H Green) who tried bravely, and often brilliantly, to channel liberalism in a more organicist direction, were, in reality, producing a hybrid theory which was no longer pure liberalism. In retrospect, as Pierre Manent remarks, the problem with their ideas was that they tried to make 'tradition' do the work of a previous religious metaphysic.[3]

Relevant here is the career of the great Anglo-American political theorist, Harold Laski. Probably because of his Jewish religious roots, Laski was initially committed to both collectivism and anarcho-libertarianism. Hence, he developed a highly influential critique of absolute state sovereignty, advocating instead a loose federal structure which involved elements of strong local government and independent self-management for co-operative economic and educational bodies (including, of course, religious ones).[4] It comes as a bewildering shock to some contemporary Americans to learn that Laski was a *socialist* thinker, for, indeed, there are some elements in common between his ideas and radically conservative corporatist theory.

It is clear that Williams—rightly and courageously in my view—is seeking to revive interest in such a socialist pluralism (even if its models now need much supplementation). And part of what the reaction to his ideas reveals is just how far we now have an horrific (but logical) collusion, especially in New-Labour (and even, to a considerable degree now, coalition Conservative-Liberal Democratic) Britain, between the unfettered market, on the one hand, and a neo-absolutist state, on the other. Such an alignment is required in order to police the anarchic consequences which extreme capitalism generates. Indeed, in the absence of trust, businesses themselves are forced to over-police their own employees. In this way, outright instrumentalist individualism on the 'Chicago' model actually *undermines* initiative, risk, and enterprise, while disguising the fact that the more one has contract based on equivalence rather than trust based upon tacit interpersonal agreement, the more the market *requires* an authoritarian state as the enforcer of contract.

Laski, thinking in purely secular terms, was ultimately forced to concede that the logic of secular liberalism is strictly individualistic and that libertarianism is incompatible with pluralism. Hence, he later became an advocate of state

---

[3] P Manent, *An Intellectual History of Liberalism* (trans R Balinski) (Princeton: Princeton University Press, 1995) 80–113.

[4] H Laski, *Liberty in the Modern State* (New York: Harper & Bros, 1937).

socialism—but on the grounds that only a strong central state could ensure an equal material and cultural basis for the genuine exercise of freedom of choice by each and every person. He rejected the kind of religious or metaphysical dimension which could have undergirded a non-liberal theory of plural sovereignty. It is clear that in some places Williams does indeed recognize the need for this dimension. Yet some of his speeches seem to fudge this issue, and with dangerous consequences.

C. Respect for Religion *as Religion*

My argument is that only a hegemonically Christian outlook, and not a secular one, can accord to Islam respect *as Islam*. A Christian polity cannot go so far as adopting Islam's own standards (about what is acceptable representation in public of its own beliefs and practices, for example). But a renewed Christendom is, I believe, far better for Islam than a secular polity (which is likely in the long term to deny most of its crucial group rights).

The positive views which I hold of Islam, I hold precisely as a Christian and one who realizes that I have much in common with what Muslims believe. This, however, does not lead me to suppose that there can be any secular basis for the acknowledgment of Muslim sacrality, nor to suppose that a Christian polity (which England technically remains) should pass laws respecting specifically Muslim sensibilities about the sacred (such as a ban on depictions of the Prophet). It to the contrary is clear that a Christian polity can only demand general respect for the 'sacrality' of other religious communities insofar as they approximate Christianity's own sense of sacrality (or are not incompatible with it).

The crucial point here is that even a vestigially Christian polity can go further in acknowledging the integral worth of a religious group as a group than a secular polity can. Christians can validly see analogies to churches in mosques and Hindu temples, similarities that lead them to accord a considerable measure of respect to these institutions. It is apparent from the reactions of many British Muslims to the Archbishop's speech, as well as from wider reports of their attitudes, that they not only welcome the detached fairness of British civil law, but also the political establishment of Christianity in the United Kingdom. Both institutions protect them from secularist extremism and preserve for them a social space for religious practice. Many of them recognize, along with British Hindus and others, that the idea of an alliance of all religions against secularization is advanced where there is one religion that is culturally and politically hegemonic. Since they are not dominated by a modern liberal mindset, they realize that a genuinely 'religious culture' has to be religious in a *specific* way. There is, for them, no such thing in practice as a 'general religiosity', and a neutral religious pluralism of the multiculturalist variety can only be an expression of secularity.

D. Challenges to Religious Liberty

The European Union, as Williams notes, still declares that religious liberty (which surely has to include some sort of recognition of religion's collective dimension) has priority over all other rights. But this priority is rooted in an ultimately Christian and not secular background, even if the EU is now loath to admit its Christian legacy (for which it is rightly criticized by the Archbishop and the Pope). There is actually nothing in a secular liberal outlook which prevents it from outlawing religious bodies that do not accord equal rights to women or to homosexuals, nor that prevents it from denying the legitimacy of the authority of a bishop over a parish congregation that wishes to control its own affairs in ways incompatible with both Church tradition and episcopal authority.

Indeed, many legal thinkers are already going in this direction, and suburban Anglican evangelicals wishing to move in a congregationalist direction exploit such an emerging climate of opinion—even though ironically it may be to their distaste in certain ways. Some secular thinkers actually now wish to abolish the right to religious freedom. For them, it privileges the religious point of view, gives rights to the 'irrational' in the public sphere, and authorizes the exercise of despotic power by non-political, non-elected bodies over vulnerable individuals.

This attack is exactly the prospect to which Williams prophetically seeks to alert us. One can only salute him—and yet I think he needs to move to much more solid intellectual ground if he is to provide a compelling case. This ground would expose the fact that post-Lockean liberalism's respect for religious freedom is actually ambivalent. By contrast, a defence of religious liberty can only be genuinely secured from a religious perspective—one which affirms that a 'faith'[5] beyond reason is needed in order to establish the socio-political order, that faith must be a matter of free consent, and that faith communities can legitimately make demands upon their members. It is arguable that only Christianity and Judaism provide this kind of religious perspective, which renders trust, rather than obedience or fearful piety, the crucial virtue.

E. Two Concepts of Pluralism

To return to the Shari'a lecture, I believe that it is critical to unravel Williams' (partial) confounding of one kind of historic, organicist, corporatist 'pluralism' from another distinct 'pluralism' of the postmodern, multicultural kind.

The origins of pluralism lie in Western 'corporatism'. Ignoring this skews nearly all modern understandings of political history, both practical and theoretical. To a

---

[5] Here I mean something like a necessary but unprovable 'trust', including a trust in the infinite reality of reason, that is required for any practical or theoretical human project to get going.

much greater extent than the Byzantine East, Western Europe developed a multitude of free associations and complex varying jurisdictions. This is traceable to the relative political power of the Church in this initially barbarian, 'politically virgin' terrain; to the conflict between pope and emperor; to the rise of relatively independent cities and towns; to the growth of all sorts of lesser corporations (monastic bodies, universities, and mendicant orders); and, finally, to the emergence of lay religious fraternities and manufacturing and trade guilds. If the Papacy retained remarkable power in the West, this was because it construed Europe as 'a corporation of corporations'. It worked with the 'subsidiary' and often (crucially) mutually balancing powers of smaller organic bodies, entities who still saw themselves as parts of the entire 'Body of Christ' (dually governed by pope and emperor).[6]

For all this to work, there had to be an increasingly sophisticated development of 'constitutionalism' throughout Europe. The famous expressions of this constitutionalism within the Anglo-French empire —Magna Carta and the growth of *parlements*/parliaments—must be considered as the outcome of a Catholic ethos. (There were similar grants of constitutional charters in Medieval Scotland and Sweden.) This High Medieval constitutionalism was the very adverse of notions of voluntarist 'Divine Right' which started to emerge at the end of the Middle Ages (in the wake of the break-up of this corporate order). The idea of 'right' residing in the Divine Will helped to encourage our modern idea of both the absolute rights of the central sovereign power and the absolute 'human' rights of the individual.[7] But in the High Medieval era, *ius* (right) meant an objective 'rightness' and *iura* (rights) were accorded diversely to corporate bodies and to individuals according to their function within the social whole.[8]

The modern Western concept of liberty and the rule of law rests far more upon this long-term instinct for 'constitution' and the 'right place and function' of diverse, relatively free corporate bodies, than it does upon the musings of a few philosophers thought to compose 'the Enlightenment'. (Is this not why, for example, Hungary and Poland, with little modern experience of either enlightenment or democracy, can still relatively quickly develop it, whereas Russia finds it extremely difficult?)

Yet Williams is right to eschew meaningless polemics against the Enlightenment. The Enlightenment represented a complex reaction against a decadent corporatism (one which served mere inherited and established power and which had corrupted the corporate role into biased privilege), and included the attempt to *restore* 'civil society', in the case of the Scottish Enlightenment, and, still more decisively, the Neapolitan one. Meanwhile its appeal to negative liberty and 'possessive' rights as a barrier against the worst abuses of feudalo-absolutism remains a valid defence mechanism. So castigating the Enlightenment is something of a

---

[6]   See J Milbank, 'On Complex Space' in *The Word Made Strange* (Oxford: Blackwell, 1997) 268–292; see also F W Maitland (1963).

[7]   See J B Elshtain, *Sovereignty: God, State and Self* (New York: Basic Books, 2008).

[8]   See J N Figgis, *The Divine Right of Kings* (Cambridge: Cambridge University Press, 1896).

red herring. Likewise, the current obsession with Darwin leads us to ignore the way in which the 'neo-religious' character of the nineteenth century gives the lie to any notions of inevitable secularization. As one aspect of this character, many nineteenth-century political thinkers, beginning with Hegel, explored the idea of some mode of 'renewed corporatism'—and this could take relatively liberal as well as relatively 'right' or 'left' forms (as in the case of 'guild socialism'). And in a real, not Giddensesque or Blairite sense, we are talking here of a 'third way', since *both* modern conservatism *and* modern liberalism/state socialism assume, along with a metaphysical voluntarism, also a metaphysical nominalism—in a direct philosophical lineage which has now been traced in detail by historians.[9] Hence, any account of modernity in terms of the emergence of individual freedom is one-sided. Just as significant is the 'conservative' idea of a single central sovereign power which achieves order, not through tacit and multiple 'organic' means, but by impositions of will and systematic discipline and regulation (of the kind which Foucault so famously illuminated). This is why dictatorship is just as endemic to modernity as democracy, and why it is meaningless to describe the Middle Ages as 'conservative'. The very idea of 'conservative' is *invented* by modernity.

Nineteenth-century 'neo-corporatism', in its diverse forms, tried to think entirely outside the 'right/left' box. However, Williams is right to see that the theory of 'pluralism' which emerged from all this was not only pluralist in the 'medieval' sense of returning, against Bodin, to an idea of graded degrees of sovereignty. It was also 'pluralist' in a newly modern sense of trying to accommodate rival and relatively private corporate bodies—and the supreme example here was probably religious denominations. Already, the Anglican monk, John Neville Figgis (one of Williams' heroes) was writing, in the early twentieth century in defence of the right of church bodies to control their membership.[10]

Regarding the 'medieval' model, there is not exactly (or at least not ideally) a positing of rival jurisdictions. Mostly we are talking about 'nests of Russian dolls', where one relatively independent jurisdiction is embedded in a higher one. In the case of parallel jurisdictions—courts for clergy and for laity, town police, and university proctors—then, in principle, they do not compete. These institutions concern different people or the same people in different roles. Of course, conflicts of jurisdiction will occasionally arise and have to be decided by a higher court. Sometimes, indeed, there could be something like a 'choice' between a civil or a canonical verdict. But this is not really tantamount to a *clash* of rival laws: the relative place, principles, and functions of civil and ecclesiastical courts are still organically *coordinated* within the overriding norms, the so-called *ius commune* of Christendom.

But even when it comes to the more modern aspect of 'pluralist' sovereignty theory, no drastic rivalry need necessarily be envisaged. Business organizations,

[9] A de Muralt, *L'unité de la philosophie Politique* (Paris: Librairie Philosophique Vrin, 2002) 181–268.
[10] J N Figgis, *Churches in the Modern State* (London: Longmans, Green, 1913).

for example, are treated as 'corporate personalities' (with powers of rule-making, self-governance, and regulation of membership) precisely because the purposes they serve can, and are, regarded by society as contributing to the common good. Likewise, the collective rights of, for example, the Baptist Union can be upheld by Anglicans and agnostics because the latter recognize at least a relative good in what the Baptist Union is trying to achieve.

F. Metaphysical 'Realism' and 'Nominalism'

By comparison with the later Laski, Williams' heroes, Lord Acton and John Neville Figgis, remained conceptually confused.[11] The nub of this confusion is metaphysical. Recall my earlier point that liberalism is simply incapable of entertaining any strong notion of group personality. How so?

Metaphysical 'realism' at the group level (the group as more than the sum of its parts), will always be outflanked by a metaphysical 'nominalism' (at the individual level).[12] The very idea of a priority of groups over a political whole *already* suggests a contradictory 'nominalism'—the groups themselves, at the meta (political) level, are so many non-related atoms. This is also mythical, because groups no more 'precede' the political whole—within which alone their functions and peaceful operations are possible—than do Locke's supposedly isolated individuals engaged in the 'original' social contract.

Acton and his followers were confused about this because they were trying to combine a British aristocratic Whig with a Catholic and Germanic pluralist-organicist legacy. But the latter (especially in Otto von Gierke's work[13]) remained more coherently Aristotelian and Thomistic: even though sovereignty should be dispersed (as in pre-modernity), 'social' groups are still inevitably positioned by a certain 'political' unity, however inchoate.[14]

This thesis is *not* the same (and this may be the key to the theoretical confusion) as the post-Bodin notion of the monopolization of sovereignty and authorized violence at the political centre. In the pre-modern era, social sub-groups (feudal manors, universities, guilds, monasteries) were *also* conveyers of dispersed sovereign political power—there existed manorial courts, for example. But the Actonian model tries to make merely social groups prior to political unity. This is

---

[11]   See especially Lord Acton, *Essays on Freedom and Power* (Boston, MA: Beacon Press, 1956).

[12]   'Realism' is a term for the medieval doctrine that there exist real 'universals', whether in material things or in the mind: there exists 'treeness' and not just individual trees. 'Nominalism' is a term for the rival medieval doctrine that there only exist individual things (like trees) and that 'universals' (like 'treeness') are mental fictions.

[13]   O Gierke, *Political Theories of the Middle Age* (Cambridge: Cambridge University Press, 1987).

[14]   See Milbank (n 6 above).

to buy into a modern liberal political model.[15] Indeed, it is covertly to buy into a Bodin/Hobbes-inspired notion of absolute sovereignty, namely that a monopoly central power will always be needed to adjudicate between the warring desires of individuals.[16]

By comparison, however, a truly Catholic, Thomist and Gierkean organicist pluralism provides a more logical bulwark to individualist liberalism. It proffers no postulate of either individuals or groups existing 'before' the political, while equally (in a tradition that is at once Aristotelian and Augustinian) it does not posit (like Hobbes and Locke) a political sphere that takes precedence over particular societies and society in general. Notably, this organicism does not rule out elements of a more heterogeneous pluralism and the toleration of different groups. This is because political society as a whole need not entirely agree with the premises of the Baptist Church, nor the Muslim *umma*, to be able nonetheless to accept that they are performing roles that contribute to the cohesion of the entire political body. Quite often, Rowan Williams seems to be indicating something like this, but he needs to make it clearer. Too often he sounds the tone of Actonian ambivalence—and this can generate language that has a 'multiculturalist' resonance.

The Actonian version of group personality falls into metaphysical incoherence (between nominalism and realism) by treating a group as a fully fledged unit 'prior' to the political whole, and therefore to the human whole. Yet even if one happens to see the human whole as represented more by a religion than by a state, this is only because a religious group like Islam or the Church *is* a kind of super-polity. A notion of group personality accordingly requires a teleological ethic: one has to be able to say that a group is aiming for a goal, that its collective character fosters desired social ends. To repeat: even if this group is the Baptist Church, and you are a Catholic (or an agnostic) and you do not agree with Baptist ideals, you can nevertheless acknowledge that, relatively speaking, they are pursuing social goals that are compatible with, and promote a shared sense of, human dignity.

An analogy here is the right of conscientious objection for pacifists. They are allowed to opt out of fighting because we implicitly say to ourselves that this hyperbolic respect for human life actually affirms—with an excess that is also usefully confirmatory—a basic principle of our social order to which we all adhere. So, in a way, a pacifist is never a rebel; instead, he is all-too-loyal a citizen, all too devoted (albeit woodenly) to the undergirding principles of law. Thus, we grant pacifists their rights of conscience.

---

[15]   See Lord Acton, 'The History of Freedom in Antiquity' in Acton (n 11 above) 53, 81 where he asserts that Adam Smith's 'doctrine of freedom and self-reliance, which is the foundation of political economy' is already to be found in the New Testament.

[16]   See A Pabst, 'Modern Sovereignty in Question: Theology, Democracy and Capitalism' (2010) 26 *Modern Theology* (forthcoming). Pabst shows that one source of modern political suspension between the absolute sovereign centre and the isolated individual is Francisco Suarez's privileging of the rights of the political community over the authority of the *ecclesia* in its 'external', juridical aspect.

It is possible then to cope with a certain degree of 'dissenting pluralism' within an 'organically pluralist' framework. This can even extend to conclusions whose very principles one disapproves of, unlike, to some degree, the instance of pacifism, or the instance of abortion—where either side can see that the other is trying to sustain respect for the human person, even if there is disagreement as to what constitutes human personhood. In the case, for example, of the exclusion of homosexuals from certain roles by certain religious bodies, it might seem that the area of agreement in principle is very thin or almost non-existent. For the argument is about what is natural, what constitutes the sexual act, and what is relevant to social virtue. Yet even here there can be a kind of displaced agreement concerning principle, because the state advocating complete neutrality as regards sexual orientation in the case, for example, of adoption, could still comprehend that the Catholic Church, in refusing this neutrality, was trying to answer the question as to which people can be regarded as suitable candidates to adopt children. The asking of this question is something which society as a whole endorses. However, the Church's perceived ethical preciosity on this subject cannot, by modern society at large, be regarded as a hyperbolic preciosity, as in the case of pacifism or even abortion. Instead, it will be seen as simply a false limiting of characteristics of what is validly human and fully capable of the human task of child-rearing. Yet this perceived outright 'error' can still be tolerated so long as other adoption agencies are prepared to consider gay parents. Catholic adoption practice would then be accepted in terms of its positive performance of the task of finding heterosexual parents, even though its judgments concerning gays are negatively and absolutely refused.

A communitarian and organicist perspective would thereby be able to tolerate in some instances even 'mistaken', besides 'hyperbolic', dissent, so long as the remit of this dissent was confined to a certain group and did not impose itself coercively upon other groups or upon society at large. Yet a rigorously liberal perspective is not capable of either toleration, because it does not think in terms of the different contributions of persons and groups to the organic whole. Instead, it thinks in terms of the direct relation of each and every individual to the whole as uniquely represented by the centre, and demands that every group treat each individual in abstraction as formally alike to all other individuals, because each individual is only to be regarded by the group with the gaze of the undifferentiated whole, which is the gaze of the absolutely sovereign state.

G. Liberalism's Priority of the Individual

Moreover, a consistent liberalism—one that no longer has any 'thick' notion of what constitutes human dignity (in excess of mere respect for negative freedom and the pursuit of material happiness)—eventually self-deconstructs. In not being able—for the reasons already seen—to tolerate group rights in the name of individual rights, it ironically lands up restricting individual freedom. Thus, increasingly, the secular press in Britain questions the right of people to opt out of legal obligations on the grounds of religious conscience. The 'public' space is effectively defined in Kantian terms that sees it as the unmediated, short-circuited relationship between the individual conscience, on the one hand, and the absolute sovereign state, on the other. To reiterate: a purely liberal argument in favour of group rights will always be trumped since, according to liberal premises, the individual always retains the right to appeal to the state over the collective 'head' of the group.

Some legal theorists now argue that, based on sexual equality laws, churches should be outlawed if they do not accept women priests. This is a serious possibility, particularly in countries where the Catholic and Orthodox Churches are relatively powerless. (While I am actually in favour of the ordination of women, I am not in favour of this being imposed by the state.) The right to religious freedom itself is now coming under suspicion. I believe that unless this right is understood in group-right terms, it will be vulnerable against assertions of the rights to freedom of expression or freedom to uncoerced assemblage. Any legal recognition of specifically 'religious' opinion and practice is starting to be seen (by 'hard-line' secularists) as allowing to religion—and therefore to 'unreason'—an unwarranted and unique public dignity and an unfairly privileged public role. For such critics, religious liberty simply licenses religious bodies to autocratically govern their members to a degree that renders these groups anomalous 'states within states'. The (individualist) liberal logic here is impeccable, if significantly ironic—since the right to religious freedom is arguably the most important theoretical and practical root of modern liberal societies.[17]

Liberal principles, when pressed to a logical extreme, will always ensure that the rights of the individual override those of the group. For this reason, undiluted liberalism cannot defend corporate religious freedom. It follows that churches will not be able to fight the threat to the integrity of religious bodies in liberal, secular terms alone; instead, they will have to adopt an outflanking manoeuvre that questions the very normativity of secular liberalism itself.[18] Liberal pluralism alone will not serve them; some kind of organicist pluralism must be deployed.

H. British Accommodation of Religious Law

How does all this relate to the English controversy over Shari'a law?

First, existing British provision for the operation of Orthodox Jewish and Shari'a law clearly falls within the remit of what remains of an organicist, pluralist model. The United Kingdom permits internal religious regulation of matters pertaining to

---

[17] See R Ahdar and I Leigh, *Religious Freedom in the Liberal State* (Oxford: Oxford University Press, 2005) 1–8.
[18] For one such sustained attempt, see Ahdar and Leigh (ibid) Ch 11.

marriage and finance insofar as these do not actually conflict with the principles of British jurisdiction. Thus, in the case of Shari'a, mortgages and banking may be operated in a way that technically avoids the notion of interest. There are, nonetheless, limits. Britain has, for example, recently moved to correct the situation under which a woman could be considered as 'not divorced' under Jewish law, and yet as 'divorced' under British law itself.

As to the potential clash between Jewish or Shari'a law and secular law, it is clear in the West that these monotheistic codes have to approximate norms which, although Christian in origin, have evolved into secular ones. Another of the perhaps strange *lacunae* in Williams' recent statements (though his academic writings are fully cognizant of this point) is his failure to note that Christianity *of itself and uniquely* secularized the law of the land. This does not imply that it also secularized organized communities and ethics.[19] Rather, it means that it regarded any use of coercive power, however necessary, as somewhat ambivalent and to be kept as far as possible from the realm of the sacred. This attitude was shared to some degree by Rabbinic Judaism, which rendered the *Torah* even more a matter of study and customary influence—'a dead letter', so to speak—than it had been in Biblical times.

Islam alone anachronistically sought to establish a rival universality to that of Christianity by way of the promulgation of an enforceable legal code. This is precisely why we cannot treat Islam in terms of full liberal pluralist equality without abandoning the principles of *both* Christianity *and* the Enlightenment. We can only accommodate Islam on our own terms—terms that require the secularization of *any* coercive religious law. If this shocks the devotees of 'the other', then they need to reflect that there is *never* any truly 'neutral', procedural ground (of a Habermasian variety[20]). Something always rules, and this something is always substantive.

I have argued that current accommodation of religious law still falls within an 'organically plural' paradigm. However, for reasons already traversed, accommodation of religion is not guaranteed, and self-regulation by religious bodies will come under greater secular scrutiny. Instances where a church's norms and regulations clash with the secular law are evident in Britain: take disputes over abortion, adoption, the rights of lesbian couples to IVF treatment, and donor-fertilization in general. Fortunately, the religious pacifists' right of conscientious objection is, as we have seen, still linked to a vestigial organic pluralism that is, at base, sustained by a generally shared, if vague, Christianity.

---

[19] As Rémi Brague seems to imply in his nonetheless illuminating book on this topic, *The Law of God: The Philosophical History of an Idea* (trans LG Cochrane) (Chicago: University of Chicago Press, 2007).

[20] See J Habermas, *Between Naturalism and Religion: Philosophical Essays* (trans C Cronin) (Cambridge: Polity Press, 2009) 24–97.

Yet because this vague Christianity is a fading sensibility, these rights of conscience are now coming under threat.[21] Already, all Catholic adoption agencies in Britain have been forced to close down because they cannot accept gay couples as prospective parents. Lesbian mothers are no longer bound to tell their children who their father is, and there is mounting pressure to force all doctors to agree to perform abortions if asked to do so.[22] Williams is wholly right to alert us to all this.

I. Back to 'Neutrality'

The Archbishop, however, endorses, like Jürgen Habermas, a public legal space marked by a 'procedural secularity' that is supposedly neutral as between non-belief and religion.[23] He appears to ignore the problem that such neutrality is itself entirely secular, and therefore unable to accord the religious perspective equal protection. If religious bodies flourish more in the United States than they do in Europe (though they are also more tacitly restricted from political interventions than in the United Kingdom), then this is partly because the United States has a collectively unembarrassed Christian political commitment—albeit of a watery, semi-deistic kind.

Group rights, whether asserted by ethical businesses or churches, can only be effectively defended pursuant to a specific and distinctly *religious* framework.[24] Williams sometimes seems to forget this. When he points to the need for courts to understand the collective 'narrative assumptions' which guide individuals' actions—if courts want to comprehend accurately their citizens' real intentions—he seems also to imply that this can take place in a liberal, pluralist framework. But the truth is that entirely 'alien' narrative settings or worldviews cannot possibly be taken into account by such a secular outlook—action incompatible with the dominant social 'narrative' will always be condemned by any secular court.

It is rather *Christianity,* and to a degree Judaism, which developed a framework—corporatist constitutionalism—that is able to comprehend 'the other'. It is certainly *not* Islam, in its historically dominant varieties. I trust that my potted history above indicates just why Catholic Christianity (in all its branches) has the theoretical resources to be able to accord religious freedom under a regime of constitutional pluralism.

---

[21] See, eg R Ahdar, 'The Vulnerability of Religious Liberty in Liberal States' (2009) 4 *Religion and Human Rights* 177.

[22] This just a few short decades after secular opinion allowed abortion only in a few extreme instances and on grounds of compassion.

[23] Habermas (n 20 above).

[24] Secularity is 'nominalist' and only a religious outlook may embrace a 'realism' about universals which metaphysically undergirds corporate personality.

J. Liberal, Multiculturalist Pluralism

If existing British accommodation of religious law and conscience is still partly based upon an 'organicist' pluralism, which is able to recognize that conscientious violation of the law may still serve the common good, then the same is not true of certain aspects of Williams' original Shari'a proposals. They appear instead to be linked to a liberal multiculturalism of a possibly Blairite variety.[25]

The Archbishop spoke (with some admitted embarrassment) of a 'market' in legal systems, implying that Muslims might choose between British law and Shari'a law. However, there can be no question of any idea of 'choice' with respect to the existing subsidiary operation of Jewish law in marriage and divorce. For while it offers procedures additional to British law and enables ratifications to be made in accordance with such law (as Church of England vicars do when they marry people), it does not offer any 'alternative' law. Williams initially entertained difference in this strong sense (or at least sounded as if he did) precisely because he insisted that all Muslims would retain the right to appeal from a Shari'a tribunal's ruling to the state, not as if from a merely local court to a higher, but as from one jurisdiction to another, even though one is taken to be ultimately prevailing. Thus, if *no* appeal was pursued, then incompatibilities between the operative principles of Shari'a and secular law could by implication still stand. This could mean, for example, that Muslim women might be married and divorced under less-advantageous circumstances. As many commentators pointed out, few Islamic women would dare to risk the social ostracism that would be consequent upon any appeal against the edicts of their local Shari'a tribunal. There also remains the murky issue of how the Muslim community might 'police' this law, given that Shari'a judgments are enforceable in a strong sense (employing coercive sanctions), not just utilizing exclusion from the faith community (as Jewish and Canon law do).

All this explains why Rowan Williams' remarks caused a furore. No doubt (as with those who proposed similar initiatives in Canada) he was seeking to avert the danger of 'back-street' Shari'a of the kind that promotes forced marriages, polygamy, and financial practices that (ironically) have covert advantages for Muslims in a capitalist market. Exposing such tribunals to public glare is a good idea, and we should salute Williams for boldly taking this initiative. But this would *not* be a good idea if we somehow thereby legitimized hitherto illegitimate backstreet legal practice on the specious grounds that its deviance can now be better controlled if done out in the open. In any case, the ensuing row made it clear that undiluted Shari'a justice is not an immediate possibility, nor one wanted by most Muslims in Britain.

---

[25]   As Phillip Blond and Adrian Pabst have argued: 'Integrating Islam into the West', *International Herald Tribune,* 4 February 2008, available at <http://www.nytimes.com/2008/02/14/opinion/14ihtedpabst.1.10050495.html>.

Nevertheless, to the extent that Shari'a *is* practised in the United Kingdom, it is very difficult to regulate its operation, and would become more difficult were it to be granted greater official recognition. Williams glosses over the fact that Shari'a, even for more moderate Shi'ite schools, is founded upon deliverances of the Qur'an and *hadith* that have to be taken literally as the commands of God, edicts that have universal human application (even if they are subject to secondary interpretation).[26] Interpretation or *ijtihad* (traditionally, reasoning by analogy from obscure cases to other definite rulings) has a more limited scope than Western hermeneutic notions of equity, and only very recently have Western techniques of interpretation begun to influence Shari'a practice. Moreover, this applies far more to Shi'ite than to Sunni jurisprudence. For many modern Sunnis—who have made all the running in shaping a modern, puritanical, totally anti-sacramental, urban 'Protestant' Islam (which appals mystical Shi'ites from the Near East)—it is taken that the 'gates of *ijtihad*' closed in the tenth century, and are never going to reopen. No mode of interpretation can, in principle, rule out the reinstatement of the full weight of Shari'a in the criminal, as well as the civil, field. Unfortunately, the extremists have it all too right here.[27]

This has to be taken account of in a globalized world where British Muslims are still strongly connected to villages in Pakistan and elsewhere. Patently, if the chopping-off of hands and the stoning of women do not feature on the British Islamic agenda, it is equally true that 'honour killings' among Muslims for sexual offences are an all-too-frequent occurrence in the United Kingdom. Furthermore, there is unclarity about the attitude to apostasy and to intermarriage: many Muslims who

---

[26] This is not how either Jews or Christians regard the laws of the Hebrew Bible/Old Testament.

[27] See M Ruthven, *Islam: A Very Short Introduction* (New York: Oxford University Press, 2000) 73–91; Sayyed Mohammed Khatami, *La Religion et la Pensée Prises au Piège de L'Autocratie* (Louvain-Paris: Peeters, 2005); Aziz al Azmeh, *Muslim Kingship: Power and the Sacred in Muslim, Christian and Pagan Polities* (London and New York: IB Tauri, 2001); B W Lewis, *The Political Language of Islam* (Chicago: University of Chicago Press, 1991). There is considerable controversy about the closing of the gates of *ijtihad*. That the gate is closed has been the majority Sunni view since the sixteenth century. However, the older scholarly view that this was the situation from the time of the tenth century or so has been recently subject to convincing challenge by Wael B Hallaq in his important article, 'Was the Gate of Ijtihad Closed?' (1984) 16 *International Journal for Middle East Studies* 3. Hallaq shows that it was not, after all, the case that Al-Ghazali and all the Asharites rejected legal interpretation by the *mujtahid* in favour of the mere citation of an absolute authority or *taklid*, as practised by a *mukallid*. The very important implication here is that one should not see Islamic hermeneutics as the exclusive preserve of the rationalistic, Mutalizite tendency. Indeed, this would make no sense of its prevalence amongst the more mystically inclined Shi'ite variant of Islam. Nevertheless, from the Kharijites onwards, a tendency to question the openness of the gate started to take hold, as with Ibn Taymiyah (1263–1328). And crucially, over time, the number of *mujtahidden* began severely to decline. The implication of this decline was more and more widely taken to be closure of the gate. This is, of course, strongly insisted upon by the *wahhabi,* and in general one can say that the more Sunnism has become hostile to mysticism then the more also it has refused a hermeneutic dimension. One can welcome a shift in axiology back towards *ijtihad* by many Sunni scholars, while wondering whether they are inclined to downplay the significance of this historical drift (intimately bound up with the later sclerosis of Islamic theology) and its sedimented impact upon modern Sunni practice the world over.

would not see themselves as 'extremists' would still take what Christians would regard as an 'extreme' attitude here.[28]

Unsurprisingly, Oriental and African Christians are alarmed by Williams' apparent public tendency to endorse (either by words or silence—for one suspects that his private opinion is very different) the scholarly inaccurate 'Religious Studies' view of Islamic history put forward by figures like Tariq Ramadan. This version tries to gloss over the historical problems of Islamic origins, Muhammed's treatment of women, the expansion of Islam by unprovoked conquest, the Qur'anic legitimation of the slaughter of polytheists, and religious war (including the massacre of civilians) against non-Islamic monotheists.[29] Similarly passed over in silence are the Islamic genocide of Hindus on a gigantic scale, and the tendency of resentful Islamic populations to turn murderously upon their Christian neighbours once the latter are given equal status—as happened in Greece and Turkey in the nineteenth and twentieth centuries.[30] Today, Ramadan has praised Sudanese leaders whose record of oppression is atrocious, while Williams cites Malaysia as relatively liberal despite the fact that it does not tolerate many aspects of Christian practice and is increasingly falling into the hands of radical Islamists.

K. The Political Sphere

Islamic and Christian attitudes to the political sphere merit attention. Williams argues that Islam has today 'something like' the Christian distinction between sacred and secular spheres, because it does not see the realm of the *umma* (the Islamic community governed by Shari'a) as totally coinciding with civil authority. But if, indeed, some modern Islamic states make this distinction, this is largely the result of Western influence. (I suspect that Williams knows this perfectly well, but understandably finds it impolitic to say so.) Historically, the scope of Shari'a was actually quite narrow, but this gap was filled almost universally (within Sunni Islam) by the tyrannical despotism of caliphs who saw themselves as vice-regents of the will of Allah.[31]

---

[28]   A 2006 poll for the London *Times* found that more than one in 10 British Muslims think that the perpetrators of 7/7 should be regarded as 'martyrs'. A report by *Policy Exchange* in 2007 found that 37 per cent of all Muslims aged 16–24 would prefer to live under a Shari'a system. In 2008, a *YouGov* poll showed that almost one-third of Muslim students at UK universities think that killing in the name of Islam is justifiable. The same poll found that 40 per cent of British Muslim students support Shari'a for all Muslims in the United Kingdom and 33 per cent advocate a global caliphate. Some 40 per cent believe that it is unacceptable for Muslim men and women to mix freely.
[29]   D Avon, *La Fragilité des clercs* (Clichy: Corlevour Publishing, 2007) Ch 2; D Avon, 'Une réponse a l' "islam réformiste" de Tariq Ramadan' (2003) 4 *Nunc* 39.
[30]   See E Karsh, *Islamic Imperialism: A History* (New Haven: Yale University Press, 2007); Marshal G S Hodgson, *The Venture of Islam,* Vols 1–3 (Chicago: University of Chicago Press, 1977).
[31]   See the works of Khatami, Azmeh, and Lewis cited in n 27 above.

Against this historical background, there is evidence that in Britain today Muslims both respect and welcome an ultimately Christian political legacy which frees them from despotism and allows them to practise their religion in peace.[32] Effectively, this is resulting in a 'Christianization' of Islam, in terms of Islam's incipient re-evaluation of the appropriate relationship of the secular to the sacred.

The relative absence of Shari'a nonetheless leaves Muslims in a sort of spiritual void. I concur with Williams in sympathizing with this predicament. However, encouraging formalization of an independent Shari'a within the British polity—which would inevitably lead to an extension of the thematic scope of its remit—is not the answer. This can only give the green light to a politicized Islamism, which is but one mode of urban Islam in our time (a mode which has flourished, in part, because of the vacuum left by the twentieth-century decline of Sufi fraternities to which many Sunni Muslims once belonged).[33] Probably it is only a return of mystical and esoteric sensibilities within Islam[34] which will allow the Mosque-centred community to take on a collectivist 'church'-like character, one that would fit well with the tacit adoption of a more critical (Christian) perspective towards the secular state. The British government itself has at times shown signs of recognizing this point.

L. An Irony: Islam's Individualistic, Non-organicist Aspect

There is a striking note of irony here. This is that revised Islamic attitudes could prove *all too modern*, and not at all in sympathy with Williams' concept of pluralism. Islamic political attitudes might prove 'all too modern' because Islamic philosophical and exemplary influence itself helped to shape late-medieval Christian thought, which in the case of William of Ockham and others provided us with the basic structure of all modern liberalism. Let me quote here the words of Malise Ruthven, a renowned scholar of Islam:

The Shari'a, both in theory and in practice, was uncompromisingly individualistic. The absence of the concept of church—the mystical 'body of Christ' that stood between the individual Christian and God through whom alone salvation was possible—militated against the creation of institutions such as the medieval Western city or trading company

---

[32] One can note here as symptomatic the fact that Muslim leaders, along with representatives of other religious minorities, were opposed to moves by various city councils across Britain to rename Christian festivities as 'Winterval'. See <http://www.telegraph.co.uk/news/uknews/1534003/Leave-Christmas-alone-say-Muslims.html>. This suggests that Muslims prefer a Christian to a secular British cultural carapace.

[33] Shi'ite mysticism is technically different from Sufism. See H Corbin, *Histoire de la Philosophie Islamique* (Paris: Gillimard, 1986) 60–154; 263–284.

[34] Islamic mystical philosophy contains enormous riches from which British Christians could profitably learn new insights and incorporate into their own orthodox beliefs, especially because it may well contain traces of the mystically apocalyptic and 'gnostic' orthodoxy of primitive oriental Christianity otherwise now lost to view: see Corbin (ibid) 49–154.

where the group interest transcended that of the individual. The Shari'a recognised no corporate entities which could be treated as persons in law. The purpose of the law, apart from enforcing God's commands, was to regulate the affairs of men. One consequence of the absence of the concept of the jural personality of groups may be seen in the proliferating alleyways of many pre-modern Eastern cities, where private territory—cafés, workshops, stalls and so forth—constantly encroaches on public space. The public domain, it is presumed, is simply the sum of its private components, not a separate entity requiring legal protection. The positive result is primarily a law that is aimed at social self-regulation.[35]

This is surely very striking. We might have imagined that 'plural organicism' belonged also to the Islamic Middle Ages. Yet their public, socio-political space was at once still antique and almost proto-modern, with almost *no* intermediary associations between the private sphere governed by Shari'a, on the one hand, and the autocratic decrees of rulers or prophets, on the other. Exactly the same 'individualism' informs the Islamic oscillation between loyalty to a law ascribed to an ultimate source (derived from one man mediating one God) and the anarchic and almost antinomian word of a desert *mullah*.[36]

Of course one can point to countervailing corporatist currents in the tradition, and supremely to the role of mystical brotherhoods. However, the gradual historical decline of the role in legal practice both of the consensus of the community (*ijmā*) and of analogy (*qiyas*), reinforced a fatal link between the dominance of a sovereign centre, on the one hand, and of the individual instance, on the other.

Hence, Muslims, based on this religious legacy, may not be natural allies in the struggle for subsidiarity and group rights. If thinkers like Said Qutb sound organicist, then that is most probably because they learned this romanticism (in an extreme right-wing form) from theorists such as Charles Maurras. Moreover, there are some commentators who—not without reason—suggest that Ramadan's 'Western Islamic' strategy disguises his hope that a Europe governed by 'natural law' will in fact increasingly conform to the understanding of natural law found in the Qur'an. This kind of natural law would contain nothing that conflicted with Qur'anic revealed law, and would also embrace many Islamic principles supposedly discoverable by reason.[37] Thus, if Islam were to assume a multiculturalist religious 'equality' with other monotheisms in Europe, this would in effect result in its superiority, because Islam's apparently purer monotheism looks closer to the lowest common denominator of basic cultural norms and belief. This is probably why some (mainly 'liberal') Muslims from all over the globe (in their document, *A Common Word*[38]) call upon Christians to recognize that the 'essence' of their monotheism is the love of God and neighbour—understood as grounded in absolute

[35] Ruthven (n 27 above) 88.
[36] Corbin (n 33 above) 122–154; C Jambet, *La Grande Résurrection d'Alamut: Les Formes de la Liberté dans le Shī'isme Ismaélien* (1990).
[37] See C Fourest, *Frère Tariq: Discours, Stratégie et Méthode de Tariq Ramadan* (Paris: Grasset & Fasquelle, 2009).
[38] See <http://www.acommonword.com/>.

submission to a clearly Qur'anic notion of divine unity, one incompatible with Christian Trinitarianism.

Meanwhile, both the desacramentalized character of Islam in general (and most of all Sunnism, and then still more Wahhabism in particular) and its one-sided indulgence of male sexuality, fits all too well into the modern world.[39] One can wonder just why Anglo-Saxon neo-conservatism has colluded with the Saudi-Arabian fomentation of the dangerous, and sometimes terroristic, Wahhabist sect. Were G K Chesterton and John Buchan right—is there something about Islamic 'simplicity' that appeals to modern wielders of 'rational' power?[40] The murky alliance of enemies that is the Saudi connection would seem to suggest so.[41]

My plea to Rowan Williams is that he should cease to (perhaps accidentally) foment confusion between postmodern, liberal pluralism and a corporatist, constitutional pluralism. It is the latter that is the real thrust of his reflections and it is amply supported by his orthodox Catholic theology. For despite his endorsement of 'procedural secularity' (which may remain necessary to a degree), there remains an extremely subtle and unnoticed point—articulated at the end of his Shari'a lecture—that goes to the heart of his theologico-political reflections.

M. The Secular Power as the Protector of Human Dignity?

Williams contends that the predominant 'negativity' of secular law should be reconceived. It can do more than merely secure 'negative liberty'; it can also act as a kind of apophatic[42] placeholder for an eschatological reality of 'positive liberty', as the final revealed truth which will set us all free beyond any known bounds. Thus he suggests that 'universal law and universal right are a way of recognizing what is least fathomable and controllable in the human subject'.[43]

---

[39] See C Caldwell, *Reflections on the Revolution in Europe: Immigration, Islam and the West* (New York: Doubleday, 2009) 199: 'The West's new "loose" sexual morality is organised more around male prerogatives than it is around female ones. It may fit traditional Muslim thinking better than it fits traditional Western thinking. If the besetting sexual failure of Christianity is prudery, the besetting sexual failure of Islam is sexism. Traditional Islam is only *partially* at odds with present-day sexual practice, not totally at odds, the way Christianity is'. One might wish to qualify that 'totally' in certain respects, but all the same this remark is surely perceptive.

[40] See G K Chesterton's prophetic novel, *The Flying Inn* (originally published 1914: New York: Cosimo, 1915) and John Buchan's equally discerning *Greenmantle* (London: Hodder & Stoughton, 1993). Hitchcock never got round to his intended filming of this (far greater) sequel to *The Thirty-Nine Steps* (Edinburgh: William Blackwood, 1915). More recent attempts to film it have been politically stalled.

[41] The willingness of several Western academics to receive Saudi-sourced money sometimes risks covert (or not so covert) links with Wahhabism. Such linkage amounts to civilisational treachery and must be strenuously opposed.

[42] 'Apophatically' means 'negatively', in the sense of 'negative' or 'apophatic' theology. According to this essential moment within orthodox theology, God is said to be 'good' (and true, one, wise, beautiful, etc) in a manner infinitely exceeding what we are able to think about goodness.

[43] See Appendix 1 at [22].

Here one can see a kind of 'Western Byzantine' balance to his usual Augustinian claim that the Church alone possesses the eternal perspective sufficient to critique any norms of merely temporary expediency.[44] This new idea implies that it is *the secular power* which has the 'sacred' function of holding open the quest for human dignity—a task which nearly all religions *internally* acknowledge as exceeding their capacity to conceive (although they do not disallow that each religion believes that its own—limited—conception comes nearest to this goal).

Williams' approach accords with traditions of political Christology within Christianity: for now, the king bows to the priest; for now, the laity submit to the priest (who represents the higher spiritual realm); for now, Jesus Christ meets us as mediating priest. But in the *eschaton* (the fulfilment or end of all things) Christ is more king than priest, the laity are equal with the priesthood, women are equal with men, and the material things that the king dealt with have also been resurrected. So if the soul for now stands above the body, then finally the entire integrated resurrected person stands above our present existence. For this reason, Christ's kingly function (which traditionally belonged also to all the laity—including women, who could be queens but not priests) ultimately exceeds His priestly one. On this basis one can see how secular rule not only deals with the lesser and ephemeral, but also apophatically anticipates an unknown integral glory.

While the Archbishop is sometimes ambivalent on this point, it should be clear that the secular power can only advance the search of 'human dignity as such' *if* it acknowledges, in some manner, a specific religious mindset—one that provides a definite metaphysical framework within which it makes sense to talk of such a thing at all. No secular, neutral, liberal perspective can do this. Rather, what Vladimir Soloviev, the great nineteenth-century Russian philosopher termed 'free theocracy' remains essential to the causes of liberty and justice.[45]

N. The Role of a Revitalized Christendom

If Anglicanism and Orthodoxy have sometimes retained a subtle sense of the reserved sacral function of the secular arm, it is Latin Catholicism that has most

[44] For 'Western Byzantinism' (which logically linked the superiority of king over pope to the doctrine of human deification and the eschatological transfiguration of the human body), see Norman Anonymous [circa 1100, York or Rouen], 'The Consecration of Bishops and Kings' in O and J L O'Donovan (eds), *From Irenaeus to Grotius: A Sourcebook in Christian Political Thought* (Grand Rapids, MI: Eerdmans, 1999) 251–259.

[45] V Soloviev, *The Philosophical Principles of Integral Knowledge* (trans Valeria Z Nollan) (Grand Rapids, MI: Eerdmans, 2008) 53–54: ' the... spiritual society or the church... forms in a free internal union with the political and economic societies a single internal organism: a *free theocracy* or *integral society*... the government and district council are completely free in their allocation of their own resources and forces, as long as they have in mind upon doing so those higher requirements by which spiritual society defines itself—a society, that in this manner, like a divine being, must move everything, while itself remaining unmovable'.

fully developed the social implications of 'the Body of Christ'. In accordance with this understanding of the Church as the continued collective resonance of the universality of the God-Man, I believe that the idea that the West (and her political and cultural extensions) is 'really the Church' alone guarantees the protection of plural political liberties against both state and capitalist market. This idea, and no other, protects us against the incipient nihilism of rulers who acknowledge no eternal standard of judgment, nor any metaphysical basis for the reality of human existence.

Note that 'Christianity' and 'Christendom' are, in most European languages, words with identical meanings. The idea of Christianity as a religion gathering 'believers' is an early modern aberration. Ever since World War II it has become dogma to distinguish these two, encouraged by the idea that ethical *kenosis* implies powerlessness. But if Christians rightly believe in the paradox that true power is attained through receptive weakness, in self-offering unto death, infinite forgiveness, and ecstatic reciprocity and reconciliation, then we must believe that such stances should prevail. We should *not* be courting the failure of these stances! We must seek to incarnate them throughout our culture and polity. That is Christendom.[46] Not to believe in Christendom is not to believe in the Incarnation, which (according to Maximus the Confessor) is a continuing dynamic reality.

Although he has verbally denied it, Williams in effect believes in Christendom, as his speech on Europe[47] clearly shows. What he says there—simply, profoundly, and directly—is that Christianity is the ultimate source of the perpetual negative critique of the West which (in part) gives the West its strange character. One could put it this way: Christianity goes beyond the law, and founds itself upon a man who died as an exception to the law, yet founded a new law of love as the basis for a new kind of community. This is why (as, curiously, far-left materialists like Alain Badiou[48] and Slavoj Zizek[49] have seen in recent times) Christianity, unlike all other religions, is only a 'particularity' in the sense that *its* particularity is paradoxically more universal than any abstract universalism.

O. The *Exemplum*

By contrast, every 'general' framework always proves in the end to be 'provincial'—as Western philosophers find when confronted with Eastern ones.

---

[46] See A Nichols, *Christendom Awake: On Re-Energizing the Church in Culture* (Edinburgh: T&T Clark, 1999).

[47] 'Europe, Faith and Culture', speech delivered on 2 January 2008 at the Anglican Cathedral, Liverpool, available at <http://www.archbishopofcanterbury.org/1547>.

[48] A Badiou, *St Paul: La Fondation de l'Universalisme* (Paris: Presses Universitaires de France, 1997).

[49] See S Zizek and J Milbank, *The Monstrosity of Christ: Paradox or Dialectic* (Cambridge, MA: MIT Press, 2009).

But one extraordinary concrete *exemplum* can be related to in ever new ways and by all cultures. If this *exemplum* is taken to be the very personification of infinite truth, then it proves indeed to be 'the concrete universal', as Hegel put it. It is this one, cosmically organic, and yet specific, 'personality' that the West presupposes. The West must continue to presuppose it if it is to continue also to 'posit' (to retain Hegelian terminology) a society and politics grounded on the ultimacy of personhood—the idea that the individual person (or the 'characterized' group, the group with 'personality') is of infinite worth, equal with the whole, and is not an atomized thing at all. This is because persons are constituted through reciprocal exchanges involving both asymmetry and delay undergirded by trust (unlike formal contract) that continuously re-establish mutual recognition within the scope of interlocking, overlapping, and organically embedded social groups.[50] Only the original outrageous claim of one man—Jesus Christ—to exceed, in His individual existence, all the truths of law and wisdom as hitherto known, permits this personalism to arise. Now even the finite, defective personalities of all other human beings can claim an infinite and all-surpassing significance through participation in Christ's divine personhood and nature.

But, unlike Hegel, we must not imagine that we have ourselves posited our Christological presupposition. False confidence that we have indubitably entrenched this cornerstone premise in modern political culture in a purely immanentist manner risks a swift descent into liberal nihilism (a polity that cannot found a community that is personally corporate 'all the way down').[51]

As Williams goes on to argue, the loss of any appeal to transcendence leaves us with a tradition of critique that nihilistically distrusts reality as much as it validly distrusts human institutions. By contrast, a Christian Europe can sustain a Europe that is critical in a doubly negative sense: *both* of established authority *and* of a malignly infinite critique that regards every positive assertion as an unwarranted intrusion upon liberty. To oppose also this scepticism is to resist our current liberal madness for which the proof of liberty supposedly requires the ceaseless destruction of the random results of precisely that positive free expression which liberalism also endorses.

At the same time, Williams does not here mention (though he does elsewhere) the cataphatic[52] aspect not just of theology, but also of social intervention. Christianity offers not just a perpetual critique of the political sphere. It also provides a specific, even if infinitely malleable, shape for the true human society to take. This is the shape of the Body of Christ itself—a community of communities, a corporation of corporations. This is *ecclesia*—a term which, for St Paul, implies

---

[50]   See L Bruni and S Zamagni, *Civil Economy: Efficiency, Equity, Public Happiness* (Bern: Peter Lang, 2007) 159–195.

[51]   And not merely in one limited sphere of modification of the capitalist market, as Hegel envisaged.

[52]   'Cataphatic' is the opposite of 'apophatic' in Christian theology. It means that which can be positively and validly attributed to God, like 'goodness' and 'wisdom'.

something like 'the ruling council of the *Cosmopolis*'. *Ecclesia* is a 'super-polity': not more particular, but more universal than the state in its very concretion and, within its super-polity, operating to protect the many diverse, but collaborating, individuals and sub-groups.

According to the strange gothic logic that is Christian personalism, persons are at once 'more' and yet at the same time 'less' than the social whole. The continuous incomplete synthesis of this 'double excess' is sustained by the series of groups, or intermediary associations, that compose 'civil society' (something at once social and political, yet not just subordinate to the state). These alone ensure that neither individualism nor a statist holism prevails, but rather render ultimate an open network of relationships.

It is hard to see how anything other than a Christologic could underwrite this principle of 'double excess', which simultaneously allows organicism and individualism to flourish, and co-ordinates the two.[53] For here the Western civil order continues secretly to borrow from ecclesiology the idea that through belonging to a social body—'the body of Christ'—a person nonetheless is offered an equal freedom (God's offer of participated 'sonship') with the sovereign head of that body (Christ, and in political translation the sovereign state) yet without denying the primacy of the corporate whole which is the personal presence of this sovereign head itself. Neither individual nor social whole is absolute, since the 'personality' comprising both is taken to be divine and therefore as transcendently in excess of our grasp, even though this transcendence is equally immanent—fully if obscurely in our midst, such that the Christological 'idea' which always outruns us remains fully tied to a past event and its complex echo which has become coterminous with the history of the West itself. By contrast, any *mere* metaphysical immanence would always have to choose between either the differentiated atomic or the identical whole as founding principles, since any mere mediation between the two would collapse back towards the pole of totality. Social mediation (neither the one nor the other) can only remain as the paradoxically non-absolute absolute when it is at once grounded in a transcendence which exceeds it and yet with which it is fully identified. This social mediation present in the West—in a sense of mediation that exceeds Hegel's dialectic, even if it remains inspired by his reflections—remains the mediation of the divine-human mediator.

This principle alone (The Exemplum) permits both organic unity and personal dignity to flourish in a co-ordinated tension, through the role of intermediary associations. Given that both the individual and the social whole enjoy an equal primacy, this twin supremacy can only be blended through its double modification in terms of a new dispersed sovereign primacy for civil society in all its multiplicity. In Christ alone, *all* things hold together.[54]

---

[53] See Milbank (n 6 above).   [54] Colossians 1:17.

10

Religious Courts, Personal Federalism, and Legal Transplants

Jean-François Gaudreault-DesBiens

A. Introduction

As evinced by the debates provoked in the United Kingdom by Rowan Williams' lecture and in Canada by the proposal of the Islamic Institute of Civil Justice, religious courts' recognition proposals seem so far to have generally been understood as raising questions of individual agency and personal choice. However, an analysis of the narratives underlying Williams' and the Islamic Institute's proposals reveals that applying in a hegemonic manner a private law grid for understanding all religious courts' recognition proposals might not be appropriate.[1] This grid certainly has something to it, but it remains heuristically limited since not all such recognition proposals can automatically be conflated with one another. As Ayelet Shachar observes, there is an important qualitative difference between the structural accommodation of religious communities in view of granting them some autonomy as far as family or personal status law is concerned (in a context where the state monitors the appointment of religious adjudicators and imposes basic norms to be respected by all) and the privatization of diversity that results from a contract-based religious arbitration regime as envisaged by the Islamic Institute.[2] This is especially so when, as in the latter case, the subtext of the claim is not the mere accommodation of religious interests but rather the sharing of sovereignty and the reconfiguration of the political structure of the state.

It is thus important to dispel the myth that the state recognition of Shari'a courts in the field of family law or personal law must inevitably be understood as leading

---

[1] See Jean-François Gaudreault-DesBiens, Ch 4 in this collection.

[2] See A Shachar, 'Privatizing Diversity: A Cautionary Tale from Religious Arbitration in Family Law' (2008) 9 *Theoretical Inquiries in Law* 573. On the 'Lochnerian' consequences of this private law bias, see J-F Gaudreault-DesBiens, 'On Private Choices and Public Justice: Some Microscopic and Macroscopic Reflections on the State's Role in Addressing Faith-Based Arbitration' in R Murphy (ed), *Public Justice, Private Justice and Community-Based Justice?* (Montreal: Canadian Institute for the Administration of Justice, 2009) 247.

to the mere application of a different set of norms to juridical acts or facts that punctuate family life, even though it may superficially look as such. This caveat is particularly important when dealing with Islamic law, which, when viewed under a conservative light, does not distinguish between the temporal and spiritual realms. Since Shari'a is more than a normative regime, but is also an *ethos* that reflects and prescribes a global normative vision of the relationship between religion, society, and the individual, the religious inevitably becomes political and, in passing, religious claims risk carrying fundamentally political ones.[3] In this respect, the fact that there are many ways to interpret Islamic law—to such an extent that it is more accurate to refer to the existence of a variety of Muslim laws than to some monolithic 'Islamic law'[4]—should not blind observers to the other fact that conservative interpretations of that *corpus juris* may promote a more radical transformation of the relations between Muslims and the state than liberal interpretations, and that nowadays these conservative voices are often more vocal than their competitors. Thus, the 'privatist' bias identified above may obscure the fact that *some* religious courts' recognition claims actually imply a partial, but still very deep, reorganization of the liberal state along the lines of the principle of personality. If, in addition, the type of authority exercised by the group over its members reflects a genuine self-government logic,[5] then we are fully immersed, so to speak, in a public law debate. More specifically, if accepted, such claims could lead to the creation of a regime of personal federalism.

B. On Personal Federalism

What is personal federalism? To put it simply, it is a form of political organization which is grounded upon the principle of personality rather than the principle of territoriality. Irrespective of its 'control' over a particular territory,[6] a community defined on the basis of race, religion, language, or history is recognized as possessing legal personhood for constitutional purposes and is permitted to exercise self-governing powers, including the power to apply a particular body of law in respect of certain matters, often in the areas of family law, personal status, or

---

[3] In this respect, the challenge posed by the state recognition of Shari'a courts in a North American liberal polity such as Canada is arguably different, from a qualitative standpoint, from the challenges posed by the recognition of other religious legal orders and institutions, such as those governing some forms of Chassidic Judaism or Anabaptist Protestantism for example.

[4] This religious *corpus juris* has been subjected to various (and often different) secular appropriations by 'Islamic states'. See R Gteri, 'Lever le voile sur le droit musulman' in J-F Gaudreault-DesBiens (ed), *Le droit, la religion et le 'raisonnable': Le fait religieux entre monisme étatique et pluralisme juridique* (Montreal: Éditions Thémis, 2009) 455.

[5] G Otis, 'L'autonomie personnelle au cœur des droits ancestraux: *sub qua lege vivis?*' (2007) 52 *McGill Law Journal* 657, 665.

[6] Personal federalism may coexist with territorial federalism, but the presence of the latter is not a precondition for the existence of the former.

education—that is, all matters that are deemed to be 'core' to that community's collective identity and desire to perpetuate itself. The meaningful exercise of these self-governing powers necessitates the recognition by the state of communal institutions that are sufficiently autonomous to exercise them,[7] the concept of autonomy implying here as broad a protection as possible from state intervention in 'core' areas under the community's jurisdiction. A regime based on the personal federalism model may also, and will often, provide non-territorialized federated communities, on par with territorialized ones, with constitutional guarantees respecting their representation within federal institutions.

Lebanese scholar Antoine Messara attributes the existence of personality-based regimes, including personal federalism, to the failure of unitary or strongly integrationist regimes to address the particular needs of multi-communal societies. These societies are generally characterized by significant, often historically rooted, cultural cleavages which overlap with political ones, and by a correlative need to ensure that the communities composing them have access to power and resources. Messara indeed stresses that such regimes tend to conceive of inter-communal equality in a manner that takes into account the disparity of power and experiences between communities. He further notes that these regimes seek to alleviate the competition between communities, instead of providing tools for the majority community to prevail over minority groups, as, he argues, unitary or strongly integrationist regimes do. Thus, rather than a struggle for political power, personality-based regimes emphasize power sharing, the question being where to draw the line between intra-communal and extra-communal matters.[8] Another challenge lies, according to Messara's Lebanese colleague Pierre Gannagé, in establishing a system of conflict rules applicable to disputes between the different legal orders, religious or secular, recognized within the state.[9]

Several critiques have been levelled against personality-based models. Geneviève Nootens identifies three important criticisms for the purposes of this essay. The first concerns the rather 'hermetic' conception of communities underpinning these models,[10] from which flows a negative vision of inter-communal interactions and, as a matter of consequence, attempts at limiting such interactions. In other words, personality-based models tend to essentialize communities, something that does not fit very well with the ideology of Western liberal states. That being said, as Messara notes, while one of the operating principles of personality-based models is that of 'self-segmentation', such can also be the case of territorial models. Delineating a physical space and drawing borders may indeed result from an act

---

[7] A N Messara, *Théorie générale du système politique libanais* (Paris: Cariscript, 1994) 25.
[8] Ibid 11.
[9] P Gannagé, *Le pluralisme des statuts personnels dans les États multicommunautaires: Droit libanais et droits proche-orientaux* (Brussels: Bruylant, 2001) 239.
[10] G Nootens, *Désenclaver la démocratie: Des huguenots à la paix des Braves* (Montreal: Québec-Amérique, 2004) 254.

of 'self-segmentation'. Moreover, if this exercise overlaps with a process of strong cultural-national affirmation, territory may serve as an anchor for attitudes that are just as essentialist as those that may emerge in a regime based on the principle of personality. Such a regime may indeed limit, perhaps paradoxically, the segmentation process to narrowly defined inter-communal contentious matters, while territorial regimes may actually expand this dynamic to non-contentious matters.[11]

The second critique raised against personality-based models deplores their overly individualist bent as well as their constraining nature: as a matter of principle, it is the individual who originally decides to self-identify with a particular community and then formally to 'register' that identification in view of making it opposable to other communities and the state.[12] For example, in a democratic context, where personal federalism primarily seeks to assuage fears related to the marginalization of non-territorialized minorities, this structure of government can take the form of 'statutory federalism', whereby individuals officially declare their belonging to a community which enjoys the level of autonomy specified in a statute.[13] As a result of this declaration, the provisions of the statute become applicable to these individuals, who then have to abide by the decisions taken by the community within the ambit of its areas of jurisdiction. Individuals thus 'adhere' to a personal status, which refers us back to the idea of 'contractualized statuses' alluded to earlier. The problem with such a process, however, is that adherence implies exclusivity, thereby contributing to the essentializing of identities. When a citizen 'chooses' a community, he or she waives the right to identify legally with another community. In that way, personal federalism tends to discourage *métissage*.

The third critique is that personality-based regimes do not always prevent the further 'minoritization' of communities.[14] Indeed, power dynamics operate irrespective of the territorial or personal structure of a state. As an example, one can think of the status of non-Muslims in the Muslim jurisdictions of the Middle Ages, where *dhimmis* could be relegated and confined to a minority status. However, from a liberal perspective, the idea that an individual belonging to a particular minority is, forever and for all public purposes, bound by his or her association with that minority is problematic. For example, a Muslim may sociologically be part of a demographic minority in a Western state, but this religious affiliation does not entirely define the individual; he or she may be part of majorities for other purposes.

The fourth critique is concerned with the fate of minorities within self-governing minorities in personality-based regimes. Some fear that the latter may be tempted to oppress the former, or, at the very least, to systematically ignore their legitimate concerns and expectations. In the particular context of religious groups, the question of the treatment of women is critically important and epitomizes what

---

[11] Messara (n 7 above) 29.   [12] Nootens (n 10 above) 155.
[13] Messara (n 7 above) 62.   [14] Nootens (n 10 above) 155.

Shachar has called the 'paradox of multicultural vulnerability'.[15] The potentially problematic treatment of smaller minorities (or otherwise minoritized groups) at the hands of larger minorities, be they territorialized or not, is not peculiar to personality-based regimes. However, it would be intellectually irresponsible to obscure the historical fact that religious groups, in addition to appealing to human beings' highest aspirations, have also, at times, been powerful vectors of oppression against individuals and of intolerance against other groups, and have seen their sacred texts or beliefs regularly instrumentalized by men who craved for power under the guise of religion and who used the comprehensive, and almost self-contained, nature of many theist ideologies as springboards for their primarily political or economic endeavours.

Now, having broadly defined personal federalism, and identified some strengths and limits of personality-based regimes, a brief examination of some experiences or theorizations of personal federalism is warranted.

The first observation that must be made is that, considering the focus of this book on Shari'a, the most relevant experiences of personal federalism originate from the Middle East or Asia, as many of them have involved the recognition of the self-governing powers of Muslim communities. These experiences generally grew out of the extremely complex composition, from a demographic and religious standpoint, of many Middle Eastern or Asian societies, and from the frequent absence of any meaningful territorial concentration of the groups composing those societies. Islam also played a major role in inspiring the legal management of intercommunal relations in states where it was dominant.

Take, for example, the Millet system, once in force in the Ottoman Empire, which arguably constitutes the original template for modern expressions of personal federalism.[16] The Millet system revolved around the recognition by the Ottoman ruler of a relative institutional, jurisdictional, and financial autonomy in non-Muslim religious communities. These communities were essentially self-governing in areas deemed essential for the preservation of their identity, ie family law and personal law. As a result of the spread of Western nationalist ideologies, particularly from the end of the nineteenth century, the soundness of the system was increasingly questioned, both by Turkish nationalists and by its immediate 'beneficiaries', ie the religious communities themselves, who began to identify with other national communities outside of the Empire. Nevertheless, after World War I and the fall of the Empire, this structure was for the most part maintained by the European powers that were given the mandate to administer territories formerly part of the Ottoman Empire. This was especially the case in what used to be known as 'Greater Syria', a territory now encompassing Israel, Jordan, Syria, Lebanon, and Palestine. While the Millet system was abandoned in many Arab countries after

---

[15] A Shachar, *Multicultural Jurisdictions: Cultural Differences and Women's Rights* (Cambridge: Cambridge University Press, 2001) 3.
[16] Messara (n 7 above) 21.

decolonization,[17] some Middle Eastern countries did maintain a legal regime to some extent based on the personality principle, most notably Lebanon and Israel. However, it is significant that the religious variable did not always play the same role in every country that adopted a regime partly based on the principle of personality. For instance, in relation to the situation in Lebanon Messara observes that the communities that are recognized for constitutional purposes are not strictly speaking recognized on the basis of religion; they are instead recognized as cultural groups, even though a particular religious faith plays a central role in their cultural identity.[18]

Islam was, of course, the dominant faith in the Ottoman Empire. Unsurprisingly, the organization of such a multi-communal political entity on the basis of the principle of personality echoed Islamic conceptions. Indeed, Islamic law privileges personality over territoriality as far as the organization of relations between the civil/religious authority and religious minorities is concerned.[19] The status of religious minorities in the Caliphate of Cordoba prior to the Spanish *Reconquista* provides a good illustration. Minorities whose religious tradition revolved around a sacred book were granted, in application of the principle of personality, some form of communal autonomy. In return, they had to remain loyal to the central (Muslim) authority and pay a special tax to retain their 'protected' status. This idea of protection, as well as the conditions that had to be met to retain it, are important, as, contrary to some idealized representations of inter-communal relations in the Caliphate of Cordoba, non-Muslims were legally treated, in today's terms, as second-class citizens since they conditionally enjoyed a limited set of rights,[20] which could be revoked at will by the Muslim ruler. In that sense, it would be misleading to depict Cordoba's golden age as evincing the existence of a covenant between equals. To illustrate this, recall that the conquest of Al-Andalus by the Almohads in the twelfth century not only ended the rule of the Almoravid dynasty, but also the relative inter-communal harmony that had prevailed for the past four centuries. Jews and Christians were left with a hard choice: convert or die, or try to flee.[21] In sum, the recognition of partially self-governing, de-territorialized religious communities, whether under classical Islamic law or under the Ottoman regime, was not the result of mere generosity on the part of the ruler: it was first and foremost a mechanism of control and a tool of pacification. Yet, in context, it often proved to be successful and the formally unequal status of non-Muslims as *dhimmis* was somehow compensated by the self-government rights they collectively enjoyed under the personal regime that was in place. Moreover, non-Muslims could, at times, become part of the regime's establishment. All this explains why non-Muslim communities often flourished under Muslim rule, at least until the

---

[17] Ibid 89.   [18] Ibid 25.   [19] Ibid 91.
[20] Ibid 89.   [21] J Attali, *Dictionnaire amoureux du Judaïsme* (2009) 45.

end of the Ottoman Empire.[22] Religious minorities could hardly do the same in Christian lands.

Political-constitutional regimes partly recognizing the personality principle also emerged in Asia, most notably in India, again as a result of the deep religious diversity and complexity of the country.[23] Interestingly, British colonizers took advantage of pre-existing structures facilitating the expression of religious personal laws, with a view to establishing and maintaining their legitimacy. In other words, following the common law rule applicable to conquered colonies, they allowed for the perpetuation of legal regimes already in force on the territory and without any direct incidence on the relations between the colonizer and the colonized, and integrated them in a broader structure of governance. In practice, by granting powers to the elites of religious communities and by helping them strengthen their status within their communities, the British ensured the collaboration of these elites and thus reinforced their own position.[24]

Personality-based models originating from the Middle East or Asia were, until recently, frowned upon by Western scholars as backward and illiberal. Messara deplores in this respect what he calls the prejudice of Western scholars against such models, and explains this by their failure to understand the context in which these models arose.[25] At the same time, he acknowledges the specificity of all—even multi-communal—societies, and shies away from making the normative argument that such models, especially that of personal federalism, offer panaceas. Hence, according to him, there is a need to be cautious when proposing transplants from one system to another.[26] That being said, some Western scholars have tried to elaborate personality-based models, and some experiments, which did not last long, were launched in European countries.

One theorization attempt is that of 'national cultural autonomy', which was promoted by Austro-Marxists Karl Renner[27] and Otto Bauer[28] at the beginning of the twentieth century as a means of managing the Austro-Hungarian Empire's numerous cultural minorities, including several that were territorially dispersed but envisaged as 'nationalities'. In stark contrast to the nation-state ideology that was dominant at the time, they considered that the state and the nation needed to

---

[22] On the cultural blossoming of Jews in the Caliphate of Cordoba, see J Peláez del Rosal (ed), *Les Juifs à Cordoue (Xème-XIIème siècles)* (2003).

[23] On India, see W Menski, *Hindu Law: Between Tradition and Modernity* (Oxford: Oxford University Press, 2003).

[24] On this dynamic, see V Narain, *Gender and Community: Muslim Women's Rights in India* (Toronto: University of Toronto Press, 2001); Z Hasan, *Forging Identities: Gender, Communities and the State in India* (Boulder, CO: Westview Press, 1994).

[25] Messara (n 7 above) 21.

[26] Ibid 23.

[27] See K Renner, 'State and Nation' in E Nimni (ed), *National Cultural Autonomy and its Contemporary Critics* (London: Routledge, 2005) 15.

[28] See O Bauer, *The Question of Nationalities and Social Democracy* (Minneapolis: University of Minnesota Press, 2000).

be disentangled, at least in multinational states. Their views are nicely summarized by Geneviève Nootens:

...in this model the principle of nationality is not seen as a principle for the creation of states as is the case in its classical expression (which posits that every nation has a right to its own sovereign state), but rather as an internal organizing principle of the multinational state. Renner understands the right to self-determination as an exclusively individual right, which itself provides the principle of the nation as a juridical institution. The right to national self-determination is conceived as the right of the individual to self-determine, and, springing from this right is the nation constituted as a body politic the competencies of which are legally protected. The nation thus becomes an intermediary juridical body, vested with powers, and the state forms a union of nations.[29]

In this model, the nation, viewed as 'a community of intellectual and emotional life, that is, a purely inward community',[30] somehow transcends its original status by becoming a fully fledged collective legal subject enjoying a constitutionally predetermined and guaranteed margin of internal autonomy and vested with the powers needed tangibly to exercise that autonomy, including legislative, judicial, and financial powers. It also participates, through various representation mechanisms, in the state's overarching system of governance. The state, however, is not left powerless, being given the powers necessary to defend and promote the interests of the larger polity and those of all its citizens, irrespective of the nation to which they personally identify. Although the nation is recognized as a collective legal subject, it somehow remains dependent on the will of its individual members, who have to declare their nationality, which implies a conscious choice on their part to be submitted to the government of one particular nationality.[31] This democratic requirement of the prior consent of the individuals governed by the laws of a given nationality distinguishes the 'national cultural autonomy' model from the Millet system, which, in contrast, represented a typical consociational, elite-based arrangement that tended to grasp minorities as innate collectives rather than as deriving from the will of their individual members.[32]

The 'national cultural autonomy' model was never formally implemented, but it inspired some initiatives of an equivalent type, notably in Estonia between the two world wars.[33] Although it almost fell into oblivion after World War II, there seems today to be a resurgence of interest in this model and for alternative models that try to reconcile the principles of autonomy and personality. On the theoretical

---

[29] Nootens (n 10 above) 149 (footnotes omitted; author translation).

[30] Renner (n 27 above) 26.

[31] In that model, belonging to more than one nation is understood as implying a relation of non-compossibility (ibid 42), hence the problems of the model for individuals who identify with more than one nationality within the state.

[32] On this, see J Lajčájková, *Ethnocultural Justice for the Roma in Slovakia*, Doctoral Thesis (Faculty of Law, University of Toronto: 2006) 208.

[33] Nootens (n 10 above) 151–152.

front, this resurgence is in part due to the influential work of Arend Lijphart on consociational theory.[34] On the practical front, personality-based models have been considered as potential templates for ancient, non-territorialized minorities who still have unresolved recognition claims,[35] and for more recent immigrant groups who increasingly refuse what used to be their fate, ie assimilation within the Western mainstream.[36]

Questions still abound, however. One of these concerns the type of minority claiming recognition through personal federalism or a variant of it. Suffice it to observe here that in the models examined above and which can be characterized either as precursors of the idea of personal federalism or as embodiments of it, the communities that were recognized were more often than not historical ones, ie communities that had a lengthy historical connection with the state from which recognition was demanded. This raises a further question: to what extent can 'newer', recently immigrated groups successfully make such a recognition claim? I will simply say for now that such a question can be answered from at least two different angles, one normative and the other pragmatic, and that any conclusion under any angle risks being highly disputable and disputed.

That being said, a preliminary conclusion can be drawn from this brief and admittedly incomplete examination of experiments and theorizations of personality-based models or personal federalism: while intellectually appealing from an abstract perspective and possibly conducive to social peace in certain circumstances, such models remain largely rooted in non-Western societies and constitute solutions to the particular ethno-religious configuration of such societies, in addition to relying on religious and political conceptions that are themselves rooted in intellectual traditions that were never dominant in modern Western states. The rather minimal success of such models in the West seems to evince the limits of their potential.[37] This thus begs the question: to what extent can such models be successfully transplanted in the West? The devil being in the details, the answer inevitably depends on the country involved. But some general observations can still be made, which in particular concern the nature of the obstacles that transplant attempts may face in Western legal systems.

[34] See A Lijphart, *Democracy in Plural Societies: A Comparative Exploration* (New Haven: Yale University Press, 1977) 41–44.

[35] For non-territorialized Aboriginal communities in Canada, see G Otis, 'Territorialité, personnalité et gouvernance autochtone' (2006) 47 *Cahiers de droit* 781. In relation to Roma populations in Europe, see Lajčáková (n 32 above) 211–228.

[36] This is the attitude adopted by *some* Muslim immigrants in Western states, which explains the existence of this collection of essays.

[37] For a survey of European experiments, see J Coakley, 'Approaches to the Resolution of Ethnic Conflict: The Strategy of Non-Territorial Autonomy' (1994) 15 *International Political Science Review* 297.

C. Transplants: Legal Traditions and Reverse Orientalism

Not all religious courts' recognition proposals are the same; the various narratives are significantly different, for two related reasons.[38] First, interpretations of Islamic law may range from liberal to very conservative and even fundamentalist interpretations. Secondly, such recognition proposals may vary widely in scope and ambition: from relatively narrow and modest accommodation projects to more radical ones (in the etymological sense) which may imply a significant constitutional restructuring of a state along the lines of personal federalism. Hence the public law dimension of the latter, and the normative questions that ensue. Indeed, the state's recognition of the legality and legitimacy of a system of parallel justice—the word *system* is critical here—allowing the use of non-state norms in the settlement of disputes simply cannot be assimilated to its validation, for example in family law contexts, of individualized settlements arrived at by the parties to such disputes, even where the arbitration agreement permitting access to this system of parallel justice itself stems from a contract. There is in my view no use in denying that the stakes involved in family law-related or personal status-related disputes, as well as the risk of significant derogations to the state's most basic norms and values allowed by the existing private arbitration framework, raise questions of a qualitatively different magnitude. Recall, first, that the parallel systems of justice so created are to be administered by groups defined on the basis of a shared socio-religious identity. As observed earlier, these groups have traditionally demanded their inclusion within society on a non-discriminatory basis, or have simply insisted on the state's non-interference in their religious affairs. However, if linked to a notion of communal autonomy understood as a form of sovereignty, the state recognition of religious tribunals' partial jurisdiction raises different stakes. The identity-based (rather than merely faith-based) legal pluralism that some personal federalism arrangements presuppose, as well as the collective definition of identity they seek to facilitate, imply the mutation of social minorities into political ones, since these minorities' identities are now grasped by the state as giving rise to a collective rights problem instead of being understood from the traditional perspective of individual rights.[39] Such a mutation implies a conscious and politically driven deepening of

---

[38] See Jean-François Gaudreault-DesBiens, Ch 4 in this collection.

[39] The distinction between political and social minorities has been proposed by Canadian legal theorist Andrée Lajoie. For her, *political* minorities are those whose primary locus of identification is a sub-state entity (which in and of itself forms a political community) rather than the global polity constituted by the state, and for whom belonging to the latter is conditional upon the respect by that polity of their primary identification with the sub-state entity. In contrast, *social* minorities are those that are in a legitimate position to advance an equality claim, but whose sense of belonging to the political community formed by the state is not conditional upon any prior, and primordial, identification with another sub-state political community. As a result, claims made by political minorities potentially threaten the integrity of the state, while those made by social minorities do not. See A Lajoie, *Quand les minorités font la loi* (Paris: Presses Universitaires de France, 2002). Using

the minority's degree of diversity.[40] This, in turn, inevitably induces that minority to require from the state recognition of its now 'deeply diverse' identity. Because of the political undertones of such a transformation, the members of this minority will 'want...an identity that is collectively negotiated',[41] and the likely result of that negotiation will be the creation of separate institutions exercising some form of *imperium* over a segment of the population. This explains the link made in this paper to the concept of personal federalism.

Let us be clear that this type of outcome is neither a necessary nor an inevitable consequence of state recognition of Shari'a courts. Nor is such a religious/political project inherently illegitimate from a normative standpoint. Conservative Muslims are free to entertain all the peaceful political projects that they want, exactly as believers of other faiths or, if one prefers, secularization activists, do. Nor am I arguing that the mutation of a social minority into a political one is normatively problematic.[42] The characteristics of a minority may evolve over time and so may its characterization. Yet, it remains important to point out that recognizing what is essentially an identity-based system of parallel justice provides the embryo of a regime of radical legal pluralism, the long-term consequences of which a democratic polity may legitimately want to examine further, be it only as a matter of *realpolitik*. Indeed, the public recognition of identity-based communities that are partially or entirely self-governing raises important questions pertaining to the nature of citizenship in a liberal polity, and the sharing of sovereignty within political communities.

That being said, it is of the utmost importance to distinguish *between* liberal states and to refine the analysis accordingly. In this respect, it may very well be a serious weakness of approaches flirting with political philosophy to evaluate the acceptability of a differentialist claim such as a Shari'a court recognition proposal in a 'liberal' society abstractly defined. This type of endeavour may be intellectually rewarding, but its usefulness is, in my view, limited because the category 'liberal society' encompasses very different realities, not all of which are entirely commensurable, especially when it comes to the ideology inspiring the management of the relations between the state and religions. 'Liberal societies' are indeed quite diverse, and while they may all adhere to basic values such as liberty and equality, we should not lose sight of the fact that these values are generally transposed as

---

Will Kymlicka's typology of group-differentiated rights, political minorities will generally demand 'self-government rights' while social minorities will more likely claim 'polyethnic rights' and, occasionally, 'special representation rights': W Kymlicka, *Multicultural Citizenship* (Oxford: Oxford University Press, 1995) 26–33.

[40] Elaborated by philosopher Charles Taylor, the concept of 'deep diversity' essentially refers to situations where belonging to a larger polity is mediated by, or conditional upon, belonging to another smaller community which can also be characterized as political. See C Taylor, 'Shared and Divergent Values' in R Watts and D Brown (eds), *Options for a New Canada* (Toronto: University of Toronto Press, 1991) 53. Note the overlap with Lajoie's concept of 'political minority'.

[41] M Walzer, *On Toleration* (New Haven: Yale University Press, 1997) 44.

[42] S Choudhry, 'National Minorities and Ethnic Immigrants: Liberalism's Political Sociology' (2002) 10 *Journal of Political Philosophy* 54.

principles in their constitutional structures. Legal principles, by definition, do not always dictate specific outcomes, and their institutionalization in particular legal contexts does not necessarily entail the same specific outcomes. Legal principles are individuated in context, which means that their very definition may be influenced by different variables pertaining to history and ideology, as well as political and legal cultures.

Take, for example, the case of Canada. While not theoretically inconceivable, the reception of a Muslim claim advocating the partial introduction of a regime of personal federalism would imply a substantial reconfiguration of the role and status of 'multicultural communities' within Canadian society. This might be the case to such an extent that it could be questioned whether such a regime would represent a desirable evolution in a fragmented federal polity like Canada, which, it bears remembering, has experienced, and still experiences, significant difficulties managing two of its minority 'constitutional communities', namely Québec and the Aboriginal peoples, sometimes to the point that the federation's unity is threatened. At some stage, *realpolitik* inevitably kicks in.

Moreover, the incorporation of a regime of personal federalism does not logically flow from Canada's commitment to multiculturalism. As observed by Joseph Magnet, the '[m]ulticulturalism policy does not intend to enable cultural communities to endure as distinctive national minorities, replete with a separate array of autonomous institutions under their control'.[43] Liberal multiculturalism, as understood in Canada, can hardly be represented as including an absolute right to institutional completeness.[44] Furthermore, legally speaking, the application of the principle of personality in that country remains the exception rather than the rule.[45] For example, even in the field of family law, the principle applicable is that the legal status of spouses is determined not by their nationality but by their domicile. Thus, as a matter of principle, two Moroccan nationals residing in Canada who wished to divorce would be submitted to Canadian law and not Moroccan law even if they

[43] J E Magnet, 'Multiculturalism and Collective Rights' in G A Beaudoin and E Mendes (eds), *Canadian Charter of Rights and Freedoms* (Toronto: LexisNexis-Butterworths, 4th edn, 2005) 1259, 1309.

[44] As observed by Will Kymlicka, Mumtaz Ali's conception of multiculturalism, as voiced in the Ontario Shari'a courts debate, was traditional rather than liberal. This conception holds that each group must be capable of practicing its own customs, applying its own laws, irrespective of whether they respect individual freedoms and human rights. Kymlicka believes that Canadian multiculturalism must be construed as a liberal and not a traditional multiculturalism. See W Kymlicka, 'Tester les limites du multiculturalisme libéral? Le cas des tribunaux religieux en droit familial' (2007) 9(1) *Éthique publique* 27, 28. See also, supporting that position, J-F Gaudreault-DesBiens, 'Constitutional Values, Faith-Based Arbitration, and the Limits of Private Justice in a Multicultural Society' (2005–2006) 19 *National Journal of Constitutional Law* 155, 180–187. Cf F Bhabha, 'Between Exclusion and Assimilation: Experimentalizing Multiculturalism' (2009) 54 *McGill Law Journal* 45.

[45] One exception can be found in the management of official bilingualism which is based on a variation of the principle of personality as opposed to, for example, Belgium, where language rights are territorialized.

were married in Morocco under the law of that country.[46] This solution—which is markedly different from that retained in many continental European countries where the law of nationality becomes a guise through which the personality principle is applied—is now somehow taken as a given and has thus permeated the Canadian legal culture. Of course, a legal culture is not something that is cast in stone and impervious to evolution.[47] However, it is one thing to acknowledge this evolutionary capacity, and it is quite another to assume that a legal culture can evolve easily and rapidly, given the ideological, institutional, and disciplinary pedigree it carries. Thus, successfully incorporating a regime of personal federalism in the Canadian context would possibly be a daunting challenge. In contrast, such incorporation could *arguably*—this word is critically important—be simpler in England, a less fragmented society with a much stronger cultural and political identity, where the Church is established and has a certain pre-eminent public status. This recognition would possibly make it easier for Muslim promoters of a form of personal federalism to legitimize their identity claim on the basis of equality rights: if the Anglican faith was granted significant privileges, which were to a certain extent extended later to Roman Catholicism and Judaism, why would Muslim religious and legal institutions not be recognized on a par with others?[48]

Ultimately, this discussion points to potential legitimization problems for a personal federalism regime that would be implemented without having first been thoroughly scrutinized from the perspective of its advantages and disadvantages, and, most importantly, of its integration within the particular constitutional, political, and cultural environment of the particular liberal society targeted by the claim. In other words, even in liberal societies, context matters. Therefore, irrespective of the abstract intellectual appeal of joint governance or personal federalism models, their successful integration in countries where the political and legal cultures do not *a priori* enshrine the presuppositions of these models can at best be characterized as a gamble.

One important variable that may influence the receptiveness of a particular legal culture to claims promoting the formal recognition of Shari'a-based adjudication, irrespective of the positive mechanism involved, is the legal tradition to which it is associated. In the West, there are two dominant legal traditions, the common law and the civil law, both of which can be subdivided into various families. Clearly, one must be careful when making generalizations, especially given the existence of country-specific variations within each tradition. I would surmise, however, that common law jurisdictions *will tend* to show more receptiveness to Shari'a courts' recognition claims than their civil law counterparts, at least when considered from a purely domestic law standpoint. (I shall explain this caveat later.)

---

[46] See J Talpis, 'L'accommodement raisonnable en droit international privé québécois' in Gaudreault-DesBiens (n 4 above) 303.
[47] D Nelken, 'Defining and Using the Concept of Legal Culture' in E Örücü and D Nelken (eds), *Comparative Law: A Handbook* (Oxford: Hart Publishing, 2007) 109.
[48] D Joly, 'Les musulmans et l'institutionnalisation de l'Islam dans la société britannique' (2008) 8(2) *Diversité Urbaine* 13, 21.

Why is that? In my view, the first reason lies in the different scope attributed to the exceptions of 'public order' (*ordre public*) in civilian jurisdictions and of 'public policy' in common law jurisdictions. These functional equivalents somehow serve as safety valves that ensure the closure of a particular legal system when faced with a claim or conduct that is allegedly irreconcilable with the most basic values of that system. But while they perform a similar function, *ordre public* and public policy are not exactly the same.[49] In common law jurisdictions, the open texture and flexibility of the public policy doctrine has raised concerns about its abusive potential at the expense of freedom of contract, thereby leading to the 'judicial censure of the doctrine'.[50] As a matter of principle, therefore, courts will tend to refrain from creating novel grounds of public policy. Additionally, at common law, the doctrine of public policy is primarily used in so-called 'private law' fields, notably contracts.[51] Civil law jurisdictions, on the other hand, tend to give a broader scope to the notion of *ordre public* and distinguish between its formal expression through an explicit enactment, in a code or an ordinary law, and its virtual expression. This means that regardless of the existence of an explicit enactment, a judge may find that a particular contract, or clause thereof, goes against public order as it contradicts the spirit of a law, an inarticulate premise of that law, or a general principle of law.[52] Further, the notion finds application in fields other than contract law or even, more broadly, private law.[53] In a way, public order in civilian jurisdictions is closely linked to a comprehensive conception of the relations between the state, individuals, and civil society, as well as reflecting presuppositions about the very nature of that society. In many cases, it refers to a legal system's 'deep conventions'.[54] All this takes place in jurisdictions where the concept of the state is often more robust (as well as the theorization of its prerogatives and those of the broader community over individual interests) and where individual freedom, while equally central in the legal ideology, is not as sacralized as in common law jurisdictions. These conceptions permeate these jurisdictions' legal culture.

Returning to Shari'a courts' recognition claims, the difference between civil and common law jurisdictions may entail an important consequence, which often finds a codified expression. In civil law systems, the private arbitration of disputes over the status of persons or family matters often tends to be prohibited because

---

[49] As Natalya Shelkoplyas observes, '[t]here is a lack of complete equivalence between the continental understanding of "ordre public" and the notion of public policy in English law ... It is generally admitted that the domain of public policy in England is remarkably more modest than its corresponding continental concept of ordre public'. See N Shelkoplyas, *The Application of EC Law in Arbitration Proceedings* (Groningen: Europa Law Publishing, 2003) 172.

[50] *Chitty on Contracts: General Principles* (London: Sweet & Maxwell, 1999) 837.

[51] S M Waddams et al., *Cases and Materials on Contracts* (Toronto: Emond Montgomery, 3rd edn, 2005) 647–693.

[52] D Lluelles and B Moore, *Droit des obligations* (Montreal: Éditions Thémis, 2007) 1007–1055.

[53] P Malaurie, *L'ordre public et le contrat (Étude de droit civil comparé France, Angleterre, URSS)* (Reims: Éditions Matot-Braine, 1953) 10.

[54] On 'deep conventions', see A Marmor, *Social Conventions: From Language to Law* (Princeton: Princeton University Press, 2009) 171–175.

these questions are deemed to be matters of public order, notably because of the vulnerability of many of the parties involved and of a greater reluctance to limit the state's normative monopoly as a tool for redressing power imbalances.[55] This prohibition applies to all potential arbitrations in those fields, and not only to arbitrations governed by religious norms. In such contexts, using multiple individual contracts to achieve some form of communal religious autonomy—what I have referred to earlier as 'contractualized statuses'—is impossible because the object of the contract is deemed inarbitrable.[56] This explains, at least in part, why a 'Shari'a court debate' could easily take place in common law Ontario, and less so in neighbouring Québec, which is a predominantly civilian jurisdiction as far as private law is concerned.[57] And it clearly points to significant hurdles for Shari'a courts' recognition claims in many such jurisdictions.[58]

Three caveats must be made to these observations. The first, to which I have already alluded, concerns the confinement of the hypothesis elaborated above to 'purely domestic law'. Indeed, the situation may be quite different when a dispute has an extraneous dimension. For instance, in many civil law jurisdictions, especially those that apply the rule of nationality instead of that of domicile, conflicts of laws are decided on the basis of an attenuated conception of public order. As a result, when faced with a foreign rule which governs the status of persons living on their territory, civil law jurisdictions may prove remarkably permissive.[59] The second caveat concerns the huge diversity of civil law jurisdictions and the importance of country-specific validations of the hypothesis examined, even if its validation remains highly plausible when envisaged from a macroscopic perspective. The public order exception may indeed be used more frequently in one civil jurisdiction than in another, and in some areas of law more than in others.[60]

I have so far focused on the political-legal *terroirs* that legal traditions offer for potential transplants of joint governance or personal federalism models. In other words, I have examined *where* such transplants may occur. But the success of a transplant is not solely determined by the circumstances of the jurisdiction where it is supposed to take place; the transplant itself must also be examined to see whether it can reasonably take root in that jurisdiction. In other words, the feasibility of the transplant is dependent upon both the specificities of the receiving

---

[55] See, eg Art 2060 of the French Civil Code and Art 2639 of the Quebec Civil Code.

[56] See, generally, T E Carbonneau (with F Janson), 'Cartesian Logic and Frontier Politics: French and American Concepts of Arbitrability' (1994) 2 *Tulane Journal of International and Comparative Law* 193.

[57] It is actually a mixed jurisdiction.

[58] See J L Halperin, *Profil des mondialisations du droit* (Paris: Dalloz, 2009) 333–337.

[59] For diverse country reports on that issue, see M F Foblets, J-F Gaudreault-DesBiens, and A Dundes Renteln (eds), *Cultural Diversity and the Law: State Responses From Around the World* (Brussels: Bruylant, 2010).

[60] For instance, see E Groffier, *Précis de droit international privé québécois* (Cowansville, QC: Éditions Yvon Blais, 4th edn, 1990) paras 103–104. Groffier signals that the public order exception is used more frequently in France than in Quebec, but that the public policy doctrine is used even less often in common law England.

system and the transplant's nature, scope, and genealogy. For, irrespective of the abstract intellectual appeal of joint governance or personal federalism models, they enshrine particular presuppositions about social ordering and the relation between groups. In addition, they have a pedigree, an *historicité*,[61] which is deeply linked to a particular society, in spite of the relatively abstract formulation of the theories or claims promoting them. Any individual norm, any system of norms, comes with intellectual and historical baggage. Thus, advocating the introduction in a given state of a particular legal model which emanates from elsewhere because this model abstractly appears to be more just from an intercultural perspective risks not yielding the desired results if some basic epistemic precautions are not taken.[62] For example, in spite of its considerable influence, Will Kymlicka's famous typology of minorities and explanation of the rights each type should abstractly enjoy was rooted in the Canadian experience. As such, if it could indeed be used as an analytical grid for the study of other multinational and multicultural democratic states, such as Belgium and Spain, its usefulness in respect of other types of states, where, for instance, national minorities are not territorially concentrated, is limited at best. In sum, the actual genealogy of a model abstractly depicted as ideal-typical or even desirable from a normative standpoint may, in certain circumstances, undermine the possibility of efficiently transplanting it elsewhere.

This applies to joint governance or personal federalism models as much as to any other legal model. Recall, here, the brief overview of the genealogy of personal federalism models that I provided above. Be it in their Ottoman, Austro-Marxist, or Muslim formulation, the modern manifestations of these models owe a debt to the historical context in which they emerged. Their fit within jurisdictions that have implemented them under one form or another can certainly be explained, at least in part, by a correspondence between a political-legal culture that has organically evolved so as to render these models not only acceptable, but 'normal' and even necessary, and the particular mode of implementation of these models privileged in a given jurisdiction.

Thus, the age-old question is raised again: can theoretical models inspired, more or less explicitly, by actual political-constitutional models implemented in other states be efficiently transplanted in a different constitutional, political, and cultural environment? The twist, however, is that this question involves an unusual situation: instead of talking of a transplant from Western legal systems to non-Western systems, which was the bread and butter of colonialism, we are by and large talking about non-Western exports to Western countries.

Predictably, the answer to that question is not clear, and certainly not univocal. This is especially so in the context of Shari'a courts' recognition claims, even when we leave aside the broader political dimensions of such claims and focus instead

---

[61] P Legrand, *Le droit comparé* (Paris: Presses Universitaires de France, 1999) 99.
[62] This implies taking stock of all the 'legal formants' that exist in a jurisdiction. On these formants, see R Sacco, 'Legal Formants: A Dynamic Approach to Comparative Law' (1991) 39 AJCL 1 and 343.

on their family law dimension. Take, again, the example of Canada, where, as noted, the law of domicile has historically been applied in private international law as regards family matters. This means that, as a matter of principle, all residents are submitted to the applicable federal and provincial norms, irrespective, for example, of where they married or procreated. As mentioned, this approach stands in stark contrast to that adopted in most continental European countries, where the law of nationality inspired by the principle of personality prevails. Under that model, even if, for example, a Moroccan national has spent most of his adult life in Belgium, the juridical resolution of his family law problems will still be governed by Moroccan law if he married and procreated in Morocco.

Suffice it to say, introducing the principle of personality into a system that has always been based on the principle of territoriality is no easy task. Anthropological and comparative law literature has long highlighted the systemic problems raised by enthusiastic, but naive, legal transplants. Interestingly, this literature came out of the realization that several norms and institutions transplanted by colonial powers into their colonies simply did not work once transplanted, although they achieved the objectives ascribed to them in the state of origin.

It is clear that the management of complex situations of legal pluralism in many non-Western societies provides an interesting counterpoint to modern Western practices and food for thought for Western states.[63] At the very least, there was an attempt to take stock of legal pluralism while Western states were ensconced in their fantasy of statist legal hegemony, when not actually devoting their energies to eliminate vectors of legal pluralism.

However, it seems to me that we are currently witnessing the repetition, but in reverse, of this naive conception of legal transplants, as evinced by the liberal reference currently made to foreign legal models which, for centuries, have been founded upon the principle of personality. Indeed, joint governance or personal federalism models universalize, by abstracting and theorizing them, particular paradigms that, for socio-historical reasons, may be perfectly adapted to meet the needs arising out of their original environment, but which could not fit so easily into a different context.

More specifically, major explicit or implicit sources of inspiration for these models nowadays come from Israel or India, where the principle of personality plays a central role in the legal order. Some advocates of these models, even when they explicitly recognize the legal regime of a particular state as their source of inspiration, purport to export them because they represent in their view a normative ideal, one that is pluralist rather than monist, as far as the legal management of ethno-religious pluralism is concerned. Clearly, not all of them are naive or seek to hide the more or less 'disagreeable facts'[64] of context.[65] Moreover, a normative inquiry into a concept or idea does not have to account for every contextual variable, as the

---

[63] On this, see W Menski, 'Beyond Europe' in Örücü and Nelken (n 47 above) 189.
[64] On such facts, see M Weber, *La profession et la vocation de savant* (Paris: La Découverte, 2003) 96.
[65] For example, Shachar (n 15 above) 6.

purpose of such endeavour is precisely not descriptive or sociological. However, scholars, irrespective of their discipline, are not alone in contemplating potential transplants of personality-based models into environments where the territoriality principle prevails. Activists and politicians also contemplate such transplantation, and this is where raising consciousness about the pitfalls of legal transplants grounded on potentially valid reasons, such as intercultural justice, or, less positively, on political expediency, becomes especially important. Whenever talking about further institutionalizing 'Shari'a councils' or formally recognizing Shari'a courts the power to issue legally binding awards, epistemic awareness is needed, not only to better evaluate the normative dimensions of such decisions but also to ensure the efficient implementation of the decisions made.

I do not want to suggest that such an implementation is absolutely impossible, nor do I wish to ascribe joint governance or personal federalism models to their historical origins or to confine them to the countries from which they initially emanate.[66] As trite as it may seem, my point is that even if some non-Western models represent a legal pluralist's normative ideal, context matters, and there is no evidence that transplanting such models, or variations of them, in a legal environment where the principle of territoriality prevails, would succeed. To blind oneself to this possibility of failure evinces, in my view, the 'reverse orientalism' that permeates many contemporary discourses on the management of diversity.

Three decades ago, Edward Said coined the term 'orientalism' to designate 'a style of thought based upon an ontological and epistemological distinction made between "the Orient" and (most of the time) "the Occident"'.[67] It is often characterized by a propensity to depict Islam and Arabs as a monolithic entity defined around stereotypical—and sometimes conflicting—characteristics such as backwardness, violence, or sensuality. In any event, it implies an 'exoticization' of the Other. In contrast, 'reverse orientalism' has been used to describe either a process under which non-Western scholars provide an idealized—and essentialized—representation of non-Western cultures to distinguish them from Western cultures,[68] or a process under which Western scholars attribute a set of positive values to essentialized non-Western cultures, for example 'in order to contrast the recent dynamic progress of Asian development with the stagnation and social disorganization of contemporary Western economies and societies'.[69] The form of reverse orientalism to which I am referring is closer to the latter definition. I thus take reverse orientalism in a comparative law setting to designate the epistemological obstacle upon which Western scholars or public actors stumble when they uncritically promote

[66] On the logics of ascription to origins, see C Castoriadis, *La montée de l'insignifiance: Les carrefours du labyrinthe IV* (Paris: Éditions du Seuil, 1996) 234.

[67] E Said, *Orientalism* (New York: Vintage Books, 1979) 2.

[68] G Khiabany, 'De-Westernizing media theory, or reverse Orientalism: "Islamic communication" as theorized by Hamid Mowlana' (2003) 25 *Media, Culture and Society* 415, 415.

[69] M Hill, '"Asian values" as reverse Orientalism: Singapore' (2000) 41(2) *Asia Pacific Viewpoint* 177, 178.

the adoption of non-Western legal regimes to 'solve' problems perceived within Western legal systems—either due to an abstract fascination for an exotic, decontextualized, and dehistoricized legal Other or to a disenchantment with Western legal systems deemed to be irredeemably blinded by their statist, monist, and universalist biases.

It is one thing to highlight the dangers of reverse orientalism when reflecting on what to do with the idea of Shari'a courts in the West; it is quite another to say that all projects seeking to address this idea through a reliance on joint governance or personal federalism are doomed to fail. There is indeed no evidence that all such projects would not succeed. Moreover, for all sorts of reasons, they may succeed better in state A than in state B, even if both states privilege the principle of territoriality. Thus, the mastery of contextual variables relating to the normative proposition to be transplanted, as well as to the circumstances of the legal system in which the transplant is to take place, remains a *sine qua non* condition for a complex approach to Shari'a courts' recognition claims. In other words, abstract philosophical considerations about some ideal state of justice are important, but blatantly insufficient to take stock of such claims.

D. Concluding Remarks

In lieu of a conclusion, I will make a few observations, which have methodological and normative implications.

First, any investigation into the acceptability of formalizing the recognition of religious courts within a liberal state needs to acknowledge that the relation between state and religion does not follow a single, universal model applicable to every liberal state. In addition, the nature and scope of recognition claims may vary significantly. As a result, overly abstract discourses about 'religious courts' recognition claims in liberal states' may be misleading. It is thus critically important to evaluate such claims—and the country-specific expressions of legal traditions—*in concreto*. We might very well find that a legal reform focused on the formal, positive law, recognition of Shari'a courts will prove acceptable in liberal state A but not in its neighbour, liberal state B.[70]

As noted, idealizations of all stripes generally tend to act as epistemological obstacles in attempting to grasp the complexities of a given situation and, more specifically, of the feasibility of legal transplants. This warning against idealization applies equally to the evaluation of secular legal systems and religious legal systems. For instance, when ascertaining the advantages and disadvantages of institutionalizing faith-based decision-making, one can hardly deny that state secular systems do not always fare very well when it comes to concretely protecting the rights and

---

[70] R A Macdonald and A Popovici, 'Le catéchisme de l'Islamophobie', in M Jézéquel (ed), *La justice à l'épreuve de la diversité culturelle* (2007) 54–55.

interests of vulnerable parties, or, more broadly, the rights of minorities. At the same time, one must acknowledge that even though most religious traditions are ideologically plural, it may very well be that at some point in time, it will be more difficult to voice either a conservative or liberal conception of a particular tradition. For example, although intellectually sustainable feminist interpretations of Islamic norms exist, these interpretations currently tend to be sociologically marginal and marginalized. At the very least, they are far from dominant. This finding points to the need to take into account power relations within secular *and* religious legal systems.

Secondly, if a decision is made to give binding legal powers (in the positivist sense) to a religious court, it is important that this court be embedded in a normative system within which it will interact with state institutions, and where religious norms must respond to the requirements of fundamental secular norms. This is what joint-governance models seek, notably through contingent accommodation schemes,[71] primarily in view of protecting the rights of vulnerable parties. Without presuming that religious courts cannot adapt the norms they apply to the basic requirements of modern liberal states in terms of equality and liberty, one must acknowledge that a certain number of such norms are hardly compatible with the realization of these values. This is not only true for Islam, but it is not Islamophobic to say that it is true for Islam. At the same time, it is important to recognize that outsiders to a particular religious or cultural group 'should not be too quick to jump to the conclusion that every practice that deviates from theirs constitutes [an] abuse'.[72]

Indeed, the perceived 'foreignness' of a norm or practice does not make it per se incompatible with a liberal state's most fundamental norms. Nevertheless, religious legal systems must accept some level of acculturation and adapt, to some extent, their norms and procedures in such a way that they become minimally intelligible from the perspective of the state. In other words, they must demonstrate their 'juridical relevance'.[73] Under that view, legal orders which recognize each other as mutually 'relevant' are expected to establish institutional relations, at least to some extent.[74] They are thus willing to open themselves to the possibility of a reciprocal acculturation, a compromise that is recognized and accepted as inevitable, if not entirely 'normal'. Given that the state remains a dominant player in liberal democracies, it must be acknowledged that this vision arguably imposes more constraints on religious legal orders than on the state itself. It is very difficult to see how this could be avoided, both in terms of *realpolitik* and from a normative standpoint. However, I would argue that modern liberal states must also reform their justice systems in such a way that they become more sensitive and hospitable to minority

---

[71] Shachar (n 15 above) 88–116.

[72] D G Réaume, 'Justice Between Cultures: Autonomy and the Protection of Cultural Affiliation' (1995) 29 *University of British Columbia Law Review* 117, 140.

[73] S Romano, *L'ordre juridique* (Paris: Dalloz, 1975) 106.

[74] Given its centrality, the state is always relevant to a certain extent even though some citizens structure their lives so as to avoid encounters with its legal order as much as possible.

cultures, including religious ones. To become meaningful, and thus legitimate, for members of minority cultural groups, state justice must be perceived as genuinely inclusive. Unfortunately, this is far from always the case.[75]

Thirdly, emphasizing the need to ensure the compatibility of faith-based adjudication with fundamental state norms implies that responses to religious courts' recognition claims can hardly lead to the implementation of juridical regimes characterized by their strong legal pluralism. More likely, the legal pluralism that will arise as a result of the acceptance of such claims will be dialogical, and rather weak.[76] Joint governance schemes emphasizing contingent accommodation offer a good illustration of this. Personal federalism regimes may also meet this expectation, even though the level of communal autonomy granted is broader.[77] However, in a federative context, it is arguably better to conceive this autonomy as implying a form of heteronomy. Indeed, federalism offers a framework under which citizens can hold many allegiances, prioritize them according to their beliefs (religious or not) and the circumstances, and change that order of priority if need be. At the same time, federalism discourages monolithic, self-contained, and essentialized identities. It encourages the development of representations of oneself as another, to paraphrase philosopher Paul Ricoeur.[78]

My last observation relates to the paradoxical dependence of some legal pluralist views on positivist-formalist conceptions of law. As already mentioned, in spite of the recurrent announcement of its imminent death, the state is still well and alive and remains a central player in most relations of interlegality. More specifically, in contexts marked by the politics of recognition, the state, through the law that it produces, is used as a tool by which social identities obtain formal institutional standing. Philosopher Marcel Gauchet observes in this respect that:–

[c]ontrary to what is in their essence to tell about themselves, communities of identification do not have a prior, spontaneous, existence, that they then seek to have acknowledged by others and global society. They constitute themselves in their distinct identity, they assert themselves in their private specificity vis-à-vis the public sphere and depending on what type of recognition they wish to obtain from that public sphere. In view of defining and reassuring themselves, they need the state outside of which they want to situate themselves and from which they seek recognition of their externality. They only exist in the mode of representation.[79]

---

[75] For a broad-ranging examination of this question, see P Noreau, *Le droit en partage: le monde juridique face à la diversité ethnoculturelle* (Montreal: Éditions Thémis, 2003).

[76] One could argue that accommodation strategies seeking to implement models conducive of dialogical pluralism could, in the long term, lead to the development of a more liberal branch of Islam in the West, which would be markedly different from that practised elsewhere.

[77] It could be argued that for the 'federal' characterization to remain, the state's monitoring of religious communities' self-governing institutions should be minimal.

[78] P Ricoeur, *Soi-même comme un autre* (Paris: Éditions du Seuil, 1990).

[79] See M Gauchet, *La religion dans la démocratie: Parcours de la laïcité* (Paris: Gallimard, 1998) 161 (author translation).

Religious courts' recognition claims, whether or not Shari'a-based, provide evidence of both the resilience and centrality of the state. But if, for a moment, we leave aside state-centered biases and acknowledge that recognition may still occur, in society, without any formal juridification process, then the question of establishing a regime of joint governance or of personal federalism takes a different twist. Discussing theoretical accounts explaining phenomena of legal diffusion, William Twining correctly observes that many such accounts rely on a number of naive and questionable assumptions, one being that 'the standard case of a reception is import-export between *countries*', another being that 'the main agents of export and import are *governments*', and a third being that 'reception involves *formal* enactment or adoption *at a particular moment of time*'.[80] If we return to the hypothesis that the implementation of joint governance or personal federalism models would constitute a form of legal transplant in most Western states, and if we forget about the state, we could construe the *current* existence of Shari'a courts in the West, even when they are not formally recognized by the state, as evidence of an already successful transplant. It is one that flows from a migration of individuals, ideas, and reasoning templates,[81] irrespective of any *country* of origin or reception, one that has been implemented absent any formal *governmental* action, and one that did not require any *formal* enactment at any time. Indeed, when we examine the behaviour of the religious believers who would constitute the clientele of formally recognized religious courts and who already consult their *imam* or rabbi on a regular basis, it is hard to escape the conclusion that, for them, a form of personal federalism is already a fact of life. Even if the principle of personality is not formally enshrined in black-letter law, it is wilfully acted upon and lived on a daily basis by agents who accept it and who, concretely, live most of their lives as if the territorial state did not exist. For them, federalism essentially becomes a psychological phenomenon.[82] Whether the state can, or should, do anything about that is the subject of another discussion.

[80] W Twining, *General Jurisprudence: Understanding Law from a Global Perspective* (Cambridge: Cambridge University Press, 2009) 270.

[81] On the migration of reasoning templates, see J-F Gaudreault-DesBiens, 'Underlying Principles and the Migration of Reasoning Templates: A Trans-Systemic Reading of the *Quebec Secession Reference*' in S Choudhry (ed), *The Migration of Constitutional Ideas* (Cambridge: Cambridge University Press, 2006) 178.

[82] On this conception of federalism as a psychological phenomenon that exists irrespective of institutions, structures, and formal norms, see R A Macdonald, 'Kaleidoscopic Federalism' in J-F Gaudreault-DesBiens and F Gélinas (eds), *The Moods and States of Federalism: Governance, Identity, and Methodology/Le fédéralisme dans tous ses états—Gouvernance, identité et méthodologie* (Brussels and Cowansville, QC: Bruylant and Éditions Yvon Blais, 2005) 261.

11

Natural Law, Democracy, and Shari'a

J Budziszewski

Should the West Accommodate to Islam?

The suggestion that Western liberal democracies accommodate[1] Islamic religious courts and Shari'a religious law might be taken in various ways. First, it might be taken as purely prudential in motive. People of different religions are just too different, the proposer might say, to live amicably under the same laws and courts. If Muslims were granted a degree of juridical autonomy, then we would all get along better. The arrangement would be much like federalism, but along religious rather than geographical lines.

This argument is surprisingly weak. Conceivably there are circumstances in which juridical autonomy for religious minorities would be the last, best hope for those who seek peace, but these circumstances would have to be desperate indeed. The contrast between Shari'a and English law is much greater than between, say, the laws of Virginia and Delaware, and they lie not only in detail but in basic philosophy. It is hard to see why separation into distinct jurisdictions would not undermine the sense of common cause among the citizens, making amicable relations among them more difficult rather than less. Besides, if Muslims were granted juridical autonomy with their own Shari'a courts, whose interpretation of Shari'a would these courts follow? Wouldn't it be necessary to establish separate jurisdictions for Sunnis and Shi'ites—at least for each of the one main Shi'a and four main Sunni schools of jurisprudence? The population would be broken into not two parts but six. But why stop there? If separate jurisdictions were established for the several varieties of Muslims, it would be difficult to explain why they should not also be established for, say, the several varieties of Jews—or is it only that their youth are not so angry? What about Christians? Notwithstanding a few decrepit 'establishments' like the Church of England, it has been a long time since anyone considered the Western democracies Christian—not to mention the fact that if the legal status of an organization such as the Church of England has any effect at all, it makes the situation of local Christians who do not belong to it more awkward,

---

[1] For discussion of the meaning of 'accommodation', see the Appendix to this chapter.

not less. How many Christian jurisdictions would we need? There is only one Catholic Church, but there are nine Orthodox patriarchates and tens of thousands of Protestant denominations. No doubt the prospect of juridical autonomy would make schism more attractive than ever.

And what about other religions? Would Theosophy count? Would Baha'i? While we are at it, what do we *mean* by religions? To be entitled to courts of their own, would believers have to believe specifically in God? If the argument for autonomy is prudential, that would be strange. Perhaps, as the US Supreme Court suggested in 1965, the juridical meaning of religion should be any 'sincere and meaningful' belief that 'occupies a place in the life of its possessor parallel to that filled by the orthodox belief in God' of groups that do believe in God.[2] Curiouser and curiouser! But then is Marxism a religion? How about utilitarianism? Perhaps the New Age sects? An especially thorny question is whether a separate jurisdiction is needed for Secular Humanists. The first *Humanist Manifesto*, in 1933, declared their creed religious; the second, in 1973, was silent on the subject; and the third, in 2000, not only denied that the creed is religious, but was indignant with anyone who said that it is. Does this show that Secular Humanism has 'evolved', or has there been a schism between New Secular Humanists and Old Regulars? Should an autonomous jurisdiction be set up just for the Olds? But then the News might be restive. Should the News be allowed courts too? Or is this unnecessary because they already get their way with the law?

Nor is the analogy between religious and geographical 'federalism' very close. How would the polity determine who belonged to each religious jurisdiction? Would juridical identity be determined by birth, ethnicity, profession of faith, simple declaration, or something else? Suppose juridical identity were immutable; what then would become of the liberty to change religions? Suppose it were *not* immutable; how then could individuals be prevented from 'gaming' the system? For example, could a man evade the bigamy laws of the majority jurisdiction by transferring to the Muslim jurisdiction, then, later, dissolve his second, third, and fourth marriages by transferring back to the majority jurisdiction? Of course legislators could set up barriers against change of jurisdiction—for example, one could forbid conversion, or allow people to convert, but require them to live according to the laws of the *former* religion in which they say they no longer believe. Needless to say, however, such solutions would merely produce new problems of their own. And if the system could be 'gamed', then wouldn't *de jure* recognition of different legal norms for different religious jurisdictions be de facto equivalent to the adoption of a single legal norm for the whole nation? It would seem that the answer is 'yes'; not only in marriage law but in every branch of law the more permissive of the various available standards would inevitably 'win'. (This also shows why jurisdictional

---

[2] *United States v Seeger*, 380 US 163, 165–166, 85 S Ct 850 (1965). The question in *Seeger* was the meaning of legal exemption from military conscription on grounds of a conscientiously held 'belief in a relation to a Supreme Being'.

autonomy for religious groups is not an authentic application of subsidiarity.[3]) If the marriage law of the majority jurisdiction were monogamous but the marriage law of the minority jurisdiction were polygamous, then the de facto norm for the whole country would be polygamy. If the marriage law of the minority jurisdiction were polygamous but the marriage law of the majority jurisdiction became 'polyamorous', God forbid, then the de facto norm for the whole country would be polyamory.

The prudential argument also assumes that the new constitutional arrangement is stable. This in turn supposes that religious minorities want nothing more than to be left alone, so that, once granted juridical autonomy, they will be content. Doubtless some religious minorities want nothing more than to be left alone, but would this not depend on the actual teachings of their religions? One observer writes that although Shari'a allows truces between Muslims and non-Muslims, such interruptions in *jihād* are but a means to an end; the fundamental teaching is 'a canonically obligatory perpetual state of war until the whole world is either converted or subjugated'.[4] If this interpretation is correct—I will return to the question later—then Muslims might accept juridical autonomy as a new stage of the truce between themselves and the non-Muslim majority. On the other hand, they might view it as the beginning of the end of the truce; that is, establishment of Shari'a in a single jurisdiction might present itself as the first step toward its imposition on everyone. In fact, the practical difficulties to which I alluded in the previous paragraph would almost compel such a step, because a legal system that can be 'gamed' is not a legal system at all.

Considering the weakness of the prudential argument, the suggestion that the Western liberal democracies accommodate Shari'a probably owes most of the attention it has received to considerations of morality, not prudence. For the typical 'hairy lefty',[5] it simply seems *wrong* not to grant juridical autonomy to Muslims. The implicit touchstone of justice seems to be something like equal treatment of all religions. Because they are not able to live under their own laws and courts, they are not treated equally.

But in the absolute sense intended, equal treatment is logically impossible. In the first place, not all religions believe in equal treatment. Shari'a, in fact, is quite explicit that different religions should *not* be treated equally. Paradoxically,

---

[3] Subsidiarity is the principle that 'it is an injustice and at the same time a grave evil and disturbance of right order to assign to a greater and higher association what lesser and subordinate organizations can do. For every social activity ought of its very nature to furnish help to the members of the body social, and never destroy and absorb them'. In particular, the state should confine itself to those functions that smaller associations, such as families, neighborhoods, and religious communities, simply cannot accomplish on their own: Pius XI, *Quadragesimo Anno* (Encyclical letter, 1931) [79]–[80]. This principle does not mean that each form of association is entitled to its own law; what it means is that the law should respect the moral work of each form of association. The overarching framework is the natural law.

[4] B Lewis, *The Multiple Identities of the Middle East* (New York: Schocken Books, 1998) 122.

[5] I allude to a self-deprecating quip by the Archbishop of Canterbury, who includes himself in that tribe. My aim, however, is to characterize the intellectual tendency of 'hairy lefties' in general.

then, insistence on equal treatment of all religions looks like just another kind of religious imperialism, privileging those religions which do believe in equal treatment over those which do not. In the second place, even if we restrict attention to religions that do believe in equal treatment, the fact remains that every view of equality is *some* view of equality. Consider, for example, equality of religious liberty. To one group, this may mean that no one may change his religion; to another, that anyone may change his religion, but no one may proselytize; to still another, that anyone may change his religion, and anyone may proselytize. Each of these three conceptions applies a uniform standard to everyone, but in each case the uniform standard is different. Clearly, to implement one view of equality rather than another is not to treat different views of equality equally, so in yet another way, different religions would fare differently. There is no such thing as being 'equal in every way'; to implement equality in one sense one must bring about inequality in another.

Moreover, a certain general view of the attainment of the truth about God and his moral requirements is usually presupposed even by 'hairy lefty' ideologies that do propose treating all religions equally. This general view is more or less agnostic; it supposes that different religions should be treated differently because they are equally in the dark about religious truth. Concerning just how dark the darkness is, different species of agnostics disagree: rigorists consider it as black as pitch, moderates hold that it is more like the thicker sort of soup. Agnostics of the former type view religious truth as utterly resistant to rational inquiry. By contrast, those of the latter type view it only as relatively resistant to it; while conceding that people may reasonably disagree about many things, they view religious truth as somehow *more* open to reasonable disagreement than the many other things about which Western liberal democracies make decisions. Presumably these other things include such easy and uncontroversial questions as how to achieve peace among nations, how to regulate their economies, and how to induce their agnostic citizens to start having children again.

The crux of the matter is that no matter which variety of agnosticism we consider, it is not theologically neutral. In fact, agnosticism closely resembles the religious view called fideism, for both fideists and agnostics agree that faith and reason are strangers to each other. The difference is that fideists view themselves as siding with faith, agnostics, usually, with reason. What makes the resemblance so important is that not all religions are fideistic—a point that often comes as a surprise to 'hairy lefties', if it is not lost on them altogether. Catholic Christianity, for example, is *not* fideistic. To be sure, it holds that certain revealed truths, such as the Trinity and the Incarnation, exceed the capacity of the human mind to have known without special assistance. Even so, in Christianity God is understood as the *Logos*, or Divine Mind, whose wisdom is reflected in the created order. This fact makes that order accessible to the finite intellect of human beings, who are made in His image. Consequently, Christianity views faith and reason not as strangers, but as complementary to each other—in the striking image of John Paul II, as the two wings of a bird, both of them are needed for flight.[6] Since not all religions are fideistic, the 'hairy lefty' is placed in the absurd position of defending his policy of treating all religions equally on grounds that fideistic religions are *right* about rational inquiry, and that non-fideistic religions are *wrong*. To say it yet again: to base public policy on such considerations is plainly not to treat all religions equally.

An even deeper problem is that if the agnostic says that religious truth is especially resistant to rational inquiry, he contradicts himself, for to know God's rational unknowability would be to know something about Him. Indeed, it would be to know a great deal about Him. First, one would have to know that even if He exists, He is infinitely remote, because otherwise one could not be so sure that knowledge about Him were rationally inaccessible. Secondly, one would have to know that even if He exists, He is unconcerned with human beings, because otherwise one would expect Him to have provided the means for humans to know Him. Finally, one would have to know that this hypothetical being is completely unlike the Biblical portrayal of Him, because in that portrayal He does care about us and has already provided such means—not only through revelation, but even, in part, through the order of Creation. So, in the end, the so-called agnostic must claim to know quite a number of things about God just to prop up his claim to not knowing. The problem is that, on his assumptions, he cannot rationally justify any of these things.

But what if the agnostics were right? What if religious truth really were specially resistant to rational inquiry; what then? Even then it would not follow, as the 'hairy lefty' thinks, that different religions should be treated equally. The consistent agnostic would have to be agnostic on this question too; he would have to concede that there is simply no rational way to decide how different religions should be treated. There might be non-rational ways, such as waiting for a bolt of illumination; one could try that. Of course the method would also require a jolt of subjective confidence that the bolt of illumination had come from on high, rather than, for example, from an electrical disturbance in the amygdala of the brain. Alternatively, one might say, 'Since I have not yet been granted a bolt of non-rational illumination, I will proceed on the basis of the things I know by purely rational means, such as the fact that I want to get along'. But that too would be irrational. After all, some religions hold that there are more important things than getting along. Others hold that reason is a 'whore', not to be trusted.[7] The agnostic is proceeding as though he knew that such claims were false, but on his premises,

---

[6] 'Faith and reason are like two wings on which the human spirit rises to the contemplation of truth; and God has placed in the human heart a desire to know the truth—in a word, to know himself—so that, by knowing and loving God, men and women may also come to the fullness of truth about themselves': John Paul II, *Fides et Ratio* (Encyclical letter, 1998) preface, citing Exodus 33:18, Psalm 27:8-9 and 63:2-3, John 14:8, and 1 John 3:2.

[7] 'As a young man must resist lust and an old man avarice, so reason is *by nature* a harmful whore. But she shall not harm me, if only I resist her. Ah, but she is so comely and glittering': M Luther, 'Last Sermon in Wittenberg' in J B Doberstein and H T Lehmann (eds), *Luther's Works* (Philadelphia: Muhlenberg Press, 1959) Vol 51, 371, 376 (emphasis added).

he has no rational grounds for such a strong conclusion. He accepts it, if he will pardon the expression, on faith—which he rejects.

Should Islam Accommodate to the West?

The contrasting suggestion is usually taken to be that Islam should accommodate itself to Western liberal democracy. But there are two different ways of taking this suggestion. According to one way, Islam must be talked into betraying itself. Though the idea is rarely expressed openly, to anyone who can read between the lines of contemporary discussions it all but shouts its presence. Shortly I will propose a different way of taking the suggestion, but first let us consider what opponents would view as the betrayal program. At least as I read between the lines, betrayalists share the following suppositions.

First, they suppose that liberal democracy is good. What this usually means for them is that it is good *as it is*—good in its present, morally relativistic form. I do not suggest that the citizens of the Western liberal democracies are all relativists, but even where they are not, their rulers tend to be.[8] Of course there is a paradox in viewing relativism about values as valuable. One may seek to escape the paradox by saying that one's preference for relativistic social arrangements reflects not a judgment about objective value, but merely a personal choice. However, such a move only pushes the paradox one step back. Rather than supposing that nothing is objectively good, it takes the act of choosing as objectively good. Choices, for so long as they last, are justified just by being choices.

Secondly, betrayalists suppose that revealed religion is bad. The usual view is that claims of access to divine revelation are dangerous to religious liberty and antithetical to government by the people. This simply ignores the testimony of history, which shows that throughout Western tradition the dominant arguments for religious liberty and for something like what we call liberal democracy were not only religious in nature but closely entwined with divine revelation. As St Hilary of Poitiers writes, God does not desire unwilling worship or forced repentance; Isidore of Pelusium agrees, adding that salvation is won not by force but by gentle persuasion.[9] According to St Thomas Aquinas, scripture and reason agree that the best form of government is 'partly kingdom, since there is one at the head of all; partly aristocracy, in so far as a number of persons are set in authority; partly democracy, ie, government by the people, in so far as the rulers can be

---

[8] As sociologist of religion Peter C Berger is said to have remarked of my own country, if India is the most religious country and Sweden the least, then America is a nation of Indians ruled by Swedes. Attribution by Richard John Neuhaus, 'The Public Square' (June/July 2002) 124 *First Things: A Monthly Journal of Religion and Public Life* 75, 90.

[9] Hilary of Poitiers, *To Constantius*; Isidore of Pelusium, *Epistles*, 2.129. For more extensive quotations and discussion, see J Budziszewski, *The Line Through the Heart: Natural Law as Fact, Theory, and Sign of Contradiction* (Wilmington: ISI Books, 2009) Ch 10.

chosen from the people, and the people have the right to choose their rulers'.[10] Unfortunately, betrayalists associate liberal democracy and religious liberty so closely with their relativism that the non-relativist origins of these ideals become invisible to them.

Thirdly, betrayalists suppose that since religious believers are unlikely to abandon their religions, what liberal democracy requires is a way to tame revelation, to make it into a wax nose, something that can be refashioned into whatever shape is desired. If Christianity appears friendly to liberal democracy today, they think, it is only because in Christianity the waxen metamorphosis has finally been accomplished; what remains is for Islam to follow suit. A case could certainly be made for this view. Consider for example Exodus 19:12–13, which reads in part, 'whoever touches the mountain [of God] shall be put to death; no hand shall touch him, but he shall be stoned or shot; whether beast or man, he shall not live'. Gregory Nazianzen, one of the Fathers of the Church, takes 'touching the mountain' to include all expressions of contempt for revealed truth whatsoever. His commentary on the passage breathes fire: to anyone who would 'tear sound doctrine to pieces by his misrepresentations', he issues the warning, 'let him stand yet afar off and withdraw from the Mount, or he shall be stoned and crushed, and shall perish miserably in his wickedness'. Yet by stoning, Gregory does not mean literal stoning, for he immediately explains that 'to those who are like wild beasts', the meaning of 'stones' is simply 'true and sound discourses'.[11] 'There', says the betrayalist, 'you see? Through sufficiently creative exegesis, Christianity can push revelation into any shape it pleases'.

If one knew nothing else about patristics but these few lines, Gregory's interpretation might indeed seem to make the Exodus passage into a wax nose. In the overall context of patristic exegesis, however, the appearance of arbitrariness disappears. Whether or not one agrees with them, writers like Gregory were not playing hermeneutical games. What lay behind their non-literal methods was the conviction that the Incarnation of Christ inaugurated a new and final phase of salvation history. The situation of Israel in Old Testament times was temporary and unique: alone among the nations of the earth, it was the nation from whom God would reveal His anointed one. But now the Messiah has come, and the gates of the covenant have been opened to the Gentiles. Torah, then, can no longer apply to the Church in the way that it applied to the Jews. Yet it is unthinkable that it has no meaning for the Church at all, for 'the word of God is living and active',[12] not like a human word, which briefly sounds and then passes into stillness. God, in whose hands all history lies, can surely arrange that His living word communicates a partial truth to Israel in one age, and a fuller truth to the Church

---

[10]   T Aquinas, *Summa Theologica* I-II, Q 105, Art 1.
[11]   Gregory of Nazianzen, *Second Theological Oration.*
[12]   Hebrews 4:12 (Revised Standard Version).

in a later one. The special case has elapsed, but the eternal realities, both spiritual and moral, endure.

Let us admit this much: the wax nose is a pretty good description of the revisionist biblical scholarship favoured by some on the left. There is no tradition behind it, as there was behind Gregory's hermeneutics. It is merely an accommodation to the shibboleths of the day, and it changes as often as they do. But revisionism of this sort is not about reconciling Christians to liberal democracy as such; it is about reconciling them to the present, relativist condition of the liberal democracies. Moreover, as a program for sustaining a flourishing social order, it seems to be a loser. Those liberal democracies which have gone farthest in the relativist direction are busily committing demographic suicide. Apparently it is true that to lose God is to lose man as well.

One could hardly expect sincere Muslims (or for that matter sincere Christians or Jews) to regard rejectionism as a good idea. The project of turning revelation into a wax nose can advance only by craft and disguise on the part of its proponents, and naive credulity on the part of those whom they seek to influence. It is a means by which an irreligious cultural elite pull the strings of a citizenry that, despite everything, retains vestiges of faith.

Should Both Accommodate to Natural Law?

There is yet another way to take the suggestion that Islam undertake an accommodation: let both Islam and the nations of the West accommodate themselves together to classical natural law—the tradition in which liberal democracy had its remote origins and that also has strong historical connections with Christianity, Judaism, and, at least in the Middle Ages, Islam. Insofar as man is a reasoning, truth-seeking creature, insofar as rightly developed reason is characterized not as bare analytical intelligence but as creaturely awareness and respect, natural law offers a common ground among all human beings. To propose such a common ground would be to abandon the shibboleths of all the 'hairy' tribe and take guidance from our shared creaturehood in a shared Creation, the moral order of which is accessible to reason. The appeal of this suggestion for Islam would be the hope it offered, not to betray itself, but to realize more fully its aspiration of submission to the Mind of God. The appeal of it for the West would be the rediscovery of its non-relativist roots, cut off from which, it is dying.

This way of taking the suggestion has a history. Natural law thinkers were no strangers to social pluralism. The 'hairy lefty' assumes that ancient and medieval thinkers were attracted to the idea of natural law because they had not yet conceived the enormous variety of possible conceptions of right and wrong. On the contrary, 'knowledge of the indefinitely large variety of notions of right and wrong is so far from being incompatible with the idea of natural right that it is the essential condition for the emergence of that idea: realization of the variety of notions of right is *the* incentive for the quest for natural right'.[13]

The classical natural law tradition must be distinguished from the thinned and flattened versions of natural law theory that emerged from the Enlightenment (and are tied up with our problems). According to their proponents, epitomized by Thomas Hobbes, civic order is based on a social covenant or contract in which we abandon the state of nature and reconcile ourselves to law merely as a desperate expedient to escape the greatest evil, death. Classical natural lawyers would reject every element of this view.

In the first place, for the unfortunate expression 'state of nature' to make any sense whatsoever, it would have to refer to the condition in which our natural potentiality can unfold, the condition in which beings of our kind can flourish. As it turns out, the condition in which that can happen is not anarchy but society, wherein we take counsel together about the common good under the rule of law, a law moreover that respects the multitude of forms of association that the various facets of human association require in order to blossom—not only or even mainly the state, but marriages, families, neighborhoods, friendships, and bodies of worship. In the second place, death is not the agreed-upon greatest evil that Hobbes took it to be. It may be that everyone dreads death, but it is also true that almost everyone views some things as worse than death. Aristotle hit the mark when he wrote that although the political community may come into existence for the sake of staying alive, it exists for living well. In the third place, law is not a necessary evil but a requirement for our good. To achieve beauty, the painter must submit to the laws of human perception, the laws of paint and canvass, and the laws of beauty themselves, as they gradually reveal themselves to the mind of man. So it is in every domain of life, including the organization of society. The right kind of discipline is not the enemy of freedom but its condition.

The central claim of the classical tradition can be expressed in just a few sentences. Law may be defined as an ordinance of reason, for the common good, made by legitimate public authority, and promulgated.[14] Nature may be conceived as an ensemble of things with particular natures, and a thing's nature may be thought of as the design imparted to it by the Creator—as a purpose impressed upon it by the divine art, so that it is directed to a determinate end.[15] The claim of the tradition is that in exactly these senses, natural law is both (1) true law, and (2) truly expressive of nature. Consider the natural law forbidding murder. It is not an arbitrary whim, but a rule which the mind can grasp as right. It serves not some special interest, but the universal good. Its author has care of the universe, for He created it. And it is not a secret rule, for He has so arranged His Creation—including the design of the created moral intellect—that every rational being knows about it.

---

[13] L Strauss, *Natural Right and History* (Chicago: University of Chicago Press, 1953) 10.
[14] *Summa Theologica* I-II, Q 90, Art 4.
[15] T Aquinas, *Commentary on Aristotle's Physics* Bk 2, Lect 14.

Has Islam Room for Natural Law?

An Islamic thinker who is writing about the natural law would of course draw from different resources than would a thinker from my own tradition. As he contemplated the moral order of Creation, a Christian thinks of scriptural passages like the following:

[F]rom the greatness and beauty of created things comes a corresponding perception of their Creator.... if [men] had the power to know so much that they could investigate the world, how did they fail to find sooner the Lord of all these things?[16]

When Gentiles who have not the law do by nature what they law requires... [t]hey show that what the law requires is written on their hearts, while their conscience also bears witness and their conflicting thoughts accuse or perhaps excuse them ... [17]

From his own scriptures, the Muslim finds a parallel for both of these reflections:

We shall show them Our signs in the horizons and in themselves until it is clear to them that it is the truth.[18]

A certain difficulty is posed by the question of how these 'signs' are to be interpreted. From medieval times to the present, some Muslim thinkers have argued that God acts not only directly, but also through secondary causes, or *ashab*. In other words, He endowed created reality with an intrinsic order of its own, both moral and physical. Natural laws are simply descriptions of this order. The many who are influenced by the medieval theologian Abu al-Hasan al-Ash'ari deny the existence of secondary causes. In their view, God produces each 'sign' we witness in the created world by a direct and unmediated exercise of His will. It may seem that the latter view is incompatible with natural law. However, the question is more complex, for order in created reality might arise not from secondary causes, but simply from the fact that the will of God habitually moves in certain regular ways. The question, then, is not whether God acts through secondary causes, but whether, if not, His will is rational and regular. If it is not, then natural law is impossible—but so, it would seem, is Shari'a! To an outsider, then, it seems that any view that would make Shari'a believable would make natural law believable too.

Just as a Christian natural law thinker also tries to be faithful to sacred scripture and apostolic tradition, so of course a Muslim natural law thinker would try to be faithful to the legal prescriptions of the Qur'an and the traditions about the Prophet, called *hadith*. However, Shari'a is not a simple transcription of these sources; it could not be, for the Qur'an and *hadith* do not provide rules for all

---

[16] Wisdom 13:5, 9 (Revised Standard Version, Catholic Edition).

[17] Romans 2:14-15 (Revised Standard Version).

[18] Fussilat (Qur'an 41) 53, cited in the open letter of Muslim scholars to Pope Benedict XVI (19 October 2006) in response to the papal address at the University of Regensburg, 'Three Stages in the Program of De-Hellenization' (12 September 2006).

possible circumstances. Rather, Shari'a is an interpretation and elaboration of these sources, much as *halakhah*, or Jewish law, is an interpretation and elaboration of Torah. In a certain sense, Shari'a requires even greater interpretive exertion, for the Qur'an contains a much smaller proportion of explicitly legal material than Torah, smaller still if one excludes those passages prescribing rules for religious ritual. The Shari'anic project of interpretation required all of the powers of Islamic moral and legal intelligence over a period of centuries.

To be sure, it is hard to see how Shari'a can be reconciled with natural law if it is regarded merely as a code, as something fixed, immutable, and dead. But a natural law-minded Islamic thinker will regard it instead as a living tradition, entering as fully as possible into the spirit of the jurists who developed it. The list of methods used by these jurists, the relations among them, and the terminology by which they are discussed differ among the various schools of Islamic jurisprudence, but in every school, jurists did much more than follow inflexible precedents and crystal-clear instructions in the holy texts. For example:

(1) They honoured historical consensus, *ijmāʿ*, although just whose consensus is to be consulted—for example, the consensus of the whole community, of the companions of the Prophet, or of Islamic jurists themselves—is a matter of disagreement among the schools.

(2) They employed analogical and 'independent' reasoning. Sunni jurisprudence calls analogical reasoning *qiyas*. Shi'a jurisprudence speaks instead of *ijtihād*, which is the exercise of ʿ*aql*, a more general term for the faculty of reason.

(3) They debated broad principles for adjudicating among conflicting precedents. This method, called *istihsān*, is characteristic of the Hanafi school of Sunni jurisprudence. Its founder, Abu Hanifa, proposed giving preference to precedents that soften or mitigate hardship or harshness. Controversy arises over whether *istihsān* is to be used only when other grounds for preference fail, or may be used more generally.

(4) They consulted widely held practices or customs of the local society. Such customs, called *urf*, are acknowledged as a basis for legal reasoning in Sunni but not Shi'a jurisprudence. The literal meaning of the term is 'knowledge', suggesting an analogy with a famous argument of Thomas Aquinas, who held that sound custom 'has the force of a law, abolishes law, and is the interpreter of law' because, by making the people's tacit reasoning about what they judge good manifest, it fulfils the criteria of all authentic law— that is, it is an ordinance of reason, directed to the common good, made by public authority, and promulgated (in this case, not by speech, but by repeated acts).[19]

---

[19] *Summa Theologica* I-II, Q 97, Art 3, in the light of Q 90, Art 4.

(5)   Finally, in some cases they tried to derive legal rules from first principles. The most famous proponent of this method was Ibn Rushd, but here the relationship with the natural law tradition is more subtle. To be sure, classical natural law thinkers view all authentic law as ultimately derivable from first principles. On the other hand, it is not ordinarily the case that the jurist or legislator begins with first principles and then reasons forward, like a devisor of geometrical proofs. Rather, it is the case that, in principle, one can always reason *backward* to the first principles in which correct judgments are grounded. The axiomatic-deductive model is more characteristic of the natural law theories of the Enlightenment than of the classical natural law tradition.

To an outsider such as myself, it seems that the spirit of these five practices within Islam would have every right to be called authentically Islamic. In so far as it employs the powers of intellect to investigate the moral order of Creation, it would also be a natural law tradition, and would make possible the authentic dialogue about rule of law that is so difficult to achieve today. It was no accident that the period during which the thinkers of my faith achieved their greatest insights into natural law coincided with the period during which they were intensely and simultaneously engaged with the pagan thought of Aristotle, the Jewish thought of Maimonides, and the Muslim thought of Ibn Rushd, whom they called Averroes.

Yet the proposal that Islam and the nations of the West accommodate themselves jointly to the natural law presents difficulties of its own—even if one can talk them into doing it. I have called natural law a common ground, but in the first place it is a *slippery* common ground, wet with the dews of self-deception, difficult to stand upon steadily. If we concede St Paul's point that a law is written on the heart of man, we must also concede that it is everywhere entangled with the evasions and subterfuges of men. Neither is it a *neutral* common ground, for if it does turn out to be the case that some truths about God and His moral requirements can be known by reason even prior to revelation, then it is unreasonable to reject these truths, and they will shape our views about which claims concerning revelation are plausible. We would not take seriously a claim that God desires, for example, the encouragement of suicide or the murder of schoolchildren, because this would put God at odds with the moral order He Himself had built into Creation. Finally, it may be an *incomplete* common ground. It is one thing to believe that the natural law determines the outlines of a just public order, but it is quite another thing to suppose that it determines all of their features without any help from revelation whatsoever.

The slipperiness, tilt, and incompleteness of the common ground may account for the reluctance of many in the Islamic world to stand on it. I mentioned earlier that Sunni jurisprudence employs analogical reason, *qiyas*, while Shi'a jurisprudence also employs 'independent' reasoning, or *ijtihād*. Most Sunni writers hold that the gates of *ijtihād* 'closed' after the tenth century and that the practice is no longer to be used—a point which the various schools dispute, and which modernist scholars within Islam deny.[20] What does it mean to say that the gates of *ijtihād* are closed? Would this view preclude a restoration of natural law reasoning in Islam, or would it preclude only the irresponsible personal philosophizing that al-Ghazali sought to criticize in his classic work *The Incoherence of the Philosophers*?[21] What would it mean to reopen the gates of *ijtihād* if reopening were generally accepted?[22]

The West has been vexed by its own version of the problem of irresponsible personal philosophizing; in the liberal democracies, it troubles relations between courts and legislatures. Some hold that judges may void legislative acts by direct appeal to natural law, because if they may not, then legislatures will be omnipotent. Others hold that judges may *not* void legislative acts by direct appeal to the natural law, because if they may, then courts will be omnipotent. What both sides overlook is that judges would not be able to avoid considerations of natural law even if they were utterly deferential and had no authority to void written law. The fact is that considerations of natural law arise willy-nilly, even in the mere interpretation of written laws whose validity is wholly conceded.

I owe my favourite illustration of this point to Professor Charles E Rice. The 1932 *Restatement of Contracts* declares in section 90,[23] 'A promise which the promisor should reasonably expect to induce action or forbearance of a definite and substantial character on the part of the promisee and which does induce such action or forbearance is binding if injustice can be avoided only by enforcement of the promise'. Put more simply, if breaking a promise would cause injustice, then the promise is binding. This formula does not explain what 'injustice' means; it expects readers to know that already. Suppose language like this were contained in written law. In such a case judges would be forced to work out some of the remote implications of the natural law, just to figure out what the written law meant by 'injustice'. One may try to avoid the problem by replacing undefined terms like 'injustice' with other terms, but then these terms will need interpretation, so the banished problem reappears. Logically, this must also be true for Shari'a.

[20] See, eg Wael Hallaq, 'Was the Gate of Ijithad Closed?' (1984) 16(1) *International Journal of Middle East Studies* 3; and Shaista P Ali-Karamali and Fiona Dunne, 'The Ijtihad Controversy' (1994) 9(3) *Arab Law Quarterly* 238.
[21] Abu Hamid Muhammad Al-Ghazali, Sabih Ahmad Kamali (trans), *The Incoherence of the Philosophers* (Lahore: Pakistan Philosophical Congress, 1963).
[22] For one form that it might take, see the approach of Mahmud Shaltut, whose work *Koran and Fighting* I discuss below.
[23] *Restatement of Contracts* (American Law Institute, 1932), Sec. 90, 'Promise Reasonably Inducing Definite and Substantial Action'.

The Question of Intrinsically Evil Acts

Considering just the slipperiness of the common ground, two areas of discussion with Muslims will prove both difficult and crucial.

The first sensitive point is likely to be whether Islam recognizes that some acts are intrinsically evil, so that they are not only categorically but irrevocably forbidden; to put it another way, whether any moral prohibitions are not only inviolable, but also immutable. Because of Islamic terrorism, the practical interest of this point is whether, if there are such acts, they include the deliberate taking of innocent life, and further, how innocence is defined.

Superficial arguments can be advanced both pro and con. Against the view that Shari'a recognizes intrinsic evil, one might call attention to the Shari'a principle, *al-daruratu tubiyh al-mahzurah*, 'necessity makes the unlawful lawful'. Taken literally, this would mean that no act is categorically prohibited; it would commit Islam to a form of consequentialism according to which, in the final analysis, right and wrong were determined only by results. The ends would justify the means.

However, it is far from clear whether Shari'a requires the principle to be taken literally. An analogous maxim can be found in classical natural law tradition, *necessitas legem non habet*, 'necessity knows no law'. Like the corresponding principle of Shari'a it is dangerously worded, and it has been subjected to endless abuse by Western consequentialists—for example to rationalize the atomic bombing of Hiroshima and Nagasaki, which was a clear violation of the 'discrimination' principle of the just war doctrine because it involved the deliberate targeting of non-combatants. But *necessitas legem non habet* was never intended literally in classical natural law, nor could it have been, because the same tradition also insisted that 'Evil must not be done that good may come'.[24] The original intention of the Western maxim about necessity seems to have been to dispense individuals from subordinate regulations in cases where these work at cross-purposes with the greater rules that they are ordained to serve. Thus, in cases of great necessity a sacred ritual may be held in an unconsecrated space, and a penitent at the point of death may seek absolution from a priest other than his own.

Thomas Aquinas sheds light on the underlying reasoning in his discussion of another example: why a person in extreme need may take the property of another. Property ownership is not absolute; it is a form of stewardship of goods that are ultimately intended for the succour of man's needs. Thus, 'whatever certain people have in superabundance is due, by natural law, to the purpose of succouring the poor'.[25] In this context the principle 'necessity knows no law' functions not

---

[24] Citing Romans 3:8, Thomas Aquinas takes the principle for granted. Eg *Summa Theologica* pt, I-II, Q 79, Art 4, ad 4; II-II, Q 64, Art 5, ad 3; and III, Q 68, Art 11, ad 3; compare Supp, Q 4, Art 1, ad 4.

[25] Ibid II-II, Q 66, Art 7. For another example, see Supp, Q 8, Art 6.

to authorize theft, but to clarify what is meant by theft; one steals not simply by taking the property of another, but taking it against his rational will. Much the same reasoning appears in Shari'a. For example, 'the jurists validate demolition of an intervening house to prevent the spread of fire to adjacent buildings, just as they validate dumping of the cargo of an overloaded ship to prevent the danger (or *darar*) to the life of its passengers'.[26]

An equally indecisive argument can be offered in favour of the opposite view, that Shari'a does recognize intrinsic evil. When Pope Benedict XVI suggested at the University of Regensburg that Islam authorizes holy war, a group of Muslim scholars protested by calling attention to 'traditional and authoritative Islamic rules of war'. These rules, they wrote, include prohibition of attacks on non-combatants, prohibition of attacks on grounds of the victims' religious belief, and the obligation to live at peace except for legitimate self-defence and maintenance of sovereignty.[27] But this argument is beside the point. The question is not whether Shari'a includes such rules; it is whether they are (1) inviolable, and (2) immutable.

Shari'a certainly classifies some acts as *haram*, categorically forbidden. On the other hand, M H Kamali holds that what is viewed as *haram* can change: 'The Qur'an thus leaves open the possibility, although not without reservations, of enacting into *haram* what may have been classified by the *fuqahā* [jurists] of one age as merely reprehensible, or *makruh*. Similarly, the recommendable, or *mandub*, may be elevated into a *wajib* [obligation] if this is deemed to be in the interest of the community in a different stage of its experience and development'.[28]

One may sharpen the question, then, as follows: is it conceivable in Muslim thought that the traditional and authoritative Islamic rules of war could change, so that even if it is now *haram* to deliberately take innocent life, it may not be *haram* in the future? To sharpen the question even further, would it be possible to argue (as some voices on al-Jazeera did argue after 9/11) that the destruction of the World Trade Centre was not a taking of innocent life, because, since Americans vote for their rulers, they all share the guilt of their government's sins? In the end, may evil be done that good may come?

The Question of Religious Compulsion

The second sticky point for discussion concerns religious compulsion. According to the classical natural law tradition, man is ordained for truth and endowed by his Creator with an inbuilt longing to attain it—not just practical truth, such as where his next meal is coming from, but the truth about the meaning of his life,

[26] M H Kamali, 'Qawa'id Al-Fiqh: The Legal Maxims of Islamic Law', sec 7 (Association of Muslim Lawyers, UK, no date), available at <http://www.sunnah.org/fiqh/usul/Kamali_Qawaid_al-Fiqh.pdf>.

[27] Open letter of Muslim scholars to Pope Benedict XVI (n 18 above).

[28] M H Kamali, *Principles of Islamic Jurisprudence* (Cambridge: Islamic Texts Society, 2003) 40.

the truth about reality as a whole, and especially the truth about God.[29] To attain such truth, however, he must have liberty to seek it. Nor are there any shortcuts, because it pertains to the very essence of religion that it be freely chosen. '[N]o one is detained by us against his will', says Lactantius, 'for he is unserviceable to God who is destitute of faith and devotedness.' A little later he explains, 'For nothing is so much a matter of free-will as religion, in which, if the mind of the worshipper is disinclined to it, religion is at once taken away, and ceases to exist'.[30]

The group of Islamic scholars who responded to Benedict XVI agreed, quoting the Qur'anic passage, 'There is no compulsion in religion'.[31] Although the Pope had quoted the same verse, he had written that 'It is one of the suras of the early period, when Mohammed was still powerless and under [threat]'. The Pope might have added that in some interpretations of Shari'a, this fact would imply that it does not provide the final word about Islamic duty, but merely expresses a norm for that time. The Islamic scholars replied:

In fact this verse is acknowledged to belong to the period of Qur'anic revelation correspond-ing to the political and military ascendance of the young Muslim community. *There is no compulsion in religion* was not a command to Muslims to remain steadfast in the face of the desire of their oppressors to force them to renounce their faith, but was a reminder to Muslims themselves, once they had attained power, that they could not force another's heart to believe. There is no compulsion in religion addresses those in a position of strength, not weakness.

These statements are most surprising. In his classic commentary to al-Misri's classic work of *Shāfiʿī* jurisprudence, *Reliance of the Traveller*,[32] 'Umar Barakat writes that '*Jihād* means to war against non-Muslims, and is etymologically derived from the word mujahada, signifying warfare to establish the religion'. To be sure, he adds, 'As for the greater jihād, it is spiritual warfare against the lower self (*nafs*), which is why the Prophet (Allah bless him and give him peace) said as he was returning from jihād, "We have returned from the lesser jihād to the greater jihād" '. On the other hand, according to 'Umar Barakat, the scriptural basis for *jihād* lies in verses like 'Fighting is prescribed for you' and 'Slay them wherever you find them',[33] as well as *haditha*[34] like the following: 'I have been commanded to fight people until they testify that there is no god but Allah and that Muhammad is the Messenger

---

[29] *Summa Theologica* I-II, Q 94, Art 2.

[30] Lactantius, *Divine Institutes* Bk 5, Ch 20.

[31] Al-Baqarah (Qur'an 2) 256.

[32] Ahmad ibn Naqib al-Misri, *Reliance of the Traveller* (revised edn, Beltsville, Maryland: Amana Publications, 1994). This is a collaborative work; only a small part comes from the original manual by Ahmad ibn Naqib al-Misri. The quotation from 'Umar Barakat is found in sec o9.0, p 599. The translator, Nuh Ha Mim Keller, omits some sections of this massive work, such as the section on slav-ery, which I am not using. Arabic and English text are presented in parallel columns. A disadvantage for readers who do not speak Arabic is that certain bracketed sections of the Arabic text are omitted from the English text, without marks of elision in the English text to show where the bracketed sec-tions belong.

[33] Al-Baqarah (Qur'an 2) 216, and An-Nisa' (Qur'an 4) 89. Here and throughout my discussion of *The Reliance of the Traveller*, I am using the translations of Qur'an and *hadith* provided in the English version of the work itself.

[34] The Arabic plural is actually *ahadith*, but it is often rendered as *haditha* or *hadiths* in English.

of Allah, and perform the prayer, and pay zakat. If they say it, they have saved their blood and possessions from me, except for the rights of Islam over them. And their final reckoning is with Allah'.[35]

Plainly, scriptures like the latter refer not to war against the lower self but to war to compel religious belief. If they supply the *basis* for *jihād*, as 'Umar Barakat asserts, then it would appear that the 'lesser' *jihād* is the *central* meaning of *jihād* even if it is the lesser one. Perhaps the *Shāfi'ī* school is eccentric, but if so then it behoves the 38 scholars to explain what school of jurisprudence they are following. To say that Shari'a *should* be interpreted as prohibiting religious compulsion is laudable; to say that normally it is so interpreted is implausible.

Even if the view of the 38 scholars were conceded, it would not settle the question. The sticky point is not just whether Shari'a prohibits compulsion in religion. Nor is it only whether such prohibitions are categorical and immutable (the question we asked about the killing of innocents). After all, a prohibition might be both permanent and exceptionless, yet narrow. The further question, then, is how broadly religious compulsion is to be understood.

Under a narrow interpretation, the only thing counted as compulsion would be forcing people to convert against their will. However, if we take seriously the considerations that ground religious liberty—the nature of man as a truth-seeker and the nature of religion as freely chosen—then this would seem to be far from sufficient. Properly understood, liberty would not only require the prohibition of forcing others to become Muslims, but protect Muslims who converted to other religions. It would include freedom to seek and to disseminate information about other religions. It would forbid hindering the rites of worship of other religions, or the construction and consecration of sacred spaces where such worship may take place. Needless to say, such freedoms are far from prevalent in Islamic states that claim to follow Shari'a, and in the light of the Qur'anic principle 'there is no compulsion in religion', it is worth asking Islamic jurists why not.

Not all 'other religions' are equivalent, either according to Shari'a or according to natural law. It would be no injury to liberty, properly understood, to hinder proselytizing for, say, a religion of kidnappers, a pederastic sect, or a cult of assassins. Such religions have existed in the past, and exist today. But in Islamic countries, even monotheistic religions that adhere to the Decalogue, such as Judaism and Christianity, suffer hindrance and persecution. Although a minority of jurists dissent, in most schools of Islamic jurisprudence the penalty for Muslims who convert to other religions remains death.

Properly understood liberty would also prohibit the imposition upon non-Muslims of civil disabilities such as a higher rate of taxation, or applying to them a different standard of justice. The customary justification for treating tolerated non-Muslims as second-class citizens, or *dhimmis*, is the verse 'Fight those who believe not in Allah nor the Last Day, nor hold that forbidden which hath been forbidden

---

[35] The speaker is Muhammad. 'Umar Barakat remarks that this *hadith* is recorded by Sahih al-Bukhari and Muslim ibn al-Hajjaj.

by Allah and His Messenger, nor acknowledge the religion of Truth, [even if they are] of the People of the Book, until they pay the jizya with willing submission, and feel themselves subdued'.[36] Although *dhimmis* are not forced to convert to Islam, an injunction to 'fight' them until they 'feel themselves subdued' would seem difficult to reconcile with the doctrine 'there is no compulsion in religion'.

In saying that citizens of different religions should be granted the protection of the same standards of justice, I am not suggesting that the natural law prohibits confessional states. Probably it does not, although prudence should also be consulted. Consider the case of the United States. Its founding document, the Declaration of Independence, not only confesses a belief in natural law, but identifies its source, avowing that the laws of Nature are the laws of Nature's God. Although it does not go so far as to identify the Creator with the God of a particular historical religion, its view of created reality is monotheistic, moral, and providential. This profession is declaratory, not coercive; nothing in it compels belief, and nothing in it requires second-class citizenship for those who do not believe. If such a profession is compatible with liberty rightly understood, then it is not obvious why the foundational documents of another nation may not go a little further and profess Catholicism, Protestantism, Judaism, or Islam—provided that one's status as a citizen were not made conditional on one's status as a believer.

Historically, the need for the latter distinction has been a hard lesson to learn, and not only in Islam. At certain notorious points in their history, Christians have also blurred faith with citizenship, confusing the body politic with the Body of Christ. What made it possible for Christians to escape this error—and it is an error—was the persistent New Testament teaching that the two bodies are *not* the same. The most emphatic statement of this theme comes at the end of a long tribute to the 'men of old who received divine approval':

These all died in faith, not having received what was promised, but having seen it and greeted it from afar, and having acknowledged that they were strangers and exiles on the earth. For people who speak thus make it clear that they are seeking a homeland. If they had been thinking of that land from which they had gone out, they would have had opportunity to return. But as it is, they desire a better country, that is, a heavenly one. Therefore God is not ashamed to be called their God, for he has prepared for them a city.[37]

Whether Islam contains resources for escaping the same error remains to be seen.

---

[36] At-Taubah (Qur'an 9) 29–30. I am using the translation of Abdullah Yusuf 'Ali from Online Quran Project, available at <http://al-quran.info>. Compare the wording of the verse incorporated into Rudolph Peters' translation of a treatise of Averroes, discussed later.

[37] Hebrews 11:2, 13–16 (RSV). Compare Philippians 3:20 (RSV), 'But our commonwealth is in heaven, and from it we await a Savior, the Lord Jesus Christ', and Ephesians 2:19 (RSV), 'So then you are no longer strangers and sojourners, but you are fellow citizens with the saints and members of the household of God'.

The Question of Holy War

To further investigate the portents for relations between Shari'a and Western liberal democracy, let us consider the question of outright war. Earlier I mentioned the view of Bernard Lewis that although Shari'a allows tactical truces between Muslims and non-Muslims, the basic teaching is 'a canonically obligatory perpetual state of war until the whole world is either converted or subjugated'. Such views are widely challenged. Rudolph Peters, for example, suggests that early Islamic treatises 'were not overly explicit' about the conditions that justify warfare against unbelievers who have not submitted to Islamic rule. 'In order to counter the rather distorted view of the jihād that is commonly held in the West', he says, modernist Islamic scholars 'profess that the jihād is essentially defensive warfare, striving to protect the Islam and the Moslems and to guarantee the propagation of the Islamic mission'.[38]

At stake here is how to construe the Qur'anic and *hadithic* passages like Al-Anfal (Qur'an 8), 39: 'Fight them until there is no more *fitna* and the deen is Allah's alone. If they stop, Allah sees'. I do not wish to be tedious, but translations of the Qur'an render the first part of the verse in strikingly different ways.[39] The reason for this variety is that the words *deen*[40] and *fitna* are broad in meaning and have no exact equivalents in English. *Deen*, usually translated as 'religion', refers to much more than a set of beliefs; it signifies a comprehensive system of life, law, morals, manners, belief, ruling authority, and subordinating power, along with the obedience, submission, and discipline resulting therefrom. *Fitna* has an even greater range. According to the authoritative lexicon of E W Lane,[41] its meanings include burning with fire; melting ore in order to separate good from bad; trial or probation; distress or affliction; chastisement or punishment; war, civil war, or slaughter; faction, sedition, or discord; madness or diabolical possession; sin, crime, or disobedience; shame, disgrace, or ignominy; error or deviation from the right way; infidelity or unbelief; difference of opinion; or anything whatsoever that tempts, misleads, or seduces.

You see where this is going. Fighting 'until there is no more *fitna* and the *deen* is Allah's alone' would appear to mean making war until nothing more remains that could give rise to distress, temptation, disagreement, or trial of faith for Muslims,

---

[38] Rudolph Peters (trans), *Jihād in Mediaeval and Modern Islam: The Chapter on Jihād from Averroes' Legal Handbook, 'Bidayat Al-Mudjtahid', and the Treatise, 'Koran and Fighting', by the late Haykh Al-Azhar, Mahmud Shaltut* (Leiden: E.J. Brill, 1977) 5.

[39] I have used the translation of Abdalhaqq and Aisha Bewley; contrast the translations of Abdullah Yusuf 'Ali, Ahmed 'Ali, Ali Quli Qara'i, Mohammed Marmaduke Pickthall, and Syed Vickar Ahamed 'Ali. These and others may be found at the Online Quran Project, available at <http://al-quran.info>.

[40] Often transliterated *din*.

[41] Edward William Lane, *Arabic-English Lexicon* (Cambridge: Cambridge University Press, 1974, reprint of 1877 ed.) Bk 1, Pt 6, 2335–2336.

and a comprehensive way of life has been fully established by force. Just how Muslims should approach non-believers in the context of such war is laid out in an authoritative *hadith* found in one of the four main collections of *haditha*, *Sahih Islam*.[42] I quoted a small portion of it earlier, but it needs to be read in its entirety. The focus in this passage is on polytheists:

[W]hen the Messenger of Allah (may peace be upon him) appointed anyone as leader of an army or detachment... [h]e would say: Fight in the name of Allah and in the way of Allah. Fight against those who disbelieve in Allah.... When you meet your enemies who are polytheists, invite them to three courses of action.... Invite them to (accept) Islam; if they respond to you, accept it from them and desist from fighting against them. Then invite them to migrate from their lands to the land of *Muhairs* and inform them that, if they do so, they shall have all the privileges and obligations of the *Muhajirs*. If they refuse to migrate, tell them that they will have the status of *Bedouin Muilims* and will be subjected to the Commands of Allah like other Muslims, but they will not get any share from the spoils of war or *Fai'* except when they actually fight with the Muslims (against the disbelievers). If they refuse to accept Islam, demand from them the *Jizya*. If they agree to pay, accept it from them and hold off your hands. If they refuse to pay the tax, seek Allah's help and fight them.

How is all of this to be taken? Rudolph Peters, whose comforting interpretation I quoted above, has helpfully presented back-to-back translations of the chapter on fighting from a classical Islamic legal handbook by Averroes, *Bidayat Al-Mudjtahid*, as well as a modernist Islamic treatise, *Koran and Fighting*, by Mahmud Shaltut.[43] A cursory glance at the two works of Averroes and Shaltut makes them seem worlds apart. Averroes says that one may war against unbelievers either for conversion, or for payment of the *jizya* or poll tax, the sign of subordination.[44] He adds that scholars disagree about the *motive* for making war against unbelievers, some saying that it is because they disbelieve, others that, in view of their disbelief, they may fight.[45]

---

[42] This particular *hadith* is *Sahih Muslim*, Bk 19, *Hadith* 4294. I am quoting it in the translation of Abdul Hamid Siddiqui (available online at the University of Southern California's Center for Jewish-Muslim Engagement at <http://www.usc.edu/schools/college/crcc/engagement/resources/texts/muslim/hadith/muslim>.

[43] Shaltut criticizes the traditional method of Qur'anic interpretation—'explaining the verses and chapters of the Koran, in their traditional order... on the basis of certain extra-Koranic assumptions or principles'—an approach which he thinks 'does scant justice to the fact that the Koran is the primary source of Islam', creates an 'intellectual anarchy', and results in an 'aversion' to the Qur'an and its interpreters. Instead he follows the second method—'collecting all the verses concerning a certain topic and analyzing them in their interrelation'—so that 'the purpose of these verses and the rule that can be derived from them, becomes clear': M Shaltut, in Peters (n 38 above) 26–27.

[44] 'The Moslems are agreed that the aim of warfare against the People of the Book, with the exception of those belonging to the Quraysh-tribe and Arab Christians, is twofold: either conversion to Islam, or payment of poll-tax (*djizyah*). This is based on [*At-Taubah* (Qur'an 9), 29], "Fight against those who do not believe in Allah nor in the last Day, and do not make forbidden what Allah and His messenger have made forbidden, and do not practice the religion of truth, of those who have been given the Book, until they pay the *jizya* off-hand, being subdued"': Averroes, *Legal Handbook* in Peters (n 38 above) 23–24.

[45] Concerning a disagreement among scholars as to whether any categories of unbelievers may be exempted from slaughter, Averroes says: 'Basically, however, the source of the controversy is to be

By contrast, Shaltut says that one may war against unbelievers *only* for protection, never for conversion. Summarizing his own conclusion, he remarks: 'How remote all this is from the smell of compulsion! How strong its aversion from the use of force as a means of propagating the Mission. Moreover, the Koran states clearly and distinctly that faith produced by force is without value and that he who yields to force and changes his faith loses his honor'.[46]

On closer examination, the difference between Averroes and Shaltut is small. Against whom is one to fight? Both give the same answer: non-believers. When does one stop fighting? Again, both give the same answer: not until all the non-believers have either accepted the 'offer' of conversion, or else submitted, signifying their submission by payment of the *jizya*. Only regarding the reason for fighting do the two seem to give different answers. Averroes says that the motive is either just that the enemy *are* non-believers, or else that, being non-believers, they may fight. Shaltut says that the motive is solely their danger to Islam. But the verbal difference is misleading, because for Shaltut, the defensive justification is astonishingly broad. At first it seems narrow, for the Qur'anic verse just quoted:

commands the Moslems to fight a certain group which is characterized by 'they do not believe in Allah etc'. Previously they had broken their pledges and hindered and assailed the propagation of the Islamic Mission. These acts constitute for the Moslems reasons for fighting them. Therefore this verse does not say that the quality of being an unbeliever etc. constitutes a sufficient reason for fighting...[47]

So far, so good, but now Shaltut goes on to explain the 'characteristics peculiar to' this group, 'in order to give a factual description and as a further incitement to attack them once their aggression will have materialized'. Notice that the 'incitement' here is the mere characteristics of the group. Although aggression may have taken place, it need not have done so. It is sufficient that unbelievers have a *disposition* to aggress against Islam, that they are the sort of people who do make aggression. What is the evidence of such a disposition? In the case of the polytheists just mentioned, the evidence is just this:

They modified the religion of Allah and took their scholars and monks for Lords apart from Him, while making things allowed and forbidden according to their whims, since they did not accept that only Allah can do so. There was nothing to hold them back from breaking pledges, and violating rights, and they were not inclined to desist from aggression and tyranny.

These are the people which, according to this verse, must be fought continuously until, by being thoroughly subjected, they can do no more harm and will desist from the persecution

---

found in their divergent views concerning the motive why the enemy may be slain. Those who think that this is because they are unbelieving do not make exceptions for any polytheist. Others, who are of the opinion that this motive consists in their capacity for fighting, in view of the prohibition to slay female unbelievers, do make an exception for those who are unable to fight or who are not as a rule inclined to fight, such as peasants and serfs': ibid 17.

[46] Shaltut, in Peters (n 38 above) 36.
[47] Ibid 47.

they used to practice. The Koran introduced a special token for this submission, viz. the payment of poll-tax (*djizyah*), which means that they actually participate in carrying the burdens of the state and providing the means for the commonweal, both for Moslems and non-Moslems.[48]

'Modifying' the religion of Allah apparently means simply believing a religion that is *not* the same as Islam. 'Taking their scholars and monks for Lords apart from [Allah]' means simply following religious leaders other than Muslim religious leaders. 'Making things allowed and forbidden according to their whims' means simply following laws other than Islamic laws. Such acts are sufficient 'incitement to attack' non-believers, just because they signify the disposition of non-believers to misbehave toward Islam: 'there was nothing to hold them back'. Indeed, Shaltut comes very close to saying that such acts not only show a disposition to aggression, but constitute aggression per se. And why shouldn't he? Let us recall the broad meaning of *fitna* in the verse examined earlier, 'Fight them until there is no more *fitna* and the *deen* is Allah's alone'.

In short, although Islam may technically oppose conversion by the sword, both the traditional authority, Averroes, and the modernist scholar, Shaltut, believe all of the following points:

(1)   That the mere fact that some are not Muslim constitutes danger to Islam.

(2)   That war is a justified response to such danger.

(3)   That such war may continue until non-Muslims are either converted or otherwise subjugated.

Between such a stance and conversion by the sword, there is a hairsplitting formal difference, but the material difference is non-existent. I very much hope that I am wrong, but I fear that I am right.

Is It Possible to Talk?

The preconditions for serious discussion about these topics are even more difficult and sensitive than the topics themselves. Foremost among such preconditions is that the parties are able to trust each other. Can they? I do not presume to say what shape this question takes for faithful Muslims. For non-Muslims, the great problem is what Shari'a says about lying. We have no space here to consider what each of the different *madhhabs* say about the matter; it will be sufficient to illustrate from the Shāfiᶜī school of jurisprudence.

The problem is not that Islam does not condemn lying; it does. According to the Qur'an, 'Allah guides not the profligate liar' and 'May liars perish'.[49] As we read in

[48]   Ibid 48.
[49]   Ghafir (Qur'an 40) 28 and Adh-Dhariyat (Qur'an 51) 10.

Reliance of the Traveller, 'Primary texts from the Koran and sunna that it is unlaw-ful to lie are both numerous and intersubstantiative, it being among the ugliest sins and most disgusting faults'.[50] Yet various traditions suggest that it *is* permit-ted to lie. The occasion of one of the most notorious such traditions, recorded by the renowned collector of *hadiths*, Muhammad ibn Ishaq, was a proposal to kill a certain Jew: 'Muhammad bin Maslamah said, "O apostle of God, we shall have to tell lies." "Say what you like," Muhammad replied. "You are absolved, free to say whatever you must"'.[51] *Reliance of the Traveller* cites a far milder *hadith*: 'I did not hear him [Muhammad] permit untruth in anything people say, except for three things: war, settling disagreements, and a man talking with his wife or she with him'.[52] But the outcome is blunt: 'This is an explicit statement that lying is some-times permissible'.

For 'the best analysis', *Reliance of the Traveller* refers the reader to the great al-Ghazali. In the sharpest possible contrast with the classical natural law tradition, which views human speech as a gift of God ordained to truth,[53] al-Ghazali flatly declares that 'Speaking is a means to achieve objectives'. 'When it is possible to achieve [a praiseworthy] aim by lying but not by telling the truth', he states, 'it is permissible to lie if attaining the goal is permissible, and obligatory to lie if the goal is obligatory', although 'it is religiously more precautionary in all such cases to employ words that give a misleading impression, meaning to intend by one's words something that is literally true... while the outward purport of the words deceives the hearer.' Although he cautions that 'strictness is to forgo lying in every case where it is not legally obligatory', this statement comes on the heels of his startling remark, 'One should compare the bad consequences entailed by lying to those entailed by telling the truth, and if the consequences of telling the truth are more damaging, one is entitled to lie'.[54]

Westerners should not feel self-righteous. The temptation to the abuse of casu-istry has been felt here too. In *The Reliance of the Traveller*, however, it seems more than a temptation. May God grant Islamic jurisprudence the grace to escape from views like al-Ghazali's, for unless it can escape from them, the preconditions for honest discussion are impossible to meet.

But suppose that Islamic jurisprudence can overcome such views. The final difficulty of discussion—and with this I conclude—concerns how to make its hoped-for achievements effectual. In Catholicism, the achievement of consen-sus and the consolidation of hard-won insight about disputed points of natural

---

[50] *Reliance of the Traveller* (n 32 above) sec r8.1, 744. The quotation is attributed to Abu Zakaria Mohiuddin Yahya Ibn Sharaf al-Nawawi.

[51] Muhammad ibn Ishaq, Alfred Guillaume (trans), *Life of Mohammad: A Translation of Ishaq's Sirat rasul Allah* (Oxford: Clarendon, 1955) *hadith* 551. A version of this *hadith* is also reported by Sahih Bukhari, M. Muhsin Khan (trans), *Hadith of Bukhari* (Charleston: Forgotten Books, 2008) Vol 4, Bk 52, *hadith* 271.

[52] *Reliance of the Traveller* (n 32 above) sec r8.2, 745.

[53] Eg *Summa Theologica* II-II, Q 110, Arts 1–4, on 'the vices opposed to truth, and first of lying'.

[54] *Reliance of the Traveller* (n 32 above) sec r8.2, 745–746.

and divine law are facilitated by the final authority of the Magisterium. As Paul Marshall has pointed out,[55] in Sunni Islam the situation is more like that in Protestantism, for:

a similar fragmentation has occurred. Despite the authority of institutions such as Al-Azhar University in Egypt, and despite the high regard given to learning, a teacher or jurist can gain authority if he can draw followers. In practice such leaders can establish their own mosques and *madrassas*, as well as radio and TV shows. Osama bin Laden, it should be remembered, is an engineer, not a jurist, but in practice he can issue *fatwās* that have tremendous influence.

It would be terrible indeed if consensus on Islamic renewal were reached among a few dozen or a few thousand Muslim thinkers, yet remained a dead letter because the rest of the population ignored it.

Let us be honest: the same dread rises when one contemplates the West. After the spectacle of Muslims rioting to protest the Pope's suggestion that Islam is too open to violence, the prospect of a renewal in Islamic thought may seem unbelievable. Yet after the meteoric advance of what the Pope has called the dictatorship of relativism, the prospect of a return of the West to its own ancient springs may seem equally unbelievable.

Aristotle wrote that in order to achieve a more beautiful story, the poet should set aside unbelievable possibilities in favour of believable impossibilities.[56] But the rule for real life is different than for stories. That Western liberal democracy could establish autonomous jurisdictions for religious minorities without destroying itself is a pleasant story and easy to imagine, but impossible. That Islam might accommodate itself to Western liberal democracy by betraying its faith is equally impossible. These poetic fictions should be set aside.

That Islam and the Western nations might mutually commit themselves to the common ground they share in the order of Creation is almost beyond our power to conceive, but it is possible. There is no hope but in the possible, even when it seems unbelievable; so let us take hold of our hope, and remember that all things are possible for God.

Appendix: The Meaning of Accommodation

To forestall confusion, it may be helpful to explain that 'accommodation' is an elastic term. In various ways, some norms of some religions are already accommodated by civil law. Consider for example the relation between civil marriage and religious marriage in Catholicism, a faith more familiar in the West. Simplifying, we can distinguish at least three levels of civil accommodation.

[55] P Marshall, 'Islamic Counter-Reformation' (August–September 2004) 145 *First Things: A Monthly Journal of Religion and Public Life* 21, 22.
[56] Aristotle, *Poetics* Bk 24, 1460a.

Level one. Provided the couple register their union with the state, the vows they take during their religious ceremony are also regarded as satisfying the requirements for civil marriage. In other words, the couple do not have to go before a civil magistrate and take separate vows in a prescribed civil form, as they do, for example, in France. Certainly this reflects a degree of accommodation. However, the two relationships remain independent. The Church concerns itself with the sacramental marriage, the state concerns itself with the civil. If the Church issues a decree of annulment, declaring that a valid sacramental marriage never actually existed, this does not affect the validity of the civil marriage in the eyes of the state. If the state issues a decree of divorce, declaring that the civil marriage has come to an end, this does not affect the validity of the sacramental marriage in the eyes of the Church.

Now let us up the ante. Agreements to submit contractual disagreements to private arbitration are increasingly common in business, and widely accepted by courts. Sometimes, depending on their religious convictions, the parties agree that such arbitration will be conducted by religious bodies. For Orthodox Jews, these will be rabbinical courts. For Muslims, they will be Shari'a courts. Suppose, then, that our Catholic couple treat their marriage in a similar way: they enter a *civil* agreement to conform their *civil* marriage to the religious norms that govern sacramental marriage as interpreted by *religious* courts. For example, they agree that neither will seek a civil divorce unless a marriage tribunal of the Church agrees that the sacramental marriage is invalid. Suppose, further, that their agreement is enforceable in civil courts; we have then reached level two. Such possibilities are not far-fetched even in the United States, where in the New Jersey case *Minkin v Minkin* a civil court ordered a man who had sued for civil divorce to obtain and pay for the costs of a *get*, or Jewish severance decree. The basis for the court's decision was that upon marrying, the man and woman had entered into a *ketuba*, an agreement to conform to Jewish marriage laws, which require the man to give his wife a *get* in the event of divorce. The wife had demanded the *get* because, under Jewish law, she would otherwise be precluded from remarrying. Taking the view that neither the *ketuba* nor the *get* is in itself a religious act, the court ordered the husband to fulfill his contract.[57]

The examples just offered are not precisely parallel; business is not marriage, and Jewish marriage is not Catholic marriage. Finer distinctions would be needed if our main concern lay in level two. But let us raise the ante higher still. At the third level of accommodation, it makes no difference whether or not our Catholic couple have entered a civil contract to abide by Catholic marriage norms. The state simply treats Catholics by different rules. If the Church says that they are sacramentally married, then the state says that they are civilly married; if not, then not. Now suppose that the state applies this approach not only to marriage but to other realms of law, and the decisions of religious authorities are enforced in civil courts. This

[57] *Minkin v Minkin*, 180 NJ Super 260 (1981).

time the nearest analogy might be the *battei din* of Israel, which have exclusive jurisdiction over a variety of matters including Jewish marriage and divorce, as well as conversion to Judaism, which has civil ramifications because it affects the Law of Return.

Which level of accommodation do the proponents of accommodating Shari'a have in mind? For our example we may take the Anglican Archbishop of Canterbury, Rowan Williams.[58] Plainly he has more in mind than level one; that is merely the status quo in the United Kingdom, as well as my own country, the United States. Almost certainly, he also means more than level two. One reason for thinking so is that although the state is already trying out experiments in level two accommodation, and has been for some time, much more so in the United Kingdom than in the United States, the Archbishop finds this approach inadequate. He is thinking of level three.

Despite his maddeningly ambiguous language, an even more important reason for thinking that the Archbishop of Canterbury has the third level in mind is that it is hard to take his words in any other way. He persistently criticizes civil law for viewing faith communities through the 'privatizing' lens of individual decisions. Instead, he calls for 'plural jurisdiction', emphasizing the need for civil law to 'recogniz[e] and collaborat[e] with communal religious discipline', to 'delegate' the authority of civil law to 'recognized authority acting for a religious group'. There is nothing like this at level two, where the state is still merely ratifying private decisions which happen to be motivated by communal religious conviction. True, the Archbishop wants to cut some exceptions. Not *everything* would be decided by the communal group. For example, no religious body would be allowed to wreak vengeance on apostates, thank you. Even so, it is the third quantum tier that he occupies.

As I suggest in the body of the chapter, the arrangement might be much like federalism. Each citizen would be automatically subject to the laws of the jurisdiction in which he 'lives', but the jurisdictional lines are religious rather than geographical. If he 'lives' in Islam, the state holds him accountable to Shari'a courts; if in Judaism, to *battei din*; if in Catholicism, to canon law tribunals. For the reasons explained in the opening section, however, this could not work.

---

[58]   R Williams, 'Civil and Religious Law in England: a Religious Perspective' (see Appendix I).

12

Negotiating the Unfamiliar: Reflections from The Netherlands on the Archbishop of Canterbury's Lecture

Sophie van Bijsterveld

A. Introduction

It is no surprise that the Archbishop of Canterbury's lecture, 'Civil and Religious Law in England: A Religious Perspective', provoked strong reactions in England and abroad. Any discussion of religion in relation to law strikes a tender chord. When 'religious law' explicitly includes the Shari'a and the presenter endorses accommodating *this* religious law in the legal system, the contentious character of the message is self-evident. That the primate of the Church of England is the speaker gives it an even sharper edge.

The Archbishop was careful to put the notion of Shari'a in context. He recognized that Shari'a is usually perceived as a phenomenon 'repressive to women and wedded to archaic and brutal physical punishments', and that occasionally an event is reported which 'powerfully reinforces the image of—at best—a pre-modern system in which human rights have no role'.[1] Of course, this primitivist version of Shari'a was not the one at stake in the lecture. Central to Dr Rowan Williams' reasoning was a Shari'a that recognized 'universal principles', but also required such principles to be 'actualized' in concrete circumstances.[2] Thus, the issue did not revolve around a notion of Shari'a as an absolute, eternal, and unchangeable set of rules, but rather one that always remains 'to some extent unfinished business'.[3] In addition, the presupposition that Shari'a assumes 'the voluntary consent or submission of the believer' and has, therefore, nothing 'intrinsically to do with any demand for Muslim dominance over non-Muslims'[4] served as a reassuring statement.

---

[1] R Williams, 'Civil and Religious Law in England: A Religious Perspective' (see Appendix 1) at [2].
[2] Ibid at [3].   [3] Ibid at [4].   [4] Ibid at [5].

Nevertheless, any suggested accommodation of Shari'a by the legal system is bound to be provocative. The central issue of the lecture was not the Shari'a. As the Archbishop explicitly stated, the issues 'around what level of public or legal recognition, if any, might be allowed to the legal provisions of a religious group, are not peculiar to Islam'.[5] Moreover, he recognized that 'there are large questions in the background about what we understand by and expect from the law, questions that are more sharply focused than ever in a largely secular social environment'.[6] The thought-provoking lecture intentionally went well beyond the scope and composition of the present legal regime. It raised fundamental questions about our understanding of law, as well as its very nature and grounding.

This essay is a reflection on the relationship between law and religion in the Netherlands in the light of the Archbishop's statements. Whereas Dr Williams provided a theological perspective on the relationship between religious and civil law, this essay's focus will be constitutional. My aim is to explore what kind of issues are at the heart of the current controversies on religion in the public domain and why they are contentious. My discussion is set in the broader context of the development of relationships between church and state and between civil and religious law.

My primary focus is not the notion of Shari'a—not so much because of the strong reactions it provokes, but because the concept is so indeterminate. Similarly, I also avoid a detailed exploration of the concept of 'religious law' as that, without any further specification, also harbours quite diverse meanings—Roman Catholic Canon Law, 'vexatious appeals to religious scruple',[7] moral insights based on a religious belief, and so on—which each connect to civil law in different ways.

B. Religion, Law, and Society in Context

Until recently, Dutch church and state relationships,[8] as well as debates on these relationships, were implicitly based on one very obvious, yet basic fact: public authorities and churches were *familiar* with each other.[9] This simple fact may be the single most overlooked of all aspects of church and state relationships. Yet, such familiarity is crucial for the development of stable relationships based on mutual trust. For public authorities, trust necessitates some basic familiarity with the religious organizations, their leaders and believers, and, of course, the beliefs themselves.

The history of Dutch church-state relationships and the law relating to religion over the past 200 years is usually described in terms of the progressive interpretation, development, and implementation of such key constitutional principles as

---

⁵ Ibid at [1].   ⁶ Ibid.   ⁷ Ibid at [9].
⁸ In this essay, the phrase 'church' also includes Jewish and, depending on the context, Islamic religious organizations.
⁹ See S van Bijsterveld, *Overheid en Godsdienst: Herijking van een Onderlinge Relatie* (Nijmegen: Wolf Legal Publishers, 2nd edn, 2009).

freedom of religion, state neutrality towards religion, and the separation of church and state. Such accounts usually abstract lofty themes from the historical events and the actual conflicts and resolutions between institutional religion, society, and the law. These historic events and interactions typically serve as a preliminary narrative—simple, albeit necessary, illustrations—to show the progress that has been made. This, however, ignores the fact that there is an *intrinsic connection* between the actual events and the development of the legal and constitutional principles.

If we step back a little and take a different look at the development of church and state in the Netherlands, we can see that the process by which public authorities *get to know* the various religious denominations (and their organizations) is critical. The societal and political tensions that originated with the first split within the formerly established Dutch Reformed Church (in the early 1830s) are an example of this. After the initial strong state reaction to this split, it took time to 'normalize' relationships and to come to terms with the new situation. Similarly, the run-up to, and aftermath of, the re-establishment of the Catholic hierarchy in the Netherlands (in 1853) can best be viewed from the perspective of a broader process of state rapprochement with the Roman Catholic Church.

When Islam first appeared in the Netherlands, around 40 years ago, familiarity between the government and Islam was clearly absent. Initially, not much effort was made by either side to start the process of 'getting acquainted'. There were many understandable reasons for this.[10] But even though those reasons no longer hold true, a mutual understanding is all the more important. Currently, religion is still regarded by many of the governing elite as a mere private matter, and the basic wisdom underlying the nurturing of religion-state relationships (between the government and the Christian and Jewish communities) seems to have disappeared from the collective consciousness. Today, we can again see how important ongoing familiarity between public authorities and religious organizations is. The process of getting to know each other is again underway—to the mutual benefit of both the state and religious communities.

Public authorities in the Netherlands are eager to learn more about religion. With a slight exaggeration, one could even say that the fact that the study of religion is presently undergoing a growth spurt is largely due to the interest that state authorities have in Islam. They may well be the greatest 'consumers' of literature on religion and sociologists of religion—through funding of advisory bodies and their research in this field.

The government realizes that it cannot afford to have a 'blindspot' regarding religion. It was not always so. Not only were there practical reasons supporting

---

[10] The dominant belief at the time seemed to be that the immigration of workers from Islamic backgrounds was a temporary matter. In retrospect it is apparent that it took some time for Muslims to organize themselves. Furthermore, the authorities could not have foreseen the full extent of ongoing Muslim immigration. A rough estimate of the present Muslim population in the Netherlands is 825,000—around five per cent of the nation's total population of 16.5 million: Centraal Bureau voor de Statistiek, *Religie Aan Het Begin van de 21ste Eeuw* (The Hague: CBS, 2009) 35.

a distance between the two realms, to some commentators it seemed wise for the state to ignore religion. Was that not required by the principles of separation of church and state, freedom of religion, and state neutrality? However, none of our constitutional principles require aloofness where religion is concerned.[11] Quite the opposite: state dealings with religion require a sound understanding of religious organizations. Only where relationships have been patiently and fully worked through and the patterns of interaction 'crystallized' can public authorities *pretend* to have a blindspot towards religion and not take an interest in it; and even then, this is only *by the grace of* this legacy. The relative 'disinterest' of the state towards religion over the last few decades can be explained by this hard-won cultural inheritance.

In this context, it is also useful to recall the challenge in the 1980s presented by 'new religious movements'. These were, numerically speaking, a marginal phenomenon and, at that time, the Netherlands was politically, socio-economically, and sociologically stable. The catch-cry 'separation of church and state' dominated any discussion on religion. Yet, the new religious movements phenomenon caused ripples of unrest and prompted an official investigation.[12]

The Netherlands has no formal state legal mechanisms for the 'recognition' of religions. Churches are legal persons *sui generis* and no formal requirements exist for their establishment.[13] Specific legislation, nevertheless, does determine access by a religious organization, to, for instance, the public broadcasting system, or its right to establish a denominational school. One could say that the fact that a *general* system of recognition is not necessary is, at least in part, due to the fact that the major religions are already 'known'. In this light, it is telling that in recent years, when the government began to engage with Islamic organizations, the word 'recognition' was used when the state organs accepted their counterparts in the conversation as (authoritative) representatives from their respective groups.

It is useful to keep in mind that church and state relationships, as well as the law relating to religion, do not develop 'autonomously', but always in relation to a particular sociological and political context. This implies that we may need constantly to revise and adapt our existing understandings of the normative aspects of these relationships (which intertwine, more often than we realize, with our actual experience). In other words, when interpreting our constitutional principles we should take account of the broader context just outlined. This may help us to understand

---

[11] Of course, the three principles of freedom of religion, state neutrality towards religion, and separation of church and state *do* require restraint on the part of public authorities with respect to religion. I simply make the point that there is more to religion-state policy than this. Dialogue and co-operation are not, *as a matter of principle*, ruled out by these three norms.

[12] See T A M Witteveen, *Overheid en Nieuwe Religieuze Bewegingen* (The Hague: Staatsuitgeverij, 1984).

[13] The Civil Code merely states that 'Churches, their independent units, and bodies in which they are united have legal personality. They are governed by their own statute in so far as this does not conflict with the law': Dutch Civil Code. Art 2:2.

the tensions that arise in this field and to develop appropriate and feasible ways of dealing with these.

C. The Extension of Public Facilities to Islam

Although Islam's presence in the Netherlands dates back some four decades, serious analysis of it was slow to develop. It is probably fair to say that, initially, Islam was regarded as an interesting and exotic new phenomenon. When it transpired that Islam was here to stay, steps were gradually taken to secure opportunities for Muslims to worship.[14] If any criticism was heard at the time, it was that these developments took too long. To be fair, one must not forget that these were truly structural societal processes, requiring a change of mindset on the side of both the state and Muslims.

In the 1980s, regulations subsidizing the building of mosques were passed. Regulations permitting animal slaughter according to Jewish ritual were also extended to Muslims. Facilities were created for spiritual care in such institutions as penal institutions, even though fully fledged chaplaincy services for Muslims were not yet feasible. Through collective labour agreements, special arrangements were made for taking time off on Muslim holy days. Burial services have also been adapted to meet Muslim needs.

Making use of existing possibilities often presupposes a certain degree of internal organization and determination. For instance, the establishment, operation, and maintenance of schools require considerable effort. The same is true of the establishment of broadcasting corporations within the public broadcasting system and the actual delivery of radio and television programmes. Differences between the various national backgrounds and the fact that educational heights attained by the first generation of immigrants was not always sufficient to take up such activities account for why this all took some time.

Although there have been hiccups and setbacks, all in all it can be said that much has been achieved over recent decades to foster the Islamic faith. In its 'ordinary' pattern, Dutch law was, and is, fairly receptive towards religion. There was much that could be readily extended to Islam. Where existing Dutch law posed an obstacle, amendments were made. Even though it generated some discussion, public funds were granted to implement the necessary changes.

---

[14] See, further, S van Bijsterveld, 'The Legal Status of Islam in the Kingdom of the Netherlands' in S Ferrari and A Bradney (eds), *Islam and European Legal Systems* (Dartmouth: Ashgate, 2000) 125. For earlier developments, see, eg N Landman, *Van Mat tot Minaret: De Institutionalisering van de Islam in Nederland* (Amsterdam: VU Uitgeverij, 1992); W A Shadid and P S van Koningsveld, 'Institutionalization and Integration of Islam in The Netherlands' in W A Shadid and P S van Koningsveld (eds), *The Integration of Islam and Hinduism in Western Europe* (Kampen: Kok, 1991) 89.

The matters I have mentioned concern mostly 'classic' religious requirements: food, festive days and worship sites, burial rites, and other items that are tangibly associated with religious practice. Other developments simply signified state action to ensure that Muslims had the same rights, benefits, and privileges enjoyed by all religions. So, here, Islam has fared well. The real challenges lie elsewhere.

D. Shari'a Courts

In 2009 public opinion was stirred by an announcement of the alleged appearance of 'Shari'a courts'. The topic was debated in Parliament.[15] A sizeable number of people insisted vehemently that this was an undesirable development. Set against the background of the discussion above, one might wonder why there was such indignation. Given the existence of ecclesiastical courts and their position in Dutch law, why would the emergence of Islamic religious courts be so contentious?

No doubt, the word 'Shari'a' itself is enough to raise alarm: it has the connotation of brutal and archaic rules. However, can this concern be totally attributed to the negative associations provoked by the word 'Shari'a'?

Let us take a look at the position of ecclesiastical courts in the Netherlands. Ecclesiastical courts perform a modest role. There exist Roman Catholic Church courts as well as Protestant and Jewish courts. In terms of Dutch law, they are *intra*-organizational or in-house mechanisms of conflict-resolution. They operate *within* the limits set by the law of the land and do not constitute a 'parallel legal system'. Their rulings may be binding upon the parties concerned. This is especially important as the state has no jurisdiction over religious issues per se. Of course, some disputes do have civil and secular law aspects—for example, business transactions within a church, hiring and firing staff, disciplinary measures, or the validity of internal decision-making. In such 'mundane' areas, the Dutch Constitution is clear: no one can be precluded from recourse to the ordinary courts.[16]

Although the relationship between ecclesiastical courts and civil courts is not unequivocally clear (in part due to the lack of cases), Dutch courts tend to refrain, albeit temporarily, from hearing a case originating in a church tribunal once such proceedings have commenced or are an option. Even then, a Dutch court reviewing an ecclesiastical decision may tread lightly. Nonetheless, the autonomy of ecclesiastical courts is not unlimited. Thus, they must adhere to basic legal values (such as the duty to act 'in good faith') and comply with certain fundamental procedural rules (for example, *audi et alteram partem*: hear the other side).[17]

---

[15] See notably *Kamerstukken* II, 2008–2009, 31 700 VI, nrs 129 and 160; and *Kamerstukken* II, 2009–2010, 32 123 VI, nrs 5 and 8.

[16] Article 17 of the Constitution: 'No one may be prevented against his will from being heard by the courts to which he is entitled to apply under the law'.

[17] See S van Bijsterveld, 'Church Autonomy in The Netherlands: The Distinctiveness of the Church, the Interplay Between Legal, Popular, and Ecclesiastical Perspectives; Church Autonomy as

Against this background, the debate on Shari'a courts may seem odd. It may become even odder if we place the debate in the context of the recent broader experimentation with alternative ways of dispute-resolution in general. The unease with Shari'a courts, therefore, cannot be explained in terms of 'ordinary' relationships between religious law and civil law, nor the expanding utilization of alternative dispute-resolution.

Here, we stumble once more on the lack of basic knowledge of, and familiarity with, the way Shari'a adjudication works in practice. As we have seen, this is an essential element in the development of stable relationships between public authorities and religious organizations as well as a workable relationship between civil law and religious law. Combined with the negative associations the word 'Shari'a' provokes, the lack of familiarity makes progress difficult. Thus, the decision of the Cabinet to commission an investigation into Muslim courts is wise.

At a deeper level, there appears to be something else at stake. In his lecture, the Archbishop asked whether greater accommodation of religious law would not prove to be a reinforcement to members of minority communities of precisely those elements of the community the legal system wants to protect them against.[18] This comment is insightful. The question takes us to the basic presuppositions governing Dutch society and religion. These guide our understanding of the law generally, and the relationship between religious law and civil law specifically.

Implicit in the state's treatment of religion are at least two presuppositions. The first is free choice in matters of religion; the second is religious believers' basic familiarity with both the law in general and the law's protection of voluntariness and consent in religious matters.

As to the first presupposition, take the occasional but tense discussions as to the extent to which the legally guaranteed right of religious freedom is a social reality for Dutch Muslims who wish to change or abandon their religion. The same issues arise for Shari'a courts. The state is rightly concerned here, not about the *theory* of the relationship between ecclesiastical courts and civil courts, but about whether *in reality* free choice exists, and whether undue social or peer pressure is in fact being exercised. As to the second presupposition, whereas there is a basic familiarity with the law in general and an appreciation of human rights protections by those taking their disputes to non-Islamic ecclesiastical courts, this is not self-evident for the (not so fully integrated) Muslim immigrants. Doubts about the fulfilment of these two presuppositions leads to concerns about the coming into existence of 'parallel legal systems'. The whole question of Shari'a tribunals is entwined with issues of cultural integration and the applicability of the fundamental presuppositions of Dutch law and society.

a "Test Case"' in H Warnink (ed), *Legal Position of Churches and Church Autonomy* (Leuven: Peeters, 2001) 147; A H Santing-Wubs, *Kerken in Geding: Burgerlijke Rechter en Kerkelijke Geschillen* (The Hague: BJu, 2002).

[18] Williams (n 1 above) at [10].

E. Religious Marriage and Civil Marriage

The societal presuppositions are evident when one turns to 'informal marriages'—unions where at least one of the two partners mistakenly assumes that a legally valid marriage exists. Such an assumption can be based on 'a ceremony, ritual, or contract'[19] and thus religious ceremonies play a role here. This type of matter is at the centre of the Archbishop of Canterbury's plea for greater accommodation of religious law into the law of the land.

Approximately a decade ago, it would have seemed strange to predict that religious ceremonies solemnizing personal relationships would be an issue. In the Netherlands, only a civil marriage has legal effect. Religious ceremonies with respect to marriage may only take place after a civil marriage has been conducted. A religious minister is obliged by law to have proof of a valid civil marriage prior to conducting a religious nuptial ceremony and, if he does not comply, he is liable to criminal prosecution.[20] In a 1971 ruling, the Supreme Court concluded that this legal arrangement constitutes a restriction of religious liberty, but one that is justified under the European Convention on Human Rights.[21]

In the early 1990s, the issue was raised whether this legal arrangement was outdated and should be abolished. It was considered a matter of common knowledge that a civil marriage is the only legally valid marriage. Besides, many people no longer opted for a civil marriage. However, they may have wished to sanction their relationship with a religious ceremony. Could they have a religious ceremony which was not related to marriage? And if so, why would religious ceremonies for other intimate relationships, including homosexual unions (if that were acceptable to the couple's particular church), be possible, and just not a ceremony related to marriage?

Ultimately, a political decision was made not to change the existing regime. One of the main reasons to retain the status quo was that this avoided any misunderstanding—for the Muslim population and others—about the status of marriage. It was also reasoned that public authorities were best equipped to assess whether there were any impediments to marriage as defined by law, such as too close a blood relationship between the two people involved or one of the partners being under age. The discussion appeared closed.

In the meantime, societal patterns of relationships and their legal status have changed considerably. Apart from simply living together, couples may draw up civil law contracts or opt for a 'registered partnership' should they not want full marital status—an option which is also open to same-sex couples. Furthermore, same-sex

---

[19] The description of an 'informal marriage' is taken from J van der Leun and A Leupen, *Informele Huwelijken in Nederland; Een Exploratieve Studie*, Universiteit Leiden/WODC 2009 (unpublished report) 11.

[20] See Civil Code, Art 1:68 and Criminal Code, Art 449.

[21] Hoge Raad, 22 June 1971, Nederlandse Jurisprudentie 1972, 31.

marriage has been introduced. Thus, we see both an 'informalization' of relationships and a wider range of possibilities for the formalization of relationships.

Given these developments, are religious (marriage) ceremonies, *without* a prior civil marriage having taken place, a problem? Leaving aside technical discussions on what the Dutch legal provisions actually do or do not allow, one could reason that there should be no problem if one sees this matter purely or predominantly in terms of the relationship between civil and religious law. But, like the concerns about Shari'a tribunals, many of the real issues fall outside the concern from the point of view of church–state relationships that the formal legal prerequisites for marriage must be satisfied.

The strongest objection to these practices relates to a fundamental value in Dutch society: marriage (and similar intimate personal relationships) should be the exercise of free will and be entered into voluntarily. Persons, notably young Islamic women, should be protected from undue social pressure to enter into monogamous conjugal relationships—and *a fortiori* polygamous ones —even if these are not, legally speaking, valid marriages.[22] This is especially the case regarding 'informal marriages'— marriages in which at least one partner assumes that a legally valid marriage exists. If a vulnerable party needs protection, the state has an obligation to provide for this.

Once again, the relative unfamiliarity with the actual situation is a handicap, as is the lack of knowledge of the participants and the social pressure exercised on them. Here the key issue appears to be not so much a matter of the accommodation of religious law per se, but a concern about the reality of the subtle cultural, peer, and other pressures exerted in these close-knit worlds. In short, there is genuine trepidation about the coming into existence—*in practice*—of a parallel legal system. All this underscores the importance of societal integration—a policy acknowledged but long neglected amidst the pressures of ongoing immigration.

F. Faith-based Social Activities

Until recently, the creed of many of the ruling elite was that religion was an exclusively private matter. This was certainly still the case when the first steps were taken to accommodate Islamic religious practices in Dutch law. Even communal religious activities were regarded as such. A combination of factors supported such a vision. First, the omnipresent social welfare state was at its peak and took care of 'public' affairs. Secondly, according to the dominant secularization thesis, religion was withering. Thirdly, the cultural climate was based on largely Christian mores, and the prevailing political ethos stressed tolerance. None of these three factors now pertains. This sea change is illustrated in the field of faith-based social activities.

---

[22] The issue should also be set against the larger background issue of forced marriages of young Muslim women when they travel abroad with their family.

Social activities by faith-based organizations have formed part of the fabric of Dutch society for many years. Education, housing, and healthcare were and are run by such entities. In the emergence of the welfare state, they became increasingly part of a system in which public authorities themselves developed initiatives in the provision of these services. Faith-based bodies became highly regulated by the state and shared in financial schemes.[23] Over time, many of these traditional activities were often subject to processes of expansion, professionalization, and specialization. The religious identity of faith-based organizations increasingly became a 'peculiar' asset that needed to be 'safeguarded' against the state, which was otherwise heavily involved in areas of policy. Due to their increasing internal 'secularization', the religious character of these bodies became less pronounced over time (a dilution that was less marked in elementary schools than in specialized hospitals).

Currently, faith-based social activities are being 'rediscovered' and are receiving renewed interest. Many social activities carried out by churches (or other organizations based on a religion or belief) occur beyond the purely voluntary domain involving highly professional organizations such as the Salvation Army. These organizations run programmes ranging from the provision of food and shelter, to dealing with addictions, providing emergency assistance at airports, and combating loneliness. Small informal groups operate at a local level and are involved in activities such as encouraging youngsters to refrain from excessive drinking or, in case of migrant churches, helping their members become socially oriented. A wide variety of churches or church-affiliated organizations, such as traditional Dutch religious denominations, Christian migrant churches, and Islamic groups, also take part in faith-based activities. The examples are endless.

Such activities are neither simply activities 'in the private sphere' nor 'activities of the state', but genuinely *social and societal activities*—social engagement from a faith background. It is not surprising that in carrying out these activities organizations often come into contact with public authorities. For example they may act simply as a two-way intermediary between clients/citizens and the public authorities; they may be part of a network of social organizations and public authorities; or they may co-ordinate their activities with public authorities and be involved in carrying out public policies (and thus acquire public subsidies).

If anything, such contact is likely to increase rather than decrease in the near future. This is not due predominantly to developments within religion, but more because *the state itself* is in a process of reshaping its role vis-à-vis its citizens. Instead of being the main provider of social services, as it was in the heyday of the welfare state, the state is now increasingly an organizer and co-ordinator of multifarious activities. These tasks are being carried out by private entities. Inevitably, this

---

[23] In the field of education, this 'dual' system of private (confessional) education and public education is entrenched in the Dutch Constitution. The revision of 1917 explicitly guaranteed public funding for private elementary education on the same footing as public education. In areas other than elementary education this system is followed in ordinary legislation.

requires the state to engage systematically with religious organizations in financial and other respects.

It is precisely at this 'interface' that tensions arise.[24] This uneasiness was clearly demonstrated in 2009, when a borough of the municipality of Amsterdam granted its responsibility for the care of youth to the evangelical organization, Youth For Christ (YFC). This body was the successful tenderer according to the official public tendering procedure. Yet, the commotion that followed caused the chairman of the borough to step down.[25] The borough is predominantly Muslim and certain features of the administration of this social service reflect its religious demography. Thus, while YFC acquiesced to an open admittance policy, it was agreed also that no 'evangelization' would take place, and that a go-between organization would be created in order to secure youth workers who were not committed to YFC's mission. The issue is still very much alive: in November 2009, the town council of Amsterdam voted in favour of a motion against any (financial) co-operation with faith-based organizations that recruit employees from their own denominational background.

How does one explain tensions that arise from arrangements that traditionally form the fabric of Dutch society? In part it concerns a change in social reality or, perhaps more accurately, a change in the dominant *perception* of reality.

First, there is some unease with the fact that faith-based organizations are engaged in social activities that were formerly perceived as *either* 'public' or 'private' in character. They are perceived as discharging responsibilities previously designed for public authorities and acquiring greater authority and standing than simple private bodies working at arm's length. Secondly, as we have seen, many of these organizations were formerly seen as secularized state agencies. A keener awareness now exists that faith-based organizations really do have a religious character and embody a particular non-secular worldview. For those who held firmly to the vision of an inexorable secular future, this alone brings some concerns. Belatedly, the realization has dawned that these organizations do things differently and work on the basis of religiously grounded moral values. Where public funding is concerned, all these delicate matters come to the fore.

The debates in the Netherlands over faith-based activities are not concerned with a greater accommodation of religion by the law as such. Rather, they resurrect supposedly bygone questions about the premises and presuppositions that undergird Dutch society—foundational matters that most hoped had quietly faded into the background over the years. The heart of the current controversy

---

[24] Positive contributions in this field have been made by the Ministry of the Interior and the Association of Dutch Municipalities (Vereniging van Nederlandse Gemeenten (VNG)) in the brochure, *Tweeluik Religie en Publiek Domein: Handvatten Voor Gemeenten* (March 2009); and in a memorandum by the Mayor and Aldermen of Amsterdam on 'Separation of Church and State' (*Notitie Scheiding Kerk en Staat*) (unpublished 2008).

[25] F de Boys, 'Jongerenwerk Aanbesteed aan God', *Binnenlands Bestuur*, 27 February 2009, 28.

seems to be angst at the real (or perceived) rise of religious thinking and influence in the public sphere,[26] combined with the reshaping of the role of the state vis-à-vis its citizens.

The debate is not primarily one concerned with Islam, although areas such as education tap into the issues discussed here. There is no doubt that Muslims have the right to establish schools, just like any other faith; and, indeed, a number of such schools exist. However, a combination of doubts on the values taught at these schools, as well as some specific incidents that have occurred at Muslim schools, have fuelled debate on their desirability. Concerns over Muslim schools can be tackled through specific legal mechanisms, while leaving the overall system of schooling intact. Besides, by their very nature, schools (just like broadcasting corporations) bring religious bodies' beliefs and activities out in the open. This transparency stimulates discussion, which may, in turn, prompt religious communities to address their societal responsibilities. To reiterate, all this healthy interaction enables public authorities (and society at large) to get acquainted with these religious organizations and their way of life.

G. Debates on 'Values'

A further belated re-discovery is also underway. A paramount concern of religion is the nature and purpose of the human person, and therefore the organization and character of society itself. Religious views, even if held personally and privately, inevitably make themselves felt in politics. Religious beliefs influence important matters such as the structuring of male-female relations (in turn, symbolized by the wearing of certain garments) and a raft of contentious matters we currently tend to summarize under the broad rubric 'values and norms'. The idea that one's religious opinions and the communication of religious beliefs is merely an 'individual' issue has been reassessed. Once again, the awareness has dawned that such opinions or communications may also have profound social implications (think of the potential impact of the utterances of a 'radical' *imam*). The West's confrontation with Islam has highlighted all this.

There is more to this than simply a heightened awareness of religion. In a dynamic society, opinions on all sorts of social and moral questions may shift in a relatively short period of time. Consider topics such as marriage and sexuality and questions related to the beginning and end of human life. The framework for assessment of the diverse opinions on these issues has changed. Traditional Christian morality, once dominant, now diverges from and often conflicts with an increasingly secular 'mainstream' public opinion.

---

[26] This is also reflected in the ambiguous and muddled debates on freedom of expression, both with regard to the right to publish 'controversial' religious messages and 'offensive' publications, artwork, etc aimed at religion.

It seems no exaggeration to say that religious contributions to contemporary debates about morality and public policy are regarded by many secular liberals as 'problematic'. The issue the Archbishop of Canterbury raised in his lecture deserves attention: is the state's monopoly ('the law is the law'[27]) and the requirements of our liberal democracy under the rule of law (the preservation of 'the great political and social advances of Western legality'[28]) at odds with certain public expressions of religious belief?

In the past, 'discordant' or heterodox religious opinions and practices tended to concern modest (numerically speaking) groups which could readily be contained or 'localized'. It was therefore relatively easy to create an ad hoc exception or to simply tolerate a particular instance of diversity. Often these dissenting ways of life were never a threat to the majority—such as religious beliefs that rejected all forms of insurance. In other cases, what were once received opinions (such as on the role of women) were now held by a tiny recalcitrant minority.

With the rise of a major faith such as Islam, official acceptance of discordant values has become much more difficult. A good example is a case which concerned a Dutch political party, the Staatkundig Gereformeerde Partij (SGP). This orthodox Reformed party is represented in both Houses of Parliament. Since 1922 it has continuously held seats in the directly elected House (currently 2 out of 150), a feat that is unique in Dutch politics. (Other parties had predecessors before World War II, but they have since changed their names or merged with other parties.) Officially, the SGP is a theocratic party, but it functions in a fashion that accords with Dutch parliamentary democracy. Until June 2006, it did not admit women as members of the party. It still does not allow women to be elected in its name.

In 2005, a claim was brought against the government by, among others, a women's rights organization. It alleged that the state was in violation of the UN Convention on the Elimination of All Forms of Discrimination Against Women ('CEDAW') by allowing the SGP to exclude women. Both the Court of First Instance and the Court of Appeal came to the conclusion that the Dutch state was in breach of the Convention.[29] For our purpose, the following recital of the Court of First Instance is of interest:

3.6 The court rejects the argument of the State. In this instance...the interest of everyone...is at stake, in particular of women, to live in a democratic society in which discrimination on the grounds of sex—resulting in the exclusion of the right to be elected—is not tolerated, and in which the State uses its power of enforcement. This interest is more compelling if one realizes that it is not unimaginable that in the (near) future other parties may also emerge that may—for religious reasons—accord women a different political and/

---

[27] Williams (n 1 above) at [14].   [28] Ibid.

[29] The violation concerned Art 7, sub a and c, of the Convention. The Court of Cassation (Supreme Court) upheld the ruling of the Court of Appeal in its ruling of 9 April 2010 (HR 9 April 2010, LJN: BK4549).

or societal role than men, and, as a result of this, there is the risk that discrimination may creep in. In this respect, the State can exercise a steering role.[30]

Clearly, the phrase 'other parties' is an allusion to parties that might base themselves on Islamic teaching.

This again underscores the importance of developing a mutual familiarity between religious communities and public authorities. Returning to the question posed by the Archbishop: in general, it is not the 'extreme' cases that are an issue here. The real difficulties seem to be in areas in which Dutch social values have already shifted or are in the process of shifting.

This is not the place to deal in depth with the vast subject of moral and religious pluralism. However, a few remarks are apposite. Cases involving conflicting values are often dealt with according to the principle of 'equal treatment' and by applying equal treatment laws. Instances include cases involving visible religious symbols (the wearing of crucifixes or headscarves, for example), customs (the refusal of Islamic men to shake hands with a woman), or conscientious objection (such as the refusal of civil marriage celebrants to marry same-sex couples). As long as equal treatment laws maintain a fair framework that leaves reasonable room for religious practice and adopt a balanced approach so far as the burden of proof is concerned, such laws are helpful. Rather than opting for sweeping statements or very general principles, such a legal framework enables a contextual assessment to be made in which the concrete circumstances of the situation at hand can be fully considered and weighed. 'Vexatious claims to religious scruple',[31] as the Archbishop put it, can also be dealt with in such a context. Of course, such assessments themselves are seldom 'neutral' and different assessments can and do occur, even in what appear to be very similar cases. However, fair and reasonable outcomes are likely to emerge over time through this incremental case-by-case approach.

H. Concluding Thoughts

The relationship between law and religion has many dimensions. Similarly, a plea such as that by the Archbishop of Canterbury for a greater accommodation of religious law can be interpreted in various ways. One must be careful to specify the *particular* aspects of the relationship between the state and the religion that one wishes to modify so as to get a clearer appreciation of the issues at stake. One also needs to undertake a *detailed* analysis of where the law currently accommodates religion (as it does without much difficulty), where the real tensions lie, and what the reasons for this might be.

[30] Rechtbank's-Gravenhage, 7 September 2005 (author's unofficial translation).
[31] Williams (n 1 above) at [9].

I have highlighted four different areas—public facilities for religious practice, ecclesiastical courts, religious marriage (and other ceremonies marking intimate personal relationships), and faith-based social services—and I have also offered some thoughts on current 'values' debates. In each of the four substantive areas mentioned, conflicts will continue to occur over concrete issues. This is not a deviation from, but rather is a *vital part* of, the ongoing dialogue between law and religion in a dynamic society. It is *in and through* such confrontations, and the discussion about these, that balances will be struck and compromises carved out. Both sides will need to listen and be calm and analytical, rather than respond hastily and from dogmatic and outdated premises.

One of the central points Dr Rowan Williams made was that if 'the law of the land takes no account of what might be for certain agents a proper rationale for behaviour ... it fails in a significant way to *communicate* with someone involved in the legal process'.[32] How has the Netherlands fared in this regard?

Any legislative accommodation presupposes a recognizable communal religious practice (food prescriptions, days of worship, conscientious objection to military service, etc). Purely 'individual' religious-based claims to exculpation from the general law are seldom or never successful. When dealing with community-wide claims to exemption, broad notions of 'reasonableness' and other public policy considerations will be assessed to determine whether the case for exemption has been made out. Similarly, determinations under equal treatment laws involve careful and contextual weighing of relevant interests.

Religious marriage and the operation of religious courts present real challenges. All those participating in these settings need to be adequately armed with sufficient knowledge to ensure that their participation is truly consensual and that their vital liberty and other interests are secured. Counteracting any overt and covert coercive pressures operating upon young people (and notably women) represents a similar challenge. It should be remembered that, in an open society, free choice is as important an ideal as any other objective—including the accommodation of religious difference.

Leaving aside the question whether certain practices are 'religious' or 'cultural', it is clear that some kinds of conduct simply cannot be tolerated—for example, the preaching of violence against groups in society (such as homosexuals), or heinous practices such as honour killings or female genital mutilation. Paradoxically, the fiercest debates on values will not take place with respect to these extreme cases. (The difficulty presented by these cases is not their merits, but the *practical* task of curtailing them.) Tensions in practice *and* theory will more likely occur in areas where core societal values are shifting, or have recently shifted, and in novel areas. It will be important here to keep the spirit of religious liberty alive.

Debates will often have a religious flavour, given the renaissance of public religion in the late twentieth century and the state's rediscovery of religion's inherently

---

[32] Ibid at [7] (emphasis in original).

social character. However, we must realize that such debates are not exclusively tied to, nor answered by, religion as such. It is important for policymakers to find new ways for law, religion, and morality to relate, and to create ample room for all sides, whatever their worldview, to inform and contribute to social policy.[33]

We must also realize that religion, society, and law are never watertight compartments. The concrete expressions of the more universally held principles in these domains are not static or etched in stone. Changes in one domain subtlety affect the other. Their mutual relationship will, therefore, in the words of the Archbishop, always to some extent remain 'unfinished business'.

---

[33] See S van Bijsterveld, *The Empty Throne: Democracy and the Rule of Law in Transition* (Utrecht: Lemma, 2002), especially Ch 6 ('The Normative Frame: The Return of Natural Law').

13

Reflections on the Establishment of Shari'a Courts in Australia

Abdullah Saeed

A. Introduction*

Recently, in a number of Western countries, a debate on establishing Shari'a courts has been generated, spurred on by Muslims who have seen the need for some form of extra-judicial institution or mechanism to assist in dispute-resolution between Muslims. Although dispute-resolution mechanisms to deal with issues between Muslims—in areas such as divorce, inheritance, and the like— do generally exist informally in Muslim communities, there is a growing recognition that more formal mechanisms or procedures could be of great benefit (particularly for some women) for resolving family law matters. However, the issue is contentious, both within Muslim communities and without. In the United Kingdom informal Shari'a tribunals have been established as a form of alternative dispute-resolution, in cases where both parties agree to recognize the tribunal's competence. On the other hand, after extensive and acrimonious debate, proposals to establish similar institutions in Canada were quashed. Following a storm of protests, all formal religion-based arbitration in Ontario (Canada) was scrapped.

In Australia, the debate is underway. Like several other Western countries, Australia has a relatively small Muslim population. Muslims in Australia can trace their presence to pre-European settlement, as Macassans (in today's Indonesia) visited and fished in the northern areas of the continent. In the mid-nineteenth century, Malay pearl divers in Western Australia, and the Afghan cameleers who were brought to Australia for the camel transport industry, represented the first significant arrival of Muslims after European settlement. Today, Australia has Muslims from over 80 countries (especially those in the Middle East, Africa, South Asia and South East Asia) all of whom are contributing to Australia's culture and religious life. Muslims, who number some 340,000, constitute the third largest

* I thank Patricia Prentice and Helen McCue for their research assistance, critical comments, and polishing-up of various parts of the draft of this essay.

faith group in Australia and around 36 per cent of Australian Muslims are born in Australia.[1] These Muslims belong to a range of Islamic theological, legal, and mystical groupings.

This essay considers whether there is room for a Shari'a court in the Australian legal system, the issues raised in the debate so far, and the kinds of challenges a Shari'a court might face if instituted in Australia.

B. Notions of Shari'a and Shari'a courts

Before considering the debate on Shari'a courts in Australia, it is important to address some issues of terminology.

Among Muslims there is no universally agreed-upon definition of the term 'Shari'a'. For some, the Shari'a represents the broad principles, values, and norms that exist in the foundation texts of Islam—the Qur'an and *Sunnah*. For others, it means the rules and regulations that are clearly spelt out in these two sources; or the 'laws' that have been constructed by Muslim jurists based on the Qur'an and *Sunnah* and Islamic principles of jurisprudence. In the West, Shari'a often simply means 'Islamic law'. In this essay I will use the term 'Shari'a' to mean Islamic law as it exists in classical Islamic legal texts written by the Muslim jurists of the pre-modern period (that is, before the mid-nineteenth century). These address areas as diverse as prayer, fasting, and pilgrimage; marriage, divorce, custody, and inheritance; financial transactions; criminal penalties; and the laws of war and peace.

In the pre-modern period, Shari'a as a body of laws, rules, regulations, and norms was operational in most Muslim societies around the world. However, during the twentieth century, its application came to be generally restricted to family law: the laws governing marriage, divorce, custody, and inheritance. Even though most Muslim-majority countries have enacted laws to regulate these matters, the extent to which the Shari'a, as existed in the pre-modern period, is reflected in their legislation differs widely.

When Muslims refer to 'Shari'a courts' in the Australian context, they usually mean an extra-judicial institution that will apply some aspects of classical Islamic family law—either formally (with some legal recognition) or informally (as a community institution), particularly for disputes related to marriage, divorce, and inheritance. These bodies would not hear criminal matters or, generally speaking, adjudicate over areas of law where the Australian legal system provides redress. They would be expected to work within the parameters of Australia's existing law. The term court in this essay thus refers to an institution that would formally or

---

[1] According to the 2006 Census, some 340,392 people, or 1.71 per cent of the Australian population, identify as Muslim. The majority of people who reported Islam as their religion were born overseas: Australian Bureau of Statistics, *Perspectives on Migrants* 2007, available at <http://www.abs.gov.au/ausstats/abs@.nsf/Lookup/3416.0Main%20Features22007?opendocument&tab name=Summary&prodno=3416.0&issue=2007&num=&view=>.

informally apply Shari'a norms, rules, and regulations in cases involving Muslims, with particular reference to marriage, divorce, and inheritance, within the broad context of Australian family law.

C. Shari'a Councils and Public Debates in the United Kingdom

Although the discussion on establishing Shari'a courts or similar institutions in Australia is relatively recent, similar debates have already occurred in other Western countries.

Various Shari'a courts, or what are better termed Shari'a 'councils', have been operating informally in the United Kingdom since the early 1980s.[2] They resolve mainly personal and civil disputes in matters of divorce, marriage, inheritance, dowry payment, and financial arrangements. While some Shari'a councils are private gatherings at a mosque (where a single *imam* or scholar presides), others operate with formal rules of procedure, an application fee, and a process for taking evidence from both parties. One important example of the latter is the Islamic Shari'a Council,[3] which primarily resolves marital disputes in Britain.

While recognition of Shari'a within the UK legal system is still being debated, there are some interesting developments unfolding. Take the establishment of Muslim Arbitration Tribunals (MATs), for example.[4] Distinct from the informal Shari'a councils, MATs were instituted under the Arbitration Act 1996 as a form of alternative dispute-resolution to provide interested Muslims with a means of resolving disputes in accordance with Islamic law. MATs have jurisdiction in cases where both parties to the dispute agree to recognize the tribunal's power to arbitrate. The decision, or award, is enforceable through county courts in England and Wales and parties have the right to seek redress by way of judicial review in the High Court. The Jewish *Beth Din* courts, which resolve civil cases, operate under the same provisions of the Arbitration Act.

Similar to the Shari'a councils, MATs have the power to arbitrate in family law cases (such as divorce and inheritance), as well as in civil and commercial disputes and disputes involving mosques. MATs do *not* have jurisdiction to arbitrate in criminal matters or child custody cases, and can only assist in reconciliation (if the parties wish this) in cases involving domestic violence; any criminal charges arising in the course of these disputes fall under the purview of the regular courts. In divorce proceedings, MATs may only grant a religious divorce, as cases involving changes to an individual's personal status in the United Kingdom must be heard by the civil courts. MATs arbitrate according to defined rules of procedure.

---

[2] See S Bano, 'In Pursuit of Religious and Legal Diversity: A Response to the Archbishop of Canterbury and the "Sharia Debate" in Britain' (2008) 10 Ecc LJ 283, 296.

[3] See the Council's website at <http://www.islamic-sharia.org>.

[4] For full details, see the official MAT website at <http://www.matribunal.com>.

A panel of two members—a scholar of Islamic law and a barrister (either male or female) qualified to practice in England and Wales—sits on each case and issues a determination within 14 days of the hearing. Parties have the option of being represented, legally or by another person, if they choose.

D. The Acrimonious Canadian Experience

Shari'a courts were first considered in Canada after 1991, when Ontario began to examine ways to ease its backlogged court system through the greater use of arbitration. The province decided to change its arbitration legislation to allow 'faith-based arbitration' so that Muslims, Jews, Catholics, and members of other faiths could use religious principles or law to settle certain aspects of family disputes without resorting to the regular court system.[5] Like MATs in the United Kingdom, faith-based arbitration was voluntary and could only be instituted if both parties recognized the arbitrator's competence. The determinations handed down by the arbitrator were designed to be binding.[6] Under the amended Ontario Arbitration Act, the Islamic Institute of Civil Justice proposed establishing Shari'a-based arbitration panels to assist with dispute-resolution for Ontario's Muslims. It was then that the debate among Muslims in Ontario intensified.

The proposal ran into fierce opposition from women's groups, legal organizations, and the Muslim Canadian Congress. Leading the charge against the proposal was a group of mainly Iranian Muslim women who had fled from Iran and Ayatollah Khomeini's Islamic state. They argued that under Shari'a law a woman was worth half that of a man and could be divorced without any rights.[7] The National Association of Women and the Law, the Canadian Council of Muslim Women, and the National Organization of Immigrant and Visible Minority Women of Canada argued similarly that men and women would not be treated equally if the Shari'a was implemented in this context.[8] In response, other Muslim women argued that Shari'a law had a bad name because of how it had been interpreted, and they stressed that Shari'a courts in Canada were important because they could lead towards developing 'a progressive and tolerant form of Shari'a, one that is consistent with 21st century notions of gender

[5] See generally N Bahkt, 'Were Muslim Barbarians Really Knocking On the Gates of Ontario? The Religious Arbitration Controversy—Another Perspective' [2006] Ottawa Law Review 67.

[6] L Weinrib, 'Ontario's Shari Law Debate: Law and Politics under the *Charter*' in R Moon (ed), *Law and Religious Pluralism in Canada* (Vancouver: UBC Press, 2008) Ch 10, 250.

[7] L Trevelyan, 'Will Canada introduce Sharia law?', *BBC News*, 26 August 2004, available at <http://news.bbc.co.uk/2/hi/programmes/from_our_own_correspondent/3599264.stm>.

[8] For a detailed analysis see S Razack, 'The "Sharia Law Debate" in Ontario: The Modernity/Premodernity Distinction in Legal Efforts to Protect Women from Culture' (2007) 15 *Feminist Legal Studies* 3; and A C Korteweg, 'The Sharia Debate in Ontario: Gender, Islam and Representations of Muslim Women's Agency' (2008) 22 *Gender & Society* 434.

equality'.[9] Moreover, they argued that Shari'a courts could be used to give women more power in contractual negotiations; for instance, when drafting pre-nuptial agreements.

The debate in Ontario—and later in Quebec—eventually sparked international protests, with human rights campaigners holding demonstrations in 11 cities in Europe and North America against the proposal to set up Shari'a tribunals.[10] The emotional furore the proposals triggered prompted the provincial government to initiate a review of the Arbitration Act, headed by former Attorney General Marion Boyd. Overall, the Boyd Report gave cautious approval to the propriety of a system of religious-based arbitration that incorporated safeguards to protect the vulnerable:

The *Arbitration Act* does contain protections, and, as a result of the Review, I will be recommending additional safeguards that recognize the values inherent in the *Charter of Rights and Freedoms*. Nonetheless, I do not believe the Constitution prohibits the use of arbitration, faith-based or otherwise, for resolving disputes about family law and inheritance.[11]

Despite the Boyd Report's thoughtful analysis and careful recommendations, the Ontario Government eventually decided to halt *all* voluntary faith-based arbitration—including the dispute mechanisms that had been used by Christians and Jews (thereby deflecting criticism that it was discriminating against Muslims).[12] In his statement to the press—on 11 September 2005—the Premier, Dalton McGuinty, was adamant: 'I've come to the conclusion that the debate has gone on long enough. There will be no Sharia law in Ontario. There will be no religious arbitration in Ontario. There will be one law for all Ontarians'.[13]

Ontario citizens could still seek religious advice on issues such as divorce and child custody; however, officially sanctioned arbitration tribunals would not play a role in family law in the province.[14] Similarly, on 26 May 2005, the Quebec National Assembly unanimously supported a motion to block the use of Shari'a law in Quebec courts.[15]

There are many who have suggested that the debate in Canada may serve as a useful reference for the debate as to whether Shari'a law could ever work in

---

[9] Trevelyan (n 7 above).

[10] E Davies, 'Protesters condemn Canada's sharia court plan', *The Independent*, 9 September 2005, available at <http://www.independent.co.uk/news/world/americas/protesters-condemn-canadas-sharia-court-plan-506063.html>.

[11] Ontario Ministry of the Attorney General, *Dispute Resolution in Family Law: Protecting Choice, Promoting Inclusion* (December 2004) 77, available at <http://www.attorneygeneral.jus.gov.on.ca/english/about/pubs/boyd>.

[12] Anne McIlroy, 'One law to rule them all', *The Guardian*, 14 September 2005, available at <http://www.guardian.co.uk/world/2005/sep/14/worlddispatch.annemcilroy>.

[13] Ibid.   [14] Ibid.

[15] For one reaction, see 'Muslim Council of Montreal condemns Quebec's decision to ban the use of Islamic tribunals', available at <http://www.montrealmuslimnews.net/shariaquebec.htm>.

the Australian context.[16] Canada and Australia are immigrant-based and have substantial Muslim populations. Both are self-governing federal democracies that follow the Westminster form of government, and each country has a free market economy with similarities in terms of natural resources, agriculture, and financial sectors. Both also have long-standing indigenous cultures and were former British colonies. The prevailing social norms are also very similar in both countries, and they share similar religious, educational, and judicial institutions in terms of family patterns, societal expectations for men and women, electoral representation, and legislation. It remains to be seen, however, whether calls for Shari'a courts, or other such forms of religious-based dispute-resolution, will be accepted in Australia.

E. The Public Debate in Australia

In response to some Muslim leaders' calls for Shari'a courts that are able to make decisions in matters such as divorce,[17] there has been public debate about recognizing Shari'a in Australia. Thus far, public figures from both sides of government, including federal and state government ministers and media personalities, have generally spoken out in opposition. For example, in February 2008, Federal Attorney-General Robert McClelland ruled out the introduction of Shari'a law in Australia: 'The Rudd government is not considering and will not consider the introduction of any part of Shari'a law into the Australian legal system'.[18] The opposition, then led by Dr Brendan Nelson, agreed: 'The idea that in some way you would change your basic values, culture and law to accommodate some people who feel that they don't want to see themselves as Australians first, above all else— under no circumstances would I support that'.[19]

As Nelson's statement indicates, some of this debate has centered around the issue of Australian values, what it means to be an Australian citizen, and the suggestion that any recognition of Shari'a law in the justice system would be contrary to Australian values. This thesis was expounded by Peter Costello (former Federal Treasurer in the Howard government) in a widely reported 2006 speech:

The radical Muslim cleric, Ben Brika, was asked in an interview on the *7.30 Report* in August last year: 'But don't you think Australian Muslims, Muslims living in Australia,

---

[16] Eg Sebastian De Brennan, 'It is only a matter of time before sharia law is proposed in Australia', *Canberra Times*, 6 March 2006, available at <http://www.canberratimes.com.au/news/local/news/opinion/it-is-only-a-matter-of-time-before-sharia-law-is-proposed-in-australia/711875.aspx?storypage=0>.

[17] P Osborne and J Turnbull, 'Govt rejects call for Islamic courts', *The Age*, 8 February 2008, available at <http://news.theage.com.au/national/govt-rejects-call-for-islamic-courts-20080208-1r0s.html>.

[18] P Coorey, 'Australia rejects call for Islamic courts', *The Sydney Morning Herald*, 9 February 2008, available at <http://www.smh.com.au/news/national/australia-rejects-call-for-islamic-courts/2008/02/08/1202234167178.html>.

[19] Ibid.

also have a responsibility to adhere to Australian law?' To which he answered: 'This is a big problem. There are two laws: there is an Australian law and there is an Islamic law'.

No, this is not a big problem. There is one law we are all expected to abide by. It is the law enacted by the Parliament under the Australian Constitution. If you can't accept that then you don't accept the fundamentals of what Australia is and what it stands for.

Our State is a secular State. As such it can protect the freedom of all religions for worship. Religion instructs its adherents on faith, morals and conscience. But there is not a separate stream of law derived from religious sources that competes with or supplants Australian law in governing our civil society. The source of our law is the democratically elected legislature.

There are countries that apply religious or sharia law—Saudi Arabia and Iran come to mind. If a person wants to live under sharia law these are countries where they might feel at ease. But not Australia.... Before entering a mosque visitors are asked to take off their shoes. This is a sign of respect. If you have a strong objection to walking in your socks don't enter the mosque. Before becoming an Australian you will be asked to subscribe to certain values. If you have strong objections to those values don't come to Australia.[20]

The Prime Minister of the time, John Howard, affirmed that his Treasurer's comments were fundamentally accurate and not designed to inflame or divide people: 'What Peter [Costello] was basically saying is that if people don't like what this country is then they shouldn't come here'.[21]

One reason for the perception that Shari'a law and 'Australian values' are largely incompatible is that debates about Shari'a are often influenced by a view that essentially reduces the Shari'a to an archaic or barbaric legal code, one that centres around the *hudūd* penalties (such as penalties for adultery, theft, murder, and consumption of wine) and the subjugation of women. As a result, Shari'a courts, especially those with jurisdiction limited to family law, are perceived to be institutions that will strip women of the rights that are afforded to them by the law of the land. There are also other arguments that have received some currency in the Shari'a courts debate. It is necessary to consider them to understand the context and intensity of the public discussion.

The first argument is that Australia is primarily a Christian country, with ethics, values, and a legal framework that has been derived from Christianity and the Anglo-Celtic tradition. For example, former Prime Minister John Howard noted, 'Australia [has] a core culture as an offshoot of western civilisation with a heavily Anglo-Saxon identity and Christianity as the great moral shaping force'.[22] It is true

---

[20] P Costello, 'Worth Promoting, Worth Defending: Australian Citizenship, What it means and How to defend it', address to the Sydney Institute, 23 February 2006, available at <http://www.treasurer.gov.au/DisplayDocs.aspx?pageID=&doc=speeches/2006/004.htm&min=phc>. See also 'If you want sharia law, move: Costello', *The Age*, 23 February 2006, available at <http://www.smh.com.au/news/National/If-you-want-sharia-law-move-Costello/2006/02/23/1140670199148.html>.

[21] 'PM: Costello comments right', *Sydney Morning Herald*, 24 February 2006, at <http://www.smh.com.au/news/national/trad-hits-back-at-islamophobia/2006/02/24/1140670236214.html>.

[22] 'Fed: Howard backs Costello over Sharia law comments', *AAP Newsfeed*, 24 February 2006. The statement appears to have been made on a Southern Cross Broadcasting radio programme. See <http://majorityrights.com/index.php/weblog/comments/prime_minister_howard_sounds_good/>.

that there are Christian underpinnings to the Australian constitution. Sir Henry Parkes, regarded as one of the Fathers of the Federation, said: 'we are a British people, pre-eminently a Christian people, and our laws, our whole system of jurisprudence, our Constitution are based upon and interwoven with our Christian belief'.[23] However, the ethnic and cultural composition of Australia has evolved considerably in recent decades and continues to evolve. Similarly, Australia's social, administrative, and legal system has adjusted to the needs of its increasingly diverse community.[24]

A second argument is that citizenship involves adherence to 'Australian' values. These values are particularly embodied in the legal structures that separate 'church' and 'state'. Consequently, the application of religious law—any religious law—is said to be inappropriate. The introduction of Shari'a law to Australia, even on a limited basis, would (the argument goes) be a fundamental threat to Australia's secular and egalitarian values. But this may not necessarily be the case. A Jewish *Beth Din* court has operated in Melbourne for a number of decades, providing rulings on divorce, conversions, and adoptions, as well as commercial matters within the Orthodox Jewish community.[25] The court has provided the Orthodox Jewish community with an institution to arbitrate in particular disputes related to the Jewish faith, without threatening or undermining the broader operation of Australia's legal system or values. Moreover, Koori courts and sentencing circles have also been established for indigenous Australians.[26]

A third contention is that Shari'a courts are merely the beginning of a greater Muslim 'agenda' to eventually see all Australians come under Shari'a law. Although there is a perception that the establishment of Shari'a courts is likely to lead to Muslim Australians pushing for the *full* introduction of Shari'a law, this is unlikely to occur. Thus far, Australian Muslims' demands for recognition of their norms have been confined to relatively few areas, such as burial places for Muslims and the recognition of Islamic burial practices, the recognition of Islamic marriages within Australian family law, and the establishment of Islamic interest-free financial institutions within the current regulatory framework. These matters relate to the recognition of certain aspects of what Muslims consider to be essential religious practices—places of worship, facilities for prayer, and the like. Moreover, they have been negotiated with local and state authorities, employers, or schools, and they

---

[23] F Nile, 'Sharia law goes against Australian tradition: Lets keep the faith', *Geelong Advertiser*, 27 October 2005, 17. See also <http://www.ourconstitution.org/constitution_creation.php>

[24] See, eg the Discussion Paper issued by the Human Rights and Equal Opportunity Commission, *Freedom of Religion and Belief in the 21st Century* (2008).

[25] See the Council of Orthodox Synagogues of Victoria website at <http://www.cosv.org.au/gsqp.php?gsqp=bethdin>.

[26] The Koori Court in Victoria, established under the Magistrates' Court (Koori Court) Act 2002, is a division of the Magistrates' Court that sentences indigenous (Aboriginal) defendants. See M Harris, 'From Australian Courts to Aboriginal Courts in Australia—Bridging the Gap' (2004–2005) 16 *Current Issues in Criminal Justice* 26.

represent a compromise between the demands of religion and the requirements of Australian society and law.

It also seems that the majority of Muslim Australians are not advocating for Shari'a law. Jamila Hussain, lecturer in Islamic law at Sydney's University of Technology, speculates that most Muslims are happy with Australian law as it is and there is little desire for the full implementation of Shari'a law, especially Islamic criminal law.[27] Many Muslims are likely to argue that they are not interested in imposing Shari'a law as more than just a set of personal religious values. Yasser Soliman, a Muslim leader who sits on the Victorian Multicultural Commission, and who is also president of the Victorian Islamic Family and Childcare Agency, stressed that any 'introduction of Shari'a law would need the approval of the wider Australian community, not just Australian Muslims'.[28]

F. The Question of Non-Muslim Rule over Muslims

The broader issue of whether Muslims can be 'fully' Muslim despite not being governed by the Shari'a in Western nations such as Australia is still a contentious issue among some parts of the Muslim community. The Qur'an views Muslim presence among non-Muslims in Mecca during the Prophet's residence there in the first 12 years of his mission (610–622 CE) as normal. It was only after the Prophet established a 'Muslim territory' in Medina, following his migration from Mecca, that the Qur'an asked Meccan Muslims to migrate to the new territory—the town of Medina[29]—to consolidate and strengthen the Muslim community there.

The Qur'an indicates on a number of occasions that what matters is not whether Muslims live among a non-Muslim majority, but whether they are free from oppression and persecution in these places. The Prophet even encouraged Muslims to seek refuge with a Christian ruler while fleeing persecution in Mecca. When his teaching spread across Arabia, the Prophet also accepted the fact that individual Muslims would live among and sometimes be ruled by pagans, Jews, and Christians.[30] However, this position changed with the writings of several classical jurists in the post-prophetic period. For instance Malik (d 769 CE), the 'founder' of the Mālikī School of law—the strictest school with regard to Muslim residence

[27] 'Sharia council an option for Australia: academic', *ABC News*, 8 February 2008, available at <http://www.abc.net.au/news/stories/2008/02/08/2157733.htm?site=news>.

[28] Osborne and Turnbull (n 17 above).

[29] Qur'an 2:218 and 4:89.

[30] While the Qur'an expected Muslims and also Christians and Jews to govern their affairs in light of God's instructions, it did not consider the implementation of Islamic law, as it was understood in the post-prophetic period, as the key determinant of the legitimacy of Muslim residence in a particular territory. Muslim jurists who supported the view that Muslims may reside in non-Muslim lands often argued that Muslims were to abide by the rules and regulations of those lands. For a discussion on Muslims under non-Muslim rule, see Khaled Abou El Fadl, 'Legal Debates on Muslim Minorities: Between Rejection and Accommodation' (1994) 22 *Journal of Religion and Ethics* 127.

under non-Muslim rule—opined that Muslims should not reside in non-Muslim territories. Malik apparently disapproved of Muslims travelling to non-Muslim lands, even for business.[31] This position, in various forms, was adopted by subsequent Mālikī jurists and has been maintained to some extent until the modern period.

While Mālikīs tended to be the strictest, other schools of law, such as Shāfiʿīs, Hanbalīs, Hanafīs, and even Shiʾa, are more flexible with regard to Muslim residence under non-Muslim rule. For instance, Tabari (d 923 CE), a commentator on the Qurʾan, argued that the ability to practise religion is the key determinant in any discussion on where Muslim residence is permissible. Shafiʾi (d 820 CE) considered that Muslims may reside in non-Muslim territories if there is no fear that they may be enticed away from their religion. The Hanafi jurist, Shaybani (d 805 CE), also argued that Muslims are not obliged to migrate from non-Muslim to Muslim territory.[32] Despite the different positions on the question of residence, there is a good degree of agreement on this point: when Muslims live under non-Muslim rule they are generally expected to follow the laws of the land. This is generally conditional upon Muslims having religious freedom to perform their basic religious duties (such as prayer).

Many of these issues are being considered by Muslim thinkers based in the West today. A key point for them is that Muslim presence in the West (and therefore under non-Muslim rule there) is permanent. In the pre-modern period, in many contexts, it was relatively easy for any religious community, even if it were a minority, to function as a single entity under its own religious law: Jews under Jewish law and Muslims under Islamic law, for instance. This is because of the way in which religious communities were treated in the great empires. Religious communities were considered quasi-independent entities with their own norms, rules, and laws in many cases. However, in the modern period, the emergence of nation-states based on the idea of common citizenship has changed this situation dramatically.

Broadly speaking, Muslim views on living in the West under non-Muslim rule can be placed into three categories:[33]

First, those who are reluctant to take part in Western societies but continue to live in the West might be referred to as 'Isolationists'. Muslims in this group argue for a strict following of the 'authorized' pre-modern interpretations of Islamic law (Sunni or Shia). For them, it is the Qurʾan and the practice of the Prophet that should guide Muslims—not modern 'needs' or concerns—and the Qurʾan (both

---

[31] S A Jackson [Abd al-Hakim], 'Muslims, Islamic Law and Public Policy in the United States' (3 July 2005) in *SunniPath: The Online Islamic Academy*, available at <http://qa.sunnipath.com/issue_view.asp?HD=1&ID=2625&CATE=124 >.

[32] See A Saeed, 'Muslims under non-Muslim Rule: Evolution of a Discourse' in A Reid and M Gilsenan (eds), *Islamic Legitimacy in a Plural Asia* (London: Routledge, 2007) 17. See also the sources cited there.

[33] Ibid 23–24

in its text and meaning) is permanent and universal in its application, regardless of the cultural context in which it is applied. According to the 'Isolationists', this means, for instance, that if the Qur'an says that a man may marry four wives, then this should remain the case forever. 'Hardline' Isolationists among Muslims in the West claim that a Muslim cannot be bound by a national constitution that allows interest, alcohol, and other behaviour which contradicts Islamic teachings.[34]

Secondly, there are those Muslims who have some admiration for the fundamental values of the West, but are undecided as to whether they want to be full members of Western societies. Muslims in this second category might be referred to as 'semi-Isolationists'. They essentially follow a range of the Isolationists' views and interpretations, but attempt to present the ethico-legal content of the Qur'an (and the guidance provided by the Prophet) in modern terms. They do so, however, without actually asking fundamental questions about the socio-historical context of the Qur'an or its subsequent interpretations.

A third category comprises those Muslims who do not see any difficulty in combining notions of being 'Western' and Muslim. We might call them 'Participants'. Muslims in this group emphasize the importance of understanding the social and historical context in which the Qur'an was revealed and how the interpretations derived from it have emerged. They argue that modern Muslim scholars should have a high degree of freedom to determine what is 'Islamic'. The role of contemporary Muslim scholars, according to them, is to determine whether a proposal, policy, or practice is based on a 'liberal' interpretation of the Qur'an and the *Sunna*, while taking into account the fundamental values of the society in which they live. A so-called 'liberal' interpretation may, from their point of view, still be firmly rooted in the Qur'an, the traditions of the Prophet, and the principles of Islamic legal thought, and the interpretation simply takes into account one more (crucial) consideration—the contemporary concerns and needs of society.

'Participants' reject the idea that a Muslim cannot be fully so unless he or she is ruled by pre-modern Islamic law. Moreover, they do not make a sharp distinction between Islamic and secular law in their daily lives—provided, that is, that the law of the land supports notions of justice, equity, equality, and public interest, and allows Muslims religious freedom to practise their fundamental beliefs.

There is no firm data that document how many Muslims support the introduction of Shari'a or Shari'a courts in Australia. Yet I would say that, as far as actual practice is concerned, most Muslim Australians probably fall into the category of 'Participants': they see the Australian legal system as, generally speaking, 'Islamic', insofar as its spirit is based on fairness, justice, equality, and non-discrimination.

---

[34] T Ramadan, *To Be a European Muslim* (Leicester: Islamic Foundation, 2003) 171.

G. Muslim Australians' Views on Establishing Shari'a courts

In Australia there is probably little support behind calls for a wholesale application of Shari'a law. Instead, certain Muslims have asked for recognition of and, where possible, the incorporation of Islamic principles into certain aspects of Australian family law. What appears to be emerging among some sections of the Muslim community is a desire for community-based conciliation and mediation mechanisms to deal with areas such as marriage, divorce, and inheritance, utilizing both Islamic norms and Australian family law.[35] For example, a number of Muslim groups and leaders have noted the need for Muslim women to be granted a religious divorce alongside the civil divorce certificate granted by the Family Court of Australia, so that their change in status is recognized by the wider Muslim community.[36] Keysar Trad, from the Islamic Friendship Association of Australia, explained:

In the case of divorce, Australian law only looks at secular divorce and does not address the Islamic marriage contract. This is a problem for some people, as some Australian Imams are not able to dissolve the Islamic marriage without the approval of both parties. In some cases the man will refuse this Islamic dissolution, making it impossible for the woman to Islamically marry again; while under Islamic law, the man can.[37]

In 2002, the Muslim Women's National Network of Australia commented that in cases where a woman's husband is overseas, his whereabouts are unknown, or he refuses to pronounce *talāq* (the unilateral decree of divorce), there was a need for another mechanism to grant women a religious divorce, such as a Shari'a court or employing a *qādī* (Islamic judge) from overseas to hear such cases.[38] According to the Network, the lack of such a mechanism in Australia has forced some women to travel to their country of birth to access a Shari'a court—an exercise that is time-consuming and expensive.[39]

In some senses this type of dispute-resolution is already happening within the community. Imams and respected community leaders with knowledge of Islam and Australian law are already involved in conciliation and mediation in the Muslim community.[40] However, these forums are extra-judicial and the obligations created

---

[35] For example, in 2005 Muslim leaders in Perth were planning to set up a special court using Shari'a law to settle disputes in divorce proceedings: D Weber, 'Muslim leaders call for Sharia divorce court', *ABC: The World Today*, 7 April 2005, available at <http://www.abc.net.au/worldtoday/content/2005/s1340348.htm>.

[36] As N Jamal notes, in some countries the power to grant an Islamic divorce to a wife is carried out by the Shari'a court through a *qādī*. Australia has no such court, so if the husband refuses to pronounce *talāq*, the wife is unable to remarry under Islamic law: N Jamal, 'Until Two Legal Systems do us Part', *Sydney Morning Herald*, 5 May 2007, available at <http://www.smh.com.au/news/national/until-two-legal-systems-do-us-part/2007/05/04/1177788404897.html?page=2>.

[37] Interview with K Trad, 8 March 2006.

[38] Jamal (n 36 above).   [39] Ibid.

[40] For example, in 2007 a group of Sydney Muslim leaders decided to form an Islamic judicial council, based at the Lakemba Mosque, to hear disputes involving marriage and divorce: ibid.

out of these processes are moral, rather than legal. Moreover, documents drawn up in such forums are not recognized by Australian courts.[41] Thus, for those who argue for Shari'a courts, the advantage of arbitration tribunals for Muslims appears to be clear. These bodies can mediate disputes at the community level (saving time, money, and unnecessary emotional distress), while the arbitrators are (or ought to be) expert, experienced persons who are sensitive to the cultural and religious needs of the parties. If these bodies are formally recognized, their rulings can be enforced (and, if need be, reviewed) via the usual legal mechanisms available to other citizens in the Australian legal system.

H. Challenges for Shari'a courts Operating in Australia

Despite the support among sections of the Muslim community for Shari'a courts (or similar mechanisms) to arbitrate certain disputes, their establishment, if it even- tuates, is likely to be problematic. A Shari'a tribunal is unlikely to be universally accepted by all or most Muslims in Australia, given the cultural, legal (in terms of Islamic legal schools), and theological differences that exist among people of this faith. Muslims are also likely to have divergent positions about *who* should admin- ister such a mechanism. For instance, should the Australian Federation of Islamic Councils (AFIC) or state Islamic Councils be involved; or should the mechanism be beyond such institutional control? How should Muslim community organiza- tions be involved? There are also likely to be substantive matters where Shari'a fam- ily law and Australian law clash.

One potential point of tension relates to Shari'a's recognition of polygamous relationships. However, according to Jamila Hussain, there are few polygamous marriages among Australian Muslims:

The Shari'a [does] permit limited polygamy. Australian law prohibits polygamy but permits de facto relationships regardless of whether one party is already legally married. Second marriages contracted under religious law are regarded as de facto relationships under Australian law and so the two can co-exist in practice.[42]

Another area of difficulty is the one-year waiting period required by Australian law before a divorce can be granted for Muslim couples. Under classical Islamic law, the waiting period is approximately three months in most cases. However, the intent of both waiting periods is the same and the longer period under Australian law could well be used to seek reconciliation of a couple through methods such as mediation.[43]

---

[41] Ibid.
[42] J Hussain, 'The myths and realities of Islam's Shariah law', *On Line Opinion*, 2 March 2006, available at <http://www.onlineopinion.com.au/view.asp?article=4211>. See also J Hussain, *Islam: Its Law and Society* (Sydney: Federation Press, 2nd edn, 2004).
[43] Interview with Ghena Krayem, 13 March 2006.

A further clash between Australian and classical Islamic law could be in the area of custody of children. It appears that some Muslim men[44] find the decision-making of the Family Court extremely difficult to accept, especially where a former wife has entered into a new relationship and has been granted custody of their children.[45] One way of overcoming such difficulties may be to remove child custody cases from the jurisdiction of the Shari'a court.

There are of course further issues that would need to be considered before the establishment of Shari'a courts could occur, even if their jurisdiction was limited simply to family law disputes. Any institution established would have to act in accordance with existing laws in Australia and fundamental Australian values—for example, gender equality. If interpretations (particularly certain classical interpretations) of the Shari'a disadvantage women and contradict existing Australian law they may have to be abandoned. Any tribunal will need to be given limited jurisdiction, perhaps, as mentioned, restricted to a few areas of family law only. Any wider jurisdiction or exercise of power is likely to be contentious.

Given that there are five legal schools in Islam, the choice of a *single* legal school to govern the courts' determinations will be highly problematic. It is therefore likely that any body established will develop an eclectic approach—either picking and choosing from various schools of Islamic law or simply using a single school where both parties to the dispute agree to this. Given the enormous diversity among Australian Muslims, there will be some who feel uneasy about using a court that does not address *their* particular understanding of what is Islamically 'acceptable' practice from *their* point of view. These questions of who should oversee such a court, how Islamic organizations and groups should be represented in its functioning and governance, and how it is to be funded are all likely to be contentious matters.

Perhaps the most important challenge for those who argue in favour of implementing classical Islamic family law in the Australian context is that many Muslim-majority countries themselves are 'reforming' their family law by taking into account gender equality and international human rights norms. In the near future this may mean that Muslim nations will increasingly be introducing laws that are more or less in line with the laws that exist in countries like Australia, and so the distinction between 'Islamic' family law and 'Australian' family law will be increasingly blurred.

A good example of this development is the recent reform of Moroccan family law. In 2004, Morocco introduced major reforms to the 1958 Personal Status Code, now called the *Code de la Famille* (Family Code). Importantly, this new Code recognizes equality between the husband and wife within the family,

---

[44] And many non-Muslim men too—although their discontent is not typically based on religious grounds.
[45] Interview with Ghena Krayem, 13 March 2006.

including their equal rights, duties, and responsibilities. The Preamble to the new Family Code states:

Doing justice to women, protecting children's rights and preserving men's dignity are a fundamental part of this project, which adheres to Islam's tolerant ends and objectives, notably justice, equality, solidarity, *ijtihād* (juridical reasoning) and receptiveness to the spirit of our modern era and the requirements of progress and development.[46]

The 2004 reforms[47] include: (a) a uniform minimum legal age for marriage of 18 years; (b) the abolition of compulsory guardianship for women; (c) the principle of gender equality, joint guardianship, and equal responsibility in the home; (d) the regulation of polygamy; (e) consensual divorce in place of unilateral repudiation;[48] (f) better recognition of maternal claims for custody of children; (g) development of separate spousal contracts detailing the management of their property; (h) recognition of a child's rights to protection, custody, alimony, paternity, and legitimacy, even if born outside of marriage; (i) recognition that orphaned grandchildren can inherit from maternal as well as paternal grandparents through obligatory bequests; and (k) a central role for judges and family courts in the resolution of family affairs. The success of this reform programme was due to the fact that it was sent to the Parliament by King Mohammed VI; it was presented as a 'project of society'; and it blended the Shari'a and human rights philosophy. 'The new Family Law', as two scholars observe, '[was] designed around three axes: equality between spouses, family equilibrium, and the protection of the children'.[49]

I. Concluding Remarks

There is interest among certain elements of the Muslim community in the question of Shari'a and its role in Australia. But I believe that most ordinary Muslims, at a practical level, probably do not take much notice of this debate and simply go about their day-to-day life in a quiet and law-abiding fashion, oblivious to the constraints of Australian law (including secular family law). It is true that there are Muslims, particularly some women, who see a need to get a 'religious' divorce, even though they may already have a civil divorce from an Australian court. This is largely due

[46] See the *Musawah* (a Malaysian non-governmental organization committed to promoting the rights of women within the framework of Islam) website's list of 'Successful Reform Efforts', available at <http://www.musawah.org/successful_reforms.asp>.

[47] V M Moghadam, 'Feminism, legal reform and women's empowerment in the Middle East and North Africa' (2009) 59 *International Social Science Journal* 9, 13–14.

[48] Different types of divorce (mutual consent, discord) allow women to initiate divorce, and divorce proceedings are now subject to judicial review.

[49] F Sadiqi and M Ennaji, 'The Feminisation of Public Space: Women's Activism, the Family Law and Social Change in Morocco' (2006) 2(2) *Journal of Middle East Women's Studies* 86, 108 (see ibid, 112 (n 12) for a detailed list of specific innovations under the new family law that give effect to 'Equality between Spouses').

to the community perception (at least within some sectors) that a civil divorce is insufficient, and the woman is still married to the man until he gives the *talāq*. Given the reforms that are taking place on this issue in the global Muslim scene, it will be interesting to see how long this practice of husband-controlled *talāq* will continue. Several Muslim countries are already taking this 'right' from the husband and forcing husbands and wives to go through regular legal proceedings to get a divorce.

In future we are likely to see a greater convergence of Australian family law and classical Islamic family law. Each—but more especially the latter—will have to take due account of gender equality and international human rights norms. The question then arises: if both systems of law converge, will there be any real need to establish Shari'a courts?

14

In the Shadow of Our Legal System: Shari'a in Australia[1]

Ann Black

A. Introduction

The Rudd government is not considering and will not consider the introduction of any part of Shari'a law into the Australian legal system.

Robert McCelland, Attorney-General of Australia, 2008[2]

This media statement was issued by Australia's Attorney-General just days after the Archbishop of Canterbury's lecture to the Royal Courts of Justice in England. Selected content of the Archbishop's lecture, particularly the notion that Shari'a law could be accommodated within the English common law system, was widely reported 'down under', with editorials, letters to the editor, talk-back radio, and blogs generally expressing concern and, in some instances, outrage. Rowan Williams' assertion that adoption of parts of Shari'a was 'unavoidable' and that the law of the land can and should be accommodating of minorities' own 'strongly entrenched legal and moral codes' saw the Archbishop described as either gullible or dangerous. The Attorney-General of Australia quickly put to rest any speculation that the views expressed by the Archbishop would be entertained in any official capacity in Australia.

In so doing, the Labor government continued the stance of previous Australian governments. This position was encapsulated in a speech entitled 'Worth Promoting, Worth Defending' given in 2006 by the former Treasurer of Australia, Peter Costello:

There is one law we are all expected to abide by. It is the law enacted by the Parliament under the Australian Constitution. If you can't accept that then you don't accept the fundamentals of what Australia is and what it stands for. Our State is a secular State. As such

---

[1] This essay develops several ideas first published in A Black, 'Accommodating Shariah law in Australia's Legal System' (2008) 33 *Alternative Law Journal* 214.

[2] B Zwartz, 'Australia's Muslims Cool on Change', *The Age*, 9 February 2008.

it can protect the freedom of all religions for worship. Religion instructs its adherents on faith, morals and conscience. But there is not a separate stream of law derived from religious sources that competes with or supplants Australian law in governing our civil society. The source of our law is the democratically elected legislature.

There are countries that apply religious or sharia law. Saudi Arabia and Iran come to mind. If a person wants to live under sharia law these are countries where they might feel at ease. But not Australia.[3]

In support of the Archbishop and in endorsing consideration of Shari'a for family law matters, Lord Phillips, Lord Chief Justice of England and Wales, soon thereafter stated that there was 'no reason why principles of Shari'a Law or any other religious code should not be the basis for mediation or other forms of dispute resolution'.[4] However, no equivalent statement or comment emanated from any senior member of the Australian judiciary. So, the official Australian position in regard to accommodating Shari'a principles or law seems clear. And yet, in fact, Shari'a does operate in Australia. Its realm is in the unofficial or extra-legal as far as the positive law of the state is concerned. Indeed, Shari'a flourishes in the shadow of the formal legal system. Like Muslims in other secular nations such as Turkey and England, Muslims in Australia do not relegate Islam to the status of personal religion or private belief but can and do apply aspects of Shari'a to a wide range of situations. This is seen as necessary, as Islam is viewed as not *merely* a religion in the contemporary liberal sense, but as a blueprint for all of life: the path to be followed as ordained by God. Muslims do not conceptualize Islam in terms of the Westernized sociological categorization of religion, which places the individual at the centre of all analyses. As Sharon Siddique has emphasized, to understand Islam, one must grapple with all of its aspects—political, economic, legal, and social—and not just the 'spiritual' relationship between God and the individual.[5] Abdullahi A An-Na'im explains that the Shari'a is the 'whole Duty of Mankind', and that in addition to the realms of moral and pastoral theology and ethics, as well as detailed ritualistic and formal observances, it encompasses 'all aspects of public and private law, hygiene and even courtesy and good manners'.[6] Shari'a cannot be excluded from daily life or from relationships with others. The challenge for Muslims in Australia is how to adhere to all that Shari'a encompasses while living within a country with very different laws, customs, and mores. The challenge for Australia is how accommodating its legal system can be for its Muslim citizens.

This essay explores Australia's response to the question 'Shari'a in the West?' It canvasses the ways in which Shari'a operates in Australia and confirms that legal

---

[3] P Costello, 'Worth promoting, worth defending—Australian citizenship, what it means and how to defend it', address to Sydney Institute, 23 February 2006.

[4] Lord Phillips, 'Equality Before the Law' (see Appendix II at [43]).

[5] S Siddique, 'Conceptualising Contemporary Islam: Religion or Ideology' in A Ibrahim, S Siddique, and Y Hussain (eds), *Readings on Islam in Southeast Asia* (Singapore: Institute of Southeast Asian Studies, 1985) 338.

[6] A A An-Na'im, *Towards an Islamic Reformation: Civil Liberties, Human Rights, and International Law* (Syracuse, NY: Syracuse University Press, 1990) 11.

pluralism is indeed a reality. Although at the level of state law 'the one law for all' mantra applies (apart from some minor concessions to indigenous peoples), Australia's ethnic and religious diversity has ensured that at other levels of society different normative orders, including Shari'a, coexist with state law. As these operate in the shadow of the formal legal system, there are concerns and challenges that arise from this unofficial status. There are, however, benefits that the informal nexus brings for both Muslim and non-Muslim Australians. Both dimensions will be explored, and family law matters will be given particular focus due to their special importance to Muslim identity. The chapter will conclude that, for now, the way forward is not to rush to establish a Shari'a court or tribunal, nor for the government to accord official recognition to aspects of Shari'a, as time is needed for an Australian Shari'a to emerge. There is scope for this to occur through contemporary *ijtihād* (legal reasoning) and *shura* (consultation) by 'home-grown' Australian scholars and *imams*.

B. Shari'a in Australia

Background

Shari'a arrived in Australia with the first Muslims to arrive on Australian shores. Although there is evidence that Muslim *Makassar* fishermen and traders may have visited northern Australia prior to European settlement, Muslims have been an integral part of Australia's multi-cultural mosaic at least since the nineteenth century. 'Mohammedans' were listed in the early musters (census) taken in the early nineteenth century. They were among the pioneers of the nation as Afghan cameleers contributed to the exploration and opening-up of remote and central Australia, including the building of railways and telegraph lines between Adelaide and Darwin. Their faith was practised and the first official Australian mosque was built in 1861, in South Australia. Today there are over 100 mosques and many more *masjids* (prayer halls) across the continent which serve the needs of a small but growing Muslim population—around 350,000[7] according to the latest official statistics. Precise numbers of Muslims in Australia are not known, however, because Australians do not have to declare their religious status for census purposes. Unofficial estimates in fact range between 400,000 and 500,000, with at least one-third of these now born in Australia. However, the pattern of migration was such that Australian Muslims are culturally, linguistically, and ethnically diverse, having come from over 70 different countries, belonging to 50 different ethnic or cultural groups, and speaking a variety of languages and dialects. Australian legal academic, Jamila Hussain, concludes that it is 'probably more correct to speak of

---

[7] Australian Bureau of Statistics, *2006 Census of Population and Housing* (2006), available at <http://www.censusdata.abs.gov.au>. Muslims are the third largest religious group in Australia, after Christians and Buddhists.

Muslim 'communities in Australia rather than the Muslim community'[8] since it is so ethnically divided. The two largest countries of origin are Lebanon and Turkey. Refugees from the Sudan are among the more recent arrivals, whereas other ethnic communities, such as the Albanians in Mareeba, North Queensland, have been established since the 1920s. The extent of this diversity must be central to the debate concerning formal recognition of Shari'a law.

Cultural navigators

As Australian citizens and residents, Muslims can retain their religious and cultural identities and in doing so regulate many aspects of their lives according to Shari'a. This extends beyond religious and devotional requirements to include the legal relationships they enter and terminate—especially marriage, divorce, custody, inheritance, and business dealings—as well as the modes for dispute-resolution that they adopt. Disputes can be settled by persons with Islamic credentials, such as *imams* of mosques, and disputes that intersect with the Australian legal system can be dealt with by Muslim lawyers, both solicitors and barristers, many of whom have an interest in harmonizing the two forms of law. Adherence to Shari'a does not amount to defiance or violation of Australian laws, but that there are choices to be negotiated within the parameters of both systems. Muslims as minorities in secular societies have been aptly described as skilled 'cultural navigators'[9] who are able to manoeuvre through the demands of different normative orders, laws, and cultures.

The process of cultural navigation is particularly important in the area of family law, especially given the strength of its religious, cultural, and historical foundations. Many verses in the Qur'an pertain to family matters and as the Qur'an is believed by Muslims to contain the direct word of God, transmitted to the Prophet through the Archangel Gabriel, these laws are considered sacred and immutable. The example of the Prophet as a married family man cements this further. In sociological terms, Poulter argues that Islamic family law embodies the 'quintessential culture of a distinctive group...which cannot be discarded lightly' and as many other aspects of Islamic law, notably in the commercial and criminal spheres, have 'given way to' Western models, family law has become increasingly 'precious and worthy of preservation worldwide'.[10] Family laws were generally not abolished by colonial powers but retained, although often codified and modified.[11] This has meant that family law remains central to Muslim identity, both at an individual and community level. It also serves as a bastion against secular society, with many

---

[8] J Hussain, *Islam: Its Law and Society* (Sydney: Federation Press, 2nd rev edn, 2004) 203.

[9] I Yilmaz, *Muslim Laws, Politics and Society in Modern Nation States* (2005) 66.

[10] S Poulter, 'The Claim to a Separate Islamic System of Personal Law for British Muslims' in C Mallat and J Connors (eds), *Islamic Family Law* (1990) 147.

[11] Eg A Black, 'The Stronger Rule of the More Enlightened European: The consequences of colonialism on dispute resolution in the Sultanate of Brunei' (2009) 13 *Legal History* 93.

Muslims believing that the best way to defend their families from 'corrupting' western influences and *haram* (not permissible) practices (such as prostitution, alcohol and drug use, pornography, child abuse, marital breakdown, extra-marital affairs, illegitimate children, same-sex relationships, and the neglect of the elderly) is to operate within the scale of values advocated in Shari'a family law.

In the navigation between the twin poles of Shari'a law and state law there are two main approaches. One is harmonization, in which the aim is to comply with both systems of law. Marriage is a good example. In Australia polygynist marriages[12] are unlawful under section 94 of the Marriage Act 1961. Otherwise the Act allows for marriages to be performed and registered by recognized marriage celebrants, who for Muslims may be their *imam*, and without the need for a separate registering event or ceremony. A single ceremony can fulfil state and Shari'a requirements.

Harmonization can also occur with divorce. A Muslim husband or wife can serve out the 12-month period of separation required in order to have a valid divorce granted under Australian law on the ground of irretrievable breakdown of marriage in accordance with the Family Law Act 1975. Shari'a allows for extra-judicial divorce by the husband which, like Australian divorce law, requires no cause or fault to be established. He can pronounce *talāq* and, provided all the legal requirements are met,[13] the divorce will also be valid under Islamic law. Therefore, either before or after a secular divorce, a husband can complete his divorce in compliance with Shari'a. Complying with both Australian and Shari'a divorce requirements is not difficult, but in effect two divorces are required. Similarly, the situation is straightforward if a husband pronounces *talāq* when his wife requests a divorce. If he refuses, however, preferring to stay married, his wife will need to take her case to an Islamic judicial authority for determination. This is significantly more onerous and can be very problematic for Muslim women.

The second navigational strategy, which is again common, especially in family law matters, is to bypass Australian legal requirements altogether, and to operate solely according to religious law. According to this strategy, Shari'a is applied alongside and in the shadow of the Australian legal system. In Australia, a Muslim can marry according to the requirements of Shari'a but not formally register the marriage and still be considered lawfully married in the eyes of the Muslim community.[14] Any children born to the union are recognized by other Muslims and the relevant mosque as the legitimate children of the marriage. If the husband or wife wishes at a later time to end the marriage, the divorce proceeds in the

---

[12] As polygamy is technically a generic term for having more than one marital (and/or sexual) partner it is more correct to use polygyny when referring to a man who has more than one wife. The rare situation where a wife has more than one husband is polyandry.

[13] These include that he understands what he is doing (is not insane, intoxicated, or asleep); is an adult; has communicated the *talāq* to his wife; and his wife is not menstruating. The pronouncement severs the marriage. There is a three-month revocation period.

[14] It would also be a de facto marriage under Australian law.

same way. The husband can divorce his wife extra-judicially through *talāq,* that is, by adhering to the three-month reconciliation period. Provided he applies the Islamic laws governing maintenance and the rules on *mahr* (money or property settled in the marriage contract) he will be considered by other Muslims to be lawfully divorced and able to re-marry without the 12-month separation period applying.

Where the wife wishes to end the marriage but mutual agreement (*mubāra'a*) for divorce is not reached, she must find an authoritative Muslim individual or body to effect an Islamic divorce through some other means. One method is *khul'a,* whereby the wife returns her *mahr* (marriage portion/dowry) and effectively buys her way out of the marriage. Another is *ta'liq* or *talāq-i-tafwīd,* where the husband is alleged to have breached a stipulated term in the marriage contract thereby ending the marriage through breach. A third mechanism is *fasakh,* which requires the wife to establish fault on the part of the husband in one of the recognized categories, such as absence, impotency, certain illnesses, cruelty, or failure to maintain his wife and child.

An empowered Muslim woman is unlikely to find these requirements a problem since there are *sheikhs, imams,* scholars, and organizations who proffer such services and who are recognized as possessing such authority. However, the absence of an established state- (such as the Shari'a Court in Singapore) or community-designated authority (such as the unofficial Shari'a courts in England) can leave many women in a vulnerable position. Shari'a can indeed present significant disincentives for a woman wanting to escape an unhappy marriage and render her vulnerable to possible spousal, religious, and community pressures to resolve the marital dispute in accordance with what is presented as a dictate of divine law. This can lead to the social phenomenon known as a 'limping marriage' in which the wife may have a civil divorce but has not been able to obtain a religious one.[15] In the eyes of her community, and even in her own eyes, she remains married to her Muslim husband and cannot remarry, as to do so would be adulterous and any children would be illegitimate. It is possible, however, for the husband to remarry since a polygynist marriage is acceptable.

While difficulties do arise, as they can in any family law paradigm, the reality is that the current system, which enables Shari'a to operate unofficially, allows Muslims within their own community to take control over these aspects of their lives. Marriage, including polygyny, divorce, custody, and financial support arrangements can and do occur without resorting to the Australian legal system. This is legal pluralism in action. State law coexists with the unofficial and unregulated Shari'a personal law.

---

[15] An analogous situation can arise for Jewish women. See A Williamson, 'An Examination of Jewish Divorce under the Family Law Act 1975 (Cth)' (2004) *James Cook University Law Review* 7.

C. Concerns and challenges

Internal pluralism

One of the main challenges for the operation of Shari'a in Australia and for according it any official recognition arises from the pluralism within the diverse and varied Muslim communities in the country. Islam is not monolithic. Islam in the Sudan is different from Islam in Iran or in Malaysia. The Islam brought to Australia by Albanians in the 1920s differs from that brought by Afghani refugees in very recent years. Although the central tenets are shared there can be considerable variation. This is a result of the Sunni-Shia schism, of differences between the schools (*madhhab*) of law,[16] political forces, levels of education and knowledge, the impact of local customs and practices, the legacy of colonial laws and governance, and, more recently, the impact of globalization and international law. Today, Shari'a is as diverse as an individual Muslim's allegiance to it. Although this can be a strength of Islam, reflecting its inherent adaptability to local situations, conversely it poses difficulties for a secular Western government considering any form of official recognition.

Whose Shari'a should be selected? This is a vexed question. It is one that generally does not have to be answered in Muslim majority nations where Shari'a law, courts, and institutions have been established for centuries. Similarly, it is not especially problematic in countries like Singapore where the Muslim minority has a shared history, adheres to the one (Shafi'i) school of jurisprudence, and has a common Malay ethnicity and language. Where individuals do not fall into these 'shared' categories, or where Muslims do not follow the same *madhhab* as the nation, Islam as it is practised in some nations provides for *takhayyur* (selection of interpretation)[17] to resolve the issue. *Takhayyur* has been extended by modernist scholars in secular Western states to permit an individual Muslim the right to have the *madhhab* of his or her heritage or choosing applied to a dispute or determination.[18] Although *takhayyur* allows for variation in the application of Shari'a, and is a valid method employed by jurists in the renewal and adaptation of Islam to contemporary times, it is too uncertain, eclectic, and unpredictable to form the basis of an official Shari'a dispute-resolution model. Making determinations according

---

[16] Within Sunni Islam (90 per cent of Muslims) there are four main schools (*madhhab* in Arabic), named after their founders: Hanafī, Mālāki, Hanbalī, and Shāfiʿī, and individuals and also governments align with one of these. There are also mystical orders of Sufis and ultra-conservative sects such as Salafī and Wahhabī. Shia Islam has its own divisions and different sects. See G Makdisi, *The Rise of Colleges* (Edinburgh: Edinburgh University Press, 1981); and M Momem, *An Introduction to Shi'i Islam* (New Haven: Yale University Press, 1985).

[17] N J Coulson, *A History of Islamic Law* (Edinburgh: Edinburgh University Press, 1994) 185.

[18] I Yilmaz, 'Muslim Alternative Dispute Resolution and *Neo-Ijtihad* in England' (2003) 1 *Alternatives* 117, 119; P Bannerman, *Islam in Perspective* (New York: Routledge for the Royal Institute of International Affairs, 1988) 259; A Marsh, *Islam and Liberal Citizenship* (New York: Oxford University Press, 2009) 83.

to each *madhhab* or Shia sect, or to the applicable Shari'a jurisprudence from 70 different nations, would make for an inconsistent and unworkable system.

Leadership and sources of authority

The extent of diversity goes some way to explain the level of factionalism among Australian Muslims. There is division: on which organization represents their interests; about who, in the individual or collective sense, has authority to speak on their behalf; on who has authority to deliver legal opinions (*fatwās*); and on who can make determinations on issues in dispute between Muslims—issues such as whether a wife should be granted a *khula* divorce and what has to be returned (*mahr*) to her husband. The Family Law Council of Australia recently noted that, in contrast to other faith communities, there is a diversity of viewpoints and a lack of consensus among Muslims about what could be done to overcome difficulties in relation to divorce in Australia.[19]

This question of authority is an important one, especially for *ifta*, the process by which leading jurists and Islamic scholars issue *fatwās*.[20] This is the legal method that allows Shari'a to be interpreted and developed to meet changing circumstances and situations. Unlike the common law, which gives this role to judges and the legislature, Islam entrusts *ifta* to its jurists and scholars, the ʿ*ulamā*, and it is their *fatwās* that have for centuries been published, disseminated, and 'cited across space and time'[21]—and not court judgments (*qada*). This means that *fatwās* fulfil a valuable role in the social and cultural transformation that occurs when Muslims live in a secular and Western society.[22] The need for *fatwās* intensifies, rather than lessens, when Muslims embark on the path of navigating two sets of laws—state law and Shari'a—and attempt to construct an Islamic identity within a secular milieu. *Fatwās* are sought on a range of issues from the apparently trivial ('is it permissible to pray while wearing nail polish?') to the vital and pressing ('is it permissible for me to have a blood transfusion when the donor may be a non-Muslim?'). *Fatwās* have been important in determining which banking and commercial transactions are Islamically acceptable in avoiding *riba* (interest) and have dealt with an array of contemporary issues, including the legitimacy of certain contraceptive methods, immunizations, genetically modified crops, recycled waste water, stem-cell research, surrogacy, cosmetic surgery, and organ donation.

---

[19] Family Law Council of Australia, *Report on Cultural Community Divorce and the Family Law Act 1975* (2001) 4 (Executive Summary 17).

[20] For an historical perspective on the institutional interaction between judges and jurists, see D Powers, *Law, Society and Culture in the Maghrib, 1300–1500* (Cambridge, UK; New York: Cambridge University Press, 2002).

[21] M K Masud, B Messick, and D S Powers, 'Muftis, Fatwas and Islamic Legal Interpretation' in M K Masud, B Messick, and D S Powers (eds), *Islamic Legal Interpretation* (Cambridge, Mass: Harvard University Press, 1996) 8, 19.

[22] A Black and N Hosen, 'Fatwas: their Role in Contemporary Secular Australia' (2009) 18(2) *Griffith Law Review* 405, 407.

In Muslim nations there may be a state-appointed jurist, the *muftī*, supported by a religious department, whose role is to issue *fatwās* for the nation, as occurs in Oman. There may also be a body of specialist scholars (*ᶜulamā*) who fulfil an *ifta* role, such as Al-Azhar University in Egypt, a government organization, such as Majlis Ugama Islam Singapura (Singapore), or several *ifta* bodies of *ᶜulamā* that are independent of the government, as occurs in the nation with the largest Muslim population, Indonesia.[23]

As *fatwās* are the means for adapting and interpreting Shari'a to new contexts, the question as to which organization or individual/s can fulfil an *ifta* role in Australia is an important one. The diversity and divisions within Australia's Muslim communities are highlighted by the paucity of *fatwās*. Australia has had two *muftīs*, Egyptian-born Sheikh Taj Din al-Hilali and Lebanon-born Sheikh Fehmi Naji El-Imam, but neither has engaged in issuing any *ifta* of significance and, for different reasons, neither has had universal support from Australian Muslims.[24] There are a range of organizations that could fulfil this role, including the Australian Federation of Islamic Council (AFIC), which consists of nine state and territory councils, and was formed to give leadership and a united voice for Muslims. However, public dissention and acrimonious disputes about leadership, even resulting in a court-appointed administrator in 2006, demonstrates that the Islamic community in Australia is profoundly divided on ethnic, political, and doctrinal lines.[25]

There also exist the Australian National Imams Council (ANIC) and the Darulfatwa Islamic High Council. The latter does issue *fatwās*, employing a collective approach and expressing generally moderate views. However, the number issued is small when compared with online *fatwās*. One of the many online *fatwās* sites on the internet, Islam Q&A, shows that Australian Muslims (based on domain reporting) have made over one million requests, placing Australia seventh after Saudi Arabia, the United Kingdom, and France, which were the highest three users of that *ifta* service. This supports Alexandre Caerio's contention that demand for *fatwās* in the West is greater than in Islamic countries due to a discontinuation in the transmission of Islamic knowledge which propels young Muslims to find ways to adapt Islamic law to their Western context.[26] *Fatwās* are thus another important navigational tool for Muslims negotiating though the two sets of laws.

Although it could be argued that the availability of guidance through online *fatwās* fills a void created by Australia's limited leadership on Shari'a interpretation on contemporary issues and thereby provides Australians with a diversity

---

[23] Ibid 421; N Hosen, 'Revelation in a Modern nation Sate: *Muhammadiyah* and Islamic Reasoning in Indonesia' (2002) 4 *Australian Journal of Asian Law* 232.

[24] Black and Hosen (n 22 above) 417.

[25] Ibid 415.

[26] A Caerio, 'The European Market for Fatwas: a case study of the European Council for Fatwa and Research' in S Allievi and M van Bruinessen (eds), *Producing Islamic Knowledge: Transmission and Dissemination in Western Europe* (New York: Routledge, 2010) Ch 5.

of opinion that may be optimal for adjustment and growth, there are two aspects of concern. The first is that there is no quality control of online *fatwās*. Unlike the scholarship and high esteem of traditional Islamic jurists, the nature of the internet is such that anyone can set themselves up as an Islamic authority, a cyber-*muftī* who issues *fatwās*. Questioners can go '*fatwā* -shopping' until a legal opinion that suits them is located. The second concern is that most of the major online *fatwā* sites are based in the Middle East, notably in Qatar and Saudi Arabia, which contain societies different from those in Australia, and it is unlikely that the cultural context of Australia is factored into their reasoning. It would be optimal if Australian Islamic scholars and organizations could collectively fulfil a greater *ijtihād* role in interpreting the classic sources of law that comprise the Shari'a, but using the methodology to give legal opinions and guidance that resonate with the local context.

The issue of leadership and authority is a problem in other secular countries where a tradition of Islamic scholarship and jurisprudence has not had time to develop. Dr Mohammad Elmasry of the Canadian Islamic Congress, in his submission to the Attorney-General of Ontario on Shari'a tribunals, highlighted this, noting, 'there are only a handful of scholars in Canada who are fully trained in interpreting and applying Shari'a law—and perhaps as few as one'.[27]

Protections are lacking

The unofficial status and the extra-legal application of Shari'a as a dominant normative force in the lives of many Australian Muslims means that its operation is not subject to scrutiny by anyone other than the participants. Nor is it subject to the protection of Australian laws and processes. If a group of Islamic scholars or sole *imams* hold themselves out as having legal authority to determine issues of marriage, divorce, gift-giving, custody, family discipline, and inheritance for Muslims, it may be accepted prima facie. In Islamic family law matters, especially the determination of marriage validity, divorce, custody, and maintenance, it has been argued that greater protections are needed to ensure fairness and justice in terms of Shari'a. This is arguably one of the main grounds for official recognition of Shari'a and any tribunal or court resolving personal disputes between Muslims. Protections could include accreditation requirements for Shari'a arbitrators, mediators, or members of any Shari'a tribunal or decision-making body; the need for independent legal advice from a qualified Australian lawyer prior to a dispute being heard and determined; the recording of transcripts and decisions; establishing avenues of appeal for an aggrieved party to another Islamic body or to the common law courts; allowing legal representation at hearings; and ensuring that there are mechanisms for addressing power imbalance between parties. Protections of this type were prominent in the Ontario model for Shari'a (and other faith-based)

[27] M Boyd, *Dispute Resolution in Family Law: Protecting Choice, Promoting Inclusion*, Report to the Attorney-General of Ontario (December 2004).

arbitration, prior to the repeal of the law in 2005. In the current unofficial system in Australia, such protections are missing and Muslims, arguably Muslim women, may be disadvantaged.

If the government, in conjunction with representatives of the Muslim community, found common ground which allowed for the application of Islamic law by a board of *imams*, a Muslim non-profit family law centre,[28] or a Shari'a arbitration tribunal or court, the opportunity for regulation and accountability becomes more likely. However, there are real questions about whether this level of scrutiny would be welcomed and whether the varied protections would be seen as secular impositions or state interference in the application of Shari'a. Would this regulated Shari'a, with common law protections, still be seen as Shari'a dispute-resolution, or merely a western form of dispute-resolution masquerading as Shari'a?

Empowering and Educative

For the Australian government to delegate legal authority and autonomy to Shari'a tribunals or similar bodies for resolving family and inheritance matters or for disputes of a contractual or commercial nature where at least both parties are Muslim would be socially empowering and would send a strong message of confidence and acceptance. It could, in turn, aid in better social integration and strengthen Muslim-Australian identity. Muslims can feel isolated from mainstream Australia. They encounter unfair stereotyping in the media, experience incidences of racism, and are confronted by a general sense of negativity against them. This is not just perception, as research shows that Muslims are the least liked of all immigrants and are seen as the most threatening.[29] The data also show that Australians have a poor knowledge of Islam[30] and this correlates directly with high levels of apprehension about Muslims—which Dunn and other commentators have called 'Islamaphobia'.[31] The more knowledge a person has about Islam and the more personal contact a person has had with Muslims, the greater the level of acceptance.[32] This suggests that official recognition of Shari'a could serve as an educative opportunity for non-Muslims. It could help non-Muslims to see that Shari'a need not conform to stereotypes derived from traditional *hudūd* punishments or from the activities of extreme political, Talibanesque-style, Islam. However, conversely, recognizing a separate system of law and institutions for one religious group could be seen as isolating, differentiating, and separating Muslims from the wider community—intensifying the ghettoization of Muslims and re-enforcing a 'them-and-us' mentality.

---

[28] A M Emon, 'Islamic Law and the Canadian Mosaic: Politics, Jurisprudence, and Multicultural Accommodation' (2009) 87 *Canadian Bar Review* 391, 422–425.

[29] S Poynting et al, *Bin Laden in the Suburbs: Criminalising the Arab 'Other'* (Sydney: Institute of Criminology, 2004).

[30] K Dunn, 'Australian Public Knowledge of Islam' (2005) 12 *Studia Islamika* 1, 8.

[31] Ibid.   [32] Ibid 22.

D. The way forward

Muslims have settled in Australia for diverse reasons, and these factor into each individual's views on the place of Shari'a in their lives. If a person has fled from persecution in a country with a comprehensive Shari'a system they may find Australia's secular system and its protections reassuring. If they were born here, were converted, or came to Australia for economic or educational reasons, they may seek to affirm or strengthen their adherence to religious laws and practices. Both dimensions are present. There are many variables that lead to different levels of commitment to the Islamic faith, from the devout to the purely nominal. Experiences in other secular common law nations reflect a similar pattern.

Ihsan Yilmaz has found that in Britain, where there are already numerous unofficial Shari'a courts, the demand for religious dispute-resolution mechanisms is growing as they are seen as a means of safeguarding Islam from the secularization of British society.[33] The desire to practice Islam intensifies particularly when migrants from Muslim countries decide not to return to their country of origin and remain in Britain, making it 'the binding force for most Muslims in their daily lives as an all-encompassing regulatory system'.[34] Yilmaz argues that British Muslims find the official legal system insensitive to their needs and look either to official recognition of decisions of the existing Shari'a courts or to formal methods of dispute-resolution compatible with Shari'a that can be incorporated within the British legal system.

In diametric contrast, however, is the experience in Ontario, Canada. When a group of *imams* set up an arbitration tribunal, which they called a Shariat Court and which complied with the existing arbitration law, the Province's community, including Canadian Muslims, divided so strongly on the issue that it drew international attention. The Muslim Canadian Congress argued that the principle of equality in the Canadian Charter of Rights demanded that Muslims be treated equally, not differently, from other Canadians. The most strident opposition and vocal criticism came from Muslim women. The National Council of Women in Canada called for repeal of the law allowing for faith-based arbitration. The 'NO Shari'a Campaign' was led by an Iranian woman, Homa Arjomand, who argued that any move to introduce Islamic laws should be opposed by everyone who believed in women's civil and individual rights.[35] Premier McGinty was persuaded by the ground-swell of opposition. He decided that religious-based arbitrations threatened 'our common ground' and that there would be 'no Shari'a law in Ontario'. Rather, he insisted, there must be only 'one law for all Ontarians'.[36] The Arbitration Act was accordingly amended to make this clear.

---

[33] Yilmaz (n 9 above) 57.   [34] Ibid.
[35] See <http://www.nosharia.com>.
[36] *Canadian Press News Agency*, 11 September 2005.

The spectrum of views demonstrated by the British and Canadian experience is also to be seen in contemporary Australia, especially given the notable diversity among Australian Muslims, as well as the significant divisions among them. This is a point of distinction from Britain where the majority of Muslims (over 80 per cent)[37] are from South Asia (India, Pakistan, and Bangladesh) according British Muslims a degree of unity of experience and culture that is not present in Australia. For this reason, Australians would be well-advised to keep the Ontarian experience in mind. Given the level of internal pluralism in Australia, there is at present no consensus concerning the establishment of a Shari'a tribunal or which aspects of Shari'a or *madhhab* should receive official recognition. Unless and until such a consensus emerges, Australian Muslims can freely practice their faith and continue to use Shari'a in their daily lives, resolving disputes within their communities without state interference, as is the current practice. Albeit in the shadow of the Australian legal system, Shari'a-informed dispute-resolution is quietly flourishing.

That is not to deny, however, that there are aspects of the Australian legal system that frustrate Muslims. Nor is it to deny that there are areas of friction or conflict between the two systems of law. And this is where Islamic scholars in Australia need to take leadership and use the tools of *ijtihād* (independent reasoning) and *shura* (consultation) to formulate a Shari'a that will resonate among Australian Muslims. There are two family law issues where a degree of friction is especially present. First, is the issue of limping marriages. Scholars should look to those Muslim nations that have addressed this problem by giving wives the same right of *talāq*—a unilateral pronouncement of divorce—as their husbands. One such nation is Brunei.[38] Alternatively, jurists in Australia could consider whether a decree of a civil divorce should be considered an automatic or at least a strong ground for a *khula* divorce, the idea being that a civil divorce provides strong evidence that the 'wife' is seriously unhappy with the marriage.

The second issue, and one featured recently in the media, concerns polygamous marriages. Muslim spokespersons, such as Kayser Trad and Sheikh Chami, have argued on religious, social, and humanitarian grounds for the practice to be made lawful for Muslim men who wish to marry a second, third, or fourth wife.[39] They point out that the practice is sanctioned in the Qur'an,[40] was practised by the Prophet, and would reduce the incidence of adultery. However, polygamous unions are currently recognized only if the marriage occurred lawfully prior to entering Australia, and recent changes to the Family Law Act in relation to de facto spouses mean that custody arrangements and property settlements for additional

---

[37] Yilmaz (n 9 above) 57.

[38] Islamic Family Law Order 1999, s 42(1) allows a husband or wife to present an application for divorce by *talāq*.

[39] 'Probing Polygamy', *The Australian*, 26 June 2008; 'Big love a bride too far for even the most secular', *The Australian*, 26 June 2008; 'Muslim Leaders Split on Polygamy', *The Australian*, 1 July 2008.

[40] Qur'an 4:3.

wives can be granted by the courts. This seems to be too accommodating of the practice, however, especially given the particular reservations[41] and requirements[42] in the Qur'an that have led to some Muslim nations, such as Tunisia and Turkey, to make polygyny a criminal offence, and others to curb and monitor the practice.[43] Doctoral research by Ghena Krayem has found that 90 per cent of Muslims interviewed did not support any change in the law in Australia.[44] Consistent with these findings, the ANIC has also issued a statement recognizing that polygamy is outside the law and claiming that its members did not request the law to be changed in this respect. Rather, the ANIC emphasized the need to strengthen existing marriages and to encourage harmony within the family unit.[45] It would appear that such opinions are generally in keeping with the views of the wider Australian population.

A recurring theme in support of official recognition for Shari'a is that formal legal pluralism, as found in the Ottoman *millet* system, various colonial regimes, and in many Muslim countries today, reveals it as a just, inclusive, and workable model. The *millet* system allowed its Christian and Jewish minorities to choose their own leader, practise their faith, and implement their personal status laws. However, one highly significant difference between Ottoman Turkey and Australia (and probably most common law countries) is that the Ottoman state operated according to Shari'a, whereas the Australian legal system is fundamentally secular. Notably, when Turkey became a secular nation and adopted its Civil Code in 1926, the *millet* members lost their differentiated status and became equal citizens under the one law of the Republic of Turkey. The rationale for the prior pluralism was gone. Similarly, the pluralism that operated effectively in colonial contexts and which has continued in many such countries since independence, was necessary to enable a tiny number of Europeans to rule and control immensely larger indigenous populations. The colonizers did not do this out of respect for the local religious law or customary practices, which were modified and diminished, but to keep their subjects pacified and to accomplish their commercial, trade, and strategic objectives. The pluralism of colonial times is thus a flawed one. In addition, the religious, cultural, and linguistic homogeneity of colonized populations contrasts markedly with the multi-religious and multi-cultural citizens of modern Australia.

[41] 'You are never able to be fair and just as between women [wives]' (Qur'an 4:129).
[42] 'The husband must support all his wives adequately and treat them equally in every respect'. Cf Qur'an 4:3 and 4:129.
[43] Islamic Family Law Order 1999, s 23(1) requires written permission of a *Syar'ie* judge and s 23(2) requires a declaration of the grounds as to why the marriage is just and necessary, present income and financial commitments, the number of dependants and future dependants, and consent or the views of existing wives.
[44] 'Probing Polygamy', *The Australian*, 26 June 2008.
[45] Imam Taj Din al-Hilali rejected this ruling as contradicting 'the wisdom and teachings of God': 'Muslim Leaders Split on Polygamy', *The Australian*, 1 July 2008.

E. Conclusion

In spite or perhaps because of Australia's longstanding ethnic and religious diversity, the concept of a formal pluralistic system in which Shari'a law would have a distinctive place has failed to gain traction at either a community or national level. Statements of successive federal governments have strongly affirmed the idea of 'one law for all'. Such a creed reassures all citizens, Muslim and non-Muslim alike, that the law aims to protect and serve all equally. In a country where most people have a migrant heritage, any Islamic exceptionalism could threaten, in Australia and elsewhere, 'the tolerance liberal societies have traditionally extended to the interface between religious and secular law'.[46] For Muslim migrants in Australia, the freedom to practice as a Muslim in a particular way, and not according to the dictates of a particular Islamic interpretation of Shari'a, is a hallmark of living in a tolerant, liberal society. The freedom to resolve disputes in accordance with the Shari'a in its current unofficial mode is unrestrained, provided there is no transgression of the law of the land. If a parallel system of government-supported Shari'a tribunals was introduced, it could be held out or perceived as being obligatory for Muslims. Concerns about coercion, especially of migrant women, featured prominently in the objections to the Ontario model.[47] Although undoubtedly welcomed by some, such a model would diminish the freedom of choice currently enjoyed by Australian Muslims and could result in substantially less beneficial outcomes, especially for women. In matters of custody, parental responsibility, maintenance, and inheritance this could be profoundly significant.

The diversity within the Islamic world is in part due to Islam's adaptability to the culture, time, and place in which it is located. The phenomenon of large numbers of Muslims coming to live in non-Muslim lands calls for this inherent adaptability to continue. German Muslims have taken the collective view that they can exist in harmony with the German political and legal system. Article 13 of their Islamic Charta states that '[t]he command of Islamic law to observe the local legal order includes the acceptance of the German statutes governing marriage and inheritance, and civil as well as criminal procedure'.[48] Researchers in Britain have discovered an *angrezi shariat* (Urdu for English Shariah, the term reflecting a South Asian dominance), which is described as a reconstruction of Muslim laws for the English socio-legal context.[49] Through scholarly *ijtihād* by jurists who identify more with Australia than with the Middle East or South Asia, a contemporary Australian

---

[46] D Houck, 'The Islamist Challenge to the US Constitution' (2006) 13(2) *Middle East Quarterly* 21, 23.

[47] M McPhredran and A Sherazee, *Submission, Review of the Ontario Arbitration Act and Arbitration Processes* (Canadian Council of Women, 30 July 2004).

[48] Islamic Charta Germany, available at <http://www.qantara.de/uploads/332/Islamic-Charta.pdf>.

[49] Yilmaz (n 9 above) 66.

Shari'a (in English, not Urdu or Arabic) could emerge. However, it needs to be an *ijtihād* that includes the reasoning of female scholars, in keeping with both the tradition of Aisha[50] and the Australian goal of gender equality. Many Muslim migrants discover that the Australian legal system has 'much room' in it: one can be a good Muslim and good Australian. While the Shari'a may be operating in the shadow of the Australian legal system, it is surviving well on the authority and respect due from those who wish Shari'a to regulate their lives. Obedience to Shari'a is not imposed by the state but comes from the heart or mind of each believer who aspires to follow Allah's path, even in a secular land.

[50] Aisha was the Prophet Mohammad's third wife. After his death, Muslims consulted Aisha for religious rulings thereby acknowledging her extensive knowledge of the Qur'an, the traditions (*hadith*) of the Prophet, and Islamic jurisprudence (*fiqh*).

15

To Shari'aticize or not to Shari'aticize: Islamic and Secular Law in Liberal Democratic Society

Erich Kolig

A. Globalization's Challenge

Modern Western society, democratized and liberalized to a degree unprecedented in human history, faces many dilemmas caused by globalization. Among them, there is a mounting need for mutual accommodation of differences in a religious, ethnic, and cultural sense. Globalization has brought about this problem on two levels. Different cultural—and to some extent religiously defined—realms, hitherto separated by geographic distance, are meeting now in close and sometimes uncomfortable socio-cultural and political proximity. This is particularly and spectacularly true for the West and the Islamic world; they now encounter each other face to face in an ever closer embrace. Samuel Huntington[1] calls these realms 'civilizations'; he sees them divided by 'fault lines' defined not only by cultural difference, but no less importantly by incompatibility, tension, and antagonism. In his major work, *The Clash of Civilizations and the Remaking of World Order*, he predicts some major altercations, especially between the West and the Islamic world. Whereas in the past they were largely geographically confined, encountering each other only in sporadic hostile sorties or cautiously exploratory episodes, globalization has changed the picture dramatically. While I do not agree with either Huntington's definition of 'civilizations' as coherent ideological and political entities which now would act as agencies of opposition to and aggression towards the West, or his prediction that this is particularly so between the West and the Islamic civilization, there are undoubtedly some tensions that have religious and cultural roots.

On an international level, globalization means finding a universal *modus vivendi* and *cooperandi*: common laws and conventions sponsored mainly by the various

[1] S Huntington, *The Clash of Civilizations and the Remaking of World Order* (New York: Simon & Schuster, 1996).

fora of the United Nations, to facilitate not only the coexistence of diverse political, commercial, and military interests of nations, but also of diverse *weltanschauungen* (worldviews and ethical-legal value systems) so as to enable the relatively peaceful coexistence of interacting collective agencies and individuals within a finite and, thanks to modern technology, ever-shrinking space. There is a pressing need to find internationally acceptable rules of conduct for nation-states and individuals on the world stage. Through migration, such issues have become transposed into the domestic jurisdiction of nation-states and have become issues of acceptable pluralism. Observation of human rights, abolishment of assimilation policies on the basis of a notion of equality of all cultures, and a didactically instilled sense of tolerance and of the worth of cultural difference, have started to clear away centuries of entrenched xenophobia and disdain for, and hostility towards, difference. Crucial are the internationally accepted human rights provisions, inspired in their formulation by the horrors of World War II and the genocide perpetrated at that time. Even though they were not designed as protection for collective minority rights and directed foremost towards the guarantee of individual rights, important foundations for minority rights (religious, cultural, ethnic) were laid.

Globalization has in various ways produced massive population shifts, displacement, and migration. Muslim minorities composed of legal (and illegal) residents, immigrants, asylum seekers, and citizens are now living in the West in relatively large numbers.[2] Second and third generation 'migrants' have obtained citizenship by way of birth or naturalization, and are increasingly engaging themselves in the political process, ideological discourses, and political debate in their respective 'host societies'. Over time, the relatively numerous presence of minorities has changed the cultural composition of Western societies. Claiming a place for themselves and their religion, they have every right as citizens to engage themselves peacefully in processes of socio-cultural change in the countries they have adopted as their home.

B. Multiculturalism: Policies and Strategies

Many Western nations have effectively become culturally pluralistic melanges. The West's traditional cultural monochrome—ignoring more subtle nuances—has given way to a religious, cultural, and ethnic multi-chromatic mosaic. Most liberal democracies have responded to pluralist conditions by devising policies that provide a certain degree of cultural accommodation, either through specific multiculturalist provisions, through adopting identity politics, or simply through studied

---

[2] Statistics diverge widely, presumably since Western countries, because of secularization, do not keep accurate records of religious affiliation. The average for Europe (without an exact definition of what constitutes 'Europe') seems to stand at about five per cent of Muslims, but the ratio can be expected to be higher in France, Germany, and the Netherlands. The United Kingdom is significantly below five per cent. See Ahdar and Aroney, Ch 1 in this collection, Figure 2.

indifference.[3] In any case, assimilative, coercive impulses of majority society—common in nation-states in the past— have to be suppressed. Many unfamiliar, and perhaps even repulsive, customs have to be tolerated in the name of minority rights, multiculturalism, human rights, or general notions of cultural liberty. The previous expectations of a nation being a melting pot—or in extreme and sinister ideologies an enclave of cultural purity—have disappeared, although lingering cultural nationalism is still present in 'right wing' political circles. There it may be masked as a protection agenda for the preservation of the 'indigenous' culture, or it may be promoted in terms of the need to preserve national political stability and a cohesive social fabric.

For other reasons too, multiculturalism has remained a highly contested concept. In some cases, opposition to multiculturalism has arisen out of disappointment and disaffection with social experiments to deal with cultural pluralism.[4] Removing the detritus of failed policies and dealing with the effects of Muslim extremism has led to some disenchantment with multiculturalist policies and has created a backlash from the political right as well as the left. 'Parallel lives' and mutual hostility of ethnic, cultural, and religiously distinct groups and the absence of conviviality[5] have turned tolerance and acceptance of cultural difference into reluctance or outright refusal, an attitudinal change more widespread now in majority society. Supporting such fears and engaging in alarmist hyperbole, the well-known Islamic studies scholar, Bernard Lewis, was reported as saying: 'Islam could soon be the dominant force in a Europe which, in the name of political correctness, has abdicated the battle for cultural and religious control'.[6] Generally speaking, there are new initiatives afoot in several Western countries to make it more difficult to gain residency and citizenship, aimed primarily, one suspects, at immigrant and asylum-seeking Muslims.

In their intent, multiculturalist policies, by and large, have rarely gone beyond a certain point. Protestations of tolerance and declarations of religious and cultural freedom notwithstanding, invisible and often undefined boundaries of accommodation have in fact been drawn, not only for in-principle reasons of upholding majority society's basic standards of justice, ethics, and aesthetics (and not only

---

[3] I am not concerned here with a review of political theory, but with sociological issues of practical cultural accommodation.

[4] D McGhee, *The End of Multiculturalism? Terrorism, Integration and Human Rights* (Maidenhead: Open University Press, 2008); W Kymlicka, *Multicultural Odysseys: Navigating the New International Politics of Diversity* (Oxford: Oxford University Press, 2007).

[5] Expressed, eg in the 'Cantle Report' commissioned by the UK Government following the ethnic riots in 2001: *Community Cohesion: a Report of the Independent Review Team chaired by Ted Cantle* (Home Office, 2001).

[6] Quoted from the *Jerusalem Post*, 2 November 2009. Earlier, he had already predicted that by century's end 'at the very latest' Europe would be Islamic: see C Caldwell, 'Islamic Europe', *Weekly Standard*, 10 April 2004, available at <http://www.weeklystandard.com/Content/Public/Articles/000/000/004/685ozxcq.asp>.

for the sake of clearly adhering to traditional notions of right and wrong)[7] but also for the sake of practical, undogmatic cohesiveness of society. Multicultural society makes conflicting demands—fostering unity and respecting diversity—which are difficult to meet.[8] Socially closely interacting agents in a nation-state can obey different rules, hold different values, and subscribe to different ontological principles—but only to a certain degree. Special group rights are appealing to modern liberalist sentiments and are rightly considered a public good, but can pose problems. Sometimes issues of having to protect the rights of citizens who do not wish to abide by the rules of a minority, even if in one sense they are part of it, come to the fore. Sometimes issues of the sovereignty of the majority appear to be critically endangered. In addition, intolerant impulses of minority customs and views have to be curbed in order to maintain the very liberties that allow minorities freely to express their differences and disaffection with, and disapproval of, majority culture. Recognizing that there is no total freedom, detractors of limited multiculturalism have variously called it 'boutique multiculturalism'[9], three Cs multiculturalism (for costumes, cooking, and concerts)[10] or three Ss multiculturalism (for saris, samosa, and steelbands).[11] Critics contend that, despite protestations of cultural freedom, only a few selected cultural features—those found harmless and not violating existing aesthetic and ethic regimes or laws of majority society—are able to find acceptance in the host society.

Societies and states react differently to cultural difference among its members and citizens. As a sweeping generalization it may be said that liberal democracies, observant of human rights conventions, react by creating laws, institutions, and rules flexible enough to accommodate some differences and by educating citizens in cultural tolerance or acceptance. Some even enact protective or exception-laden laws and rules for minority cultures (eg through restorative justice provisions for indigenous minority groups in settler states).[12] In some cases the social rulebook is riddled with exceptions. And some states create group categories to which different rules and laws are applied. (This 'communitarian' approach, however, runs the risk of aiding discrimination and ultimately being seen as a form of apartheid, even when it is devised with the best humanist

---

[7] E Kolig, 'Romancing Culture and Its Limitations: Policies of Cultural Recognition, Multiculturalism and Cultural Boundaries in New Zealand' in R Openshaw and E Rata (eds), *The Politics of Conformity in New Zealand* (Auckland: Pearson, 2009) 63.

[8] B Parekh, *Rethinking Multiculturalism* (Basingstoke: Palgrave, 2000) 196.

[9] S Fish, 'Boutique Multiculturalism, or Why Liberals Are Incapable of Thinking about Hate Speech' (1997) 23 *Critical Inquiry* 378.

[10] S Gunew, *Haunted Nations: the Colonial Dimensions of Multiculturalism* (London: Routledge, 2004) 17.

[11] J Donald and A Rattansi, *'Race', Culture and Difference* (Newbury Park CA: Sage, 1992) 2.

[12] B Bashir and W Kymlicka (eds), *The Politics of Reconciliation in Multicultural Societies* (Oxford: Oxford University Press, 2008).

intentions. Beneficial positive discrimination, by marking out minorities, can inflect to a negative one.)[13]

Excessive liberalism—in a sense of *vive la différence!*—challenges even tolerance as too narrow, ethnocentric, or restrictive. Not only celebrating difference, it aims at respecting illiberal features of minority cultures, even when they infringe on people who do not wish to come under minority cultural jurisdiction. Especially impressive cases from Europe can be found in the writing of the Norwegian anthropologist, Unni Wikan, and her work on Muslim women in Norway who become the football between customary ethno-religious rights and the human and civil rights of a citizen. Wikan describes how the sanctioning of Moroccan marriage customs by Norwegian authorities has led to bizarre cases of abuse.[14] Muslim women may be citizens of Norway's liberal democracy but, by virtue of their, or their family's, ethnic origin, they are forced into under-age or arranged marriages. Similarly, the Dutch-Somali author, Ayaan Hirsi Ali, exposed domestic violence in Muslim families—such as wife beating—being ignored by the Dutch police in the interest of multiculturalism and respect for Islamic teaching that supposedly prescribes absolute obedience of the wife vis-à-vis her husband.[15] Will Kymlicka and Bhikhu Parekh argue consistently that the realization of liberal values in a situation of deep value pluralism necessarily entails recognition and respect for groups that may be hostile or indifferent to a hegemonic culture and may even be adverse to liberalism.[16]

One wonders what happens if Thugism (the worship of the Hindu goddess of death Kali) were to be revived in the large Indian community resident in the United Kingdom; would authorities condone sacrificial random killings in the name of religious freedom? Hardly. So-called 'honour killings' in some ethnic minority groups do not seem to enjoy legal immunity. Clearly some boundaries setting limits to accommodation are being drawn, even in the most liberal society. In fact, tolerance seems to have diminished in recent years: the fear of terrorism, apparently Islam-inspired violence, and a perceived lack of adjustment on the part of some Muslims are ready explanations. Preaching violent *jihād* against the West in mosques in Western countries, which was seemingly widely tolerated in the past, more recently has become a focus of investigation and criminal prosecution. A shift in tolerance has thus criminalized a religious practice—considered a religious duty and often referred to as the sixth pillar of Islam—where previously it may have fallen under provisions of religious freedom or freedom of expression.

---

[13] It is perhaps for this reason that Jytte Klausen (*Islamic Challenge: Politics and Religion in Western Europe* (Oxford: Oxford University Press, 2005)) has found that European Muslim leaders reject multiculturalism.

[14] U Wikan, 'Citizenship on Trial: Nadia's Case' in R Shweder, M Minow, and H R Markus (eds), *Engaging Cultural Differences: the Multicultural Challenge in Liberal Democracies* (New York: Russell Sage Foundation, 2002) 128; U Wikan, *Generous Betrayal: Politics of Culture in the New Europe* (Chicago: University of Chicago Press, 2002).

[15] H A Ali, *The Caged Virgin* (London: Free Press, 2006).

[16] Much of that argument predates the 9/11 and 7/7 terrorist attacks.

C. A Catalyst: The Archbishop's 2008 Lecture

Inspired by a very tolerant perspective of liberalism and cultural freedom, the Archbishop of Canterbury, Dr Rowan Williams, in a public lecture in 2008 seemed to suggest that Islamic law, the Shari'a, be officially recognized as a worthy companion complementing Western secularized law.[17] He appeared to recommend conceding an official status to Shari'a in the United Kingdom, even though one must be careful to come to that conclusion: the thrust of his argument is difficult to discern clearly from his rhetorical circumambulations. If Dr Williams meant to refer to the creation of Shari'a courts to adjudicate in a limited range of family matters on a voluntarist basis, his argument lacks novelty.[18] If his intention was to advocate a more comprehensive recognition of Shari'a, it warrants a closer inspection.

The question posed by Dr Williams is pertinent to a highly globalized and pluralist society within a nation-state in which citizens of different cultures and religious faiths are enjoying a relatively high degree of personal liberty.[19] It is also useful as it brings to the fore issues of practical social feasibility of legal pluralization. While on the international level, the coexistence of various quite different juridical systems and philosophical-ethical viewpoints may be able to coexist and still allow for a *modus vivendi* —though sometimes laboured and tense—the fully fledged and total recognition of two very different systems (such as secular Western law and Shari'a law) side-by-side within a nation runs into serious issues of compatibility and reconcilability. (The piecemeal concession-making of liberal democracies, on the basis of an individualist liberal political perspective, is not at issue here. If not general humanism, then certainly the global human rights agenda reflected in policies and laws such as multiculturalism, cultural and religious freedom, freedom of choice and expression, and so on demand and justify it.) The purely technical-juridical issues cannot be dealt with here. Instead, I will examine reasons that lie in the irreconcilable difference of *weltanschauungen*, and practical sociological reasons will be discussed relating to why the total application and recognition of Shari'a in all its consequences is not feasible in a liberal democracy.

---

[17] 'Civil and Religious Law in England: a Religious Perspective' (see Appendix I).

[18] The United Kingdom appears to have had five Shari'a 'courts' since 2007 and, according to Islamineurope.blog of June 2009, it now has 85. These courts operate under the aegis of the Muslim Arbitration Tribunal. Under the Arbitration Act 1996 they can make legally binding decisions, but such rulings must not contravene British law and recourse to the ordinary courts is not precluded.

[19] Williams' speech has reinvigorated a debate that has been going on for some years in several Western nations: to what extent, if at all, Shari'a could be tolerated or accommodated in liberal democracy so as to better enfranchise sizeable Muslim minorities; and how it could be made compatible with human rights provisions and constitutional requirements. (An example is the work of Maurits Berger in the Netherlands: see, eg M Berger, 'Sharia in Europa? Welke Sharia?' 11 *Eutopia* (2005), available at <http://www.clingendael.nl/staff/publications.html?id=6&&type=offline&& start=2>.).)

Liberal sycophantism in Western Europe is more than counterbalanced by the rising tide of harsh ideologies preaching anti-immigration views, Islamophobia, and general xenophobia. The cries of opinion-makers and politicians like Geert Wilders in the Netherlands, Jean-Marie Le Pen in France, Nick Griffin in the United Kingdom, the late Jörg Haider and his political successors in Austria, and others, are getting louder. The brutish notion that Muslims simply have to adjust totally to Western norms and values, or they may not be welcome, not only shows an alarming absence of democratic flexibility, but suggests a standpoint that is unworthy of the doctrines of individual liberty and scientific humanism. Jews and other religious, cultural, and ethnic minorities in Europe—eg Romas, Saami, perhaps even Basques, and other groups that did not comfortably fit into national cultural and religious majorities, let alone indigenous minorities in settler states—have suffered from that approach for centuries. Minority cultural peculiarities had to survive either in the very private sphere, or in the darker nooks and crannies of society. The full force of the dictatorship of the majority was brought to bear in various ways ranging from discrimination to extermination.

In comparison to Europe's harsh practices of earlier centuries the Islamic *dhimma* system, an early and admittedly imperfect form of official multicultural-ism and religious liberalism, seemed positively enlightened—although now it is clearly thoroughly outdated and discredited for being in violation of present-day human rights conventions and liberal sensitivities.[20] (In the Islamic world it persists in one form or another.) Even if it were practically possible to apply it now in reverse order for Muslims in Western society, human rights conventions (especially those relating to equality) would prohibit it and modern forms of social interaction would make it virtually impossible to police and enforce, or only so under a staggering amount of public surveillance.

A few philosophers and sociologists have argued that Islam might have an important future role as a redeemer of ethics: as an antidote to Western decadence and immorality, it could tighten the prevailing laxity and set new strict standards of morality.[21] For them, Christianity, too enfeebled by secularization and

---

[20] While some descriptions of the *dhimma* system in elevating its discriminatory features to prominence may have a political agenda, it is clear that traditionally this is not a system under which minorities would voluntarily choose to live. Marking minorities out for special treatment was to some extent for their protection, but also holds significant disadvantages, mainly in terms of politically emasculating them. It represents a denial of power. When the Taliban, shortly before their downfall, tried officially to introduce this system (by ordering religious minorities to wear badges) it was met with universal protest because of its similarities with the badge-system of the Nazi regime that singled out Jews, homosexuals, and communists. See, eg D Arzt, 'The Treatment of Religious Dissidents under Classical and Contemporary Islamic Law' in J Witte and J van der Wyver (eds), *Religious Human Rights in Global Perspective: Religious Perspectives* (The Hague: Nijhoff, 1996) 387; B Ye'or, *The Dhimmi* (Rutherford NJ: Farleigh Dickinson, 1985); B Ye'or, *Islam and Dhimmitude: Where Civilizations Collide* (Cranbury NJ: Assoc. Univ. Press, 2002). In her latest book, *Eurabia: The Euro-Arab Axis* (Cranbury NJ: Assoc. Univ. Press, 2005), Ye'or engages in exaggerated polemics. See also J Waardenburg, *Muslims and Others: relations in context* (Berlin, New York: De Gruyter, 2003); B Tibi, *Political Islam, World Politics and Europe* (London, New York: Routledge, 2008).

[21] See, eg F Allam, *Der Islam in einer Globalen Welt* (original: *L'Islam Globale*, 2002) (Berlin: Klaus Wagenbach, 2004) 69–71.

compromises, and riddled with laissez-faire tolerance, cannot do the job and is irredeemably lost to society as a moral force. In the search for new ethical principles and a moral *terra firma*, Islam may come to the rescue. However, in the cold clear light of realism it is obvious that the universal embracement of Islamic ethical and juridical viewpoints can hardly be counted on, nor can it be foreseen, even with the largest of crystal balls, to ever happen.

It is not my intention to argue in favour of a profound universalism or superiority of ethics. (Doing so would all too easily fall into the trap of 'occidentalism'.) As the philosopher Max Horkheimer of the Frankfurt School, marvelling about the relativity of ethics and the impossibility of scientifically supporting a hierarchy of ethical systems, once observed: arguing that one set of ethics is better than another is like arguing that 'red is better than blue or an egg is better than milk'.[22] Some of the answers why the future of global morality does not lie with the Shari'a are these.

Putting aside the global trajectory of secularization,[23] the West's rampant hedonism, its individualistic egotism and general anthropocentric outlook constitute an overwhelming, irrepressible force and account for the fact that much of the rest of the world is following suit (or seems poised to do so sooner or later). All that militates against the universal adoption of a strongly theocentric *weltanschauung* in which humanity has duties of discipline and sacrifice but basically no rights of enjoyment. Conservative Islam does not show any preparedness to compromise. *Islamiyun* (Islamists) in particular mistake the forces of intellectual globalized interlocking as 'unfreedom' and slavery to the West that have to be rejected. De-colonization and post-modernist liberalism in the West have not invoked an equivalent epistemological response on the other side. In fact, a conservative Islamic point of view condemns liberalism, humanism, and enlightenment as intellectual imperialism and as a form of secularist arrogance which would not allow an epistemology outside the materialistic order.[24] Enlightenment liberalism preaches human enjoyment and benefit and a quantifiable anthropocentrism quite in contrast to the Islamic sense of devotion and duty to God.

It seems implausible that such views will globally gain traction any time soon. Putting the *zeitgeist* aside, another reason lies in the nature of Shari'a. Its social and temporal specificity—through the minuteness and detail of divinely commanded rules—if taken literally creates a time-bound character that threatens to alienate Islam more and more from the social patterns of modern global society. The sense of gender inequality that pervades Islam and relegates women to a state of subservience and legal immaturity intrudes on all gender relations and women's abilities

---

[22] H Gumnior and R Ringguth, *Max Horkheimer* (Hamburg: Rowohlt, 1973) 103. M Horkheimer, *Zur Kritik der instrumentellen Vernunft* (A Schmidt ed) (Frankfurt aM: Suhrkamp, 1967) 33.

[23] Here is not the space to discuss and refute arguments about the current momentum of global re-religionization that some social analysts claim to have observed.

[24] A particularly crass example is provided by Abdulwahab al Masseri, 'The Imperialist Epistemological Vision' (1994) 11 *American Journal of Islamic Social Sciences* 403.

for public functioning in a modern liberal society;[25] strict codes of honour and responsibility that bind collectively whole families and groups, and a rigid family structure are phenomena that are fast vanishing in the face of social fluidity, individual ambition, and individuality in choosing a lifestyle different from one's group of origin; the exponential increase in genetic, gender, and cosmetic manipulations to satisfy new aesthetic notions conflicts with the rigidity of the bi-polar gender and descent views of conservative Islam; the unbridgeable universal dichotomy between 'true believers' (the *umma*) and 'infidels' (derisively termed *kafirs*), and so on. Thus, to radically 'modernize' Islamic dogma requires an extraordinary reformatory effort. On the whole there is overwhelming resistance by 'true believers' for whom the need to stay true to Islam precludes the radical exegesis and reformation needed to speedily create a 'privatized', profoundly modernized and 'secularized' Islam.[26]

To reduce a difficult philosophical debate to the practical dynamics of a democratized and globalized world in search of rules, worldviews, values, and doctrines held in common, at least superficially, may simply come down to a question of numbers: Muslims constitute about 1.4 billion[27] —of whom not all may be happy to live by Shari'a in any form (so-called nominal or 'secularized' Muslims) and others who may baulk at being ruled by a certain version of it—as against around five billion non-Muslims, most of whom are absolutely opposed to the idea.

[25] Gender relations in Islam are a contentious issue in terms of whether Islam is misogynistic and discriminatory vis-à-vis women in the practices it prescribes. But more important to the present discussion is the claim that Islamic doctrine violates domestic and international human rights, laws which have great currency in Western nations and which insist on absolute equality of the genders. Lila Abu-Lughod's apologist argument ('Do Muslim Women really need saving?' (2002) 104 *American Anthropologist* 783) extolling the virtues of cultural relativism and of withholding judgment on other cultures is more than counter-balanced by a host of Muslim women authors and activists who are critical of Muslim gender relations dictated by Islamic doctrine and habituated by social practice. See, eg Fatima Mernissi's various writings, Irshad Manji, Hirsi Alyaan Ali, Amina Wadud, Seyran Ates (eg her book, *Der Multi-Kulti-Irrtum* (Berlin: Ullstein, 3rd edn, 2007)), innumerable Muslim blog sites, websites of Muslim feminist organizations, etc. The current diatribes against the gender situation in Muslim society and the allegations of Islam's misogyny are to some extent a product of contemporary global discourses—admittedly Western hegemonic in provenance—on equality, rights, gender, and freedom. Cultural relativism, and the recognition of different histories that are very modern and New Age, do encourage an acceptance of alien cultural practices and beliefs; and yet there is unease that Muslim gender conditions do not fit into a globalized and globalizing world. To acknowledge Islam's ill-adjustment in this area of doctrine and social practice is not Orientalist (in Said's sense) but strikes a chord with current global preoccupations.

[26] This means an Islam that is reduced to largely ceremonial importance and an abstract worldview held as a matter of personal choice in believers' private lives.

[27] This amounts to between 20 to 23 per cent of the world's population. See Ahdar and Aroney, Ch 1 in this collection, Figure 1.

D. Is There One Shari'a?

Shari'a primarily refers to commandments, ordinances, rules, and recommendations contained in various form in the sacred scriptures (the Qur'an and *Sunna*);[28] or abstractly put, the concept refers to the regulative ontological aspects of Islamic doctrine. As a cohesive text, Shari'a delivers not only rules of worship, but much more comprehensively sets out a blueprint for human existence as a whole. It is more like an ontology as it spells out in varying degrees of clarity (or obscurity, as the case may be) the meaning of human existence, a life which largely lies in the duty to please God by following the divinely devised rules of social conduct. These rules apply to individual existence as much as they render structural norms for an Islamic society or the global community of believers (*umma*) as a whole. From conducting personal hygiene, behaviour in the privacy of the bedroom and performing sex, the ringtone of one's cellphone, to laws of inheritance, conducting business and wars, giving witness in a court of law, divorce, political leadership—everything is at least potentially, if not overtly and clearly, contained in this belief system. Insofar as these rules are grounded in metaphysical, kerygmatic considerations, Shari'a, it can be argued, even goes beyond the purely regulative, world-immanent aspects. Mainstream Sunni Islam is often regarded by its followers as in essence a legal code—a complex juristic system of divinely ordained rules and laws by which believers must live and the close observation of which promises God's grace in the form of redemption and eternal reward. Theology becomes jurisprudence.

It is instantly clear why this perspective runs into difficulties in secularized Western societies and states, where 'religion' refers to a much narrower section of human social and spiritual existence. Religious freedom as understood in the West is therefore never so comprehensive as to span all of Islam. When Sebastian Poulter says that Islam (in the United Kingdom) can only be lived as a 'religion',[29] he underscores the point that religion in the modern Western sense is a product of decades, if not centuries, of secularization. Religion provides a vague moral background and a system of metaphysics and transcendence with little direct application in daily social life. Bluntly put, Christian ethics and canon law have been relegated to a backseat in society, where they no longer dictate moral and social rules or perform a supervisory function for social interaction. At best they relate to the sphere of privacy that is meant to stay out of public affairs. The previous, universally valid function of a religion, any religion, of regulating society by establishing benchmarks of lawful and ethical behaviour, providing checks on socio-political matters, and delivering and

---

[28] Islamic law is (mostly implicitly) contained in the Qu'ran and to a much greater extent in the *Sunna* (see, eg Frank Vogel, *Islamic Law and Legal System* (Leiden, Berlin, Köln: Brill, 2000) for succinct summaries and useful definitions). The complex body of law is derived from these texts through exegesis and interpretation (*ijtihād*). Essence, spirit, and letter of the sacred texts together form the basis of Islamic law.

[29] S Poulter, *Ethnicity, Law and Human Rights: The English Experience* (Oxford: Oxford University Press, 1998) 236.

vetting laws has been shed. (Liberal secularized society, in the Durkheimian sense, is in the transition phase between elementary society in which religion performs an indispensable social function and modern society in which rational education takes over the vital function previously monopolized by religion.) Excepting socio-politically inconsequential enclaves comprising sects, so-called 'cults', and reclusive groups, Christianity has virtually abdicated its social role in favour of secular institutions and agencies. Christianity hovers uneasily in the remote background, occasionally critiquing secular social, political, and juridical agencies whenever secularized society is prepared to pay attention. In this situation of diminished governance by religion, the maintenance and formation of ethical standards and social rules are taken over by the secularist state and its law-making and enforcement institutions. From a devout Muslim's viewpoint, this signifies a religion in its death-throes. The Islamic maxim, held high by Islamism, *din wa daulah* (belief and state) is the exact opposite of the church-state separation so cherished in the West.

Shari'a canon law is contained principally in the sacred scriptures (above all in the Qur'an, but also the *Sunna*, the tradition, and exemplified in hundreds of *Ahadith*, primarily the sayings of the Prophet or exemplary episodes in his life). Exegesis is almost always necessary with both texts to establish the narratives' relevance to present-day conditions. This body of revelations is usually supplemented by *qiyas* (analogical reasoning, deductive interpretation) and also by the *ijmāᶜ* (the consensus among eminent jurist-scholars at various stages of the past). Another source of wisdom and licit clarification may be *ijtihād* (interpretation). In one view, it may still be carried out by present-day authorities, while, under another view, *ijtihād* has been concluded centuries ago and if carried out today would constitute illicit innovation (*bida*). Individual clarification when required in specific cases may come through *fatawā* (rulings) of accredited jurist-scholars. Many eminent experts maintain websites or blogs to answer enquiries by the believers. Cases in which their opinions, invited or not, coincide are rare.[30]

In effect, all this contributes to the rich and complex tapestry of Shari'a, which even for the believer can grow into a bewildering maze. Acceptance of the various parts of this ethic-legal corpus, its metaphysical underpinnings, the authority of the sources and their interpretations, collectively and individually, is not universal among Muslims. Most Sunni accept the precedents set by the *Rashidun*, the four rightly guided caliphs who assumed succession to the role of spiritual and temporal leadership of the Prophet Muhammad after his death. Extreme Salafism rejects as heresy or illicit innovation any interpretation or consensus after that, while others draw the line somewhat later.[31] Shi'a Islam does not accept the *Rashidun* part of the

---

[30] There are many variations and differences in ranking the relative gravity of these and other sources where they are not consonant in detail. This cannot be discussed here.

[31] There are several versions of Salafism placing emphasis on different aspects of Islam for revival. Bernard Haykel (eg *Revival and Reform in Islam* (Cambridge: Cambridge University Press, 2003)) has extensively published on this topic; and see also B Tibi, *Der Islam und das Problem der kulturellen Bewältigung sozialen Wandels* (Frankfurt a.M.: Suhrkamp, 1985) and B Tibi, *Political Islam, World Politics and Europe* (London, New York: Routledge, 2008).

doctrine at all and looks more to ongoing spiritual leadership among the leading clergy who are supposed to step in the footsteps of Ali, the cousin and son-in-law of the Prophet and last of the *Rashidun*. The charismatic guidance of top *ayatollahs* contrasts with the dry scriptural juridical interpretations of Sunni Islam experts (*uluma, fuqahā, muftīs, mujtahidun*).

To partly overcome individual or sectional variation, Shari'a has been codified in the *fiqh* (science of Islamic law). This codification was achieved mainly by the law-schools (*madhāhib*) of which there are four in Sunni Islam, and two or three in Shi'ism. The schools all offer different interpretations. For instance, three Sunni schools utterly condemn homosexuality as a sin worthy to be punished in the severest form, while one does not. There are also variations in the application of the five major rubrics of divine commands relating to human actions and normative behaviour: obligatory, recommended, permissible, recommended against, and prohibited. In any case, Islam contains strong impulses for a society to have jurisdictional functions that are careful in trying to obey all rules laid down, be it overtly or obliquely, and in dispensing justice that strives to completely espouse the divine spirit of their foundation.

Another important feature of Shari'a is that no wilful changes are allowed through human agency and authority. Therefore, the law-making processes of secular democratic society, which operates without reference to religious law, is considered illicit and would only be tolerable if it at least takes its cues from the Shari'a. The basic doctrine which lies at the root of Islam's denial of man's law-making capacity is that sovereignty does not reside in people (no matter whether or not they are citizens of a sovereign nation), but only in God.

In Islam, no historical or sociological interpretation of the scriptures is allowed.[32] The argument that the *zeitgeist* of the Prophet's era and Arabic culture and society may have shaped the revelation, or that the revelation may have been influenced by the temporal issues of that society and culture, would be considered by many as the grossest heresy and blasphemy. Proposing that the Shari'a be stripped of time-specific issues and views sails close to the wind of heresy. The Mutazilah tradition since the nineteenth century has made attempts to modernize doctrines and thereby create a greater degree of conformity with and relevance to modern times and contemporary society,[33] but they are not universally appreciated by the *umma*. (For instance, the female immaturity in legal and political matters can be interpreted as a feature of social conditions in ancient Arab society, while nowadays

---

[32] I am referring here to a much more critical historical engagement than that provided by traditional *tafsir* (exegesis) and *asbab al-nusul* (circumstances of descent)—an engagement that understands the texts as historical testimonies and historical narratives mirroring Arabic culture, its mindset, values, and the particular (limited, 'pre-scientific') cognitive horizon at the Prophet's time.

[33] I am referring here to Mutazilah's engagement with modernity where it differs distinctly from conservative or traditionalist viewpoints. For a general overview, see, eg R Martin, M Woodward, and D Atmaja, *Defenders of Reason in Islam: Mu'tazilism from Medieval School to Modern Symbol* (Oxford: One World, 1997).

education prepares women for responsible roles in society and for equality before the law.)

Only a few radical Islamic thinkers have had the courage of seeking to increase the relevance of Islam for diasporic Muslims and undertake efforts to make Islam compatible with the twenty-first century. Modernizing the Shari'a faces another difficulty. The traditional minuteness of regulative detail, although giving a secure guide for the lives of believers in seeking eternal bliss, makes this a timeless and fixed blueprint for human existence. Even though advanced for its time—conceding, for instance, rights to women where previously they may have had none—Islamic dogma risks being stuck in a groove by reason of its apparent freeze-framing every aspect of human life forever.

Some aspects of the Shari'a are spelt out in relative clarity, while others are obscure and require intricate and laborious exegesis. Hand amputation for theft, for instance, is unambiguously commanded in the Qur'an—which being God's word 'verbatim', all Muslims accept as the most authoritative source of legal wisdom. Other rules need interpretation, requiring consultation with the experts. Take the right, and even duty, of a man (usually the *pater familias*) to exercise authority over the family and enforce the law of obedience on the women under his jurisdiction. A husband has the god-given right to administer a beating to a recalcitrant or insubordinate wife. Some experts interpret this to mean that a real and painful punishment should be administered, while others insist that the respective *Ayat* (Qu'ran verse) requires only a very light beating (recommended for instance by the official Saudi version of the Qu'ran) or even only a symbolic one (carried out with a *miswak*, a tooth pick, as recommended by al-Azhar scholars).

Another complicating feature of the Shari'a are regional variations. Islam being spread over a vast geographic expanse in its history has accepted regional customs as part of Shari'a. Customary practice, some of it probably pre-Islamic in its origin, has created some significant differences in perceived orthodoxy between scriptural Islam and that practised in some regions.[34] For the practitioners of such customs, they are an integral part of the integrative function of Islamic law, while for others they are simply illicit accretions bordering on heresy (*bida*).

Finally, one has to realise that Shari'a varies in the severity of its implementation. The severity in which Shari'a is followed officially by the Saudi, Sudanese, and Iranian states (and enclaves in Nigeria, Somalia, and other tribal areas) is surpassed by the Talibanic version, which is unique in its harsh restrictiveness, misogyny, and uncompromising intolerant and absolute nature.

---

[34] The Taliban's version of Islam, for instance, draws heavily on *pashtunwala*; that is, it is saturated with local customs of the Pashtuns in Afghanistan and the adjoining regions in Pakistan.

E. Shari'a in the West[35]

Muslims living in the West come from a multitude of different countries, regions, and places, and are of disparate sectarian and ethnic backgrounds. Consequently, they have divergent views of what exactly constitutes proper Shari'a. Most prominently, the sectarian difference between Sunni and Shi'i entails distinctly different interpretations of Shari'a. Many Shi'ites accept the political and spiritual leadership and juridical legacy of Ayatollah Ruollah Khomeini and his dictates, while Sunni abhor it on principle. A *Salafiya*–inspired interpretation would find little sympathy from among assimilation-ready, 'modernized' Muslims, and so on. It is fair to assume that few Muslims living in the Western diaspora would appreciate the enforcement of Talibanic Shari'a in their lives.

Tariq Ramadan,[36] a leading light of Islamic reform in Europe, suggests extracting the essence of doctrine and discarding the time- and culture-specific shell in which the doctrinal principles are clad, so as to allow a timely accommodation of faith. Conservative Muslims reject this as *bida* (error, heresy). At the very least, ejection of the baggage of regionally or ethnically based customs, considered integral parts of the Shari'a, has to be achieved for at least a semblance of being a firm member of national Muslimhood or, more expansively, of Muslimhood in the West.[37] Some Western Muslims defend a severe, 'literal' form of Shari'a, that includes the *hudūd* provisions (corporal punishment for what are considered severe transgressions), but as a concession to modern circumstances argue that it is only apposite to a truly Islamic society. However, this God-pleasing condition, they argue, does not yet exist anywhere—not even in the so-called Islamic world. Only when Islamic doctrinal principles are collectively and unreservedly embraced, based on sound Islamic education, and fully applied in society, can the Islamic law in all its severity come into force. For instance, hand amputation for theft would be permissible only when Islamic charity and fair distribution of wealth secure a standard of living in which the need to steal out of hunger has been eradicated and moral education causes embezzlement out of greed to disappear. This reasoning provides a comforting excuse for living in an emphatically non-Islamic society, as

[35] In considering the difficulties of aligning Islamic law with the secular law of a liberal democracy, I am drawing on an 'essentialized' view of Shari'a. Strictly speaking, this is not only a violation of current anthropological mantras, but also contradicts what I have said before about internal differences and fluidity of Shari'a. But for the sake of brevity it is unavoidable.

[36] See T Ramadan, *Western Muslims and the Future of Islam* (Oxford: Oxford University Press, 2004).

[37] See the statements of a British Muslim leader, Sheikh Zaki Badawi, and the readiness he expresses for Muslims to adapt their doctrines to fit diasporic life in modern Western conditions and Muslim multi-ethnicity: J Wolffe, 'Fragmented Universality: Islam and Muslims' in G Parsons (ed), *The Growth of Religious Diversity* (London: Routledge, Open University, 1993) 133, 164. I suspect that today few Muslim leaders would openly show this readiness.

does the concept of *Dār ul-Ahd*, the Abode of Truce,[38] standing in between the House of Islam (*Dār ul-Islām*) and the Realm of War (*Dār ul-Harb*). In the traditional Islamic perspective of the world, finding oneself living in the infidel realm under infidel governance and law would theoretically force a devout Muslim to leave, to become a *muhajir* (after the example of the *hijra*, the Prophet's departure from 'godless' Mecca to migrate to Medina.)

There are many 'lawful' contradictions at many levels and a noticeable degree of incompatibility between Shari'a and the letter of Western law and its spirit of justice. Leaving aside the manifold and tangled variations in the Shari'a, several aspects of it are not just deviating by degree from Western laws, norms, values, practices, and customary conventions, but are in direct conflict to the point of total incompatibility. Islamic idiomatic understanding of 'justice' can be very different from the secularized, Western understanding. (It certainly places greater emphasis on punitive rather than restorative functions.) Even though the question of precisely which core values of the West are beyond compromise has never been satisfactorily answered, there is obvious evidence that many important Western juridical notions are largely incompatible with Shari'a.

The strict application of the demand that there be only 'one law for all' can lead to great injustice.[39] Citizenship too is not necessarily legally totally uniform. There are differentiated forms of citizenship: minors, intellectually impaired persons, prison inmates, and convicted criminals on probation have different rights and duties; members of some sects may be freed from military service (in countries with general conscription or in a war situation), and have a right not to vote and to abstain from democratic involvement (in countries and elections in which voting is obligatory); some citizens may have rights in an electoral system from which others are barred. So why not create a citizen category for Muslims?

F. How Much Accommodation?

How far can legal pluralism go in the course of cultural accommodation? This question confronts a paradox: in the name of liberty, the right to be less liberal is handed over to a minority to be used at will. The moral norms and practices of minorities may conflict with liberal democratic core values at many points. Some of the cardinal sins for minorities (worthy of the most severe forms of punishment) hardly raise an eyebrow, or are even counted among cherished freedoms, in secularized liberal society. The right of individual choice, so elevated in liberal political theory, has collective ramifications that go beyond the sum total of individual choices. Demanding 'interactive pluralism' instead of social parallelism

---

[38] Similar concepts are Ramadan's *darul shahada* and *darul dawa, darul amn*, etc.
[39] J Waldron, 'One law for all? The logic of cultural accommodation' (2002) 59 *Washington and Lee Law Review* 3.

not only gives rise to a conflict of contradictory principles, but also creates a great danger to social harmony. Because of social interpenetration, the liberty to be illiberal is not confinable to the minority and its conscious choices. In fact, liberal democracy would be in danger of negotiating away its own fundamental liberties hard-won over centuries of struggle and bloodshed. In other words, the personal choice of being a Shari'a-abiding Muslim may also have severe repercussions on majority society.

A liberal democracy will educate its citizens to refrain from wilfully insulting a religion and attempt to instil a measure of respect for the beliefs of minorities. But it is not expected to legislate to confine, circumscribe, and remove fundamental freedoms that define it as a liberal polity. Conversely, minorities retain the right to protest and demand respect, but ought not to expect the state to apply *their* illiberal or restrictive notion of what is permissible.

One of the most cherished public goods is freedom of opinion (including religious belief) and expression. Some of these 'rights' (some may say privileges) are severely proscribed by Shari'a. Most prominently, exercising religious choice may constitute apostasy (*irtidad* or *ridda*) and freedom of opinion may lead to expressions considered heresy (*bida, kufr*) or blasphemy (*ridda* or *kufr*, a concept that goes beyond the divine sphere and includes disrespect shown towards the exalted person of the Prophet Muhammad and, in some interpretations, other sacred persons).[40] The controversies surrounding the Danish cartoons and Salman Rushdie's book, *The Satanic Verses*, graphically brought this home, but they are just the more widely known examples of what is a continuous clash.[41] Demands to apply the death penalty, assassination attempts (some of which have succeeded), and demonstrators with placards demanding the death of the perpetrators and the destruction of the West, are just some of the outcomes that have starkly highlighted the cultural and religious differences. In addition, the 'wrong' choice of sexuality (referred to as sodomy (*luwat*) in Islam) and adultery are cardinal sins, in some interpretations ranking in severity with blasphemy. Most of these 'crimes' attract the death penalty in many understandings of the Shari'a, but in secular Western society they would be tolerated or ignored.

Although realizing that there is no total freedom of expression even in liberal democracies,[42] by elevating the Shari'a to official status could have the consequence of placing constraints on the production of certain forms of knowledge and altering the definition of truth.[43] Islamization of knowledge could mean even

---

[40] The overlapping terminology indicates that the Shari'a sees these 'crimes' as closely related, if not identical, in intent and severity, hence punishable by the same measure.

[41] It is less well-known, for example, that Dan Brown's *The Da Vinci Code* has been banned in some Muslim countries. He has not, however, been threatened with a death *fatwā*.

[42] For examples of how freedom of expression is hedged in with taboos and interdictions, see E Kolig, *New Zealand's Muslims and Multiculturalism* (Leiden: Brill, 2010) 157.

[43] See, eg L Stenberg, 'Islam, Knowledge and the "West"' in B Schaebler and L Stenberg (eds), *Globalization and the Muslim World* (Syracuse: Syracuse University Press, 2004) 93.

more trenchant curbs, for example, on journalism, the literary and fine arts, and the social sciences.

The sociologist Bassam Tibi,[44] himself a Muslim of a moderate persuasion, has persistently argued that Islam should accept not only the fruits of Western science and technology, but also the intellectual and epistemological conditions that have enabled these advances to come about. Above all, Islam should accept critical rationalism; which means, as Karl Popper convincingly argued, that all knowledge is open to scrutiny, critique, and, if need be, ridicule. There must, from the Western perspective, be no dogmatic sanctuaries that can induce intellectual *rigor mortis* of a whole society. From a juridical position, Ahdar spells it out candidly: if people want to live in a liberal democracy enjoying religious and other liberties, they have to accept the liberty of others to criticize and even ridicule them.[45]

G. Some Practicalities of Accommodation

Liberal democratic society has made many concessions, some of which are now enshrined in law and in other social institutions. Some countries, in the name of multiculturalism, seem to allow, on an ad-hoc basis, supplementary Shari'a functions within the legal system for certain kinds of civil cases involving consenting parties. Charged with settling family matters, they may have limited jurisdiction, confined mainly to inheritance, divorce settlements, financial matters, and family disputes.[46] 'Transformative accommodation' in the form of limited Islamic jurisprudential functions may place some matters in the hands of the Shari'a,[47] but that opens up a range of problems. For instance, the claim that honour killing, *izzat*, is a 'family matter' presumably would fall outside the powers of Shari'a tribunals. Even the law of wifely obedience to her husband, when it concerns domestic violence, should not be under the jurisdiction of such courts. Strictly speaking, conservative Islamic justice implies the notion of a religiously prescribed gender imbalance. This bias forces these tribunals to severely impinge on the basic

---

[44] B Tibi, *Islamischer Fundamentalismus, moderne Wissenschaft und Technologie* (Frankfurt a.M.: Suhrkamp, 1992) 94–103.

[45] R Ahdar, 'The Right to Protection of Religious Feelings' (2008) 11 *Otago Law Review* 629, 656.

[46] Shari'a courts have probably operated unofficially in mosques and backyards in many Western countries with sizeable Muslim minorities. (Some so-called honour killings are rumoured to have been sanctioned by such unofficial judicial panels.) Some countries seem to have experimented with co-opting Shari'a experts in disputes between consenting parties with the rider that verdicts do not conflict with fundamental rights or constitutional issues. The European Court of Human Rights in 2003 concluded that Shari'a is not compatible with fundamental rights of democracy and European values (see Ahdar and Aroney, Ch 1 in this collection), while Ontario, Canada, rejected a proposal for Shari'a tribunals (see Gaudreault-DesBiens, Ch 4 in this collection). There is much confusion about terminology: whether it is appropriate to speak of Shari'a courts versus arbitration tribunals, and rulings, verdicts, *fatawā*, recommendations etc.

[47] A Baumeister, 'The Limits of Universalism' in B Haddock and P Sutch (eds), *Multiculturalism, Identity and Rights* (New York: Routledge, 2003) 109, 122.

human rights guaranteeing equal treatment of men and women before the law. For instance, Islamic inheritance rules divide up an estate unevenly, according to the gender of the beneficiaries and, most conspicuously, the testimony of a woman is, according to the Qur'an, worth only half of a man's. Critics point out that it is not unusual when violent domestic disputes come before a Shari'a court for women to struggle to get protection. It is alleged that women may be forced into sexual obedience to their husband or coerced to acquiesce in covert polygamous arrangements. In mixed marriages or situations where one party does not wish to submit, grave problems can arise.

In fact, the whole question of voluntarism in the submission to Shari'a is a thorny question. Should the system operate on the basis of individual choice? What if not all the parties agree on the judicial system they wish to govern them? Or should it be on the basis of prior categorization, on the basis of one's declared 'Muslimness'? Should liberal states enforce this? If jurisdiction is on an individual voluntary basis, must the parties submit to potentially harsh orders issuing from the Shari'a tribunal? Would, for instance, women be forced to abide by Shari'a rulings that required them to submit to sexual activity in furtherance of rights of their husbands?

Leaving aside conflicts in matters of principles, the close social interpenetration of minorities with majority society makes a clear separation of groups and their social conduct impossible. Even if all parties and persons involved agree to a *Shari'atic* approach to conflict resolution the ruling may be in clear breach of international human rights provisions.[48]

Great problems can arise when Muslims convert to Christianity or atheism: are they to be regarded and judged as Muslim apostates or are they escaping harsh Shari'a rules? How can homosexuality of Muslim men and women be judged? Other jurisdictional quandaries arise. What if a Muslim steals from a non-Muslim, or vice versa? Is the shoplifter to be judged by the Shari'a justice system and lose his hand—and, if so, through a humane surgical amputation or something worse? In some interpretations of Shari'a, a crime committed against a non-Muslim is not as grievous as one perpetrated upon a Muslim victim. What of appeals from a Shari'a verdict: does Western law overrule Shari'a? The questions are endless, and I suspect that contemporary jurisprudence has no firm answers.

Among the most serious challenges to Western legal and aesthetic regimes are transgressions which warrant the most serious of punishments (*ḥudūd*) according to the most severe interpretation of Shari'a and its punitive aspects. The enforcement of such punishments in some Muslim-majority countries highlights the respective conceptions of justice (Western versus Islamic), not only because of the disproportionate relationship between the offence and the

---

[48] Some Muslim-majority countries have signed up to the various UN human rights conventions, but only with the proviso that, in situations of conflict, the Shari'a shall prevail. Islamic nations have also drawn up their own charter of Islamic human rights that differs in important aspects from the UN Convention, ie the Cairo Declaration on Human Rights in Islam 1990 (drawn up by the Organization of the Islamic Conference, a body representing all Muslim majority nations).

severity of the punishment, but because of the types of punishment seemingly prescribed by the Shari'a. (Hand amputation, beheading, stoning, and incarceration until death by starvation occurs, are probably the penalties most repulsed in the West.) The Taliban regime in Afghanistan, which was practising an archaic form of Shari'a widely condemned even in the Muslim world, was known for carrying out death sentences on murderers by allowing a relative of the victim's to publicly execute the offender with a Kalashnikov. Clearly this is in serious breach of Western laws and aesthetics. The law of retaliation (*qisās*) provides for other forms of physical punishment (blinding, removal of teeth, foot amputation, etc) considered 'cruel' and 'unusual' according to contemporary human rights norms. Another matter alien to Western law is the possibility of the death penalty being commuted to the payment of a fine, if this is acceptable to the murdered victim's family.

H. *Jihād* and Veils

The concept of *jihād* is, due to its doctrinal importance, often referred to as the sixth pillar of Islam. It provides a moral imperative that ranges from personal moralization to waging war on the enemies of Islam. This, for example, is Al Qaeda's ideological justification for its campaign of terror. In some *Shari'atic* interpretations, the defence of Islam allows strategies which the West labels terrorism ('striking fear into the hearts of the enemy') and even suicide bombing may be permitted—even though suicide is condemned—as virtuous self-sacrifice.

As seemingly innocent an accoutrement as the head covering for women, the *hijab*, is subject to varying interpretation. In some interpretations, the covering of head and hair is absolutely required and some women see it as an important statement of their Muslim identity. Others view it as a fashion statement and yet others as a protective device against molestation. Some dispense with it altogether, while insisting that they are no lesser Muslims than those women who even cover their faces with a *niqab*. France, priding itself as the cradle of enlightenment and routinely placing *laicité* in the public sphere above religious freedom, has given a particularly forceful response to the *hijab*. For the French, religious impartiality, secularity of public education, and the importance of instilling a common French secular identity in the citizenry rank above the freedom of religious expression. Turkey—an officially secular state, but overwhelmingly Muslim society—apparently also considers the wearing of the *hijab* to be non-essential for the maintenance of a Muslim identity.

Even greater controversy has been aroused by the *burqa*. It has aroused suspicion and hostility, not only as a marker of religious conservatism and an ultra-orthodox adherence to Islamic doctrine, but also as a hint of extremist leanings. France is considering a general ban on the *burqa*, and in other countries partial bans are mooted. Recognizing Shari'a would add a new dimension to the debate.

Some cultural differences can be resolved by concessions by majority society: for instance, by recognizing various marriage arrangements. The 'partnership' concept has emerged in modern society, with de facto arrangements and same-sex marriage in many countries enjoying equal status with traditional heterosexual and formal forms. Furthermore, the traditional ideal of the nuclear family is losing its primacy through the necessary acknowledgement of solo parenting. Muslim polygamy may also gain legitimacy. Shi'ism recognizes short-term contractual marriage, which may also come to find increasing acceptance in majority society. Problems may well arise in mixed religious marriages with regard to divorce, financial regulations, maintenance of family discipline, religious education of children, and so on.

I. Shari'a and Democracy: Friends or Foes?

It is often claimed that Islam is fundamentally against democracy.[49] This is not exactly true and *Shari'atic* notions of proper government may not necessarily, or in principle, be adverse to democratic rule.[50] Islam does not specify a particular type of political regime, other than preferring one that is essentially Islamic, or at least sympathetic to Islam. But for the West, the unwanted result would be that religious, judicial, and political functions would lose their vital distinctiveness. A stream of Islamic thought cultivates a sense of indifference, if not hostility, towards the legitimacy of secularized, non-Muslim governance. There is also a certain degree of scepticism towards the process by which such democratic rule is established. Majority principle (through voting) contrasts with Islamic mechanisms such as the *shura*-system (council of the learned) reaching *ijmāᶜ* (consensus).

The degree to which Shari'a is officially adopted will determine the extent of the blurring of the state-religion division. As decision-making in many areas is surrendered to religious experts—individuals and institutions possessing doctrinal knowledge without electoral mandate or accountability to the public—secular and democratic structures may be weakened. Although the degree of religious influence would vary depending on particular leadership qualities, power structures, and organizational matters, adoption of Shari'a may have a much more immediate and profound impact on religion-state relations than what remains of the historic compacts between Western nations and their majority Christian churches.

[49] See, eg Khaled Abou El-Fadl, *Islam and the Challenge of Democracy* (Princeton, Oxford: Princeton University Press, 2004).

[50] Bhiku Parekh, *A New Politics of Identity: Political Principles for an Interdependent World* (Basingstoke: Palgrave, 2008) 263 considers that Islamic democracy is possible where the Qur'an is the basis of constitution. But it will not be liberal. It will also have a 'secular thrust', he says, insofar as the privileged official role of the 'mullahs' has to be curtailed. This form of Islamic democracy seems a *contradictio in se* since for governance to be Islamic the balance of power will necessarily be in favour of religious supervision. This is not to say that Islam in its political dimension has an inevitable tendency towards repressive theocracy. As political Islam shows today, it contains liberationist impulses directed against secular and religious autocracies.

J. What If…? Some Consequences of *Sharia's* Recognition

Let me briefly speculate on some possible social consequences subsequent to elevating Shari'a to an officially recognized position.[51] I am referring to the hypothetical situation of recognition of Shari'a beyond the usual, familiar, piecemeal, multiculturalist accommodation that modern liberal democracies have undertaken. If Shari'a is officially recognized as a repository of national, cultural identity, demands for state support of Muslim education and faith-based schooling, welfare organizations, mosques construction (especially in countries where the established churches receive state support) will increase. There will be demands for greater sensitivity to *Shari'atic* aesthetics (curbs on sexual permissiveness, restrictions on 'offensive' art and literature, challenges to immodest dress codes, implementation of special sporting and bathing arrangements), restraints in journalistic freedom (in religious matters), limits in portraying Islam in a derogatory manner, new sabbatarian arrangements, and a closer watch on scientific, medical, and genetic research that undermine religious conceptions of personhood (eg cloning). These challenges may find an ally in conservative Christianity. All this will require a re-thinking of the nature and scope of the public sphere in order to avoid chronic social disharmony. Many significant consequences, foreseeable and unforeseeable, would result from elevating Shari'a from an occasionally accommodated faith (among the many) to a code that is formally recognized and thus empowered to demand apposite changes.

K. Where To From Here?

The integration of minorities, whatever the precise form it takes from country to country, is the stated policy goal of most Western countries.[52] Since integration is not based on assimilation, but accommodation, it raises the vexed question: How far can liberal democracy go, both in accommodating minority groups in public policy and, more profoundly, in granting official legal recognition to their beliefs, customs, practices, and worldviews, especially when minority religious conduct and values are not congenial to the majority?

One answer is to educate Muslims through a state-controlled education system that would seek to inculcate a version of Islam that is fully compatible with liberal democracy. This constitutes, I suggest, a slight infringement on strict church-state separation, but in some countries it has come to be considered the preferred

---

[51] As a social anthropologist, I will leave the constitutional measures that would be necessary to give Shari'a an official status to the lawyers.

[52] See, eg J S Fetzer and J C Soper, *Muslims and the State in Britain, France and Germany* (Cambridge: Cambridge University Press, 2005).

option to allowing religious separatism and hostile extremism to fester. Inculcating a privatized and 'sanitized' (in the sense of purged of impulses hostile to or incompatible with liberal society) Islam is the policy goal of education in countries in which accredited religious faiths enjoy state support. The long-term goal is that a form of Islam that fits the Western conception of 'religion' will emerge and become the subject of free choice.

I do not mean for a moment to advance the argument that immigrants have an obligation to succumb to absolute assimilation, nor to surrender their identity to that of the host nation.[53] However, the official attitude in the West so far has been that, one way or another, a line in the sand has to be drawn. This is so whether the boundary is enshrined by way of a blanket policy or on a tentative case-by-case basis (grounded in notions of individual liberty, equality of religions, and cultural relativism). Social synergy between majority and minority, if not conviviality, can only be achieved if the principles of recognition of minority rights, as well as the values and laws on which equality and acceptance are founded, remain intact. The crafting of these principles and their associated safeguards lies entirely in the hands of the state. In future, this may be increasingly achieved in concert with minorities and those policymakers who recognize that the path forward lies in the *shared* maintenance of the principles of liberal democracy. There is, of course, a fear that ultra-conservative-minded Muslims may come to gain disproportionate influence and may be able democratically to tip the balance, thus preventing liberal democracy from defending itself against religious illiberality. It would certainly demonstrate a cryptic paradox: liberalism and democracy have the potential to metamorphose into their opposites by adhering too rigidly and dogmatically to their own cherished principles of freedom and democracy.[54]

Realistically, given the ascendancy of multiculturalism over assimilation,[55] the integration of Muslim minorities can only be achieved by incorporating sufficient features of Shari'a to allow Muslims to maintain their religious identity. Developing an identity that is based on religion (in a modern, secularized sense), that is 'Muslim' (in the rather vague sense of belonging to *umma*, the worldwide community of believers), and that largely disregards finer nuances as identity markers, represents a steep learning curve for many Muslims.[56] For many, it may

---

[53] Bhikhu Parekh (n 50 above) 85 maintains that there is little difference between assimilation and integration. An argument can be made, however, that there is a major difference in social intent.

[54] Parekh (ibid) 263 takes a peculiar look at this conundrum. In a liberal democracy, he argues, liberalism is the dominant partner which, in the interest of preserving itself, is entitled to set limits to democracy.

[55] Tariq Modood argues that multiculturalism and integration are complementary (but not assimilation) and are based on mutual respect: see 'Rethinking Multiculturalism after 7/7', *Open Democracy*, 28 September 2005, available at <http://www.opendemocracy.net/conflict-terrorism/multiculturalism_2879.jsp>. But indications are (see, eg Klausen (n 13 above)) that European Muslim leaders are sceptical of the policy of multiculturalism as well as integration.

[56] It has been argued that second and third generation immigrants find it easier to embrace a pan-Muslim identity, but it also harbours the danger of creating a kind of solidarity that may transmute to extremism.

demand as much of an effort as assuming the national identity of their adopted country. Furthermore, it is dependent on achieving as wide a consensus as possible among Muslims concerning just what are the most deeply held and indispensable religious and doctrinal values, Muslim essentials that can and must be adhered to without violating the basic principles of justice or liberal democracy. It is hoped that globalization will create translocal forms of Islam that fit into the intercultural spaces the West is prepared to concede, and create a Muslim identity of diminished exclusivity.

But let us dare to take a glimpse into a possible wider future. The well-known philosopher of multiculturalism, Bhikhu Parekh, in his recent book[57] sketches the outlines of a new identity that transcends the social identity on which religious, ethnic, and ideological separatism, often magnified to assume intolerance and cultural fascism, can grow. A new global awareness requires an identity that reflects the fact that we are members of the human race and have a common fate and destiny. It is an identity defined by human rights, enriched with pan-human dignity, with an emphasis on the distinctiveness of humans as a species. The recognition of our commonality as a species, with basically similar moral and ontological outlooks, is becoming, in a practical sense, more important than emphasizing differences (of a cultural, ethnic, or religious kind) and elevating them to the pinnacle of human freedom and dignity. In this bold vision of humanity's goal, fanatical religious distinctiveness has no place. Currently, and more modestly, one can only hope that practical reason[58] prevails over ideological doctrine and purist political theory to pacify the troubled waters of deep pluralism.

[57] Parekh (n 50 above).
[58] See the discussion by Bruce Haddock, 'Practical Reason and Identity' in B Haddock and P Sutch (eds), *Multiculturalism, Identity and Rights* (London: Routledge, 2003) 10.

16

The Future of Muslim Family Law in Western Democracies

John Witte Jr

A. Introduction

Anglican Archbishop Rowan Williams set off an international firestorm on 7 February 2008 by suggesting that some accommodation of Muslim family law was 'unavoidable' in England. His suggestion, though tentative and qualified, prompted more than 250 articles in the world press within a month, the vast majority denouncing it. England, his critics charged, will be beset by 'licensed polygamy', 'barbaric procedures', and 'brutal violence' against women encased in suffocating *burqas*. Muslim citizens of a Western democracy will be subject to 'legally ghettoized' Muslim courts immune from civil appeal or constitutional challenge. Consider Nigeria, Pakistan, and other former English colonies that have sought to balance Muslim Shari'a with the common law, other critics added. The horrific excesses and chronic human rights violations of their religious courts—even ordering the faithful to stone innocent rape victims for dishonoring their families—prove that religious laws and state laws on the family simply cannot coexist. Case closed.

This case will not stay closed for long, however. The Archbishop was not calling for the establishment of independent Muslim courts in England, let alone the enforcement of Shari'a by English courts. He was, instead, raising a whole series of hard but 'unavoidable' questions about marital, cultural, and religious identity and practice in Western democratic societies committed to human rights for all. What forms of marriage should citizens be able to choose, and what forums of religious marriage law should state governments be required to respect? How should Muslims and other religious minorities with distinctive family norms and cultural practices be accommodated in a society dedicated to religious liberty and self-determination, and to religious equality and non-discrimination? Are legal pluralism and even 'personal federalism' necessary to protect Muslims and other religious believers who are conscientiously opposed to the liberal values that inform modern state laws on sex, marriage, and family? Is every constitutional accommodation of

Muslim family law and Shari'a courts not a dangerous step on the slippery slope toward empowering a faith, some of whose leaders subvert the very democratic and human rights values that now offer them protection? These and other hard questions are becoming 'unavoidable' for many modern Western democracies with growing and diverse Muslim communities, each making new and ever louder demands. If current growth rates of Muslim communities in the West continue, a generation from now the Danish cartoon 'crisis' is going to seem like child's play.

The chapters in this volume —centred on Australia, Canada, England, and the United States—have unpacked these questions with particular candor, acuity, and awareness of the high stakes involved. Some authors deftly employ the sharp new tools of multiculturalism and post-modern liberal theory to carve out legal and cultural space for semi-autonomous Muslim minority communities in the West— something of a reverse millet system. Others provide enlightening descriptions of the depth and diversity of Muslim laws and cultures, raising caveats about which of these sundry Muslim laws should govern these diaspora communities. Others offer trenchant analysis of the serious constitutional and cultural implications of accommodating faith-based family laws like Shari'a, warning of the real dangers of maintaining dual religious and political sovereigns to govern domestic life.

We learn from these chapters that these four democratic nations, despite their common law heritage and common commitment to human rights, have taken quite different approaches. England, with the largest groups of Muslim minorities, has been the most accommodating of Muslim schools, charities, banks, and arbitration tribunals that govern the family, financial, and other private issues of their voluntary faithful. In particular, English courts have regularly upheld the arbitration awards of Muslim tribunals in marriage and family disputes, provided all parties consent to participate and arbitration takes place without physical coercion or threat. The same deference is accorded to the marital arbitrations of Jewish, Christian, Hindu, and other peaceable religious authorities. Canada, though the most constitutionally liberal of these four nations, debated seriously the development of Shari'a marital tribunals in Ontario, but ultimately rejected religious arbitration in favour of a single provincial marriage law for its citizens. Canadian Muslims, however, enjoy ample religious freedom to engage in their own worship, education, banking, and religious rituals and apparel. Australia, with smaller and more scattered Muslim minorities, grants Muslims general religious freedom. But it is only beginning to grapple with how to accommodate Muslim demands for state enforcement of Muslim marriage contracts and state deference to Muslim religious arbitration of family law and other disputes. The United States, though with sizeable and diverse Muslim populations, has become the least accommodating of its Muslim citizens. Like Muslims in France, Turkey, and elsewhere, American Muslim litigants have not fared well of late when they have challenged state denials of charters or exemptions for their schools, charities, or mosques. Nor have they often succeeded in challenging prohibitions to wear traditional religious apparel while teaching in public schools, testifying in state courts, or serving in public places. American states have also not readily accommodated Muslim family law, let alone Shari'a courts. Most American state courts have only sporadically upheld private Muslim marriage contracts. They have often sided with non-Muslim spouses in divorce and child custody cases involving mixed marriages. They have held a firm line against Muslim polygamy, and have granted little deference to arbitration awards or mediation settlements by Muslim marital tribunals or religious officials. But American Muslims have continued to agitate for greater religious freedom, autonomy, and self-determination in marriage and other subjects.

B. The Evolution of the Law of Marriage

It is no surprise that it is the law of marriage and family life that has triggered this new contest between law and religion in Western democracies. For marriage has long been regarded as both a legal and a spiritual institution—subject at once to special state laws of contract and property, and to special religious canons and ceremonies.[1] Marriage has also long been regarded as the most primal institution of Western society and culture. Aristotle and the Roman Stoics called the marital household the 'foundation of the republic' and 'the private font of public virtue'. The Church Fathers and medieval Catholics called it 'the seedbed of the city', 'the force that welds society together'. Early modern Protestants called it a 'little church', a 'little state', a 'little seminary', the first school of love and justice, charity, and citizenship. John Locke and the Enlightenment philosophers called marriage 'the first society' to be formed as men and women moved from the state of nature to an organized society dedicated to the rule of law and the protection of rights.

Because of its cultural importance, marriage was also one of the first institutions to be reformed during the divisive battles between church and state in the history of the West. In the fourth century, when Constantine and his imperial successors converted the Roman Empire to Christianity, they soon passed comprehensive new marriage and family laws predicated directly on Christian teachings. In the later eleventh and twelfth centuries, when Pope Gregory VII and his successors threw off their civil rulers and established the Catholic Church as an independent legal authority, the church seized jurisdiction over marriage, calling it a sacrament subject to church courts and to the church's canon laws. In the sixteenth century, when Martin Luther, Henry VIII, and other Protestants called for reforms of church, state, and society, one of their first acts was to reject the Catholic canon law of marriage and the sacramental theology that supported it, and to transfer principal legal control over marriage to the Christian magistrate. In the later eighteenth century, when the French revolutionaries unleashed their fury against traditional institutions, they took early aim at the Catholic Church's complex marital rules,

---

[1] See generally J Witte Jr, *From Sacrament to Contract: Marriage, Religion, and Law in the Western Tradition* (Louisville, KY: Westminster John Knox Press, 2nd edn, 2011).

roles, and rituals, consigning marriage to the rule of secular state authorities. And, in the early twentieth century, when the Bolsheviks completed their revolution in Russia, one of Lenin's first acts was to abolish the legal institution of marriage, as a bourgeois impediment to the realization of true communism.

Modern Western democracies have not abolished marriage as a legal category, but they have dramatically privatized it and thinned out many of its traditional elements. Half a century ago, most Western states treated marriage as a public institution in which church, state, and society were all deeply invested. With ample variation across jurisdictions, most Western states still generally defined marriage as a presumptively permanent monogamous union between a fit man and a fit woman with freedom and capacity to marry each other. A typical state law required that engagements be formal and that marriages be contracted with parental consent and witnesses after a suitable waiting period. It required marriage licences and registration and solemnization before civil and/or religious authorities. It prohibited sex and marriage between couples related by various blood or family ties identified in the Mosaic law. It discouraged, and sometimes prohibited, marriage where one party was impotent or had a contagious disease that precluded procreation or endangered the other spouse. Couples who sought to divorce had to publicize their intentions, petition a court, show adequate cause or fault, and make provision for the dependent spouse and children. Criminal laws outlawed fornication, adultery, sodomy, polygamy, contraception, abortion, and other perceived sexual offences. Tort laws held third parties liable for seduction, enticement, loss of consortium, or alienation of the affections of a spouse. Churches and other religious communities were given roles to play in the formation, maintenance, and dissolution of marriage, and in the physical, educational, and moral nurture of children.

Today, by contrast, a private contractual view of sex, marriage, and family life has come to dominate the West, with little constructive role left to play for parents or peers, religious or political authorities. Marriage is now generally treated as a private bilateral contract to be formed, maintained, and dissolved as the couple sees fit. Prenuptial, marital, and separation contracts that allow parties to define their own rights and duties within the marital estate and thereafter, have gained increasing acceptance. Implied marital contracts are imputed to longstanding lovers in some states, supporting claims for maintenance and support during and after the relationship. Surrogacy contracts are executed for the rental of wombs. Medical contracts are executed for the introduction of embryos or the abortion of fetuses. Requirements of parental consent and witnesses to the formation of all these contracts have all largely disappeared. No-fault divorce statutes have reduced the divorce proceeding to an expensive formality, and largely obliterated the complex procedural and substantive distinctions between annulment and divorce. Payments of alimony and other forms of post-marital support to dependent spouses and children are giving way to lump sum property exchanges providing a clean break for parties to remarry. Court-supervised property settlements between divorcing spouses are giving way to privately negotiated or mediated settlements, confirmed with little scrutiny by courts. The functional distinctions between the rights of the married and the unmarried couple and the straight and the gay partnership have been considerably narrowed by an array of new statutes and constitutional cases. Marriages, civil unions, and domestic partnerships have become veritable legal equivalents in many states. The roles of the church, state, and broader community in marriage formation, maintenance, and dissolution have been gradually truncated in deference to the constitutional principles of sexual autonomy, laïcité, or church-state separation. Traditional criminal prohibitions against most voluntary sexual conduct and contact, short of obscenity or child abuse, have become dead or discarded letters. Traditional prohibitions against contraception and abortion have been held to violate the constitutional right of privacy. Traditional tort suits for sexual interference with one's spouse have become largely otiose.

These exponential legal changes in the past half century have, in part, been efforts to bring greater equality and equity within marriage and society and to stamp out some of the patriarchy, paternalism, and plain prudishness of the past. These legal changes are also, in part, simple reflections of the exponential changes that have occurred in the culture and condition of Western families—the stunning advances in reproductive and medical technology, the exposure to vastly different perceptions of sexuality and kinship born of globalization, the explosion of international and domestic norms of human rights, and the implosion of the traditional nuclear family born of new economic and professional demands on wives, husbands, and children. But, more fundamentally, these legal changes represent the rise of a new theory of private ordering of the domestic sphere and the growth of a new 'democracy of desire'. A fantastic range of literature—jurisprudential, theological, ethical, political, economic, sociological, anthropological, and psychological—has emerged in the past four decades vigorously describing, defending, or decrying these legal changes.

C. Muslim Responses and Arguments for Accommodation

Many Muslims living in the West decry these massive changes to prevailing state laws of sex, marriage, and family—and they want out. Some Muslims have gone back to their Muslim-majority homelands shaking their heads in dismay at what Western libertinism has wrought. Others have stayed put and quietly ignored the state's marriage and family law, using the shelter of constitutional laws of privacy and sexual autonomy to become, in effect, a law unto themselves. Others have developed elaborate premarital contracts that seek to exempt Muslim couples from much of the state law in favour of the internal norms and practices of their religious communities. Still others have led bicultural lives, dividing their time between Western homes and Muslim-majority lands that allow them to form Muslim marriages and families, including those that license polygamy, patriarchy, and primogeniture.

All of these informal methods of cultural and legal coexistence, however, can only be temporary expedients. Not only do some of these arrangements put in jeopardy many of the state's rights and privileges for spouses and children that depend on a validly contracted marriage, but these creaky accommodations and concessions that now exist in various Western lands can easily fall apart. Eventually a Muslim citizen will appeal to the state for relief from a marriage contract, religious family practice, or worship community that he or she cannot abide but cannot escape. Eventually an *imam* or (shadow) Shari'a court will overstep by using force or issuing a *fatwā* that draws the ire of the media and the scrutiny of state courts. Eventually, an aggressive state case worker or prosecutor will move upon a Muslim household, bringing charges of coerced or polygamous marriage. Eventually, a Muslim school or charity will find itself in court faced with a suit for gender discrimination or child abuse owing to its practice of corporal punishment and single-sex education. Eventually, another major media event like that surrounding the Ontario Shari'a court of 2005 or the stray Rowan Williams' comment of 2008 will bring a bright spotlight back on Western Muslim communities. And, once such a major case or controversy breaks and the international media gets involved, many of these informal and temporary arrangements might well unravel—particularly given the cultural backlash against Muslims prompted by 9/11, 7/7, and now Fort Hood, or by the bloody wars against Islamicist extremists in Iraq, Afghanistan, and beyond.

It is precisely this vulnerability that advocates of faith-based family law and Shari'a courts want to avert. They want to put Shari'a, and its voluntary use by Muslim faithful, on firmer constitutional and cultural ground in the West. Rather than denouncing Western liberalism, however—and the sexual, moral, and marital lassitude it has occasioned—sophisticated advocates now press their case for Shari'a in and on the very terms of Western constitutionalism and political liberalism.

Part of the case for Shari'a is an argument for religious freedom. Both Western constitutional laws and international human rights norms give robust protection to the religious freedom of individuals and groups. Why should peaceable Muslim citizens not be given freedom to opt out of state laws on sex, marriage, and family that run afoul of their core claims of conscience and central commandments of their faith? Why should they not have the freedom to choose to exercise their domestic lives in accordance with the norms of their own voluntary religious communities? Why does freedom of religion not provide a sincere Muslim with protection against a unilateral divorce action or a child custody order by a state court that directly contradicts the rules of Shari'a? Why does freedom of religious exercise not empower a pious Muslim man to take four wives into his loving permanent care in imitation of the Prophet, particularly when his secular counterpart can consort and cavort freely with four women at once and then walk out scot free? And, in turn, why should Muslim religious authorities not enjoy the autonomy and freedom to apply their own internal laws and procedures for guiding and governing the private domestic lives of their voluntary faithful? Religious groups in the West have long enjoyed the corporate free exercise rights to legal personality, corporate property, collective worship, organized charity, parochial education, freedom of press, and more. Why cannot Muslim religious groups also get the right to govern the marriage and family lives of their voluntary members—particularly when such domestic activities have such profound religious and moral dimensions for Islamic life and identity.

Part of the case for Shari'a is an argument for religious equality and non-discrimination. After all, many Western Christians do have religious tribunals to govern their internal affairs, including some of the family matters of their faithful, and state courts will respect their judgments even if their cases are appealed to Rome or Canterbury, Moscow or Constantinople. No one is talking of abolishing these church courts, or trimming their power, even after recent discoveries of grave financial abuses and cover-ups of clerical sexual abuse of children in some churches. No one seems to think that these Christian tribunals are illegitimate when some of them discriminate against women in decisions about ordination and church leadership. Similarly, Jews are given wide authority to operate their own Jewish law courts to arbitrate marital, financial, and other disputes among the Orthodox Jewish faithful. Indeed, in New York State by statute, and in several European nations by custom, courts will not issue a civil divorce to a Jewish couple unless and until the *beth din* issues a religious divorce, even though Jewish law systematically discriminates against the wife's right to divorce. And again, Amish, Mennonites, Hutterites, and other ascetic religious minorities have been exempted from compliance with general laws concerning education, child labour, workplace and employment relations, and more, and have had their laws of excommunication and banishment upheld by the courts. If Christians can have their canon laws and consistory courts, if Jews can have their *Halacha* and *beth din*, and if even indigenous peoples can have their ancestral laws and tribal rulers, why cannot Muslims be treated equally in their use of Shari'a and Islamic courts?

Part of the case for Shari'a is an argument from political liberalism. One of the most basic teachings of classic liberalism is that marriage is a pre-political and pre-legal institution. It comes before the state and its positive laws, both in historical development and in ontological priority. As John Locke put it famously in *Two Treatises on Government* (1689), the marital contract was 'the first contract' and 'the first society' to be formed as men and women came forth from the state of nature. The broader social contract came later, presupposing stable marital contracts. And contracts to form state governments, churches, and other voluntary associations within this broader society came later still. Why, on this simple contractarian logic, should the state get exclusive jurisdiction over marriage? After all, it was sixteenth-century Protestants, not eighteenth-century Enlightenment philosophers, who first vested the state with marital jurisdiction. But why is state jurisdiction over marriage mandatory, or even necessary? Before the sixteenth century Protestant Reformation—and in many Catholic lands well after the

Reformation—the Catholic canon law and Catholic Church courts governed marriage. Moreover, even in Protestant England until the nineteenth century, the state delegated to ecclesiastical courts the power to decide many marriage and family questions. There is evidently nothing inherent in the structure of Western marriage and family law that requires that it be administered by the state. And there is nothing ineluctable in liberalism's contractarian logic that requires marital couples to choose the state rather than their own families or their own religious communities to govern their domestic lives—particularly when the state's liberal rules diverge so widely from their own beliefs and practices. On this latter argument, conservative Muslims sometimes join hands with selected conservative Christians and critical liberals who call for exemption from, or the abolition of, state marriage law—conservative Christians because the state has betrayed traditional Christian teachings on marriage, critical liberals because the state is encroaching on individual privacy and sexual autonomy.

D. The Limits and Lessons of Accommodation

The problem with the pro-Shari'a argument from religious freedom is that it falsely assumes that claims of conscience and freedom of religious exercise must always trump. But this is hardly the case in modern democracies, even though religious freedom is cherished. Even the most sincere and zealous conscientious objectors must pay their taxes, register their properties, answer their subpoenas, obey their court orders, swear their oaths (or otherwise prove their veracity), answer their military conscriptions (even if by non-combat duty), and abide by many other general laws for the common good that they may not in good conscience wish to abide. Their eventual choice if they persist in their claims of conscience is to leave the country or go to prison for contempt. Even the most devout religious believer has no claim to exemptions from criminal laws against activities like polygamy, child marriage, female genital mutilation, or corporal discipline of wives, even if their particular brand of Shari'a commends it or if their particular religious community commands it. The guarantee of religious freedom is not a licence to engage in crime. Muslims who are conscientiously opposed to liberal Western laws of sex, marriage, and family are certainly free to ignore them. They can live chaste private lives in accordance with Shari'a and not register their religious marriages with the state. That choice will be protected by the constitutional rights of privacy and sexual autonomy so long as their conduct is truly consensual. But it also leaves their family entirely without the protections, rights, and privileges available through the state's complex laws and regulations of marriage and family, marital property and inheritance, social welfare, and more. And if minor children are involved, the state will intervene to ensure their protection, support, and education, and will hear nothing of free exercise objections from their parents or community leaders. Western Muslims enjoy the same religious freedom as everyone else, but some of the special accommodations pressed by some Muslim advocates today in the name of religious freedom are simply beyond the pale for most Western democracies.

Even further beyond the pale is the notion of granting a religious group sovereignty over the sex, marriage, and family lives of its voluntary faithful. Allowing religious officials to officiate at weddings, testify in divorce cases, assist in the adoption of a child, facilitate the rescue of a distressed family member, and the like are one thing. Most Western democracies readily grant Muslims and other peaceable religious communities those accommodations. Some democracies will also uphold the religious arbitration awards and mediation settlements over discrete domestic issues. But that is a long way from asking the state to delegate to a religious group the full legal power to govern the domestic affairs of its voluntary faithful in accordance with its own religious laws. No democratic state can readily accommodate a competing sovereign to govern such a vital area of life for its citizens—especially since family law is so interwoven with other state public, private, procedural, and penal laws, and especially since so many other rights and duties of citizens turn on a person's marital and familial status. Putting aside the formidable constitutional obstacles to such a delegation of core state power to a private religious body, surely a democratic citizen's status, entitlements, and rights cannot turn on the judgments of a religious authority that has none of the due process and other procedural constraints of a state tribunal. Moreover, the proud claim of Muslim advocates that Shari'a provides a time-tested and comprehensive law governing all aspects of sex, marriage, and family life for the Muslim faithful is, for some, an even stronger strike against its accommodation. Once a state takes the first step down that slippery slope, sceptics argue, there will eventually be little to stop the gradual accretion of a rival religious law over sex, marriage, and family life, particularly as Muslim communities grow larger and more politically powerful. Some Western states thus resist even religious arbitration and mediation of marital disputes by Muslim tribunals.

The pro-Shari'a argument from liberal contractarian logic—since marital contracts are pre-political, coming before the contracts that form the society, the state, or religious associations, marital parties should be free to choose whose laws govern them —is clever but incomplete. It ignores another elementary teaching of classical liberalism, namely that only the state and no other social or private unit can hold the coercive power of the sword. The government contract does grant this coercive power over individuals but only in exchange for strict guarantees of due process of law, equal protection under the law, and respect for fundamental rights. A comprehensive system of marriage and family law—let alone the many correlative legal systems of inheritance, trusts, family property, children's rights, education, social welfare, and more —cannot long operate without coercive power. It needs police, prosecutors, and prisons, subpoenas, fines, and contempt orders, and material, physical, and corporal sanctions. Moral suasion and example, and communal approbation and censure can certainly do part of the work. But a properly functioning marriage and family law system requires resort to all these coercive instruments of government. And only the state, not a religious body, can properly use these instruments in a modern democracy.

The pro-Shari'a argument from religious equality and non-discrimination takes more effort to parry. A useful starting point is the quip of US Supreme Justice Oliver Wendell Holmes Jr: 'The life of the law has not been logic: it has been experience'.[2] This adage has bearing on this issue. The current accommodations made to the religious legal systems of Christians, Jews, First Peoples, and others in the West were not born overnight. They came only after decades, even centuries of sometimes hard and cruel experience, with gradual adjustments and accommodations on both sides.

The accommodation of and by Jewish law to Western secular law is particularly instructive.[3] It is discomfiting but essential to remember that Jews were the perennial pariahs of the West for nearly two millennia, consigned at best to second class status, and periodically subject to waves of brutality—whether imposed by Germanic purges, medieval pogroms, early modern massacres, or the twentieth century Holocaust. Jews have been in perennial diaspora since the destruction of Jerusalem in 70 CE, living in a wide variety of legal cultures in the West and well beyond. One important legal technique of survival they developed after the third century CE was the concept of *dina d'malkhuta dina* ('the law of the community is the law'). This meant that Jews accepted the law of the legitimate and peaceful secular ruler who hosted them as the law of their own Jewish community, to the extent that it did not conflict with core Jewish laws. This technique allowed Jewish communities to sort out which of their own religious laws were indispensable, and which more discretionary; which secular laws and practices could be accommodated, and which had to be resisted even at the risk of life and limb. This technique not only led to ample innovation and diversity of Jewish law over time and across cultures; it also gave the Jews the ability to survive and grow legally even in the face of ample persecution.

Western democracies, in turn—particularly in the aftermath of the Holocaust and in partial recompense for the horrors it visited on the Jews—have gradually come to accommodate core Jewish laws and practices. But it is only in the past two generations, and only after endless litigation and lobbying in state courts and legislatures, that Western Jews have finally gained legal ground to stand on, and even that ground is still thin and crumbles at the edges at times. Today, Western Jews generally have freedom to receive Sabbath day accommodations, to gain access to kosher food, to don yarmulkes, distinctive grooming, and other forms of religious dress in most public places, to gain zoning, land use, and building charters for

---

[2] *The Common Law* (Boston: Little Brown, 1881) 1–2.

[3] The accommodation of the First Peoples of Canada, Australia, or the United States are simply not precedents for any others besides First Peoples. These arrangements are products of ancient treaties worked out, in no small part, as compensation for massive atrocities and dislocation of native or Aboriginal peoples committed during earlier colonial days. The courts of all three lands have stated clearly that these accommodations and benefits are *sui generis*, not to be imitated by and for others.

their synagogues, charities, and Torah schools, to offer single-sex and bilingual education, and more. Jewish law courts have gained the right to decide some of the domestic and financial affairs of their faithful who voluntarily elect to arbitrate disputes before these courts rather than suing in secular courts. Jewish law courts are attractive to Jewish disputants because they are staffed by highly trained jurists, conversant with both Jewish and secular law, and sensitive to the bicultural issues that are being negotiated. Unlike their medieval and early modern predecessors, these modern Jewish law courts claim no authority over all of Jewish sex, marriage, and family life, leaving many such issues to the state. Jewish law courts have also abandoned their traditional authority to impose physical coercion or sanctions on the disputants; in particular, they claim no authority beyond persuasion to stop a disputant from simply walking out of court and out of the Jewish community altogether.

The modern lessons in this story for Shari'a advocates are four-fold. First, it takes time and patience for a secular legal system to adjust to the realities and needs of new religious groups and to make the necessary legal accommodations. The hard-won accommodations that modern Jewish law and culture now enjoy are not fungible commodities that Muslims or any others can claim with a simple argument from equality. They are individualized, equitable adjustments to general laws that each community needs to earn for itself based on its own needs and experiences. Muslims simply do not have the same history of persecution that the Jews have faced in the West, and do not yet have a long enough track record of litigation and lobbying. Concessions and accommodations will come, but only with time, persistence, and patience.

Secondly, it takes flexibility and innovation on the part of a religious community to win accommodations from secular laws and cultures. Not every religious belief can be claimed as central; not every religious practice can be worth dying for. Over time, and of necessity, diaspora Jewish communities learned to distinguish between what was core and what more penumbral, what was essential and what more discretionary to Jewish legal and cultural identity. Over time, and only grudgingly, Western democracies learned to accommodate the core religious beliefs and practices of Jewish communities. Diaspora Muslim communities in the West need to do the same. As several chapters in this volume have made clear, Islamic laws and cultures have changed dramatically over time and across cultures, and modern day Islam now features immense variety in its legal, religious, and cultural practices. That diversity provides ample opportunity and incentive for Muslim diaspora communities to make the necessary adjustments to Western life, and to sort out what is core and what is more discretionary in their religious lives. Cultural adaptation, though not assimilation, is what is needed to win the accommodations of the state.

Thirdly, religious communities, in turn, have to accommodate, or at least tolerate, the core values of their secular host nations if they expect to win concessions for their religious courts and other religious practices. No Western nation will long accommodate, perhaps not even tolerate, a religious community that cannot accept its core values of liberty, equality, and fraternity, or of human rights, democracy, and rule of law. Those who wish to enjoy the freedom and benefits of Western society have to accept its core constitutional and cultural values as well. So far, only a small and brave band of mostly Western-trained Muslim intellectuals and jurists have called for the full embrace of democracy and human rights in and on Muslim terms. These are highly promising arguments. But these arguments can hardly be heard amid all the loud denunciations from sundry traditional Muslims in and beyond the West. Moreover, even liberal Muslims are hard-pressed to point to modern examples of a Shari'a-based legal system that maintains core democratic and human rights values. Until that case can be reliably made out, deep suspicion will remain the norm. Western-based Muslims have an ideal opportunity to show that Shari'a and democracy can coexist and complement each other.

Finally, Muslim tribunals must become more legally sophisticated and procedurally equitable to be both attractive to voluntary Muslim disputants and acceptable to secular state courts. Like the Jewish *beth din* that sits in New York or London, the Muslim law court needs to be staffed by jurists who are well trained both in Muslim law and in secular law, and who maintain basic standards of due process and representation akin to those in secular courts or arbitration tribunals. A single *imam* pronouncing legal judgments in an informal proceeding at the local mosque will get no more deference from a state court than a single priest or rabbi making legal pronouncements in a church or synagogue. In addition, Western state courts will have little patience with claims that this lack of deference violates the religious liberty of the mosque or its *imam* and members. The courts' suspicions will be the opposite: that the disputing parties who appeared before the *imam* either did not understand the full legal options available to them at state law, or were coerced to participate in the internal religious procedures. It is much harder for a court to have such suspicions when educated Muslim parties, eyes wide open, choose a legally sophisticated Muslim arbitration tribunal over a secular court that does not share their core values but still offers a serious jurisprudential option for them to state marriage law.

Lest the foregoing seems like an unduly patronizing argument for religious minorities to 'wait and see' or 'change and hope for the best', it is worth remembering that majority Christians also went through much the same exercise in the area of religion and education. The American story offers a good illustration of how this developed, and how common educational standards were eventually raised and maintained. In the later nineteenth century, a number of American states wanted a monopoly on education in public (that is, state-run) schools. Some of this agitation was driven by anti-Catholicism, and some by anti-religious animus altogether. For half a century, churches, schools, and religious parents struggled earnestly to protect their rights to educate their children in their own private religious schools. In the landmark case of *Pierce v Society of Sisters* in 1925,[4] the US Supreme Court finally held for the churches and ordered American states to maintain parallel public and private education options for their citizens. But in a long series of cases thereafter, courts also made clear that states could set basic educational requirements for all schools—mandatory courses, texts and tests, minimal standards for teachers, students and facilities, common requirements for laboratories, libraries, gymnasia, and the like. Religious schools could add to the state's minimum requirements, but they could not subtract from them. Religious schools that sought exemptions from these requirements found little sympathy from the courts, which instructed the schools either to meet the standards or lose their accreditation and licences to teach.

This compromise on religion and education, forged painfully over more than half a century of wrangling, has some bearing on questions of religion and marriage. Marriage, like education, is not a state monopoly, even if marriage law must be a state prerogative. Religious parties in the West have long had the right to marry in a religious sanctuary, following their religious community's preferred wedding liturgy. Religious officials have long had the right to participate in the weddings, annulments, divorces, and custody battles of their voluntary members. But the state has also long set the threshold requirements of what marriage is and who may participate. Religious officials may add to these threshold state law requirements on marriage but cannot subtract from them. A minister may insist on premarital counseling before a wedding, even if the state will marry a couple without it. But if a minister bullies a minor to marry out of religious duty, the state could throw him in jail. A rabbi may encourage a bickering couple to repent and reconcile, but he cannot prevent them from filing for divorce. An *imam* may preach of the beauties of polygamy, but if he knowingly presides over a polygamous union, he is an accessory to crime.

If religious tribunals do eventually get more involved in marriage and family law, states might well build on these precedents and set threshold requirements in the form of a licence—formulating these licence rules through a democratic process in which all parties of every faith and non-faith participate. Among the most important licence rules to consider would be:

- no child or polygamous marriages or other forms of marital union are recognized by the state;[5]

- no compelled marriages or coerced conversions before weddings that violate elementary freedoms of contract and conscience;

- no threats or violations of life and limb, or provocations of the same;

- no blatant discrimination against women or children;

- no violation of basic rules of procedural fairness.

---

[4] 268 US 510 (1925).
[5] I put the case against religiously based polygamy briefly in 'The Legal Challenges of Polygamy in the USA' (2009) 11 *Ecclesiastical Law Journal* 72.

Religious tribunals may add to these requirements but not subtract from them. Those who fail to conform will lose their licences and will find little sympathy when they raise religious liberty objections.

This type of arrangement worked well to resolve some of the nation's hardest questions of religion and education. And it led many religious schools to transform themselves slowly from sectarian isolationists into cultural leaders. Muslims in the West have already begun some of this exercise in the development of grade and high schools, which are now attractive to non-Muslims because of their discipline and high academic standards. This should continue, and eventually give rise to major colleges and universities on the order of Notre Dame, Brigham Young, Wheaton, or Pepperdine.

Such an arrangement holds comparable promise for questions of religion and marriage in Muslim diaspora communities. It not only prevents the descent to 'licensed polygamy', 'barbaric procedures', and 'brutal violence' that the Archbishop's critics feared, but also encourages today's religious tribunals to reform themselves and the marital laws that they offer. Even hardened and prejudiced local communities in democratic lands will eventually find room for new Muslim minorities who are skilled at 'cultural navigation' and who are both consistent and persistent in pressing their main case for accommodation. And, in the process of adjusting to the legal and cultural realities of their new homes, Muslim religious minorities may eventually become legal and cultural leaders in succeeding generations of the West.

APPENDIX I

Civil and Religious Law in England: a Religious Perspective*

The Archbishop of Canterbury The Rt Rev Dr Rowan Williams
7 February 2008

The Archbishop of Canterbury, Dr Rowan Williams, gave the Foundation Lecture at the Royal Courts of Justice.

[1] The title of this series of lectures signals the existence of what is very widely felt to be a growing challenge in our society—that is, the presence of communities which, while no less 'law-abiding' than the rest of the population, relate to something other than the British legal system alone. But, as I hope to suggest, the issues that arise around what level of public or legal recognition, if any, might be allowed to the legal provisions of a religious group, are not peculiar to Islam: we might recall that, while the law of the Church of England is the law of the land, its daily operation is in the hands of authorities to whom considerable independence is granted. And beyond the specific issues that arise in relation to the practicalities of recognition or delegation, there are large questions in the background about what we understand by and expect from the law, questions that are more sharply focused than ever in a largely secular social environment. I shall therefore be concentrating on certain issues around Islamic law to begin with, in order to open up some of these wider matters.

[2] Among the manifold anxieties that haunt the discussion of the place of Muslims in British society, one of the strongest, reinforced from time to time by the sensational reporting of opinion polls, is that Muslim communities in this country seek the freedom to live under *Shari'a* law. And what most people think they know of *Shari'a* is that it is repressive towards women and wedded to archaic and brutal physical punishments; just a few days ago, it was reported that a 'forced marriage' involving a young woman with learning difficulties had been 'sanctioned under *Shari'a* law'—the kind of story that, in its assumption that we all 'really' know what is involved in the practice of *Shari'a*, powerfully reinforces the image of—at best—a pre-modern system in which human rights have no role. The problem is freely admitted by Muslim scholars. 'In the West', writes Tariq Ramadan in his groundbreaking *Western Muslims and the Future of Islam*, 'the idea of *Shari'a* calls up all the darkest images of Islam...It has reached the extent that many Muslim intellectuals do not dare even to refer to the concept for fear of frightening people or arousing suspicion of all their work by the mere mention of the word' (p 31). Even when some of the more dramatic fears are set aside,

---

* Reproduced with the kind permission of The Rt Rev Dr Rowan Williams.

there remains a great deal of uncertainty about what degree of accommodation the law of the land can and should give to minority communities with their own strongly entrenched legal and moral codes. As such, this is not only an issue about Islam but about other faith groups, including Orthodox Judaism; and indeed it spills over into some of the questions which have surfaced sharply in the last twelve months about the right of religious believers in general to opt out of certain legal provisions—as in the problems around Roman Catholic adoption agencies which emerged in relation to the Sexual Orientation Regulations last spring.

[3] This lecture will not attempt a detailed discussion of the nature of *Shari'a*, which would be far beyond my competence; my aim is only, as I have said, to tease out some of the broader issues around the rights of religious groups within a secular state, with a few thoughts about what might be entailed in crafting a just and constructive relationship between Islamic law and the statutory law of the United Kingdom. But it is important to begin by dispelling one or two myths about *Shari'a*; so far from being a monolithic system of detailed enactments, *Shari'a* designates primarily—to quote Ramadan again—'the expression of the universal principles of Islam [and] the framework and the thinking that makes for their actualization in human history' (32). *Universal* principles: as any Muslim commentator will insist, what is in view is the eternal and absolute will of God for the universe and for its human inhabitants in particular; but also something that has to be 'actualized', not a ready-made system. If *shar'* designates the essence of the revealed Law, *Shari'a* is the *practice* of actualizing and applying it; while certain elements of the *Shari'a* are specified fairly exactly in the Qur'an and *Sunna* and in the *hadith* recognized as authoritative in this respect, there is no single code that can be identified as 'the' *Shari'a*. And when certain states impose what they refer to as *Shari'a* or when certain Muslim activists demand its recognition alongside secular jurisdictions, they are usually referring not to a universal and fixed code established once for all but to some particular concretization of it at the hands of a tradition of jurists. In the hands of contemporary legal traditionalists, this means simply that the application of *Shari'a* must be governed by the judgements of representatives of the classical schools of legal interpretation. But there are a good many voices arguing for an extension of the liberty of *ijtihad*—basically reasoning from first principles rather than simply the collation of traditional judgements (see for example Louis Gardet, 'Un prealable aux questions soulevees par les droits de l'homme: l'actualisation de la Loi religieuse musulmane aujourd'hui', *Islamochristiana* 9, 1983, 1–12, and Abdullah Saeed, 'Trends in Contemporary Islam: a Preliminary Attempt at a Classification', *The Muslim World*, 97:3, 2007, 395-404, esp 401–2).

[4] Thus, in contrast to what is sometimes assumed, we do not *simply* have a standoff between two rival legal systems when we discuss Islamic and British law. On the one hand, *Shari'a* depends for its legitimacy not on any human decision, not on votes or preferences, but on the conviction that it represents the mind of God; on the other, it is to some extent unfinished business so far as codified and precise provisions are concerned. To recognize *Shari'a* is to recognize a *method* of jurisprudence governed by revealed texts rather than a single system. In a discussion based on a paper from Mona Siddiqui at a conference last year at Al Akhawayn University in Morocco, the point was made by one or two Muslim scholars that an excessively narrow understanding *Shari'a*

as simply codified rules can have the effect of actually undermining the universal claims of the Qur'an.

[5] But while such universal claims are not open for renegotiation, they also assume the voluntary consent or submission of the believer, the free decision to be and to continue a member of the *umma*. *Shari'a* is not, in that sense, intrinsically to do with any demand for Muslim dominance over non-Muslims. Both historically and in the contemporary context, Muslim states have acknowledged that membership of the *umma* is not coterminous with membership in a particular political society: in modern times, the clearest articulation of this was in the foundation of the Pakistani state under Jinnah; but other examples (Morocco, Jordan) could be cited of societies where there is a concept of *citizenship* that is not identical with belonging to the *umma*. Such societies, while not compromising or weakening the possibility of unqualified belief in the authority and universality of *Shari'a*, or even the privileged status of Islam in a nation, recognize that there can be no guarantee that the state is religiously homogeneous and that the relationships in which the individual stands and which define him or her are not exclusively with other Muslims. There has therefore to be some concept of common good that is not prescribed solely in terms of revealed Law, however provisional or imperfect such a situation is thought to be. And this implies in turn that the Muslim, even in a predominantly Muslim state, has something of a dual identity, as citizen and as believer within the community of the faithful.

[6] It is true that this account would be hotly contested by some committed Islamic primitivists, by followers of Sayyid Qutb and similar polemicists; but it is fair to say that the great body of serious jurists in the Islamic world would recognize this degree of political plurality as consistent with Muslim integrity. In this sense, while (as I have said) we are not talking about two rival systems on the same level, there is some community of understanding between Islamic social thinking and the categories we might turn to in the non-Muslim world for the understanding of law in the most general context. There is a recognition that *our social identities are not constituted by one exclusive set of relations or mode of belonging*—even if one of those sets is regarded as relating to the most fundamental and non-negotiable level of reality, as established by a 'covenant' between the divine and the human (as in Jewish and Christian thinking; once again, we are not talking about an exclusively Muslim problem). The danger arises not only when there is an assumption on the religious side that membership of the community (belonging to the *umma* or the Church or whatever) is the only significant category, so that participation in other kinds of socio-political arrangement is a kind of betrayal. It also occurs when secular government assumes a monopoly in terms of defining public and political identity. There is a position—not at all unfamiliar in contemporary discussion—which says that to be a citizen is essentially and simply to be under the rule of the uniform law of a sovereign state, in such a way that any other relations, commitments or protocols of behaviour belong exclusively to the realm of the private and of individual choice. As I have maintained in several other contexts, this is a very unsatisfactory account of political reality in modern societies; but it is also a problematic basis for thinking of the legal category of citizenship and the nature of human interdependence. Maleiha Malik, following Alasdair MacIntyre, argues in an essay on 'Faith and the State of Jurisprudence' (*Faith in Law: Essays in Legal Theory*, ed, Peter Oliver, Sionaidh Douglas Scott and Victor Tadros, 2000, pp 129–49) that there is a

risk of assuming that 'mainstream' jurisprudence should routinely and unquestion-
ingly bypass the variety of ways in which actions are as a matter of fact understood by
agents in the light of the diverse sorts of communal belonging they are involved in. If
that is the assumption, 'the appropriate temporal unit for analysis tends to be the basic
action. Instead of concentrating on the history of the individual or the origins of the
social practice which provides the context within which the act is performed, conduct
tends to be studied as an isolated and one-off act' (139–40). And another essay in the
same collection, Anthony Bradney's 'Faced by Faith' (89–105) offers some examples
of legal rulings which have disregarded the account offered by religious believers of
the motives for their own decisions, on the grounds that the court alone is competent
to assess the coherence or even sincerity of their claims. And when courts attempt to
do this on the grounds of what is 'generally acceptable' behaviour in a society, they
are open, Bradney claims (102–3), to the accusation of undermining the principle
of liberal pluralism by denying someone the right to speak in their own voice. The
distinguished ecclesiastical lawyer, Chancellor Mark Hill, has also underlined in a
number of recent papers the degree of confusion that has bedevilled recent essays in
adjudicating disputes with a religious element, stressing the need for better definition
of the kind of protection for religious conscience that the law intends (see particularly
his essay with Russell Sandberg, 'Is Nothing Sacred? Clashing Symbols in a Secular
World', *Public Law* 3, 2007, pp 488–506).

[7] I have argued recently in a discussion of the moral background to legislation about
incitement to religious hatred that any crime involving religious offence has to be
thought about in terms of its tendency to create or reinforce a position in which a religious person or group could be gravely disadvantaged in regard to access to speaking in
public in their own right: offence needs to be connected to issues of power and status,
so that a powerful individual or group making derogatory or defamatory statements
about a disadvantaged minority might be thought to be increasing that disadvantage.
The point I am making here is similar. If the law of the land takes no account of what
might be for certain agents a proper rationale for behaviour—for protest against certain unforeseen professional requirements, for instance, which would compromise
religious discipline or belief—it fails in a significant way to *communicate* with someone
involved in the legal process (or indeed to receive their communication), and so, on at
least one kind of legal theory (expounded recently, for example, by R A Duff), fails in
one of its purposes.

[8] The implications are twofold. There is a plain procedural question—and neither
Bradney nor Malik goes much beyond this—about how existing courts function and
what weight is properly given to the issues we have been discussing. But there is a
larger theoretical and practical issue about what it is to live under more than one jurisdiction, which takes us back to the question we began with—the role of *Shari'a* (or
indeed Orthodox Jewish practice) in relation to the routine jurisdiction of the British
courts. In general, when there is a robust affirmation that the law of the land should
protect individuals on the grounds of their corporate religious identity and secure
their freedom to fulfil religious duties, a number of queries are regularly raised. I want
to look at three such difficulties briefly. They relate both to the question of whether
there should be a higher level of attention to religious identity and communal rights
in the practice of the law, and to the larger issue I mentioned of something like a

delegation of certain legal functions to the religious courts of a community; and this latter question, it should be remembered, is relevant not only to Islamic law but also to areas of Orthodox Jewish practice.

[9] The first objection to a higher level of public legal regard being paid to communal identity is that it leaves legal process (including ordinary disciplinary process within organizations) at the mercy of what might be called vexatious appeals to religious scruple. A recent example might be the reported refusal of a Muslim woman employed by Marks and Spencer to handle a book of Bible stories. Or we might think of the rather more serious cluster of questions around forced marriages, where again it is crucial to distinguish between cultural and strictly religious dimensions. While Bradney rightly cautions against the simple dismissal of alleged scruple by judicial authorities who have made no attempt to understand its workings in the construction of people's social identities, it should be clear also that any recognition of the need for such sensitivity must also have a recognized means of deciding the relative seriousness of conscience-related claims, a way of distinguishing purely cultural habits from seriously-rooted matters of faith and discipline, and distinguishing uninformed prejudice from religious prescription. There needs to be access to recognized authority acting for a religious group: there is already, of course, an Islamic *Shari'a* Council, much in demand for rulings on marital questions in the UK; and if we were to see more latitude given in law to rights and scruples rooted in religious identity, we should need a much enhanced and quite sophisticated version of such a body, with increased resources and a high degree of community recognition, so that 'vexatious' claims could be summarily dealt with. The secular lawyer needs to know where the potential conflict is real, legally and religiously serious, and where it is grounded in either nuisance or ignorance. There can be no blank cheques given to unexamined scruples.

[10] The second issue, a very serious one, is that recognition of 'supplementary jurisdiction' in some areas, especially family law, could have the effect of reinforcing in minority communities some of the most repressive or retrograde elements in them, with particularly serious consequences for the role and liberties of women. The 'forced marriage' question is the one most often referred to here, and it is at the moment undoubtedly a very serious and scandalous one; but precisely because it has to do with custom and culture rather than directly binding enactments by religious authority, I shall refer to another issue. It is argued that the provision for the inheritance of widows under a strict application of *Shari'a* has the effect of disadvantaging them in what the majority community might regard as unacceptable ways. A legal (in fact Qur'anic) provision which in its time served very clearly to secure a widow's position at a time when this was practically unknown in the culture becomes, if taken absolutely literally, a generator of relative *insecurity* in a new context (see, for example, Ann Elizabeth Mayer, *Islam and Human Rights. Tradition and Politics*, 1999, p 111). The problem here is that recognizing the authority of a communal religious court to decide finally and authoritatively about such a question would in effect not merely allow an additional layer of legal routes for resolving conflicts and ordering behaviour but would actually *deprive* members of the minority community of rights and liberties that they were entitled to enjoy as citizens; and while a legal system might properly admit structures or protocols that embody the diversity of moral reasoning in a plural society

by allowing scope for a minority group to administer its affairs according to its own convictions, it can hardly admit or 'license' protocols that effectively take away the rights it acknowledges as generally valid.

[11] To put the question like that is already to see where an answer might lie, though it is not an answer that will remove the possibility of some conflict. If any kind of plural jurisdiction is recognized, it would presumably have to be under the rubric that no 'supplementary' jurisdiction could have the power to deny access to the rights granted to other citizens or to punish its members for claiming those rights. This is in effect to mirror what a minority might themselves be requesting—that the situation should not arise where membership of one group restricted the freedom to live also as a member of an overlapping group, that (in this case) citizenship in a secular society should not necessitate the abandoning of religious discipline, any more than religious discipline should deprive one of access to liberties secured by the law of the land, to the common benefits of secular citizenship—or, better, to recognize that citizenship itself is a complex phenomenon not bound up with any one level of communal belonging but involving them all.

[12] But this does not guarantee an absence of conflict. In the particular case we have mentioned, the inheritance rights of widows, it is already true that some Islamic societies have themselves proved flexible (Malaysia is a case in point). But let us take a more neuralgic matter still: what about the historic Islamic prohibition against apostasy, and the draconian penalties entailed? In a society where freedom of religion is secured by law, it is obviously impossible for any group to claim that conversion to another faith is simply disallowed or to claim the right to inflict punishment on a convert. We touch here on one of the most sensitive areas not only in thinking about legal practice but also in interfaith relations. A significant number of contemporary Islamic jurists and scholars would say that the Qur'anic pronouncements on apostasy which have been regarded as the ground for extreme penalties reflect a situation in which abandoning Islam was equivalent to adopting an active stance of violent hostility to the community, so that extreme penalties could be compared to provisions in other jurisdictions for punishing spies or traitors in wartime; but that this cannot be regarded as bearing on the conditions now existing in the world. Of course such a reading is wholly unacceptable to 'primitivists' in Islam, for whom this would be an example of a rationalising strategy, a style of interpretation (*ijtihad*) uncontrolled by proper traditional norms. But, to use again the terminology suggested a moment ago, as soon as it is granted that—even in a dominantly Islamic society—citizens have more than one set of defining relationships under the law of the state, it becomes hard to justify enactments that take it for granted that the only mode of contact between these sets of relationships is open enmity; in which case, the appropriateness of extreme penalties for conversion is not obvious even within a fairly strict Muslim frame of reference. Conversely, where the dominant legal culture is non-Islamic, but there is a level of serious recognition of the corporate reality and rights of the *umma*, there can be no assumption that outside the *umma* the goal of any other jurisdiction is its destruction. Once again, there has to be a recognition that difference of conviction is not automatically a lethal threat.

[13] As I have said, this is a delicate and complex matter involving what is mostly a fairly muted but nonetheless real debate among Muslim scholars in various contexts. I

mention it partly because of its gravity as an issue in interfaith relations and in discussions of human rights and the treatment of minorities, partly to illustrate how the recognition of what I have been calling membership in different but overlapping sets of social relationship (what others have called 'multiple affiliations') can provide a framework for thinking about these neuralgic questions of the status of women and converts. Recognizing a supplementary jurisdiction cannot mean recognizing a liberty to exert a sort of local monopoly in some areas. The Jewish legal theorist Ayelet Shachar, in a highly original and significant monograph on *Multicultural Jurisdictions: Cultural Differences and Women's Rights* (2001), explores the risks of any model that ends up 'franchising' a non-state jurisdiction so as to reinforce its most problematic features and further disadvantage its weakest members: 'we must be alert', she writes, 'to the potentially injurious effects of well-meaning external protections upon different categories of group members here—effects which may unwittingly exacerbate preexisting internal power hierarchies' (113). She argues that if we are serious in trying to move away from a model that treats one jurisdiction as having a monopoly of socially defining roles and relations, we do not solve any problems by a purely uncritical endorsement of a communal legal structure which can only be avoided by deciding to leave the community altogether. We need, according to Shachar, to 'work to overcome the ultimatum of "either your culture or your rights"' (114).

[14] So the second objection to an increased legal recognition of communal religious identities can be met if we are prepared to think about the basic ground rules that might organize the relationship between jurisdictions, making sure that we do not collude with unexamined systems that have oppressive effect or allow shared public liberties to be decisively taken away by a supplementary jurisdiction. Once again, there are no blank cheques. I shall return to some of the details of Shachar's positive proposal; but I want to move on to the third objection, which grows precisely out of the complexities of clarifying the relations between jurisdictions. Is it not both theoretically and practically mistaken to qualify our commitment to legal monopoly? So much of our thinking in the modern world, dominated by European assumptions about universal rights, rests, surely, on the basis that the law is the law; that everyone stands before the public tribunal on exactly equal terms, so that recognition of corporate identities or, more seriously, of supplementary jurisdictions is simply incoherent if we want to preserve the great political and social advances of Western legality.

[15] There is a bit of a risk here in the way we sometimes talk about the universal vision of post-Enlightenment politics. The great protest of the Enlightenment was against authority that appealed only to tradition and refused to justify itself by other criteria—by open reasoned argument or by standards of successful provision of goods and liberties for the greatest number. Its claim to override traditional forms of governance and custom by looking towards a universal tribunal was entirely intelligible against the background of despotism and uncritical inherited privilege which prevailed in so much of early modern Europe. The most positive aspect of this moment in our cultural history was its focus on equal levels of accountability for all and equal levels of access for all to legal process. In this respect, it was in fact largely the foregrounding and confirming of what was already encoded in longstanding legal tradition, Roman and mediaeval, which had consistently affirmed the universality and primacy of law (even over the person of the monarch). But this set of considerations alone is not

adequate to deal with the realities of complex societies: it is not enough to say that citizenship as an abstract form of equal access and equal accountability is either the basis or the entirety of social identity and personal motivation. Where this has been enforced, it has proved a weak vehicle for the life of a society and has often brought violent injustice in its wake (think of the various attempts to reduce citizenship to rational equality in the France of the 1790's or the China of the 1970's). Societies that are in fact ethnically, culturally and religiously diverse are societies in which identity is formed, as we have noted by different modes and contexts of belonging, 'multiple affiliation'. The danger is in acting as if the authority that managed the abstract level of equal citizenship represented a sovereign order which then *allowed* other levels to exist. But if the reality of society is plural—as many political theorists have pointed out—this is a damagingly inadequate account of common life, in which certain kinds of affiliation are marginalized or privatized to the extent that what is produced is a ghettoized pattern of social life, in which particular sorts of interest and of reasoning are tolerated as private matters but never granted legitimacy in public as part of a continuing debate about shared goods and priorities.

[16] But this means that we have to think a little harder about the role and rule of law in a plural society of overlapping identities. Perhaps it helps to see the universalist vision of law as guaranteeing equal accountability and access primarily in a negative rather than a positive sense—that is, to see it as a mechanism whereby any human participant in a society is protected against the loss of certain elementary liberties of self-determination and guaranteed the freedom to demand reasons for any actions on the part of others for actions and policies that infringe self-determination. This is a slightly more gentle or tactful way of expressing what some legal theorists will describe as the 'monopoly of legitimate violence' by the law of a state, the absolute restriction of powers of forcible restraint to those who administer statutory law. This is not to reduce society itself primarily to an uneasy alliance of self-determining individuals arguing about the degree to which their freedom is limited by one another and needing forcible restraint in a war of all against all—though that is increasingly the model which a narrowly rights-based culture fosters, producing a manically litigious atmosphere and a conviction of the inadequacy of customary ethical restraints and traditions – of what was once called 'civility'. The picture will not be unfamiliar, and there is a modern legal culture which loves to have it so. But the point of defining legal universalism as a negative thing is that it allows us to assume, as I think we should, that the important springs of moral vision in a society will be in those areas which a systematic abstract universalism regards as 'private'—in religion above all, but also in custom and habit. The role of 'secular' law is not the dissolution of these things in the name of universalism but the monitoring of such affiliations to prevent the creation of mutually isolated communities in which human liberties are seen in incompatible ways and individual persons are subjected to restraints or injustices for which there is no public redress.

[17] The rule of law is thus not the enshrining of priority for the universal/abstract dimension of social existence but the establishing of a space accessible to everyone in which it is possible to affirm and defend a commitment to human dignity *as such*, independent of membership in any specific human community or tradition, so that when specific communities or traditions are in danger of claiming finality for their own boundaries

of practice and understanding, they are reminded that they have to come to terms with the actuality of human diversity—and that the only way of doing this is to acknowledge the category of 'human dignity as such'—a non-negotiable assumption that each agent (with his or her historical and social affiliations) could be expected to have a voice in the shaping of some common project for the well-being and order of a human group. It is not to claim that specific community understandings are 'superseded' by this universal principle, rather to claim that they all need to be undergirded by it. The rule of law is—and this may sound rather counterintuitive—a way of honouring what in the human constitution is not captured by any one form of corporate belonging or any particular history, even though the human constitution never exists without those other determinations. Our need, as Raymond Plant has well expressed it, is for the construction of 'a moral framework which could expand outside the boundaries of particular narratives while, at the same time, respecting the narratives as the cultural contexts in which the language [of common dignity and mutually intelligible commitments to work for certain common moral priorities] is learned and taught' (*Politics, Theology and History*, 2001, pp 357–8).

[18] I'd add in passing that this is arguably a place where more reflection is needed about the theology of law; if my analysis is right, the sort of foundation I have sketched for a universal principle of legal right requires both a certain valuation of the human as such and a conviction that the human subject is always endowed with some degree of freedom over against any and every actual system of human social life; both of these things are historically rooted in Christian theology, even when they have acquired a life of their own in isolation from that theology. It never does any harm to be reminded that without certain themes consistently and strongly emphasized by the 'Abrahamic' faiths, themes to do with the unconditional possibility for every human subject to live in conscious relation with God and in free and constructive collaboration with others, there is no guarantee that a 'universalist' account of human dignity would ever have seemed plausible or even emerged with clarity. Slave societies and assumptions about innate racial superiority are as widespread a feature as any in human history (and they have persistently infected even Abrahamic communities, which is perhaps why the Enlightenment was a necessary wake-up call to religion ...).

[19] But to return to our main theme: I have been arguing that a defence of an unqualified secular legal monopoly in terms of the need for a universalist doctrine of human right or dignity is to misunderstand the circumstances in which that doctrine emerged, and that the essential liberating (and religiously informed) vision it represents is not imperilled by a loosening of the monopolistic framework. At the moment, as I mentioned at the beginning of this lecture, one of the most frequently noted problems in the law in this area is the reluctance of a dominant rights-based philosophy to acknowledge the liberty of conscientious opting-out from collaboration in procedures or practices that are in tension with the demands of particular religious groups: the assumption, in rather misleading shorthand, that if a right or liberty is granted there is a corresponding duty upon every individual to 'activate' this whenever called upon. Earlier on, I proposed that the criterion for recognizing and collaborating with communal religious discipline should be connected with whether a communal jurisdiction actively interfered with liberties guaranteed by the wider society in such a way as definitively to block access to the exercise of those liberties; clearly the refusal of a

religious believer to act upon the legal recognition of a right is not, given the plural character of society, a denial to anyone inside or outside the community of access to that right. The point has been granted in respect of medical professionals who may be asked to perform or co-operate in performing abortions—a perfectly reasonable example of the law doing what I earlier defined as its job, securing space for those aspects of human motivation and behaviour that cannot be finally determined by any corporate or social system. It is difficult to see quite why the principle cannot be extended in other areas. But it is undeniable that there is pressure from some quarters to insist that conscientious disagreement should always be overruled by a monopolistic understanding of jurisdiction.

[20]   I labour the point because what at first seems to be a somewhat narrow point about how Islamic law and Islamic identity should or might be regarded in our legal system in fact opens up a very wide range of current issues, and requires some general thinking about the character of law. It would be a pity if the immense advances in the recognition of human rights led, because of a misconception about legal universality, to a situation where a person was defined primarily as the possessor of a set of abstract liberties and the law's function was accordingly seen as nothing but the securing of those liberties irrespective of the custom and conscience of those groups which concretely compose a plural modern society. Certainly, no-one is likely to suppose that a scheme allowing for supplementary jurisdiction will be simple, and the history of experiments in this direction amply illustrates the problems. But if one approaches it along the lines sketched by Shachar in the monograph quoted earlier, it might be possible to think in terms of what she calls 'transformative accommodation': a scheme in which individuals retain the liberty to choose the jurisdiction under which they will seek to resolve certain carefully specified matters, so that 'power-holders are forced to compete for the loyalty of their shared constituents' (122). This may include aspects of marital law, the regulation of financial transactions and authorized structures of mediation and conflict resolution—the main areas that have been in question where supplementary jurisdictions have been tried, with native American communities in Canada as well as with religious groups like Islamic minority communities in certain contexts. In such schemes, both jurisdictional stakeholders may need to examine the way they operate; a communal/religious *nomos*, to borrow Shachar's vocabulary, has to think through the risks of alienating its people by inflexible or over-restrictive applications of traditional law, and a universalist Enlightenment system has to weigh the possible consequences of ghettoizing and effectively disenfranchising a minority, at real cost to overall social cohesion and creativity. Hence '*transformative* accommodation': both jurisdictional parties may be changed by their encounter over time, and we avoid the sterility of mutually exclusive monopolies.

[21]   It is uncomfortably true that this introduces into our thinking about law what some would see as a 'market' element, a competition for loyalty as Shachar admits. But if what we want socially is a pattern of relations in which a plurality of divers and overlapping affiliations work for a common good, and in which groups of serious and profound conviction are not systematically faced with the stark alternatives of cultural loyalty or state loyalty, it seems unavoidable. In other settings, I have spoken about the idea of 'interactive pluralism' as a political desideratum; this seems to be one manifestation of such an ideal, comparable to the arrangements that allow for shared

responsibility in education: the best argument for faith schools from the point of view of any aspiration towards social harmony and understanding is that they bring communal loyalties into direct relation with the wider society and inevitably lead to mutual questioning and sometimes mutual influence towards change, without compromising the distinctiveness of the essential elements of those communal loyalties.

[22] In conclusion, it seems that if we are to think intelligently about the relations between Islam and British law, we need a fair amount of 'deconstruction' of crude oppositions and mythologies, whether of the nature of *Shari'a* or the nature of the Enlightenment. But as I have hinted, I do not believe this can be done without some thinking also about the very nature of law. It is always easy to take refuge in some form of positivism; and what I have called legal universalism, when divorced from a serious theoretical (and, I would argue, religious) underpinning, can turn into a positivism as sterile as any other variety. If the paradoxical idea which I have sketched is true—that universal law and universal right are a way of recognizing what is least fathomable and controllable in the human subject—theology still waits for us around the corner of these debates, however hard our culture may try to keep it out. And, as you can imagine, I am not going to complain about that.

Transcript of the Question and Answer Session following the Lecture

[Questions and Answers relating to Islam only are reproduced]

The Lord Chief Justice, Lord Phillips of Worth Matravers ('LP'), read out questions to the Archbishop ('RW') that been submitted in advance or which had been written on slips of paper by the audience during the lecture.

[23] LP: Another fairly down to earth [question]. 'Our existing world order is based upon usury with control by manipulation of rates of interest. In Islam this is not just illegal but sinful. How can this be reconciled with Christianity? And this Christianity also condemns the existing order as the law of Mammon.'

[24] RW: I've often been rather surprised by the ease with which the Christian church changed its mind about usury in the sixteenth century, without any very great public fuss. Martin Luther strongly disapproved of it; he was a good medieval Catholic in all sorts of ways, and he disapproved of it like his medieval predecessors on the basis of the Bible, tradition and the authority of Aristotle. But within about fifty years of the beginning of the Reformation, virtually everybody had mysteriously and imperceptibly decided that there wasn't a problem.

[25] Now, without going into details of the history of that fascinating issue, I think that in all seriousness what theologians and moralists have said about lending at interest in the modern economy, is simply to raise the question 'Is *this* what is prohibited in Jewish scripture?' And they've answered on the whole, 'No'. And yet I have to say there remains, or should remain for the Christian moralist, a level of discomfort around this. Taking absolutely for granted the manipulation of rates of interest as the engine of an economy, ought to leave us with some unfinished moral business, let's say, and I believe that rather than, so to speak, address that head on, we need to look—and this has been said by many people—at what are the alternative protocols and ethical frameworks for banking that are around. And that is one reason why I am personally so very interested in the ethics and practice of micro-credit as a way of addressing serious poverty.

[26] LP: Thank you. 'How can the civil law distinguish between religious principles and cultural customs when Islam's own religious leaders cannot agree on what constitutes faith and what constitutes culture?'

[27] RW: A very salient question which I think would be much better answered by some within the Islamic community, but that there is a distinction seems to me clear. As I said in the body of the lecture, what we need is a high level of shared ownership of any means of distinguishing between culture and religious prescription, and a very well resourced body to advise on that nationally. Internationally it remains complicated. I don't think there is a short answer to this but Muslim jurists when writing about some of these very difficult issues, will recognize precisely the compromising character of presenting custom as if it were religious prescription and will be very uneasy about the blurring of boundaries.

[28] LP: 'I would have no difficulty with people being able by agreement, to opt into private religious legal systems, if it suited their purposes—it seems to work with Beth Din—but how do you ensure that the consent to jurisdiction is genuine?' I think that's another way of saying 'what is the nature of the scheme you are postulating?'

[29] RW: Well, I think I must come clean and say I'm not postulating a detailed scheme, but raising a question about what the most fruitful kinds of relationship might be between the law of the state and what I have been calling 'supplementary jurisdiction'. But I think were there to be—and I regard this as an open question—were there to be further forms of accommodation, then there would need to be I think, some element of transparency of monitoring which expressed a cooperative relationship rather than just parallel tracks.

[30] I noticed that one of the questions that was posted in advance was the very simple one, 'did I think that *Shari'a* could ever exist as a parallel legal system in Britain?' And I would want to say very firmly that I am not talking about parallel systems, but about how the law of the land most fruitfully, least conflictually, accommodates practice, and that will I think involve a degree of transparency on the part of communal practice, which might help to answer that question.

[31] LP: 'What role do you feel Islamic law can play in finding a solution to the Israel Palestine conflict?'

[32] RW: Yes, this is where I feel that a good answer would either qualify me for the Nobel Peace Prize or guarantee my assassination. (audience laughter) Now because those are somewhat extreme alternatives, I shall give you a poor answer, because I don't know what a good answer really is here. And the poor answer is I think along these lines. The principles of Islamic law, as outlined by the Muslim jurists I've read, are principles which lay heavy stress on dignity, respect; which even though they are crafted in the context of a good deal of fierce conflict, none-the-less retain a sense that the 'otherness' of the Other's identity is not something that can be extinguished by force. Now that is an ethical principle which Islam holds entirely in common with Judaism and Christianity; the otherness of the Other can't be ironed out by force. I think in that sense there is a real convergence, which ought to help us look at this and other situations, at depth.

[33] Having said that, the level of convergence there is so abstract and so general, that it is very hard indeed to apply. Yet if that's the question; "what role can Islamic law play?",

I can only say it will play the role that Jewish and Christian legal and moral commitments also play in underlining the right of the Other to be; to be there. (applause)

[34] LP: Here is a robust question. 'Must we accommodate Islam or not, as Christians?'

[35] RW: Must we accommodate Islam or not as Christians? Must I love my Muslim neighbour? Yes, without qualification or hesitation. Must I pretend to my Muslim neighbour that I don't believe my own faith? No, without hesitation or qualification. Must I as a citizen in a plural society work for ways of living constructively, rather than tensely or suspiciously with my Muslim neighbour? Yes, without qualification or hesitation.

[36] LP: This is, again, a question on a premise but it might be interesting to know whether you agree the premise. 'Why are Muslims so scared to debate and question *Shari'a* law?'

[37] RW: Well, I can't speak for Muslims. There are quite a lot of them in the world and I'm not one of them. But I think that precisely because of the convergence of faith and custom in so many contexts, the way in which people construct and pin down their identities becomes very much allied to these issues about how disputes are resolved and what protocols are observed. And I think therefore there is an understandable sense, often confused and I would say misguided, that touching any bit of the cultural complex, undermines your whole identity. That has to do with the perceived political and social insecurity of many Muslim communities in our world. And I've said it before, I'll say it again, the paradox is that from the Western perspective we frequently see the Muslim world as powerful, aggressive, coherent and threatening. From the other side of the world, the Muslim world, or a great deal of it sees us as powerful, coherent and threatening in very much the same way. Now, when those are the perceptions, you don't have a very fertile ground for critical, relaxed, long-term discussions of some legal and cultural issues, and I think that's a question that can't really be answered without looking at those larger, global, political questions.

[38] LP: 'Is there a danger that if religions rely on secular law to provide a safety net for where human dignity is not protected by religious norms, that these norms are not reassessed and re-evaluated as they should be?'

[39] RW: I take it that that is a question about some of what was entailed in the last few minutes of my lecture about 'transforming accommodation'; that is the way in which a wider public discourse over time impacts on a religious community as it thinks through its own standards and philosophies.

[40] I think that where there is a good communicative relationship involved; where there is transparency, it's inevitable. And this may again, seem threatening. It's inevitable that some of the questions raised in a wider society about the scope of human dignity, will get raised within the subsidiary, the minority, community. And that is uncomfortable, but it's part of our pluralist environment.

[41] LP: 'Do you think the inclusion of some Islamic history in the national curriculum could help generate a wider cultural understanding of Islam?'

[42] RW: Mindful of the potential headlines, 'Archbishop calls for Muslim history in schools,' (audience laughter) I think I'd say two things. One is that of course there is already some of that orientation going on in good-curricula religious studies around

the place. I would hope that any teaching of British, European or global history would contain a sensible amount of well perspectived and proportioned Islamic history as well; it's part of the story.

[43] And just another word on that, because there is a bigger question. Partly thanks to (our) post-sixteenth century situation, it is quite easy for us now in the modern West to forget that there is a high degree of shared history. A very interesting book, some years ago, talked about the three successor states to the Roman empire. The Byzantine empire, the Papacy and Islam; all Mediterranean realities disputing an imperial legacy which in very, very different ways they were all exploiting, trading on, in certain respects. I think it helps to remember that. It's not just the history of some world that is totally 'Other'.

[44] LP: 'Are there not situations in which communal customs would merit recognition, regardless of religious authority?'

[45] [45] RW: I'll assume that's a question about good practice within religious communities from which the law of the land might learn. If so I suspect there is something to be said there about the way in which unofficial styles of mediation could be more widely adopted, or encouraged by the law in general.

[46] LP: This is perhaps a slightly parallel question. 'Why are we not asking similar questions of non-Abrahamic faiths, such as the increasingly marginalized Hindu society?'

[47] RW: A very good question. I think there are many, many people of Hindu affiliation in this country who see themselves, understandably, as having been rather 'ruled out' by the great focus, the great concentration on issues around Islam. And I don't think that's healthy. I think that there are many issues about how we relate to Hindu minorities here which need addressing. The difference of course is that you are not there dealing with, obviously not a single body, but a tradition, a shared practice of jurisprudence, in the way that you are where Islam is concerned.

[48] LP: This is a slightly aggressive question. 'Contrary to the Archbishop's suggestion, the State does not delegate legal authority to Jewish religious courts, and Jewish law is not recognized by, or incorporated into English law. Why then does he think Islam should be given unique status in challenging majority cultural and legal norms?' I think there are about three premises there which are perhaps false. (laughter)

[49] RW: I don't think I said, or at least I hope I didn't say that Jewish law was incorporated in any way into the law of the land; I am well aware that it's not. What I mean is that there is an established, recognized practice in Orthodox Jewish communities, particularly with regard to marital practice, which the law of the land does not seek to override or replace, as I understand it. Now I'm open to correction on this because I'm not a lawyer, but I used the analogy not to try and claim a privileged place for Islam—which I'm not seeking to claim—simply to look for parallel situations where a highly developed, well resourced and sophisticated system of communal law was *de facto* at least, embedded in our social practice.

[50] LP: This is a question that I was discussing with you before this lecture and I thought you might decline to answer it as it rather seems to be a question for me, but you seem to be prepared to do so, so I will ask it. 'How could the court obtain a full

understanding of a female defendant or witness if that person is covered entirely, or only has the eyes visible?'

[51] RW: Yes, there is in fact a long question submitted in advance about the use of the full veil in a legal setting.

[52] My views about the veil, as an outsider, are these. First of all, the routine reminder that we are here dealing with cultural, customary reading of legal prescription, rather than a detailed order provision. But second, a degree of cultural sensitivity is part of the ordinary good manners of a pluralist state and there are plenty of contexts where it seems to me unproblematic to grant that freedom.

[53] And there are some contexts where—back to my earlier point—there are some contexts in which the wearing of a full facial veil actively disadvantages others. The school-teaching setting has been mentioned; the legal setting can be another one. And that's where it becomes problematic and I would not see it as self evidently right. But in saying that, whether in the school or in the law court, again one needs to explore what the cultural sensitivities are that would make it difficult and make the appropriate provision; for example in certain cases for a woman wishing to wear the veil to be interviewed in some circumstances by another woman, that kind of thing. Ordinary cultural good manners in a plural society.

[54] LP: 'Surely belief in God is a personal matter between the believer and the god in which he believes. Why should this give the believer any rights *vis à vis* those who do not believe in his God?'

[55] RW: Well, I don't think that belief in God does give the believer any rights over anyone else. But because society recognizes liberty of belief, the believer can claim that measure of legal respect at least. God forbid, if you allow the expression, that any religious group should seek to be dictating; setting the agenda for a society from the top down on behalf of a minority. When somebody from a religious community makes a bid in an argument in the public sphere, on religious grounds, he or she is doing so not because of any belief that there is a prescriptive right to override what anyone else believes, but because the law of our society at the moment secures the liberty to say these things as part of public argument.

[56] But I would just add a little qualification to the way in which the question is phrased. Yes, the believer relates in free and personal ways to the god he or she believes in. At the same time, as my lecture rather takes for granted, no religious believer lives in a vacuum and most of the major religious traditions of the world would say that your belief, your relationship with God, is inextricably tied up with how you relate to other believers, to a tradition and a community practice. That's not to say that that gives it any more public status or power to dictate; simply to say that's the nature of belief as many understand it.

[57] LP: 'Do you foresee a time when people domiciled in this country, whose religion permits polygamy, will be allowed to marry polygamously in this country, and would you be content with that?'

[58] RW: No, I don't think I would. Again, as a number of Muslim scholars have pointed out, the prescriptions about polygamy in the Qur'an are permissive, not mandatory. In other words, nobody has to have more than one wife. In that sense, I would say

that it's never going to be a question of a religious duty being—demanding respect from the law of the land. And because most aspects of our public law assume, as axiomatic, certain attitudes to the rights of women which are not readily compatible with the practice of polygamy, I can't really see this as an option.

[59] LP: Here's rather a nice one. 'If the State was to acknowledge the legal status of *Shari'a* law in whatever respect, would it not be appropriate for the Monarch to become Defender of the Faiths?' (laughter)

[60] RW: Yes, yes I get asked this from time to time. My fallback reply, and don't worry, there will be another one in a moment, but my fallback reply has tended to be: the title Defender of the Faith, is one that has a very specific historical setting, and I don't believe in revising historical titles on the hoof.

[61] But that the British Monarchy should, as part of its responsibility for the cohesion of our society, take seriously the reality of corporate faith and, in certain circumstances speak on its behalf in the most general way, yes.

[62] LP: And there's another premise to this one. 'Looking at this society, which is spiralling out of control in terms of moral or behavioural conducts that are embedded in both Christian and Islamic jurisdiction, do you believe inter-faith intervention is the solution to restoring the diminishing moral fibre of this imperialistic society?' (laughter)

[63] RW: Yes, there is a premise there I think, but not one with which I would quarrel too violently. That's to say I think we are a fragmented and fragmenting society in all kinds of ways, and we probably ought to be more rather than less anxious about some aspects of that. But that does mean that certain kinds of collaboration on issues of common concern are going to be socially very important.

[64] About three years ago we had a meeting at Lambeth Palace for a number of, I hope representative faith leaders, in which we discussed some of the anxieties we shared. Anxieties around education; around the security of children. Anxieties around the infrastructure of communities and around the environmental crisis; and spoke there of how we needed to develop better ways of consulting, speaking and acting across these boundaries. It is quite hard to bring this into practice, I must admit, but particularly in the Christian-Muslim context, I would point to the work of the Christian-Muslim Forum in this country, which has in some areas, precisely taken up some of these issues of community regeneration and cohesion.

[65] LP: It is the time to draw this discussion, reluctantly, to a close. Could I thank you Archbishop, for so brilliantly introducing us to this difficult area, for raising questions over which we shall be pondering in the weeks ahead, and for answering all the questions which have been thrown at you in the last half hour. Thank you very much.

Equality Before the Law

Lord Phillips of Worth Matravers,
*Lord Chief Justice of England and Wales**
East London Muslim Centre
3 July 2008

[1] In 1903 two young immigrants arrived in England. They were Sephardic Jews and had eloped to this country from Alexandria because they understood that England was a country in which they would enjoy freedom. Not merely freedom from their families, who did not approve of their marriage, but freedom under the law from all forms of discrimination. They believed that England was a country where all were treated equally, regardless of their colour, race, religion or gender. They were my maternal grandparents, and to a large extent they were correct. England was a country that prided itself on the freedom accorded to those who lived here. But, as we shall see, this very freedom permitted some who lived here to discriminate in the way that they treated others. It is only in my own lifetime that the law has moved to outlaw almost every form of discrimination, so that those who live in this country really are entitled to be treated as equals.

[2] I propose to explain to you the ways in which the law has changed, with the result that Muslim men and Muslim women are entitled to be treated in exactly the same way as all other men and women in this country. And there is, of course, another side to this coin. Rights carry with them obligations, and those who come to live in this country and to benefit from the rights enjoyed by all who live here, also necessarily come under the same obligations that the law imposes on all who live here. The title of my talk is 'equality before the law', and it may be helpful to consider at the outset what 'the law' is. The law that I am to talk about is the set of rules that govern how we live in society. They are rules made by those with authority to make them and rules that are enforced by those with authority to enforce them.

[3] In some countries those who make the law are the same as those who enforce it. In this country that is not the case. We have what is known as the separation of powers. Parliament makes our laws. The government administers the country in accordance with those laws and, if anyone alleges that an individual or a government authority has broken the law, it is the judges who have to determine whether the law has been broken or not and, if it has, to rule on what sanction or remedy is to be imposed.

---

* Lord Phillips is now President of The Supreme Court of the United Kingdom.

[4] The judges of this country are independently appointed. We are fiercely proud of our independence. When we are appointed we take an oath or affirmation that we will administer justice 'to do right to all manner of people after the laws and usages of this realm'. We act in accordance with that oath. We treat equally all who come before us, regardless of whether they are men or women, regardless of their race or religion and whether they are rich or poor.

[5] We are not influenced by the wishes of the government, and no Government Minister would dare to attempt to influence a judge to decide a case in a particular way. Each individual judge is independent, which means that I as Lord Chief Justice would not think of directing another judge how to decide a case.

[6] So I can give you this assurance. Any man or woman who appears before a judge in this country will receive equal treatment in the administration of the law. The judge will treat each litigant in the same way. But the judge's duty is to apply the law, whether he agrees with the law or not. So the important question is not 'does the judge treat everyone equally?' but 'does the law treat everyone equally?' In any society the answer to that question depends upon the motives, the beliefs, the attitudes, the prejudices or lack of prejudices of those who make the law.

[7] At this point, you will forgive me I hope, as I must say a little about history, for our law today is, to some extent, a product of this country's history. Before this country became a democracy, those responsible for the laws were not very enthusiastic about equality. There is a popular perception that the freedoms that we all enjoy had their root in the Magna Carta. That is a misconception. Before the Magna Carta England had a feudal system, in which the King was supreme. Below the King came the noblemen and below the noblemen the serfs. The law imposed by the King was imposed for his own benefit and made very substantial demands on his noblemen, who themselves made exacting demands on their serfs. The King's rights included, by way of example, the right to dictate to whom the widow of a nobleman should be re-married. Ultimately the nobles revolted against the demands made on them and the Magna Carta set out an agreement made by King John in 1215 that he would moderate those demands. Thus Chapter 8 of the Charter provided 'no widow shall be forced to marry so long as she wishes to live without a husband.'

[8] It is not for provisions such as these that the Magna Carta is remembered, but for the following pledges:

No freeman shall be arrested or imprisoned or disseised or outlawed or exiled or in any way victimised, neither will we attack him or send anyone to attack him, except by the lawful judgment of his peers or by the law of the land. To no-one will we refuse or delay right or justice.

[9] This came to be regarded as setting out the fundamental rights of British citizens. King John subsequently renounced the agreement that he had made in Magna Carta, but later Kings agreed to abide by an amended version and so this became an important part of the law. Magna Carta dealt with relations between the subject and the State, in the form of the monarch. Other laws dealt with disputes between the King's subjects. How were these laws created? Initially they were created by judges, appointed by the King to act on his behalf in resolving those disputes. The law created by the judges came to be called the 'common law'. The common law covered aspects of life common to most societies—the right to own property, rules in relation to inheritance,

the right to compensation if one person injured another and so on. These are aspects of what we call civil law; the law governing the reciprocal rights and duties of citizens towards each other. But the judges created another kind of common law—the law that we call criminal law. This law exists not for the benefit of the individual citizen, but for the benefit of society as a whole, and it lays down acts that are prohibited because they are anti-social. Those who break those laws commit crimes against the state and are liable to be punished by the state. In the old days we used to talk about crimes as being a 'breach of the King's peace'. Examples of acts that have always been recognized as crimes are murder, rape, assault and theft.

[10] The common law still exists and, indeed, it is the foundation of the law that is applied today. But it has been largely replaced by statute law, that is law enacted by Parliament, and that is the usual way that laws are made in a democracy. The supremacy of Parliament dates back to 1689 when King William III signed the Bill of Rights. This provided for free elections and freedom of speech in Parliament and removed the power of the King to suspend the laws which Parliament had passed. Under the parliamentary system the people elect representatives who then make the laws that govern the people.

[11] I said earlier that laws tend to reflect the motives, beliefs, attitudes and prejudices of those who make the law. Parliament tends to enact legislation that reflects the attitudes and wishes of the majority of the electorate. If everyone has the right to vote that is a fact that tends towards laws which apply equally to everyone. But for a very long time not every citizen of this country had the right to vote. Men tended to dominate society and to consider that they were more important and superior to women. When parliamentary democracy was introduced to this country, it was a very biased democracy, because only men were allowed to vote and only men were allowed to become members of Parliament. So it is perhaps not surprising that the laws passed by Parliament tended to discriminate in favour of men.

[12] Slowly there was a change in attitude, a change that was partly brought about by protests of the women themselves. In 1918 Parliament voted for a limited right to vote for women and permitted those eligible to vote to become Members of Parliament. In 1928 women gained the right to vote to the same extent as men. Thereafter, so far as relations between the citizen and the State were concerned, women came to be treated equally with men.

[13] There were other respects in which prejudices on the part of those who made the laws resulted in inequality of treatment of citizens of this country. This was certainly true of religion. Historically Christianity has been the religion of the majority of the British people, but the United Kingdom has a long tradition of accommodating other religions. This has not always been the case however. Jews came to this country with William the Conqueror in 1066. But in 1290 all Jews were expelled from Britain by the Edict of Expulsion proclaimed by King Edward I. They were allowed back in 1656 by Oliver Cromwell and have since then been a valued element of our society. Paradoxically at that time we had a much less charitable attitude to some members of the Christian faith. The history of the Christian religion has been marred by schism and, in particular by strife between the Protestant and the Roman Catholic branches of the faith.

[14] King Henry VIII broke with the Catholic Church in 1534 and after that, with one or two very short exceptions, Protestant Christianity has been the official religion of this country. In 1700 an Act of Parliament provided that the sovereign had to be a member of the Church of England and that remains the position to this day. Laws were passed that discriminated severely against Catholics, so that they were prevented from owning property, inheriting land, joining the army, holding public office or voting. It was only at the end of the 18th Century and the beginning of the 19th Century that a series of Acts of Parliament were passed removing all these disqualifications.

[15] I have so far been concentrating on the negative side of our history; areas where our laws have positively discriminated on grounds of race, religion or gender. In general, however, the approach of our law has been that of liberty. As Sir John Donaldson, one of my distinguished judicial predecessors, put it in this way:

The starting point of our domestic law is that every citizen has a right to do what he likes, unless restrained by the common law or by statute.[1]

[16] That statement today is true not merely of British citizens, but of anyone who is lawfully within this country. Personal liberty is a right to which the courts of this country have long attached the highest importance. Anyone who is deprived of his liberty, whether by the state or by anybody else, can bring proceedings in the courts to challenge the legality of his detention. One way that he can do so is by the writ of habeas corpus, a remedy that has existed since the 17th Century. A famous example of this remedy was *Somerset's Case* in 1772. A Mr Stewart had purchased an African slave called Somerset in Jamaica and had brought him on a visit to England, not bringing him ashore but keeping him detained in the ship which was to take them both back to Jamaica. A gentleman called Granville Sharpe, who was vehemently opposed to slavery brought habeas corpus proceedings before the English court claiming that Somerset was being unlawfully detained. His claim succeeded and Lord Mansfield ordered that Somerset should be released. This set a precedent and led the Lord Chancellor to say in a subsequent similar case 'As soon as a man sets foot on English ground he is free.'[2]

[17] But freedom of individuals from State interference can itself lead to unequal treatment in the way that those individuals behave towards each other. Life in a modern society involves the interdependence of those who live and work together. There is scope for discrimination in many areas if the law does not place restraints on the way people may behave. I have already described how women were not given the vote until 1918. But this was not the only way that a male dominated society tended to discriminate against them. The first university college for women was not opened until 1869. By 1910 there were over a thousand women students at Oxford and Cambridge, but they still had to obtain permission to attend lectures and were not allowed to take a degree. It was not until 1918 that the first woman became entitled to qualify as a barrister, and the first woman solicitor was not admitted until 1922. Until more recently employers were permitted to refuse to employ women, or to offer women employment on less generous terms than male employees.

---

[1] *Attorney-General v Observer Ltd* [1990] 1 AC 109, 178.
[2] *Shanley v Harvey,* 2 Eden 126, 126 (1762).

[18] It is only in my lifetime that Parliament has legislated to stamp out discrimination in all areas and aspects of society. The catalyst for change was perhaps the horrifying racism of the Nazi regime in Germany before and during the Second World War. This led in 1948 to the Universal Declaration of Human Rights, which included the following statement:

recognition of the inherent dignity and the equal and inalienable rights of all members of the human family is the foundation of freedom, justice and peace in the world.

[19] More significantly, the United Kingdom helped to draft and, in 1951, signed the European Convention on Human Rights. This required all the signatories to ensure that there was no unlawful interference with the fundamental human rights set out in the treaty. Furthermore, Article 14 of the Convention provided:

The enjoyment of the rights and freedoms set forth in the Convention shall be secured without discrimination on any ground such as sex, race, colour, language, religion, political or other opinion, national or social origin, association with a national minority, property, birth or other status.

[20] The requirement to ensure equal treatment applies in respect of the fundamental human rights protected by the Convention. In 1998, the Human Rights Act was passed which requires all public authorities to comply with the Convention, so that individuals now have a legal right to compensation if they are subject to discrimination by agents of the government in relation to their fundamental human rights.

[21] In 1976 the United Kingdom ratified a Convention that imposes a general obligation to prohibit civil and political discrimination. Article 26 of the International Covenant on Civil and Political Rights 1966 provides:

All persons are equal before the law and are entitled without any discrimination to the equal protection of the law. In this respect, the law shall prohibit any discrimination and guarantee to all persons equal and effective protection against discrimination on any ground such as race, colour, sex, language, religion, political or other opinion, national or social origin, property, birth or other status.

[22] I propose to outline some of the laws that Parliament has passed to ensure that people in this country receive equality of treatment. I say some of them, because in 2000 it was calculated that there were no less than 30 Acts of Parliament, not to mention statutory Regulations and Codes of Practice, dealing with discrimination.

[23] The prohibition against racial discrimination is a good place to start. There has been legislation prohibiting discrimination on the grounds of race for over 40 years, but the most important statute is the Race Relations Act 1976. This prohibits anyone from treating a person less favourably on the grounds of race; that means on the grounds of 'colour, race, nationality or ethnic or national origins'. No longer could a landlady hang a sign in her window saying 'Bed and Breakfast. No blacks or Irish.'

[24] Perhaps the most significant area where the prohibition against discrimination matters is in relation to employment. People cannot be refused employment on the ground of their race. There has been quite a lot of litigation, however, as to what constitutes a racial group for the purposes of the Act. Jews, Sikhs and Gypsies have all been held to be protected by the legislation. In 1976, the House of Lords ruled that it had been unlawful for a school to exclude a Sikh boy on the ground that he refused to

cut his hair. [3] The House of Lords held that Sikhs were historically descended from a recognized group and thus qualified as a racial group.

[25] That case can be contrasted with a decision of the Court of Appeal ten years later. A Rastafarian had been refused a job as a van driver because he refused to cut his hair. The court held that Rastafarians did not constitute a racial group. [4]

[26] Muslims have been held not to fall within the definition of a racial group. In a decision in 1998 the Employment Appeal Tribunal observed that 'Muslims include people of many nations and colours who speak many languages and whose common denominator is religion and religious culture.' [5] Thus they form a group defined by religion rather than race. I shall refer to legislation that prohibits discrimination on the ground of religion in a moment. First, however, I would like to deal with discrimination on the ground of gender.

[27] The Sex Discrimination Act 1975 forbids discrimination against women and provides that a person discriminates against a woman if he treats her less favourably than he treats or would treat a man. Once again the most important area where this applies is probably the field of employment, but the prohibition is of general application. I remember a famous case when I was practising at the Bar where a woman brought proceedings against a well known wine bar frequented by barristers and journalists in Fleet Street called El Vino. They had a strict rule that only men were allowed to drink standing at the bar—women would only be served if they were sitting at a table. This rule was supposed to be out of consideration for women, but the court held that it constituted wrongful discrimination. This may not seem to be a case where the right involved was of great importance, and it is a fact that many of the cases brought to court have not involved the most serious forms of discrimination, being concerned with dress, or length of hair.

[28] I now want to consider the protection that the law provides against discrimination that can be of great significance; discrimination on the ground of a person's religion. Article 9 of the Human Rights Convention provides:

Everyone has the right to freedom of thought, conscience and religion; this right includes freedom to change his religion or belief and freedom, either alone or in community with others and in public or private life, to manifest his religion or belief, in worship, teaching, practice or observation.

[29] This human right is one that, as I have already said, this country has long recognized. In this country everyone is free to follow their own religion. The different Christian denominations can build their own churches, Jews can build synagogues, Hindus can build temples and Muslims can build mosques, of which the mosque here is a magnificent example, and each of these is free to practise his own faith in his own way.

[30] There is another fundamental human right that is relevant in this context, and that is freedom of speech. Article 10 of the Human Rights Convention provides:

Everyone has the right to freedom of expression. This right shall include freedom to hold opinions and to receive and impart information and ideas without interference.

---

[3] *Mandla v Dowel Lee* [1983] AC 548.
[4] *Crown Suppliers v Dawkins* [1993] ICR 517.
[5] *Nyazi v Rymans Ltd*, EAT/6/88, 10 May 1998.

[31] Freedom of speech has long been prized and protected in this country. Any person is free to preach the merits of his own religion, and freedom of religion includes the right to change one's faith, or apostasy.

[32] These religious freedoms of which I have been speaking relate to the relations between those practising a religion and the State. Many States are less ready than the United Kingdom to permit the practice and preaching of religions other than that officially recognized by the State. But, just as in other fields, it is possible for one citizen to discriminate against another on the grounds of a person's religion or belief. Until recently there was no law in this country that prohibited such discrimination. European Law was ahead of English law, and it was in order to give effect to a European Directive that, in 2003, Regulations were introduced that prohibited discrimination in the field of employment on the ground of a person's religion or belief.[6] In 2006, the Equality Act extended the prohibition against discrimination on the ground of religion or belief to cover other areas such as the provision of goods, facilities and services, the letting of premises and the provision of education.

[33] Let me try to summarize the position. British law has, comparatively recently, reached a stage of development in which a high premium is placed not merely on liberty, but on equality of all who live in this country. That law is secular. It does not attempt to enforce the standards of behaviour that the Christian religion or any other religion expects. It is perhaps founded on one ethical principle that the Christian religion shares with most, if not all, other religions and that is that one should love one's neighbour. And so the law sets out to prevent behaviour that harms others. Behaviour that is contrary to religious principles, but which is detrimental only to those who commit it, is not, in general, contrary to our law. A sin is not necessarily a crime.

[34] Those who come to live in this country must take its laws as they find them. British diversity is valued and the principles of freedom and equality that the law protects should be welcomed by all. Laws in this country are based on the common values of tolerance, openness, equality and respect for the rule of law. Whilst breaches of the requirements of any religion in the UK may not be punished by the law, people are free to practise their religion. That is something to be valued.

[35] I said that the law sets out to prevent behaviour that harms others. In a modern society there are many ways in which the behaviour of some can harm others, and there have been passed thousands of laws and regulations that are designed to try to prevent such behaviour. These laws and regulations can run into conflict with the freedoms that I have been discussing. The law can sometimes, quite unintentionally, have an adverse impact on a particular minority. Where this happens we will sometimes be able to make exceptions in order to prevent this. Let me give you two examples. Regulations require special headgear to be worn in a number of different situations. Advocates are expected to wear wigs, policemen to wear helmets, servicemen to wear caps, construction workers to wear safety helmets. These regulations would have a discriminatory effect on Sikhs, who could not comply with them because they do not cut their hair but encase it in the turban, and so Sikhs have been given an exemption from complying with these requirements.

---

[6] The Employment and Equality (Religion or Belief) Regulations 2003 (UK).

[36] Principles of Shari'a prohibit the earning or paying of interest. This means that a conventional mortgage offends the principles of Islam. The banks managed to devise an alternative system of financing house purchases that did not offend Shari'a principles. This involved the bank itself buying the house and then reselling it to the Muslim purchaser. There was one problem with this. English taxation law charges stamp duty on a house purchase and under this system of mortgage stamp duty had to be paid twice, once on the sale to the bank and again on the resale to the purchaser. This was not fair and so the law was changed in April 2003 so that stamp duty only had to be paid once on an Islamic mortgage.

[37] This example brings me onto the topic of Shari'a law. It is not a topic on which I can claim any special expertise, but I have been reading quite a lot about it in preparation for this talk. I have also recently been on a visit to Oman and discussed with lawyers there the manner of the application of Shari'a law in that country. It has become clear to me that there is widespread misunderstanding in this country as to the nature of Shari'a law. Shari'a consists of a set of principles governing the way that one should live one's life in accordance with the will of God. These principles are based on the Qu'ran, as revealed to the Prophet Muhammad and interpreted by Islamic scholars. The principles have much in common with those of other religions. They do not include forced marriage or the repression of women. Compliance with them requires a high level of personal conduct, including abstinence from alcohol. I understand that it is not the case that for a Muslim to lead his or her life in accordance with these principles will be in conflict with the requirements of the law in this country.

[38] What would be in conflict with the law would be to impose certain sanctions for failure to comply with Shari'a principles. Part of the misconception about Shari'a law is the belief that Shari'a is only about mandating sanctions such as flogging, stoning, the cutting off of hands, or death for those who fail to comply with the law. And the view of many of Shari'a law is coloured by violent extremists who invoke it, perversely, to justify terrorist atrocities such as suicide bombing, which I understand to be in conflict with Islamic principles. There can be no question of such sanctions being applied to or by any Muslim who lives within this jurisdiction. Nor, when I was in Oman, did I find that such penalties formed any part of the law applied there. It is true that they have the death penalty for intentional murder, but they do not apply any of the other forms of corporal punishment I have just listed.

[39] It remains the fact that in Muslim countries where the law is founded on Shari'a principles, the law includes sanctions for failure to observe those principles and there are courts to try those who are alleged to have breached those laws. The definition of the law and the sanctions to be applied for breach of it differ from one Muslim country to another. In some countries the courts interpret Sharia law as calling for severe physical punishment. There can be no question of such courts sitting in this country, or such sanctions being applied here. So far as the law is concerned, those who live in this country are governed by English law and subject to the jurisdiction of the English courts.

[40] In February this year I chaired a lecture given by the Archbishop of Canterbury in the Royal Courts of Justice on the topic of Civil and Religious Law in England. It was a profound lecture and one not readily understood on a single listening. It was,

I believe, not clearly understood by all, and certainly not by sections of the media which represented the Archbishop as suggesting the possibility that Muslims in this country might be governed by their own system of Shari'a law. That is certainly not what he was suggesting. On the contrary he made it plain that there could not be some subsidiary Shari'a jurisdiction which, I quote, 'could have the power to deny access to rights granted to other citizens or to punish its members for claiming those rights.' Speaking more specifically of apostasy he said: 'In a society where freedom of religion is secured by law, it is obviously impossible for any group to claim that conversion to another faith is simply disallowed or to claim the right to inflict punishment on a convert.'

[41] A point that the Archbishop was making was that it was possible for individuals voluntarily to conduct their lives in accordance with Shari'a principles without this being in conflict with the rights guaranteed by our law. To quote him again 'the refusal of a religious believer to act upon the legal recognition of a right is not, given the plural character of society, a denial to anyone inside or outside the community of access to that right'.

[42] The Archbishop went on to suggest that it might be possible to contemplate, and again I quote, 'a scheme in which individuals retain the liberty to choose the jurisdiction under which they will seek to resolve certain carefully specified matters'. He suggested by way of example 'aspects of marital law, the regulation of financial transactions and authorized structures of mediation and conflict resolution'.

[43] It was not very radical to advocate embracing Shari'a law in the context of family disputes, for example, and our system already goes a long way towards accommodating the Archbishop's suggestion. It is possible in this country for those who are entering into a contractual agreement to agree that the agreement shall be governed by a law other than English law. Those who, in this country, are in dispute as to their respective rights are free to subject that dispute to the mediation of a chosen person, or to agree that the dispute shall be resolved by a chosen arbitrator or arbitrators. There is no reason why principles of Shari'a Law, or any other religious code should not be the basis for mediation or other forms of alternative dispute resolution. It must be recognised, however, that any sanctions for a failure to comply with the agreed terms of the mediation would be drawn from the laws of England and Wales. So far as aspects of matrimonial law are concerned, there is a limited precedent for English law to recognize aspects of religious laws, although when it comes to divorce this can only be effected in accordance with the civil law of this country.

[44] Those who provide financial services in this country are subject to regulation in order to protect their customers and that regulation accommodates financial institutions or products that comply with Shari'a principles. There are three Islamic banks authorized by the Financial Services Authority to carry on business in the United Kingdom. A number of Sukuk issues have been listed on the London Stock Exchange. In May this year, Europe's first Islamic insurance company or 'takaful' provider was authorized by the Financial Services Authority. Speaking earlier this year, Kitty Ussher, the Economics Secretary said:

We want to make sure that no-one has their choice of financial services limited by their religion, and to help ensure that Muslims have the same access to financial services as anyone else in Britain.

[45] Having heard what I have had to say this evening, some of you may be thinking 'this equality in law is all very well, but some of those in authority with whom we come into contact do not treat us as equals and, anyway, how can we be expected to know our legal rights when we are not lawyers?' As to the first point I am well aware that Muslims sometimes feel that they are being unfairly singled out simply because a small minority, who purport to share their religion, have ignored its teachings by turning to a violent extremism that is a threat to society. There are I know here this evening some whose job it is to enforce the law and to them I would say this. It is not enough that all in this country are entitled by law to equal treatment. It is up to you to make sure that you, and those for whom you are responsible, treat every man and woman on equal footing, entitled to the same personal dignity and respect.

[46] As to the problem of knowing what your rights are, that is a problem shared by most citizens who are not in a position to pay for legal advice. Happily here the London Muslim Centre has supported the provision of a 'pro bono' legal advice service, that is, the provision without charge by volunteers of legal advice and representation to Muslim and non-Muslim alike. I strongly commend that service and those who generously provide it.

[47] There are now about 1.6 million Muslims living in this country. They form a vital and valued element of British Society. They are well represented by a variety of groups and individuals, including the Muslim Council of Britain, whose aims include the fostering of better community relations and working for the good of society as a whole. That aim is undoubtedly promoted by this impressive Centre, whose buildings appropriately embrace one of the East End's oldest synagogues, fostering Jewish-Muslim relations which have been described as the best in the country. I know that this centre does much to encourage inter-faith relations and community cohesion—one of its stated aims. It has—as I said at the beginning—been a privilege to have been invited to talk to you here today.

[48] If I may summarize the message that I have sought to give, the courts of this country offer the same justice to all who come before them, regardless of gender, race or creed. The point is sometimes made that this is not easy to accept when the judiciary is not representative of those whom they are judging. Judges are now appointed by an independent appointment Commission and they are appointed on merit. The Equal Treatment Advisory Committee, whose members represent all parts of the legal profession, is working hard to assist judges in recognizing the role of social and cultural differences in the determination of cases before them. There has, however, been a dearth of applicants from the ethnic minorities for appointment to the bench. Both the Appointments Commission and the judiciary are concerned about this. I have no doubt that there are, in the Muslim community, many men and women alike who would make outstanding lawyers and outstanding judges. It is important that they should recognize that they have a valuable potential role to play as judges, administering the law of this country to all who come before them, without fear or favour affection or ill-will.

Glossary

ʿAda	The customs of a particular people or nation
Ahad gharīb	A tradition which has a single source and only one chain of narrators
Ahadith	The body of reports attributed to the Prophet (singular *hadith*)
Al-daruratu tubiyh	Necessity makes the unlawful lawful (Shari'a principle)
Ashab	The action of God through secondary causes
Ayah	Verse
Bida	Illicit innovation, heresy
Burqa	An enveloping outer garment
ʿAql	The mind, intellect, reason
Chachnāmah	The ancient chronicle of the Muslim Conquest of the Sindh
Dār ul-Ahd	The abode of covenanted treaty
Dār ul-Harb	The abode of conflict or war
Dār ul-Islām	The abode of faithfulness and surrender to Allah
Dār ul-Sulh	The abode of peace by agreement
Darar	Danger
Darul-qada	Islamic Court of Justice
Dhimma	'Protection' or 'responsibility'; applying in Islamic law to non-Muslims who accept the conditions for living under Muslim rule
Din wa daulah	Belief and state
Dīn	Belief, religion, or worldview
Diya	Compensation
Dustūr	The customs of a particular people or nation
Fard	Mandatory
Fatwā	Non-binding legal opinion issued in response to a legal problem
Fiqh	Codified Islamic law (literally, the understanding)
Fitna	Calamity, corruption, civil disorder
Fuqahā	Jurists, ones learned in Islamic law
Furūʿ Al-fiqh	The 'branches' of the law; the systematic elaboration of how the law, derived from the sources, was to be applied
Hadith	A report or tradition of what the Prophet said or taught (plural *ahadith*)
Halal	Permissible
Hanafī	Adherent of the Sunni juristic school named after its eponym Abu Hanifah al-Nu'man
Hanbalī	Adherent of the Sunni juristic school named after its eponym Ahmad b Hanbal
Haram	Forbidden acts or practices
Hijab	Islamic headscarf

Hijra	Historic migration of the Prophet from Mecca to Medina
Hudna	A temporary truce, for the sake of trade
Hudūd	Punishment for severe transgressions
ʿIbādāt	Matters such as worship, ritual, prayer, fasting, and pilgrimage, where Muslims have an obvious duty towards God
Ifta	The process by which leading jurists and Islamic scholars (the *ʿulamā*) issue *fatwās*
Ijmāʿ	Consensus of scholarly opinion
Ijtihād	Reasoning by analogy from obscure or non-explicit cases to definite rulings (literally, effort or exertion)
Imam	Religious leader, leader of prayer (literally, one who stands out in front)
Istihsān	Juristic method for adjudicating between conflicting precedents
Istislāh	Juristic consideration of equity or public interest in the formulation of a legal decision
ʿIzza	Dignity
Izzat	Honour killing
Jihād	Struggle for the sake of God, whether for self discipline and self-purification or against oppression and injustice
Jihād Al-Akbar	The greater *jihād*
Jihād Al-Asghar	The lesser *jihād*
Jilbab	Loose fitting outer garment
Jizya	Poll-tax
Kafir	Non-believer; someone who is ungrateful to God
Khalifa	Head of the Islamic state after the death of the Prophet
Kharāj	Tribute; tax
Khula	Divorce whereby the wife retains her marriage portion/dowry
Khulʿ	A decree of divorce by the courts
Kufr	Ingratitude or infidelity to God
Luwat	Sodomy
Madhāhib	Law schools (singular *madhhab*)
Mahr	Money or property settled on marriage
Makruh	Acts merely reprehensible, discouraged
Māl	Property
Mālikī	Adherent of the Sunni juristic school named after its eponym Malik b Anas
Mandub	Recommended, commendable
Masjids	Prayer halls
Maslaha	Applying or withholding the application of the law in terms of the public good
Mubāraʾa	Divorce by mutual agreement
Muftī	Scholar who is qualified to issue a legal ruling
Mujahada	Warfare to establish religion
Mujtahid	A jurist who performs *ijtihād*
Murtadd	Apostate
Nafs	The person, the lower self

Nasl	Everything connected with the propagation of humanity
Niqab	A veil that leaves only the area around the eyes exposed
Nizam Islami	The Islamic order
Qada	Judgment of God; the judiciary
Qādī	Islamic judge
Qisās	The law of retaliation
Qiyas	Collective name for a variety of legal methods, such as analogical reasoning; deduction by analogy
Rashidun	The four rightly guided caliphs who assumed the spiritual and temporal leadership of the Prophet Muhammad after his death
Ra'y	Opinion, judgment based on precedent
Riba	Interest
Ridda	Apostasy
Sabb	Insulting the Qur'an or the Prophet
Sahīfat Al-Medīna	The Constitution of Medina
Salafiya	Inspired interpretation
Shāfiʿī	Adherent of the Sunni juristic school named after its eponym Muhammad b Idris al Shafi'i
Shāriʿ	A thoroughfare, way or main road leading to a source
Shura	Consultation, advice
Sunna	The example of the Prophet embodied in his statements, actions, and those matters that he silently approved or disapproved as reported in *hadith* literature
Sura	Chapter
Tafsir	Exegesis or commentary, particularly as it relates to the Qur'an
Takhayyur	Selection of interpretation
Talāq	Unilateral decree of divorce
Talfiq	Borrowing and mixing from the different law schools to reach the most prudent result
Taqlīd	The following of a legal precedent (literally, imitation)
ʿUlamā	The jurists; scholars of eminence
Umma	The community of Muslims—understood as a socio-political, as well as religious or spiritual, entity
Urf	The customs of local society as a basis for legal reasoning
Usūl Al-fiqh	The four sources of law
Wahhabī	Follower of the strict puritanical teachings of Muhammad b Abd al-Wahhab
Wajib	An obligation
Zakat	Alms tax given as an act of worship

Further Reading

Books

Abou El Fadl, Khaled, *Speaking in God's Name: Islamic Law, Authority and Women* (Oxford: OneWorld, 2001)
—*The Great Theft: Wrestling Islam from the Extremists* (San Francisco: Harper Collins, 2005)
Allawi, Ali A, *The Crisis of Islamic Civilization* (New Haven: Yale University Press, 2009)
Amanat, Abbas and Frank Griffel (eds), *Shari'a: Islamic Law in the Contemporary Context* (Stanford: Stanford University Press, 2007)
An-Na'im, Abdullahi Ahmed, *Towards An Islamic Reformation: Civil Liberties, Human Rights, and International Law* (Syracuse, NY: Syracuse University Press, 1990)
—*Islam and the Secular State: Negotiating the Future of Shari'a* (Cambridge, MA: Harvard University Press, 2008)
Asad, Talal, *Formations of the Secular: Christianity, Islam, Modernity* (Stanford: Stanford University Press, 2003)
Aslan, Reza, *How to Win a Cosmic War: God, Globalization and the End of the War on Terror* (New York: Random House, 2009)
Baderin, Mashood A, *International Human Rights and Islamic Law* (Oxford: Oxford University Press, 2003)
Bashir, Bashir and Will Kymlicka (eds), *The Politics of Reconciliation in Multicultural Societies* (Oxford: Oxford University Press, 2008)
Bauer, Otto, *The Question of Nationalities and Social Democracy* (Minneapolis: University of Minnesota Press, 2000)
Benhabib, Seyla, *The Claims of Culture: Equality and Diversity in the Global Age* (Princeton: Princeton University Press, 2002)
Boyd, Marion, *Dispute Resolution in Family Law: Protecting Choice, Promoting Inclusion* (Ontario Ministry of the Attorney General, 2004)
Caldwell, Christopher, *Reflections on the Revolution in Europe: Immigration, Islam and The West* (New York: Doubleday, 2009)
Carroll, Lucy, and Harsh Kapoor, (eds), *Talaq-i-Tafwid: The Muslim Woman's Contractual Access to Divorce: Women Living Under Muslim Law* (Lahore, 1996)
Chapman, Colin, *Islam and the West: Conflict, Coexistence or Conversion?* (Carlisle: Paternoster, 1998)
Coulsen, Noel J, *A History of Islamic Law* (Edinburgh: Edinburgh University Press, 1994)
Cragg, Kenneth, *The Arab Christian: A History in the Middle East* (Louisville, KY: Westminster/John Knox Press, 1991)
Esposito, John L, *Unholy War: Terror in the Name of Islam* (Oxford: Oxford University Press, 2002)
Feldman, Noah, *The Fall and Rise of the Islamic State* (Princeton: Princeton University Press, 2008)

Fetzer, Joel S and J Christopher Soper, *Muslims and the State in Britain, France and Germany* (Cambridge: Cambridge University Press, 2005)

Hallaq, Wael B, *A History of Islamic Legal Theories: An Introduction to Sunni Usul Al-Fiqh* (Cambridge: Cambridge University Press, 1997)

—*Authority, Continuity and Change in Islamic Law* (Cambridge: Cambridge University Press, 2001)

—*The Origins and Evolution of Islamic Law* (Cambridge: Cambridge University Press, 2005)

Hussain, Jamila, *Islam: Its Law and Society* (Sydney: Federation Press, 2nd rev edn, 2004)

Ipgrave, Michael (ed), *Building a Better Bridge: Muslims, Christians and the Common Good* (Washington DC: Georgetown University Press, 2008)

Juergensmeyer, Mark, *Global Rebellion: Religious Challenges to the Secular State from Christian Militias to Al Qaeda* (Berkeley: University of California Press, 2008)

Kamali, Mohammad H, *Principles of Islamic Jurisprudence* (Cambridge: Islamic Texts Society, 2003)

Karsh, Ephraim, *Islamic Imperialism: A History* (New Haven: Yale University Press, 2007)

Kelsay, John, *Arguing the Just War in Islam* (Cambridge, MA: Harvard University Press, 2007)

Kepel, Gilles, *Jihad: The Trail of Political Islam* (Cambridge, MA: Harvard University Press, 2002)

Klausen, Jytte, *Islamic Challenge: Politics and Religion in Western Europe* (Oxford: Oxford University Press, 2005)

Kolig, Erich, *New Zealand's Muslims and Multiculturalism* (Leiden: Brill, 2010)

Kymlicka, Will, *Multicultural Citizenship* (Oxford: Oxford University Press, 1995)

—*Multicultural Odysseys: Navigating the New International Politics of Diversity* (Oxford: Oxford University Press, 2007)

Lewis, Bernard W, *The Political Language of Islam* (Chicago: University of Chicago Press, 1988)

March, Andrew, *Islam and Liberal Citizenship: The Search for an Overlapping Consensus* (Oxford: Oxford University Press, 2009)

Maudūdī, S Abul, *Rights of Non-Muslims in an Islamic State* (Lahore: Islamic Publications, 1982)

McGhee, Derek, *The End of Multiculturalism? Terrorism, Integration and Human Rights* (Maidenhead: Open University Press, 2008)

Muthuswamy, Moorthy S, *Defeating Political Islam: The New Cold War* (Amherst, NY: Prometheus Books, 2009)

Narain, Vrinda, *Gender and Community: Muslim Women's Rights in India* (Toronto: University of Toronto Press, 2001)

Nazir-Ali, Michael, *Islam: A Christian's Perspective* (Philadelphia: Westminster Press, 1983)

—*Conviction and Conflict: Islam, Christianity and World Order* (London: Continuum International, 2006)

Nielsen, Jørgen S and Lisbet Christoffersen, *Shari'a As Discourse: Legal Traditions and the Encounter with Europe* (London: Ashgate Press, 2010)

Noreau, Pierre, *Le droit en partage: le monde juridique face à la diversité ethnoculturelle* (Montreal: Éditions Thémis, 2003)

Oliver-Dee, Sean, *Religion and Identity: Divided Loyalties?* (London: Theos, 2009)

Parekh, Bhiku, *Rethinking Multiculturalism* (Basingstoke: Palgrave, 2000)

—*A New Politics of Identity: Political Principles for an Interdependent World* (Basingstoke: Palgrave, 2008)

Phillips, Anne, *Multiculturalism Without Culture* (Princeton: Princeton University Press, 2007)

Poynting, Scott, Greg Noble, and Paul Tabar, *Bin Laden in the Suburbs: Criminalising the Arab 'Other'* (Sydney: Institute of Criminology, 2004)

Rahman, Fazlur, *Revival and Reform in Islam* (Oxford: OneWorld, 2000)

Ramadan, Tariq, *To Be a European Muslim* (Leicester: Islamic Foundation, 1999)

—*Islam, the West and the Challenges of Modernity* (Leicester: Islamic Foundation, 2001)

—*Western Muslims and the Future of Islam* (Oxford: Oxford University Press, 2004)

—*Radical Reform: Islamic Ethics and Liberation* (Oxford: Oxford University Press, 2009)

Razack, Sherene H, *Casting Out: The Eviction of Muslims from Western Law and Politics* (Toronto: University of Toronto Press, 2008)

Ruthven, Malise, *Islam: A Very Short Introduction* (New York: Oxford University Press, 2000)

Schacht, Joseph, *An Introduction to Islamic Law* (Oxford: Oxford University Press, 1964)

Shachar, Ayelet, *Multicultural Jurisdictions: Cultural Differences and Women's Rights* (Cambridge: Cambridge University Press, 2001)

Taylor, Charles, *A Secular Age* (Cambridge, MA: Belknap Press of Harvard University Press, 2007)

van Bruinessen, Martin and Stefano Allievi (eds), *Producing Islamic Knowledge: Transmission and Dissemination in Western Europe* (London: Routledge, 2010)

Vikør, Knut S, *Between God and the Sultan: A History of Islamic Law* (Oxford: Oxford University Press, 2005)

Wikan, Unni, *Generous Betrayal: Politics of Culture in the New Europe* (Chicago: University of Chicago Press, 2002)

Witte Jr, John and Johann van der Vyver (eds), *Religious Human Rights in Global Perspective: Religious Perspectives* (The Hague: Kluwer, 1996)

Ye'Or, Bat, *The Dhimmi: Jews and Christians Under Islam* (London: Associated University Presses, 1985)

— *Islam and Dhimmitude: Where Civilizations Collide* (Madison/Teaneck, NJ: Dickinson University Press, 2001)

Yilmaz, Ihsan, *Muslim Laws, Politics and Society in Modern Nation States* (Aldershot: Ashgate, 2005)

Essays and Chapters in Anthologies

Baumeister, Andrea, 'The Limits of Universalism' in Bruce Haddock and Peter Sutch (eds), *Multiculturalism, Identity and Rights* (New York: Routledge, 2003) 111

Gaudreault-DesBiens, Jean-François, 'On Private Choices and Public Justice: Some Microscopic and Macroscopic Reflections on the State's Role in Addressing Faith-Based Arbitration' in R Murphy (ed), *Public Justice, Private Justice and Community-Based Justice?* (Montreal: Canadian Institute for the Administration of Justice, 2009) 247

Kolig, Erich, 'Romancing Culture and Its Limitations: Policies of Cultural Recognition, Multiculturalism and Cultural Boundaries in New Zealand' in Roger Openshaw and Elizabeth Rata (eds), *The Politics of Conformity in New Zealand* (Auckland: Pearson, 2009) 63

Laden, Osama bin, 'Crusader Wars' in Bruce Lawrence (ed), *Messages to the World: The Statements of Osama bin Laden* (New York: Verso Press, 2005) 135

Magnet, Joseph E, 'Multiculturalism and Collective Rights' in Gerard A Beaudoin and Errol Mendes (eds), *Canadian Charter of Rights and Freedoms* (Toronto: LexisNexis-Butterworths, 4th edn, 2005) 1259

Moosa, Ebrahim, 'Colonialism and Islamic Law' in Muhammad Khalid Masud, Armando Salvatore, and Martin van Bruinessen (eds), *Islam and Modernity* (Edinburgh: Edinburgh University Press, 2009) 158

Otto, Jan Michiel, 'The compatibility of *shari'a* with the rule of law. Fundamental conflict: between civilisations? Within civilisations? Or between scholars?' in Adriaan in't Groen, Henk de Jonge, Eduard Klasen, Hilje Papma, and Piet van Slooten (eds), *Knowledge in Ferment: Dilemmas in Science, Scholarship and Society* (Leiden: Leiden University Press, 2007) 137

Poulter, Sebastian, 'The Claim to a Separate Islamic System of Personal Law for British Muslims' in Chibli Mallat and Jane Connors (eds), *Islamic Family Law* (London: Graham and Trotman, 1990) 147

Ramadan, Tariq, 'Islamic Views of the Collective' in Michael Ipgrave (ed), *Building a Better Bridge: Muslims, Christians and the Common Good* (Washington DC: Georgetown University Press, 2008) 73

Shachar, Ayelet, 'What We Owe Women? The View From Multicultural Feminism' in Debra Satz and Rob Reich (eds), *Toward a Humanist Justice: The Political Philosophy of Susan Moller Okin* (New York: Oxford University Press, 2009) 143

Siddique, Sharon, 'Conceptualising Contemporary Islam: Religion or Ideology' in Ahmad Ibrahim, Sharon Siddique, and Yasmin Hussain (eds), *Readings on Islam in Southeast Asia* (Singapore: Institute of Southeast Asian Studies, 1985) 337

Stenberg, Leif, 'Islam, Knowledge and the "West"' in Birgit Schaebler and Leif Stenberg (eds), *Globalization and the Muslim World* (Syracuse: Syracuse University Press, 2004) 93

Taylor, Charles, 'Shared and Divergent Values' in Ronald Watts and Douglas Brown (eds), *Options for a New Canada* (Toronto: University of Toronto Press, 1991) 53

Tibi, Bassam, 'War and Peace in Islam' in Terry Nardin (ed), *The Ethics of War and Peace: Religious and Secular Perspectives* (Princeton: Princeton University Press, 1998) 130

Waldron, Jeremy, 'Status versus Equality: The Accommodation of Difference' in Omid A Payrow Shabani (ed), *Multiculturalism and Law: A Critical Debate* (University of Wales Press, 2007) 129

Weinrib, Lorraine E, 'Ontario's Sharia Law Debate: Law and Politics under the *Charter*' in Richard Moon (ed), *Law and Religious Pluralism in Canada* (Vancouver: UBC Press, 2008) 250

Wikan, Unni, 'Citizenship on Trial: Nadia's Case' in Richard A Shweder, Martha Minow, and Hazel Rose Markus (eds), *Engaging Cultural Differences: the Multicultural Challenge in Liberal Democracies* (New York: Russell Sage Foundation, 2002) 128

Williams, Melissa S, 'The Politics of Fear and the Decline of Multiculturalism' in John E Fossum, Paul Magnette, and Johanne Poirier (eds), *Ties That Bind. Accommodating Diversity in Canada and the European Union* (Brussels: Peter Lang, 2009) 53

Articles

Afsaruddin, Asma, 'Absolutism vs. Pluralism in Islam Today' (2008) 6 *Review of Faith and International Affairs* 23

Akhavi, Shahrough, 'Islam and the West in world history' (2003) 24 *Third World Quarterly* 545

Aslan, Reza, ' "A" Source of Law?' (2008) 36 *Harvard Divinity Bulletin* 14

Bakht, Natasha, 'Were Muslim Barbarians Really Knocking On the Gates of Ontario? The Religious Arbitration Controversy—Another Perspective' [2006] *Ottawa Law Review* 67

Bano, Samia, 'In Pursuit of Religious and Legal Diversity: A Response to the Archbishop of Canterbury and the "Sharia Debate" in Britain' (2008) 10 *Ecclesiastical Law Journal* 283

Bhabha, Faisal, 'Between Exclusion and Assimilation: Experimentalizing Multiculturalism' (2009) 54 *McGill Law Journal* 45

Black, Ann, 'Accommodating Shariah law in Australia's Legal System' (2008) 33 *Alternative Law Journal* 214

—and Nadirsyah Hosen, 'Fatwas: their Role in Contemporary Secular Australia' (2009) 18 *Griffith Law Review* 405

Borovali, Murat, 'Islamic headscarves and slippery slopes' (2009) 30 *Cardozo Law Review* 2593

Carroll, Lucy, 'Muslim Women and "Islamic Divorce" in England' (1997) 17 *Journal of Muslim Minority Affairs* 97

Choudhry, Sujit, 'National Minorities and Ethnic Immigrants: Liberalism's Political Sociology' (2002) 10 *Journal of Political Philosophy* 54

Dunn, Kevin M, 'Australian Public Knowledge of Islam' (2005) 12 *Studia Islamika* 5

Emon, Anver M, 'Conceiving Islamic Law in a Pluralist Society: History, Politics and Multicultural Jurisprudence' [2006] *Singapore Journal of Legal Studies* 331

—'Islamic Law and the Canadian Mosaic: Politics, Jurisprudence, and Multicultural Accommodation' (2008) 87 *Canadian Bar Review* 391

Farr, Thomas F, 'Islam's Way to Freedom' (2008) 187 *First Things* 24

Fish, Stanley, 'Boutique Multiculturalism, or Why Liberals Are Incapable of Thinking about Hate Speech' (1997) 23 *Critical Inquiry* 378

Gartenstein-Ross, Daveed, 'The Role of Consensus in the Contemporary Struggle for Islam' (2008) 6 *Review of Faith and International Affairs* 13

Gaudreault-DesBiens, Jean Francois, 'Constitutional Values, Faith-Based Arbitration, and the Limits of Private Justice in a Multicultural Society' (2005–2006) 19 *National Journal of Constitutional Law* 155

Hallaq, Wael, 'Was the Gate of Ijtihad Closed?' (1984) 16 *International Journal for Middle East Studies* 3

—' "Muslim Rage" and Islamic Law' (2003) 54 *Hastings Law Journal* 1705

Hirschl, Ran and Ayelet Shachar, 'The New Wall of Separation: Respecting Diversity, Prohibiting Competition' (2009) 30 *Cardozo Law Review* 2535

Hosen, Nadirsyah, 'Revelation in a Modern Nation State: Muhammadiyah and Islamic Reasoning in Indonesia' (2002) 4 *Australian Journal of Asian Law* 232

Houck, David K, 'The Islamist Challenge to the US Constitution' (2006) 13 *Middle East Quarterly* 21

Idriss, Mazher, '*Laïcité* and the Banning of the "Hijab" in France' (2005) 25 *Legal Studies* 260

Khan, Liaquat Ali, 'Jurodynamics of Islamic Law' (2009) 61 *Rutgers Law Review* 231

Khiabany, Gholam, 'De-Westernizing Media Theory, or Reverse Orientalism: "Islamic Communication" as Theorized by Hamid Mowlana' (2003) 25 *Media, Culture and Society* 415

Korteweg, Anna C, 'The Sharia Debate in Ontario: Gender, Islam and Representations of Muslim Women's Agency' (2008) 22 *Gender and Society* 434

Macklem, Patrick, 'Militant Democracy, Legal Pluralism, and the Paradox of Self-Determination' (2006) 4 *International Journal of Constitutional Law* 488

Marshall, Paul, 'Islamic Counter-Reformation', *First Things,* August–September 2004, 21

Masseri, Abdulwahab al, 'The Imperialist Epistemological Vision' (1994) 11 *American Journal of Islamic Social Sciences* 403

Moghadam, Valentine, 'Feminism, Legal Reform and Women's Empowerment in the Middle East and North Africa' (2009) 59 *International Social Science Journal* 9

Mottahedeh, Roy P, 'The Clash of Civilizations: An Islamicist's Critique' (1995) 2 *Harvard Middle Eastern and Islamic Review* 1

Razack, Sherene, 'The "Sharia Law Debate" in Ontario: The Modernity/Premodernity Distinction in Legal Efforts to Protect Women from Culture' (2007) 15 *Feminist Legal Studies* 3

Réaume, Denise, 'Justice Between Cultures: Autonomy and the Protection of Cultural Affiliation' (1995) 29 *UBC Law Review* 117

Sadiqi, Fatima and Moha Ennaji, 'The Feminisation of Public Space: Women's Activism and Family Law and Social Change in Morocco' (2006) 2 *Journal of Middle East Women's Studies* 86

Shachar, Ayelet, 'Religion, State, and the Problem of Gender: New Modes of Citizenship and Governance in Diverse Societies' (2005) 50 *McGill Law Journal* 49

—'Privatizing Diversity: A Cautionary Tale from Religious Arbitration in Family Law' (2008) 9 *Theoretical Inquiries in Law* 573

Tibi, Bassam, 'Islamist Parties: Why They Can't be Democratic' (2008) 19 *Journal of Democracy* 43

Tucker, Adam, 'The Archbishop's unsatisfactory legal pluralism' [2008] *Public Law* 463

Volpp, Leti, 'The Culture of Citizenship' (2007) 8 *Theoretical Inquiries in Law* 571

Waldron, Jeremy, 'One Law For All? The Logic of Cultural Accommodation' (2002) 59 *Washington and Lee Law Review* 3

Wilken, Robert, 'Christianity Face to Face with Islam', *First Things,* January 2009, 19

Index

334